Competing Through
Productivity and Quality

Competing Through Productivity and Quality

Edited by Y.K. Shetty and
Vernon M. Buehler
College of Business
Utah State University

Foreword by Colby H. Chandler
Chairman and CEO, Eastman Kodak

Productivity Press
Cambridge, Massachusetts   Norwalk, Connecticut

Productivity Press
P.O. Box 3007
Cambridge, Massachusetts 02140
U.S.A.
telephone: (617) 497-5146
telefax: (617) 868-3524

Library of Congress Catalog Card Number: 88-43106
ISBN: 0-915299-43-7

Jacket design by Joyce C. Weston
Text design by Caroline Kutil
Typeset by Rudra Press, Cambridge, Massachusetts
Printed and bound by Maple-Vail Book Manufacturing Group
Printed in the United States of America

Grateful acknowledgement is made to the following for permission to reprint previously published material:

"Secrets of Super Achievers" from *Peak Performers: The New Heroes of American Business* (New York: William Morrow & Co., 1986), by Charles Garfield, copyrighted by Garfield Enterprises Inc., reprinted in the June 1986 issue of *Reader's Digest*.

Library of Congress Cataloging-in-Publication Data

Competing through productivity and quality
  Bibliography: p.
  Includes index.
  1. Industrial productivity — United States — Case studies.
2. Quality control — United States — Case studies.   3. Competition, International — Case studies.   4. Industrial management — United States — Case studies.   5. United States — Foreign economic relations — Japan.   6. Japan — Foreign economic relations — United States.
I. Shetty, Y. Krishna. II. Buehler, Vernon M.
HC110.I52C655 1988   658.5   88-43106
ISBN 0-915299-43-7

89   90   91   10   9   8   7   6   5   4   3   2   1

Contents

List of Tables and Illustrations   xi

Dedication   xiii

A Note From the Publisher   xv

Foreword   xvii

Preface   xix

Acknowledgements   xxiii

PART I: Competing in Global Markets   1

1   Productivity and Quality: Keys to Competitive Advantage   3
    Y.K. Shetty and Vernon M. Buehler
    The Editors

2   Productivity for All Seasons: Yesterday, Today,
    and Tomorrow   17
    C. Jackson Grayson
    Chairman, American Productivity Center

3   Exploiting Technology to Regain Markets   33
    Bobby Inman
    Chairman, Westmark Industries

4   Managing in an Information-Rich World   45
    Herbert Simon
    Nobel Laureate, Carnegie-Mellon University

5   The Work Ethic   55
    James Buchanan
    Nobel Laureate, George Mason University

 6   **Competitiveness and the Union**   63
     Lynn Williams
     President, United Steelworkers

 7   **Responding to the New Reality of Global Competition**   79
     John Young
     President and CEO, Hewlett-Packard

 8   **Challenge to America's Industrial Leadership**   95
     Armand V. Feigenbaum
     President, General Systems

 9   **The Reckoning: Made in America or Japan**   117
     David Halberstam
     Pulitzer Prize Winner

10   **Merger Strategies and Goals**   129
     Richard Bierly
     Senior Corporate Vice President, Unisys

11   **New Skills and Productivity**   143
     Ray Marshall
     Professor, University of Texas

12   **Cost Containment**   159
     Carl Reichardt
     CEO, Wells Fargo Bank

PART II: Human Dimensions of Productivity   167

13   **Constraints and Opportunities Faced by Women Managers**   169
     Mylle Bell
     Director of Corporate Planning, BellSouth

14   **Women in Management: View from
     Adolph Coors Company**   175
     Rosa M. Bunn
     Director of Community Affairs, Adolph Coors

15 Successful Women at Transamerica   181
    Patricia J. Blair
    Corporate Personnel, Transamerica

16 How Ford's HR Staff Supports Strategic Planning   189
    Raymond H. Johnson
    Corporate Employee Development, Ford Motor Company

17 HR's Impact in Strategic Planning at Xerox   201
    Douglas Reid
    Senior Vice President of Human Resources, Xerox

18 Compensation Strategies of John Hancock   209
    Kathleen Dole
    Executive Consultant, John Hancock Insurance

19 Union Carbide's 1987 Benefit Plan Initiatives   217
    Roger Wolff
    Director of Corporate Benefits, Union Carbide

20 Cost Effective Benefits Programs   223
    Harold Loeb
    Senior Vice President, Hay Huggins

21 Employee-Driven Productivity   233
    Neal Orkin
    Professor, Drexel University

22 Internal Decision to Excel: Secrets of Super Achievers   241
    Charles Garfield
    President, Peak Performance

23 Total Employee Involvement   247
    Norman Bodek
    President, Productivity Press

24   Upgrading Workforce Ethics at General Dynamics   255
Kent Druyvesteyn
Director of Ethics, General Dynamics
   Appendix: General Dynamics' Standards of Business
      Ethics and Conduct

25   Creativity at Bonneville International   279
Jean Bishop
Bonneville International

PART III: Exploiting Information Technology   285

26   Networking Is the Organization   287
Ellen S. Quackenbush
Group Manager, DEC

27   Networking in the 1990s   301
Gil Piddington
Vice President of Networking, Unisys

28   Working Toward Open Systems Interconnection (OSI)   305
George Chang
Research Scientist, Bell Communications

29   Competing with Standards   311
Lincoln Faurer
President and CEO, Corporation for Open Systems

30   Integrated Services Digital Networks (ISDN)   321
Edward Botwinick
Timeplex

31   Planning Operations Systems Networks   327
Daniel Minoli
Scientist, Bell Communications

32   The Information Explosion   337
Susan Hitchcock
Operations Manager, Southern Bell

33 **Administrative Productivity Through
    Information Technology**   341
    Ronald Whittier
    Vice President of Direct Marketing, Intel

34 **Du Pont Exploits Emerging Technologies**   347
    John Taylor
    Manager, Du Pont

35 **Computer Simulation in Manufacturing**   355
    W. David Kelton
    Professor, University of Minnesota

36 **Hidden Costs of Computing**   371
    Charlotte Cook Hofmann
    President, Information Ideas

**PART IV: Company Practices for Enhancing Productivity
           and Quality**   381

37 **SMED: The Heart of JIT Production**   383
    Shigeo Shingo
    President, Institute of Management Improvement (Japan)

38 **Putting Shingo Methods to Work in U.S. Business**   399
    Daniel Bills
    President, Granville-Phillips

39 **Employee-Driven Productivity at Omark Industries**   405
    Lawrence White
    Plant Manager, Omark Industries

40 **Ford's Use of Shingo's Methods**   413
    James Torvinen
    Ford Motor Company
        Appendix: Ford's Experience with Shingo Methods

41 **Computer Integrated Manufacturing:
    The Continuous Journey**   423
    Jodie Ray
    Senior Vice President I.A., Texas Instruments

42   **Kodak's Copy Products Quality Program**   431
     Dale Esse
     Manager of Product Quality, Eastman Kodak

43   **Total Quality Control: A Breakthrough Approach to**
     Teamwork at Hewlett Packard   443
     Julie Holtry
     Marketing Manager, Hewlett Packard

44   **Managing Quality/Productivity Improvement**
     at McDonnell Douglas   451
     Henry "Hank" Todd
     Vice President, McDonnell Douglas

45   **The Quest for Sustaining Quality Improvement**   457
     James Talley
     Vice President of Quality, General Dynamics

46   **Improving Service Sector Productivity**   463
     William McCormick
     President, Fireman's Fund

47   **ConAgra's Approach to Quality and Productivity**   473
     John Phillips
     Assistant to the Chairman, ConAgra

PART V: Guidelines for Managerial Action   483

48   **Managerial Guidelines for Productivity**
     and Quality Improvement   485
     Y.K. Shetty and Vernon M. Buehler
     The Editors

Bibliography   491
Biographical Notes   511
Index   523

List of Tables and Illustrations

Table 15.1	Women in Line vs. Staff Positions	184
Table 16.1	Strategic Planning Terms	191
Table 20.1	Levels of Coverage/Cost Within Features	227
Table 20.2	Health Plan Redesign: Potential Plan Reductions	228
Table 20.3	Plan Reductions	230
Table 21.1	U.S. Innovation	234
Figure 28.1	What Is OSI?	306
Figure 35.1	Methods of Studying Systems	357
Figure 35.2	Manufacturing Simulation Model	361
Figure 35.3	Putting Capacities on the Buffers	364
Figure 35.4	Information Flow and Transformation in Simulation	368
Table 36.1	One Approach To "Rapture of the Deep"	374
Figure 37.1	The Economic Lot Size	385
Figure 37.2	Structure of Production	391
Figure 39.1	Model for Meaningful Work	408
Table 39.2	Investment in Training	410
Table 39.3	Productivity Results	411
Figure 42.1	Copy Products Quality (Product Quality vs. Product Shipment)	437
Figure 44.1	A Sample Organization Chart	453
Table 45.1	General Dynamics Corporate Quality Policy	459
Table 45.2	Quality Improvement Parameters	460
Table 45.3	Corporate Common Parameters	461

Dedication

August 2, 1988

Gratefully dedicated to Shigeo Shingo

As a world famous consultant, Shigeo Shingo lectured at Utah State University's 13th Annual Productivity Seminar, April 7-8, 1988, on his manufacturing methods for improving quality and productivity. USU proudly awarded him an honorary doctoral degree at its commencement ceremonies on June 4, 1988. In recognition of the prominence of USU's Partners Program for promoting quality and productivity, Dr. Shingo designated USU as the center for annually awarding the new "Shingo Prizes for Manufacturing Excellence" to businesses, students, and faculty, nationwide. He also announced the creation of a USU-endowed professorial chair for teaching, research, and promotion of improved manufacturing methods.

Shigeo Shingo is the originator of several production systems. His genius is in his understanding of why and how products are manufactured and transforming that understanding into a system for low-cost, high-quality production. He was instrumental in helping Toyota become the most productive automobile manufacturer in the world, and his work now helps numerous U.S. companies save billions of dollars in manufacturing costs. The originator and president of Japan's highly regarded Institute of Manufacturing Improvement, Shigeo Shingo obtained his education at the Yamanashi Technical Institute. He has authored numerous books and articles and has trained more that 10,000 executives. His latest book, *Non-Stock Production: The Shingo System for Continuous Improvement* (Cambridge, MA: Productivity Press, 1988), concentrates on expanding American manufacturers' understanding of stockless production. Mr. Shingo has helped raise international standards of living by reducing industrial waste. He has raised the human dignity and pride of the worker by introducing methods that treat the worker as a valuable creative asset for solving production problems. His understanding of production processes and his creativity have resulted in innovations that match the watershed contributions of the great industrial engineers of the late nineteenth and early twentieth centuries.

A Note
From the Publisher

As publisher of *Competing through Productivity and Quality*, I wish to make special mention of Utah State University's College of Business. The University is taking a lead in the United States in the field of quality and productivity. Its Partners Program seminars attract the very best in North American business and have raised the consciousness of many corporate executives, professors, and students.

In the course of his 50-year career, Dr. Shigeo Shingo has written over 20 books that reveal his depth of insight into the principles of industrial engineering. Along with Taiichi Ohno, he is the creator and teacher of the Toyota Production System (JIT). On June 4, 1988, during Utah State's commencement ceremonies, the school awarded Shigeo Shingo an honorary doctorate in management for a lifetime of work in improving manufacturing productivity in the world. Dr. Shingo was delighted and very moved. Being recognized in America for his contribution to improving industry was a highlight of his career.

With this in mind, Dr. Shingo and Utah State's College of Business have established the Shigeo Shingo Endowed Chair and the "Shigeo Shingo Prizes for Manufacturing Excellence," to be funded by contributions from Dr. Shingo's clients and associates worldwide. The Shingo Prize will be awarded annually to as many as six companies that improve productivity by best applying Shingo techniques in areas such as Single-Minute Exchange of Die (SMED), JIT techniques, Poka-yoke (Mistake-Proofing), Zero Defects, and the total elimination of non-value-added waste. Companies will submit papers to a review committee detailing their improvements.

Annual monetary awards will be given to three faculty members and to five undergraduate and five graduate students submitting the best papers on manufacturing excellence based on Dr. Shingo's teachings. A new curriculum to teach manufacturing excellence to more students will be developed at Utah State. By helping further the teachings of this great man, Utah State is strengthening American industry.

As publisher of Dr. Shingo's books in English, I have long been acquainted with this remarkable man. I have witnessed the miracles he has accomplished in production plants in Japan and North America and the creative spark he ignites in people whenever he speaks. At a time when industry is often critical of education in America, Utah State University should be commended.

Norman Bodek
Publisher, Productivity Press
and Chairman, Shingo Prize Committee

Foreword

Can America compete?

The editors of these 1988 seminar proceedings on quality and productivity, their sixth volume covering Utah State University's seminars, answer with a confident "Yes!" They agree with most experts that the improvement from the highly over-valued dollar that is fueling some of the surge in manufacturing exports is only a temporary route to improved competition. Long-term improvements must come from innovative manufacturing methods that provide better quality, reduced inventories, and faster response times. The editors are encouraged by seminar speakers who discussed the adoption of time-based strategies for restoring our competitive strength. Included are improved manufacturing methods that save time by drastically cutting set-up times for quick changeovers, lead times on customer orders, and rework time by eliminating defects.

Buttressing these promising developments are the encouraging prospects for new products and processes that are evolving from our science and technology base. The editors are awed by the predictions of a ten-fold increase in technological progress by the year 2000 as compared to that in the past dozen years. Again, cutting time in commercializing new technology provides crucial time-based competitive advantages. On the other hand, the editors concur with those who state that our science and technology base is suffering from weaknesses in our education system and inadequate funding of public and private sector R & D. However, they feel that shifts in public policy are afoot to restore our long-standing strength in these areas as demanded by society. They offer one caveat, namely, that the hoped-for savings in time from applying new technology depends on our elimination of excessive administrative layers and other inefficiencies. Otherwise, the addition of new technology will result in "automated inefficiency."

They also are encouraged by the movement away from adversarial labor-management practices toward a teamwork approach. Seminar speakers stressed the need for change in the way workers, supervisors, and managers interact. Both labor and business leaders recognize that increased employee involvement will speed the adoption of factory practices that improve quality, shorten product delivery times, lower inventories, and upgrade productivity. Again, this conserves time, a vital competitive force.

Starting in the 1970s, USU's Partners Program has conducted these state-of-the-art management seminars on quality, productivity, information systems, human resources, innovation, world trade, banking, and accounting. It represents a model of the teamwork between business and academics that is essential in restoring our competitive position. Other institutions would benefit by adopting this model to enable students to test their theoretical learning against proven, innovative practices that often are not yet in textbooks.

Colby H. Chandler
Chairman and CEO
Eastman Kodak Company

Preface

This is our sixth volume that reports on company experiences and public policy measures for improving U.S. competitiveness. The lessons from these industry-academic co-sponsored seminars become increasingly more vital in meeting the growing complexities caused by rapidly evolving technologies and expanding global markets. For example, some experts are confident that by the year 2000 we will see ten times as much progress in computer technology as we have experienced in the last ten years. They predict that computers will recognize handwriting and will be voice- and gesture-controlled. Converging with these electronic advances will be low-cost and highly productive telecommunications networks that will link computerized facilities for processing voice, data, and video worldwide.

This volume again carries messages by gurus on productivity and quality improvements. Many focus on manufacturing methods that will enhance quality, flexibility, and speed. They stress the need for time-based strategies to compete in global markets. Shigeo Shingo, one of the contributors who is known in Japan as the "Dean of Quality Consultants," advocates a time-saving strategy with his single-minute-exchange-of-die (SMED) technique for quick change-overs and his non-stock production (NSP) system which emphasizes short response time and minimal inventories. Shingo's manufacturing methods were the cornerstone of Toyota's JIT production system where response time for one Toyota supplier was reduced from 15 days to 1 day by cutting lot sizes and streamlining the factory layout.

These proceedings also stress the need for teamwork. Shingo is joined by others in emphasizing employee participation as one of the best approaches for eliminating defects, reducing response time, and improving quality, flexibility, and speed. High tech additions must be accompanied by changes in the way workers, supervisors, and managers interact. In fact, many contend that total employee involvement is the most important force for enhancing productivity.

Lessons from these experiences continue to raise our confidence in the competitive ability of the United States. Favorable trends are being reported in U.S. trade balances. We believe this stems not only from a declining dollar but, more importantly, from progress by U.S. manufacturers on such fronts as wage constraints, improved quality, increased capital, R & D spending, and efficiencies from organizational changes and restructuring. We are confident that U.S. manufacturers will continue to practice enlightened and adaptive management practices, and that the dynamism of the American free enterprise system will enable us to be competitive in an expanding global market place.

Utah State University's Partners Program of the College of Business is committed to improving U.S. competitiveness through academic-business exchanges. Dating from 1970, this student-driven program provides a forum for interaction between practitioners and our entrepreneurial-minded students. Each year some 100 business experts from top U.S. firms come at company expense to our scenic campus. They share their experiences on evolving global management practices with thousands of young aspiring managers and business friends. Realism is injected into the classroom by discussing creative approaches that are headlined in the *Wall Street Journal* but are not yet in textbooks. Several are world-renowned such as Harvard professor Rosabeth Moss Kanter, Hewlett-Packard's President John Young, corporate raider T. Boone Pickens, and Harvard economist John Kenneth Galbraith. So, in seven annual student-managed seminars, USU's Partners Program enables students and friends from the community to discuss cutting-edge issues in banking, accounting, real estate, world trade, human resources, information systems, quality, and productivity.

This volume contains the proceedings of three Partners Program Seminars held in 1988 on managing productivity, human resources, and information systems. The manuscripts reported here were selected from over 100 presentations.

Has the Partners Program been successful in helping students and executives understand how to rebuild U. S. competitiveness? This can be partially answered by examining the extent of annual participation by students and industry:

- As many as 3,000 students with business and other majors attend selected sessions of the seminars. Some students earn academic credit by submitting research papers and passing examinations on the seminar topics.
- Some 150 to 500 executives attend each of the seven seminars and hear world-class keynoters. Attendees may earn 70 units of Continuing Professional Education and/or eight Continuing Education Units.
- One hundred speakers nationwide participate by traveling to USU at their own expense. They are hosted by 300 to 400 students and several student associations while discussing career and job opportunities and speaking at class sessions as well as at seminars.
- Close coordination is maintained with 500 to 600 dues-paying Partners by plant visits, newsletters, and luncheon meetings. Partners often participate as seminar panelists, lecturers, and moderators.
- Over 40 firms and individuals nationwide qualify as Life Members by making significant financial contributions and/or speaking at Partners events annually.
- Some 30 professional societies representing approximately 5,000 members in the area serve as co-sponsors of seminars and assist in planning, promoting, and conducting these Partners events.
- Seminar proceedings similar to this volume are published annually.
- Fifteen to 20 students plan and conduct Partners events with minimal supervision, involving an annual $250,000 budget. Over 100,000 student-produced program brochures, semi-annual newsletters, and other Partners literature are distributed annually.
- Partners seminars generate net revenues for awarding over 20 modest scholarships annually. Twenty-five $500 assistantships are granted annually from earnings on Partners endowments that exceed $200,000.
- Over $150,000 has been endowed from donations and seminar revenues to support distinguished executive lectures annually. These lectures are endowed in the names of such leaders as W. Edwards Deming, Henry Kaufman, Robert Noyce, Joseph M. Juran, Philip Crosby, and William Hewlett.
- The effectiveness of the Partners Program in promoting practices for improving U.S. competitiveness has been recognized by statements from Congress and U.S. Commerce Secretary Verity.
- Shigeo Shingo, a leading Japanese consultant on manufacturing methods, has designated the Partners Program to administer the awarding annually of the "Shingo Prize for Manufacturing Excellence" to businesses, students, and faculty. He is establishing a USU endowment for the awarding of the prize and for creating a professorial chair for teaching, research, and promoting manufacturing methods.

Acknowledgements

The materials for this volume come from Utah State University's student-driven Partners Program. The success of the Partners Program stems from many sources, but the predominant factor is its small, industrious student staff, supported by several student associations. The student staff works with minimal direction in developing and conducting a comprehensive program for infusing cutting-edge issues into the classroom. These new ideas are not yet in texts but they are causing major changes in the workplace and the boardroom. Students have a bone-deep desire to better understand how managers cope with such complex forces as fast-changing information and other technologies, shifting work force demographics, global competitive pressures for improved quality and productivity, innovative manufacturing strategies, and the evolving government-business relations. Meeting and exchanging views with executives fresh from the trenches of the competitive battlefield provide a lasting learning experience. These managers are eager to share their insights in this life-span learning endeavor and to close the gap between the worlds of business and academics.

Our Partners, who provide the life blood for these programs, are our industrious faculty and students, managers throughout the nation, and our loyal alumni. They generously contribute their time, advice, and resources. A few deserve special recognition.

The late George S. Eccles, and his charming wife, Dolores Dore Eccles, founded our prestigious George S. Eccles Distinguished Lecture Series in 1974. It has financed over 50 lectures by national leaders and is continuing under the generous sponsorship of Spencer F.

Eccles, who is chairman, president, and CEO of First Security Corporation, Salt Lake City.

To recognize the exceptional generosity of those who have helped promote the interaction of academia and business, Partner Life memberships and memorial awards were recently presented to the following:

Life Members:
Joseph A. Anderson, ZCMI, Salt Lake City, Utah
Russell V. Anderson, RVA Service Corporation, Logan, Utah
Apple Computer Company, Cupertino, California
Samuel Barker, Attorney at Law, Ogden, Utah
Norman Bodek, Productivity Inc., Norwalk, Connecticut
Val Browning, Industrialist, Ogden, Utah
Charles Bullen, Bullen's Inc., Logan, Utah
Reed Bullen, Legislator/Businessman, Logan, Utah
M. Anthony Burns, Ryder Systems Inc., Miami, Florida
G.H. "Herb" Champ, Mortgage Banker, Logan, Utah
John E. Clay, CPA, Logan, Utah
Philip B. Crosby, Quality Consultant, Winter Park, Florida
Thomas D. Dee II, Dee Company, Ogden, Utah
W. Edwards Deming, Statistical Consultant, Washington, DC
Spencer F. Eccles, First Security Corp., Salt Lake City, Utah
Armand V. Feigenbaum, General Systems, Pittsfield, Massachusetts
C. Jackson Grayson, American Productivity Center, Houston, Texas
Ronald S. Hanson, Zion's First National Bank, Salt Lake City, Utah
Jay Dee Harris, Harris Truck and Equipment, Tremonton, Utah
William R. Hewlett, Hewlett-Packard, Palo Alto, California
Bobby Inman, Westmark Systems, Austin, Texas
J.C. Penney Company, Salt Lake City, Utah
Joseph M. Juran, Juran Institute, Wilton, Connecticut
Henry Kaufman, Salomon Brothers, New York, New York
John W. Kendrick, George Washington University, Washington, DC
Jack Lampros, First Security Bank, Ogden, Utah
J.W. Marriott, Jr., Marriott Corporation, Bethesda, Maryland
Ore-Ida Foods Inc./Heinz Co. Foundation, Pittsburgh, Pennsylvania
D.B. "Bud" Ozmun, Selway Foundation, Wheeling, Illinois
Jack B. Parson, Jack B. Parson Construction, Logan, Utah
T. Boone Pickens, Mesa Petroleum, Amarillo, Texas
Rex G. Plowman, Lewiston State Bank, Lewiston, Utah
Ralph H. Redford, Tetrotech International, Arlington, Virginia
Lynn A. Richardson, Banker, Ogden, Utah
Richard E. Shea, Pepperidge Farms, Norwalk, Connecticut
Shigeo Shingo, Institute for Management Improvement, Japan
Kenneth O. Sorensen, Cache Mortgage Corporation, Logan, Utah

Fred H. Thompson, Banker, Logan, Utah
Robert and Patricia Wangsgard, Stimson Inc., Ogden, Utah
Lynn R. Williams, United Steelworkers, Pittsburgh, Pennsylvania
Morris H. Wright, Wall Street Banker, New York, New York
John A. Young, Hewlett-Packard, Palo Alto, California

Posthumous Memorial Awards:

George S. Eccles, First Security Corporation
Howard & Evelyn Larson, Larson Foundation
D. Wade Mack, Mack Foundation
Samuel C. Powell, Attorney at Law
Bert L. Thomas, Winn-Dixie Stores

Utah Manufacturers Association has assisted in the promotion
and conduct of the annual productivity seminars for 12 years. It is one
of some 30 professional and industrial societies that co-sponsor annual seminars. Most noteworthy of these is the Utah Bankers Association which has co-sponsored highly successful annual banking
seminars starting in 1970 and has endowed $16,000 for student assis-
tantships.

Generous assistance was received from over 100 seminar speakers in 1988 representing organizations such as the following that have
participated in the past:

3M Company*, St. Paul, Minnesota
ACME Electric, New York, New York
Adolph Coors, Golden, Colorado
AFL-CIO, Washington, DC
Allen-Bradley, Milwaukee, Wisconsin
American Express, Salt Lake City, Utah
American Productivity Center, Houston, Texas
American TV & Communications, Englewood, Colorado
AMFAC, San Francisco, California
Amgen, Thousand Oaks, California
Analog Devices*, Norwood, Massachusetts
ARCO Oil & Gas, Dallas, Texas
Arthur Andersen*, Salt Lake City, Utah
Ashton-Tate, Chicago, Illinois
ASK Computer Systems, Altos, Colorado
A.T. Kearny, Chicago, Illinois
AT&T*, New York, New York
Aubrey G. Lanston Company, New York, New York
Bakke Company, Walnut Creek, California

---

* Indicates multiple visits

Bank of America*, San Francisco, California
Bell Communications, Piscatawny, New Jersey
BellSouth, Atlanta, Georgia
Beneficial Life*, Salt Lake City, Utah
B.F. Goodrich*, Cleveland, Ohio
BioActives, Salt Lake City, Utah
Boeing Aerospace*, Seattle, Washington
Bonneville, Salt Lake City, Utah
Borg-Warner*, Chicago, Illinois
Boston University*, Boston, Massachusetts
Bourns Networks, Logan, Utah
B. P. Minerals, Salt Lake City, Utah
Bureau of National Affairs, Washington, DC
Burroughs, Camarillo, California
Campbell Scientific, Logan, Utah
Celanese, New York, New York
Cetron & Associates, Miami Lakes, Florida
Cetus, Emeryville, California
Chrysler Corporation, Highland Park, Michigan
Cincom Systems*, Cincinnati, Ohio
Citibank*, New York, New York
Coasts Productions, Hollywood, California
Coca-Cola, Atlanta, Georgia
Collagen, Palo Alto, California
Comshare, Ann Arbor, Michigan
ConAgra, Omaha, Nebraska
Contexture, Salt Lake City, Utah
Control Data*, Minneapolis, Minnesota
Corporation for Open Systems, McLean, Virginia
CRSS Inc., Sterling, Virginia
Cullinet*, Atlanta, Georgia
Dana Corporation*, Toledo, Ohio
Dataquest, San Jose, California
Dayna Communications, Salt Lake City, Utah
DEC*, Maynard, Michigan
Deere & Company, Moline, Illinois
Delta Air Lines, Salt Lake City, Utah
Dialogic Systems, Sunnyville, California
DMS Systems, Salt Lake City, Utah
Do-It Systems, Albuquerque, New Mexico
Dow Chemical, Midland, Michigan
Du Pont*, Wilmington, Delaware
Eastman Kodak*, Rochester, New York
Eaton Corporation*, Cleveland, Ohio
Epsilon Data Management, Burlington, Massachusetts
Federal Express*, Memphis, Tennessee
FHP, Salt Lake City, Utah

Fidelity Investments, Boston, Massachusetts
Fireman's Fund, Novato, California
First Interstate*, Torrance, California
Florida, University of, Gainesville, Florida
FMC, Chicago, Illinois
Forecasting International, Arlington, Virginia
Ford Motor Company*, Dearborn, Michigan
Gandalf Technologies*, Ontario, Canada
Gartner Group, Stamford, Connecticut
General Dynamics*, St. Louis, Missouri
General Electric, Selkirk, New York
General Foods, White Plains, New York
General Motors*, Detroit, Michigan
General Systems Inc., Pittsfield, Massachusetts
Goetze, Muskegon, Michigan
Golder Thoma & Cressey, Chicago, Illinois
Gompertz Management Group, San Anselmo, California
Granville-Phillips, Boulder, Colorado
Hay Huggins, Los Angeles, California
Hercules*, Magna, Utah
Hewlett-Packard*, Palo Alto, California
Honeywell, Minneapolis, Minnesota
Hughes, Los Angeles, California
IBM*, San Jose, California
Information Builders, New York, New York
Information Ideas, Oakland, California
Inland Steel, Chicago, Illinois
Institute of Management Improvement, Japan
Integrated Circuits, Scottsdale, Arizona
Intel*, Santa Clara, California
International Trade Commission, Washington, DC
Internal Revenue Service, Washington, DC
Irvine Sensors, Costa Mesa, California
Jacquelyn Wonder, Denver, Colorado
J.C. Penney*, New York, New York
Jetway Systems, Ogden, Utah
J.I. Case, Racine, Wisconsin
John Hancock Insurance, Boston, Massachusetts
Johnson Wax, Racine, Wisconsin
Kellogg, Battle Creek, Michigan
Kimberly-Clark, Neenah, Wisconsin
Leaseway Transport, Cleveland, Ohio
Lee Scientific, Salt Lake City, Utah
Lincoln Electric, Cleveland, Ohio
Litton Systems*, Salt Lake City, Utah
LTV Steel, Cleveland, Ohio

Maridean Enterprises, Los Angeles, California
Marriott*, Washington, DC
Mary Kay, Dallas, Texas
Maxicare Inc., Los Angeles, California
McDonald's, Oak Brook, Illinois
McDonnell Douglas*, St. Louis, Missouri
McKesson, San Francisco, California
McKinsey & Company*, Los Angeles, California
Mead, Dayton, Ohio
Metropolitan Life, New York, New York
Micro DB Systems, West Lafayette, Indiana
Massachusetts Institute of Technology, Cambridge, Massachusetts
Mitchell Fein, Hillsdale, New Jersey
Molecular Computer, San Jose, California
Monsanto, St. Louis, Missouri
Moore Business Forms*, Glenview, Illinois
Moore Financial, Boise, Idaho
Morton Thiokol*, Brigham City, Utah
Motorola, Scottsdale, Arizona
Mutual Benefit Life*, Newark, New Jersey
Mutual of Omaha, Omaha, Nebraska
NASA, Washington, DC
National Advanced Systems*, Mountain View, California
National Science Foundation*, Washington, DC
National Semiconductor, West Jordan, Utah
Nestar Systems*, Palo Alto, California
Nolan, Norton & Co, Lexington, Massachusetts
Nordstroms, Salt Lake City, Utah
Northern Research & Engineering, Woburn, Massachusetts
Northern Telecomm*, Nashville, Tennessee
Northwest Mutual Life*, Milwaukee, Wisconsin
Novel Data Systems*, Orem, Utah
Nucor Steel, Charlotte, North Carolina
NYC Partnership Inc., New York, New York
Omark Industries, Portland, Oregon
Omnidata, Logan, Utah
Ore-Ida Foods*, Boise, Idaho
Organization Consultants, Ann Arbor, Michigan
Otis Elevators, Farmington, Connecticut
Pacific Bell, San Francisco, California
Pacific Northwest Bell, Seattle, Washington
Peak Performance, Palo Alto, California
Peat Marwick*, Salt Lake City, Utah
Penwalt, Philadelphia, Pennsylvania
Pepperidge Farm, Norwalk, Connecticut

Personnel Corporation of America, Norwalk, Connecticut
Pillsbury, Minneapolis, Minnesota
Pizza Hut, Wichita, Kansas
PPG Industries*, Pittsburgh, Pennsylvania
Price Waterhouse, New York, New York
Procter & Gamble, Cincinnati, Ohio
Productivity Inc., Norwalk, Connecticut
Psychological Consultants, Richmond, Virginia
QCI International, Red Bluff, California
Rainier Bank, Seattle, Washington
Rockwell International, Pittsburgh, Pennsylvania
RTE Corporation, Waukesha, Wisconsin
Rutgers University, New Brunswick, New Jersey
Ryder Systems*, Miami, Florida
Salomon Brothers, New York, New York
Sanders Associates, Nashua, New Hampshire
Satellite Software*, Orem, Utah
Schreiber Foods*, Green Bay, Wisconsin
Security Pacific Automation, Los Angeles, California
Security Pacific National, Los Angeles, California
Shell Oil, Houston, Texas
Software AG of North America, Reston, Virginia
Southern Bell, Atlanta, Georgia
Southland Corp, Dallas, Texas
Southwestern Bell Labs, St. Louis, Missouri
Sperry, Blue Bell, Pennsylvania
SRI International, Menlo Park, California
Steelcase, Grand Rapids, Michigan
Tandem Computer*, Cupertino, California
Tandy, Fort Worth, Texas
TeleVideo Systems, San Jose, California
Tennant Company, Minneapolis, Minnesota
Texas Instruments*, Dallas, Texas
TIAA, New York, New York
Timeplex, Woodcliff Lake, New Jersey
Toshiba, Tustin, California
Transamerica, San Francisco, California
Travelers Insurance, Hartford, Connecticut
TRW*, Cleveland, Ohio
Twin City Federal Bank, Cleveland, Ohio
Union Carbide, Danbury, Connecticut
Unisys*, Detroit, Michigan
United Energy Resources, Houston, Texas
United Steel Workers, Pittsburgh, Pennsylvania
United States Congress, Washington, DC
U.S. West Information Systems, Salt Lake City, Utah

Utah Tech-Financial Corporation*, Salt Lake City, Utah
Wang Laboratories*, Lowell, Massachusetts
Westinghouse Electric, Grand Rapids, Michigan
Westin Hotel, Seattle, Washington
Westmark, Austin, Texas
Weyerhaeuser*, Tacoma, Washington
Xerox*, Stamford, Connecticut

Assistance in arranging for these Partners seminars was provided by many individuals and organizations, including USU's President Stanford Cazier, Provost Peter E. Wagner, and Vice President William Lye.

Our College of Business Dean, David Stephens, and his faculty provided guidance and support in planning and conducting the seminars.

Assistance was willingly and conscientiously provided by numerous students. Kevin Baugh typifies the work ethic orientation of our students; with the the assistance of Kris Hammer and Jay Ward, he prepared the manuscripts with flawless accuracy and exceptional timeliness. Invaluable assistance in the planning and execution of the seminars was provided by the student staff including Brett Bagley, Rochelle Bassett, David Bland, Julie Hall, Mark Hazelgren, Kristen Henrie, Shaun Henrie, Jennifer Jenkins, Laurie Jenkins, Lee Jenkins, Paul Johnston, Glenn Morris, Daryl Nielson, David Pierce, Paula Rosson, Lauri Staheli, Larry Ward, Dave Whitehead, and Bill Wilcox. Several have graduated and are expertly applying their new understanding.

Competing Through Productivity and Quality

PART I

Competing in
Global Markets

1

Productivity and Quality: Keys to Competitive Advantage

Y.K. Shetty and Vernon M. Buehler, the Editors

Corporate America has experienced an era of competitive crisis in global markets. During the 1960s, the United States accounted for more than one-fourth of the manufacturing exports of the industrial nations and supplied 98 percent of its domestic markets. Since then it has lost much of its competitive position in international and domestic markets despite the encouraging note that U.S. manufactured exports rose 15.3 percent in 1984 and have risen again in 1988. The annual trade deficit grew to $171 billion or 4 percent of the gross national product (GNP) in 1987. It is expected to fall by $30 billion in 1988. America's trade balance in manufacturing goods has gone from a surplus of $18 billion in 1980 to a deficit of more than $160 billion in 1987. In the early 1960s, the United State produced nearly 90 percent of the color TVs made in the world. In 1987, more than half were made in Japan. In 1960, nearly half of the world's automobiles were made in America. In 1987, nearly half were made in Japan.

Evidence of the decline in U.S. competitiveness is all around us — in trade deficits that are huge despite the drop in the dollar, in slow productivity growth, in stagnant real wages, and in a declining share of world markets, even for high technology products. These threatening trends have added new urgency to the national quest for competitive renewal. Our ability to provide a continual rising standard of living is threatened.

The declining competitiveness of American business is well-documented. How to reverse this trend has become a major challenge confronting corporate America. The President's Commission on Industrial Competitiveness has made a number of recommendations in this critical area. Measures aimed at improving American competitiveness include new capital investment, reduced government regulation, restructuring corporate management, improving education (more specifically, technical education), improved labor-management cooperation, increased research and development, increased emphasis on manufacturing technology, and improved productivity and quality. Of all the proposals, productivity, quality, and innovation have attracted most business attention. By general consensus, improved productivity and quality and a strong commitment to innovation are considered to be essential for regaining sustainable competitiveness.

Many of the current studies on the competitive future of U.S. manufactured goods come down on both sides of the question of whether or not U.S. factories need a further decline in the exchange rate. Those that feel U.S. industrial competitiveness should continue to improve without more drastic dollar declines point to favorable factors such as:

1. Recent U.S. wage restraints and healthy productivity gains,
2. Efforts by manufacturers to improve quality control,
3. Recent U.S. manufacturing investments in relation to sales and factory employment that compare favorably with those in Japan and elsewhere,
4. U.S. industrial R & D spending as a percentage of manufacturing sales that has exceeded those in Japan and elsewhere, and
5. Restructuring of U.S. industry and other organizational changes that promote efficiency.

Opposing studies that see a need for further decline in the dollar feel that the United States is making progress in the above areas but overseas competitors are also moving ahead rapidly, such as in Japan, where increases in manufacturing productivity outpace those in America. These skeptics cite (1) larger Japanese investments per unit of output than in the United States, (2) smaller U.S. investments in civilian R & D on a relative basis than its major overseas competitors, and (3) America's losing race in the practical application of technology in such areas as computer controlled flexible manufacturing. It is clear from this debate that no aspect of the race for competitive advantage can be ignored. However, the editors of this volume are optimistic about the prospects for regaining U.S. competitiveness, provided that the trend toward reliance on free market forces in foreign exchange and other areas continues with minimal political interference.

The business sector has definitely gotten the message. As Allan F. Jacobson, chairman and CEO of 3M so aptly puts it, "There are only three issues critical to business success — innovation, productivity, and total quality." John Young, CEO of Hewlett-Packard and chairman of the President's Commission on Industrial Competitiveness says, "In today's competitive environment, ignoring the quality issue is tantamount to corporate suicide. Companies that continuously produce high-quality products have lower manufacturing cost, higher profit margins, and capture a larger and larger share of the market."

Major corporations throughout the United States are vigorously addressing this challenge. They have launched a variety of initiatives to improve productivity, to produce better quality products and services, and to unlock the innovative potential of their organizations to meet the challenge of international competition.

Productivity and Quality. Productivity can be defined simply as a ratio of output to input. The output is the number of units produced in a given period by a worker, a plant, a firm, or a nation's economy. Inputs are the resources used to produce certain outputs. A typical product is a combination of raw materials, machinery, labor, energy, and many other factors. Inputs are combined in the manufacturing process into products or outputs. Productivity indicates how well an organization utilizes its labor, capital, and raw material resources. The fewer resources per unit of output, the more productive. There is a direct link between productivity and competitive advantage. Improved productivity clearly reduces cost and enhances competitiveness and profitability.

Quality is a complex concept. In simple terms, quality is a key attribute that customers use to evaluate products or services. However, attributes associated with quality vary among products. For an automobile, for example, quality may include performance, durability, styling, comfort, safety, finish, speed, competence of repair, and value. Airline quality may include ease of check-in, cabin cleanliness, food, flight attendants' courtesy, and other aspects. Quality attributes may also vary between firms — for instance, quality standards probably differ between Lord & Taylor department stores and K-Mart discount stores and between Mercedes and Volkswagen automobiles. It is often difficult to precisely define quality since it has a number of components or dimensions. However, definitions usually consider performance features: reliability, conformance, durability, serviceability, aesthetics, and overall reputation or perceived quality. The relative importance of these factors and how they are defined can vary from market to market.

Quality must be defined from the customer's perspective and a firm's products and services must be compared to the products or services offered by competitors. American business tends to examine quality largely from the perspective of management. However, the customer defines quality, and management must accept the customer's perspective. It is not easy to identify customer requirements. Customer requirements must be examined continuously. Companies known for product or service quality use several methods to determine desirable quality-related attributes, including customer surveys, focus groups, customer comments, constant interaction with the customer and other methods. Once quality has been defined, a firm can test conformance and correct any problems.

Finally, quality must also include the criteria that customers use when they perceive value, a perspective that involves the concept of relative value. Relative value can be envisioned as:

$$\text{Value} = \frac{\text{Quality}}{\text{Price}}$$

Thus, product preference is determined by the value of the perceived quality/price ratio of one product in relation to another competing product.

Quality and Profitability. Is a strategy to improve product quality profitable? While the literature on product quality is voluminous, the linkage between quality and profitability has not been carefully explored. U.S. firms have traditionally viewed quality and productivity as distinctly different concepts. Efforts to improve quality have, therefore, been perceived to increase costs and reduce productivity and profitability. In recent years scholars such as W. Edwards Deming, Joseph Juran, Philip B. Crosby and others have attempted to correct this misconception. According to Deming, quality is productivity. He contends that productivity improves and costs decrease as quality is improved. A company captures the market and becomes more profitable when it couples lower prices with higher quality. Crosby says quality is free, and disregarding quality is costly. In short, it pays to do jobs right the first time.

Peters and Waterman in their popular book, *In Search of Excellence: Lessons from America's Best-Run Companies*, documented that well-managed U.S. corporations that are most profitable also emphasize product and service quality. Their research confirmed that companies such as Hewlett-Packard, IBM, Marriott, Procter and Gamble, Johnson and Johnson, Maytag, Merck, and Walt Disney provided quality products and services and also ranked in the top of their respective industries in at least four out of six financial criteria over a 20-year period. The financial criteria included compound asset growth, compound equity growth, the average ratio of market value to book value, average return on total capital, average return on equity, and the average return of sales. The results clearly show that America's best-run companies use product quality to enhance profit performance.

A large-scale study, conducted by the Strategic Planning Institute of Cambridge, Massachusetts, provided more quantitative data concerning the link between quality and profitability. This study, "Profit Impact of Marketing Strategies" (PIMS), involved 1,200 businesses. The quality ratings were based on executives' estimates of the proportion of sales of (a) products clearly superior in quality to those of its largest competitors, (b) those of equivalent quality, and (c) those of inferior quality. Both return on investment and net profit as a percentage of sales rose as relative quality increased. The return on investment ranged from 13 percent for the businesses ranked in the lowest one-fifth product quality category to 30 percent for those ranking in the highest one-fifth, a statistically significant difference. Businesses selling high-quality products or services are generally more profitable than those whose product are of lower quality.

How does product quality affect profitability? Quality can increase profits by lowering costs, increasing sales, or a combination of both factors.

Quality Improves Productivity. "Doing it right the first time" reduces costs, and thus increases productivity, in several ways. Eliminating defects or errors reduces labor and/or machine hours. It also reduces inspection costs and the level of inventories for replacements. Reducing scrap and waste reduces the cost of materials. Fewer warranty claims decrease the material and labor required to repair defective products. A reduction in service costs decreases labor costs. A low-cost producer can use its cost advantage to increase profit margins and/or lower prices for improved sales.

Substantial cost savings accrue from reduced rework, scrap, and lower inspection, warranty, and product liability costs. IBM estimates that 30 percent of its manufacturing cost — the total cost of detection and appraisal — was the direct result of not doing it right the first time. Hewlett-Packard calculated that as much as 25 percent of its manufacturing assets was tied up in reacting to quality problems. Eliminating these costs could increase output by a similar percentage, thus triggering a comparable percentage increase in profitability.

Calculating the cost of poor quality is one of the best ways to convince top managers and employees that quality significantly affects productivity and profitability. Cost of poor quality is simply any expenditure, manufacturing and service, above that incurred if the product was built right the first time. Total quality costs typically include expenditures concerning:

1. *Prevention costs* — steps taken to assure tasks are always done right the first time, which include quality planning, worker training, and supplier education.
2. *Appraisal costs* — costs associated with evaluating whether a task, in fact, has been done right the first time, typical costs include product inspection and testing.
3. *Internal failures* — costs associated with correcting mistakes. These costs include rework and scrap.
4. *External failures* — costs associated with any failures experienced by the customer, including costs of warranty and product liability.

In most companies, however, such cost information is not readily available. Accounting information systems focus on financial data and not on data concerning the cost of poor quality. Despite the fact that many companies seem to recognize the need for better quality, their financial and accounting systems do not yet reflect product quality information.

Quality Enhances Sales. Quality also affects a firm's sales and market share. First, the reputation for higher quality decreases the elasticity of demand and provides opportunities for companies to charge higher prices and earn higher profit margins. Second, a reputation for quality also improves chances of enhancing sales and market share. PIMS data confirm that high-quality products and services increase sales and market share. Businesses that improved quality increased their market share five or six times faster than those whose products declined in quality, and three times faster than those whose quality was similar to that of their competitors. Even when increasing quality required more expensive materials and manufacturing processes, the price differentials typically exceeded the higher costs.

Quality improvement is a powerful means of building market share. Research based on PIMS data concerning the relationship between advertising, price, product quality, and market share showed that (a) changes in the relative product quality are strongly related to changes in market share, (b) relative advertising had only a modest relationship to changes in market share, and (c) the relative changes in price were not related to changes in market share. The benefits of simply lowering prices are short-lived as competitors quickly match decreases in price. Quality improvement, on the other hand, is much more difficult for other companies to match; it requires more time, money, and creativity.

A reduction in quality can suddenly reduce sales, harm the competitive position of a company, and reduce customer loyalty. Failure to correct quality errors can lead to incalculable losses. A leading manufacturer of appliances estimates that one in three dissatisfied customers will complain to the company; however, each dissatisfied customer complains to at least 15 friends and acquaintances. One "Big-Three" automobile company estimated that a single dissatisfied owner of a luxury car costs the company no fewer than 100 lost sales in a single year. Recent studies conducted by Ford Motor Company show that satisfied customers tell eight other people about their car, while dissatisfied customers complain to 22 people.

Recognizing the importance of productivity and quality, many companies have taken initiatives aimed at improving productivity and quality to gain competitive advantage. Though some companies have made substantial improvements, many have not yet fully recaptured the reputation for product quality. A recent study conducted by the American Society for Quality Control (ASQC) showed that eight out of ten executives believe that product quality plays a very important role in making U.S. companies more competitive with foreign nations and quality will be essential to their own companies' ability to compete in intensely competitive marketplaces.

Productivity Investments Based on Intangibles. There is a growing concern over the fact that American manufacturers have been plowing billions into high-tech equipment and automation without paying off in higher productivity. Investment has been done using conventional accounting methods based on projected direct labor savings. This fails to account for such intangibles as better quality, greater flexibility, faster time to market, quicker order processing, and higher customer satisfaction. The latter factors contribute significantly to the bottom line but most capital decisions still use the classical return-on-investment calculations that seek to recover funds only from labor cost savings and not from gains in business.

To correct this, enlightened management is adopting a "new math" of productivity that points to "time" as being the manufacturers' most valuable commodity. New technologies such as flexible manufacturing enable factories to rapidly shift from one product to another, cut lead time, and speed their response time to customer demands. This drives down economies of scale so that producing in batches of one can be done about as cheaply as larger batches. By doing so, inventories are also minimized.

This "new math" recognizes that investments must be made to improve competitive advantage which increasingly depends on higher quality standards, more timely response, and increased flexibility to meet a greater variety of products. Many ideas of this "new math" are being tested by companies. A task force of a U.S. and European non-profit research consortium called Computer Aided Manufacturing-International is examining new ways that will replace old-time accounting practices and revolutionize the way business calculates costs.

As noted, "time" is being increasingly recognized as a manufacturer's chief strategic weapon. It represents an important competitive advantage. Leading manufacturers world-wide are focusing on gaining this critical time-based competitive advantage in all phases of their operations. They are shortening the planning loop in the product development cycle, trimming process time in the factory by short production runs and small lot sizes, cutting sales and distribution cycle times by speeding information flow, and accelerating product innovation by making continuous smaller increments of improvements in new products. Time, then, together with cost, is the critical competitive force.

Major Seminar Themes. This book is based on the material presented in the 1988 annual seminars on managing productivity, quality, human resources, and information technology. It provides a variety of perspectives, approaches, and views concerning productivity and quality and many suggestions for improvement at the national and business level. Major themes of this book are discussed in four parts: Part I, Competing in Global Markets; Part II, Human Dimensions of Productivity; Part III, Exploiting Information Technology; and Part IV, Company Practices for Enhancing Productivity and Quality.

Competing in Global Markets. The papers in this part provide a wide variety of perspectives that describe and prescribe different points of view aimed at improving U.S. competitiveness. These perspectives range from C. Jackson Grayson's fairly wide-ranging reviews of productivity and its role in influencing business success, national strength, and the world's standard of living to Herbert A. Simon's view of managing information to enhance productivity and John Young's prescription on how to respond to global competition at the national and business level. The general tone of these papers is that the world is becoming a global market and that America's competitive problem is growing, and that, on a positive note, the U.S. business sector has the resources and imagination to face its challenge. The general theme of this section is that there is a need to better understand the problem of global competition and to examine appropriate solutions aimed at reversing America's declining ability to compete.

Human Dimensions of Productivity. Experiences of a large number of companies suggest that human resource is the key to productivity and quality. Companies unanimously agree that where proper attention is paid to people, productivity and quality naturally follow. At least, there are two basic rationale for this contention.

First, all inputs required to attain and sustain consistent productivity and quality — modern technology, statistical quality control, automation, process control, investment, control over suppliers, computer-based design and manufacturing, and all else that a firm uses to make improvement — is unproductive except for human efforts. All activities required to improve productivity and quality are initiated and sustained by human efforts. Every aspect of improvement effort is determined by the competence, motivation, and attitudes of its employees. Of all tasks required to make productivity and quality a top priority in an organization, managing the human side is the central task, because all else depends on how well this task is performed.

Secondly, poorly served employees perform and serve company customers poorly. In many companies employees are treated poorly and managed ineffectively. They are treated as valueless and unintelligent. The employees in turn are not only less productive but convey the identical message to the customer. If management treats employees' concerns with indifference, then employees will not care about their work and customer satisfaction. It is a rare employee who can rise above the effects of such poor management treatment and be productive.

Papers in this part contain material on how to make the human organization effective for better productivity and quality. Topics discussed cover the experiences of a number of companies, including Ford Motor Company, Xerox, General Dynamics, Westinghouse, Transamerica, and many others. They cover areas such as the HR role in strategic planning, employee involvement, creativity, pay for performance, women in management, compensation strategies, and innovative management. The general theme is clear: Employees are the key to improving productivity, quality, and customer service. Hence, human resources must be managed with utmost care for successful outcome.

Exploiting Information Technology. Information technology is growing and has become a major tool for productivity enhancement and quality. This part contains a number of papers on the topic. Some deal with certain aspects of information technology while others discuss how companies are using this technology for improving business performance. The topics range from the development of standards for exchanging data among disparate systems to the increasing use of networks through interconnectivity and interoperability, and to the exporting of information technology for increasing productivity through simulations and improved administrative practices. All these themes are relevant for companies that are interested in exploiting information technology for gaining productivity, profitability, and competitive edge. It is an evolving theme and companies will gain by closely monitoring its evolution on a continuous basis.

An overriding message surfaces from all papers without exception, namely that the future of the Information Age depends on the adoption of international agreements for openness and standardization of computer systems. The effective use of the world's 50 million computers depends on a fundamental revolution in the economics of information management that is presently in progress. As these papers indicate, the computer industry after four decades of delay is gradually adopting reliable, vendor-neutral standards that permit dissimilar computer systems to run the same software programs and communicate openly with one another.

When this standardization and openness is achieved as it has long existed in the telephone and other fields of communications, immense benefits will be realized. Productivity by users will improve, computing costs will decrease, competition among vendors will increase, and technological progress will be advanced. All the papers in this part, whether dealing with networking, simulation, Integrated Services Digital Networks (ISDN), or administrative productivity stress the desirability of single-vendor-neutral standards. And they feel this will be realized in the 1990s, provided users will speak out and assert their interests. This optimism for interconnectivity and software portability comes from such developments as OSI, ISDN, COS, and the new efforts of the members of the Open Software Foundation.

Company Practices for Enhancing Quality and Productivity. This part provides material on company practices and experiences in enhancing productivity and quality. These papers answer the question of how to improve productivity and quality in a direct manner by examining company experiences as they relate to improvement efforts. They discuss computer integrated manufacturing, total quality control, employee driven productivity, teamwork, and many other topics. Many techniques and approaches have the potential for improving productivity and quality, such as statistical quality control, automation, computer-based design and manufacturing, quality circles, and many others. Quality and productivity experts such as W. Edwards Deming, Philip B. Crosby, Joseph M. Juran, Armand Feigenbaum, and others have developed specific programs.

The experiences of numerous companies examined in this book and elsewhere suggest an important point: Programs and techniques must be tailored to specific problems and business situations. No single approach or technique is best for all companies. Productivity and quality problems facing different companies must be precisely defined and the attributes and limitations of different approaches must be recognized before the actions are taken.

Several of the papers address practices for improving manufacturing which many authorities feel have been neglected and thus have become a key cause of our lagging growth in productivity. In contrast, Japan, Taiwan, and Korea have proven extremely adept at adopting innovative processing technologies, embedding them in new capital equipment, and creating the skilled work force that can effectively use them. This has led to dramatic improvements in manufacturing efficiencies and quality that have made countries of East Asia such formidable competitors in world markets.

The paper by Shigeo Shingo typifies the improved manufacturing methodologies used in Japan and elsewhere. Shingo is known as the world's leading expert on improving the manufacturing process. In his paper he describes his SMED (single-minute exchange of die) concept, his Poka-yoke defect prevention system, and his non-stock production (NSP) system for eliminating or reducing inventories. Using these and others of his manufacturing methods including active employee involvement, he helped make Toyota the most productive auto manufacturer in the world. His work helped hundreds of companies worldwide (including Ford, Omark Industries, and Granville-Phillips whose papers are included herein) save billions of dollars in manufacturing costs annually. These savings come from cuts in defects, inventories, lead time, floor space, and costs of transportation and delays. Probably most important, these improved methods have saved time in responding to customer orders and in designing new products. And by saving time, these improvements have created a valuable competitive advantage.

Taken together, papers in this volume provide a wide variety of views, approaches, techniques, and tools for improving productivity and quality and gaining competitive advantage. The particular merits of each paper as well as the collection as a whole now await your closer inspection. In today's highly competitive global marketplace, learning to effectively manage productivity and quality may, in fact, provide the single greatest managerial challenge. A strong commitment to productivity and quality is the best way to reduce costs, increase sales, and enhance profitability and competitiveness.

2

Productivity for All Seasons: Yesterday, Today, and Tomorrow*

C. Jackson Grayson, Chairman, American Productivity Center

Productivity, in the long run, is the single most important factor that influences (a) the survival of businesses, (b) the economic, political, and military strength of nations, and (c) the world's standard of living.

It provides profits, jobs, real wages, education, health care, roads, defense, and — ultimately — productivity determines the rank of nations.

Given this critical and central role of productivity in the well-being of all nations, it is incredible how relatively under-used productivity is in determining public policy in governments, how often productivity is misused or not used at all in running profit and non-profit organizations, how many myths and misunderstandings there are about productivity, and — compared to other economic concepts — how relatively little is done to measure it, to integrate it into economic theory, or to understand very well why it grows and why it declines.

---

* Adapted from the book by C. Jackson Grayson, Jr. and Carla O'Dell, *American Business: A Two-Minute Warning* (New York: Free Press, 1988). Originally given as the Shirley Kallek Memorial Lecture, Bureau of the Census, April, 1988.

I want to share with you a few of my views, based on ten years of work in the American Productivity Center, about productivity — yesterday, today, and tomorrow.

Productivity Yesterday: The Rise and Decline of Nations. Why is productivity yesterday important? For the same reasons we find history of value.

We can learn from the past — clues as to what caused productivity to grow, to stagnate, and to decline in nations, and attempt to arrive at some lessons from history to guide us in the future.

When I first did reading in history focusing on productivity, I presumed, as do most people, that growth through productivity started fairly soon after man stopped his nomadic wanderings around 8000 BC and settled down to agriculture and that it accelerated even more around 4500 BC when the first civilizations were formed. That's not quite right.

There was almost no growth in income per person (or population) from 8000 BC until the 1700s — almost a 10,000 year period! There was some absolute growth in population and incomes but, spread out over thousands of years, the rate of growth was almost imperceptible.

Of course, there were wealthy civilizations — Babylon, Persia, Phoenicia, Egypt, Rome. All accumulated fabulous wealth. The annual income per person in Rome is estimated by some to have been about $250 to $300 in today's dollars; not bad considering the 1987 estimate for the Peoples' Republic of China is about $230. But their wealth didn't come from growth as we know it today. It came primarily from taking it away from one another — thighbone bashing, war and plunder, expropriation, and "beggar-thy-neighbor" trading. It was mostly a win-lose world.

Growth through productivity — win-win — is really an invention of Western civilization, and it is only about 200 to 250 years old. Since then, only three nations have led the world in productivity growth. Can you guess who they are?

Most people immediately assume England, as the home of the Industrial Revolution, was the first leader. That is wrong. The world's first productivity leader was the Netherlands. Angus Maddison, former chief economist of the Organization for European Cooperation and Development (OECD), names the Dutch as the world's first real productivity leader, pacing the world for most of the 18th century — from about 1700 to 1785. As the world leader, they grew rich, powerful, and finally, complacent. They shouldn't have: The British were coming.

England began to improve its productivity growth in the last quarter of the 18th century, as the first effects of the Industrial Revolution were felt. Hargreave's Spinning Jenny (1764) permitted a 16-fold productivity increase in spinning soft welt. Arkwright's spinning frame (1768), Watt's steam engine (1776) and other technical developments began to increase the rate of England's productivity growth. The word "productivity" first appeared in print in 1766 interestingly not in England, but in France.

England's average rate of productivity growth was a steady, though tiny, 0.5 percent per year for the last few decades of the 18th century. But that rate of growth — plus Dutch stagnation — was sufficient for the British to pass the Dutch in productivity level around 1785.

England became number one — the world's second productivity leader. It became the technological wonder and workshop of the world, as David Landes put it, ". . . the very model of industrial excellence and achievement," and had incredible world economic power.

But the British, like the Dutch before them, became complacent, idealized themselves and their own past, and didn't look back to see if anybody was gaining. They should have. Two major competitors — America and Germany — were growing faster in productivity than the British.

It was very important to note that even though British productivity was still growing at an average rate of 1.3 percent during this period, England was losing. America's productivity was growing faster, at a rate of 2.1 percent. Though the difference in productivity growth rates was very small — only 0.8 percent — this small difference, compounded over time, was enough for the United States to pass England in productivity level in the 1890s.

The United States became number one, the productivity leader of the world, the position it still holds today.

To recap:

	Leader	Years as #1
1700–1785	Netherlands	85
1785–1890	England	105
1890–present	United States	98

The rise and decline of nations is the tale of long distance runners. Relative positions change slowly, but they do change. It is, as Landes said, "a race without a finishing line."

Now, the trillion-dollar question: Is there to be a fourth number 1? Who? When? And what are the implications if the leadership changes hands?

No one can answer any of those questions with certainty, but from my review of the history of productivity, ten lessons emerged that we would do well to remember as we turn to productivity today:

1. Complacency is the cancer of leadership and seems to infect all leaders.
2. Leaders overlook the relative growth rates of their challengers.
3. Productivity changes are so slow that leaders fail to sense, in time, the cumulative gains made by challengers.
4. Initial size of nations is not a predictor of winners.
5. Gainers have drive, hunger, desire — the "eye of the tiger" that focuses their energies.
6. Challengers stress education very heavily.
7. Gainers copy the leaders, adapt, and improve.
8. Quality improvement and customer focus are key strategies of challengers.
9. Protection helps challengers; it hurts leaders.
10. The leader's ability to adjust diminishes over time.

As the present world productivity leader, the United States would do well to keep these lessons in mind as it contemplates the 21st century, and those now challenging it for economic leadership. And there are challengers.

Productivity Today: Competitiveness. It would be hard to find anyone who does not now know that there has been a serious decline in the rate of American productivity (GNP/hour, business sector):

Year	Rate of Growth
1948–65	3.2%
1965–73	2.1
1973–77	1.1
1977–87	1.0
1987–	0.9

Numerous researchers have attempted to find the causes of the slowdown. They have rounded up a number of traditional economic suspects: inadequate capital investments and R & D, age/sex work force composition, energy costs, inflation, government regulations, and more.

However, none of the suspects has been convicted, for there is still wide disagreement on the degree of influence of the various sus-} ʿcts, plus there are those among us who do not believe that the tradiuonal list contains all suspects. To make matters worse, nearly every researcher, even after exhaustive econometric calculations, has been left with as much as 40 to 50 percent of the slowdown simply unexplainable. This "residual" has been appropriately called by some the "measure of ignorance." In other words, we still don't completely understand it.

While we are trying to figure out what caused our slowdown, other nations, particularly Asian, have been growing much faster in productivity and now challenge the productivity leadership of the United States. There are problems measuring and comparing productivity across nations which I will discuss later, but for the moment, let's use the most widely available yardstick: gross domestic product (GDP) per employee.

GDP Per Employee

	1986 U.S. Dollars (Purchasing Power)	Growth Rates 1973-1986
United States	$37,565	0.5%
Canada	35,670	1.2
Netherlands	32,415	0.7
France	31,667	2.2
Belgium	30,543	2.0
Germany	30,390	2.2
Norway	30,114	2.4
U.K.	26,448	1.5
Japan	25,882	2.8

Though the United States is still the world productivity leader, if one assumes that the trend rates of 1973 to 1986 were to continue, then the United States would lose its leadership to a number of nations in the next few decades.

Country	Year Lead Lost
Canada	1994
France	1996
Norway	1998
West Germany	1999
Belgium	2000
Japan	2003

Of course, trend rates do not have to continue. But if they do, by the year 2003, the United States will rank seventh in productivity level (GDP/employee) among leading industrialized nations. History shows that when a nation loses the productivity lead, in subsequent decades it also loses the world economic and political leadership. That could occur in the early part of the 21st century.

There is, however, some encouraging news and some factors that argue against the decline possibility:

1. The United States has recently had a surge in manufacturing productivity and the problem is solved.
2. The measures of service sector productivity are imperfect and the slowdown may not be as extensive as believed.
3. The challengers, having almost "caught up" will now slow down their faster pace and not overtake America.
4. The United States is now sufficiently awake to the problem and will adjust and retain its leadership.

I hope that the above is true. But I do not think so. That is why I wrote a book just published in February co-authored with Carla O'Dell, called *American Business: A Two-Minute Warning*, which says, among other things:

- The United States is still losing (not "has lost") the productivity lead.
- While the news about manufacturing productivity is encouraging, the trend in productivity growth of the service sector (nearly 70 percent of the GNP) is almost zero, and trends do not change quickly.
- Though some of the productivity measures are imperfect, especially in services, we have not changed the measures and the trends are still essentially telling the right story.

- The overall U.S. response is still not sufficient.
- History shows that challengers do not have to slow down when they reach the leader's level — almost everyone passed England. And, in one of history's lessons, relative differences matter. A small difference of even less than 1 percent compounds slowly, but inexorably, and topples leaders.

If the United States, as England, becomes a "weary Titan" — to borrow Joseph Chamberlain's phrase — and declines, it will be because of a failure to maintain its productivity leadership in a hotly competitive global economy. Should that occur, the implications for this nation and for the world are enormous.

That is why it is very important for the United States and other nations to pay more attention to productivity — how to measure it, how to compare relative productivities across nations, what the sources and obstacles are to productivity growth, and how we can make productivity growth the win-win strategy for all citizens of this earth.

That's the challenge of productivity tomorrow.

Productivity Tomorrow: The Global Economy. Plate tectonics is the study of the ebb and flow of land masses — continents — and the forces that affect them. Similarly, forces are at work producing major changes in world economies which might be called "economic tectonics." Both are processes of destruction and creation, changing the face of the globe.

Economic tectonics is reshaping international competition, entire industries, notions of comparative advantage, even the concept of national economies. Instead of breaking apart like the continents, the 186 economies of the world are flowing together — imploding — becoming more integrated, interrelated, and interdependent.

As Dorothy in *The Wizard of Oz* said, "Toto, I don't think we're in Kansas anymore." She's right. While the world has not yet become Marshall McLuhan's global village, the first outline of the competitive characteristics of this new global economy are becoming apparent:

1. *Global Production*: Products made and services delivered everywhere by everybody.
2. *Technology*: Technology no longer the monopoly of advanced nations; copying, improving, and rapidly applying may pay off better than inventing.

3. *Comparative Advantage*: Dynamic and man-made, not static and fixed by nature. Natural resource-poor nations can become strong international competitors.
4. *Human Capital*: The greatest value-added source, not physical capital or natural resources.
5. *Financial*: Incredible financial power coming from the Orient, especially Japan — the financial powerhouse of the 21st century.
6. *Flexibility*: A premium on rapid adaptation, not specialized skills.
7. *Protection*: Increased danger of world trade barriers and retaliatory trade wars.
8. *Quality*: Ever more important, especially in service/information oriented economies.
9. *Arbitrage*: Jobs and factories moving across nations to obtain lower costs, highest productivity, and quality.
10. *Commoditization*: Declining importance of traditional commodities and quick commoditization of technical advancements.
11. *Centrally Planned Economies*: The entrance and integration of centrally planned economies into the world economy.
12. *Have's and Have-Not's*: The wealth gap that is likely to grow between economically advanced and less developed nations.
13. *Multi-Polar World*: The end of U.S. economic hegemony and the emergence of a multi-polar economy.
14. *Pacific Basin*: The economic center of the world in the 21st century. The Asian-Pacific nations alone will create over 20 percent of the world GDP by the year 2000 — the equal of America or Europe. And one of every two people on earth will live in Asia.

You know the world is changing when Coca-Cola earned more in 1987 in Japan than it did in the United States, when Italy passed England in 1987 in GDP/capita, and when seven of the top ten banks in the world are Japanese. Given these system-wrenching changes, how can firms, industries, and nations monitor and adjust to the changes?

Productivity is the one factor more than any other that can help to monitor, organize, and channel the destructive-creative economic tectonic forces for tomorrow. I suggest productivity as the organizing theme for the global economy. If that is to happen, we have a lot of work to do.

The main points I want to stress up front are:

1. A major effort must be made to raise the level of productivity understanding, productivity consciousness, productivity education, and usage of productivity in business, government, and non-profit organizations in all nations.

2. Better international comparative productivity data are needed. All nations need to work together to improve comparability standards.
3. The United States has the best productivity data system in the world right now. But it needs major improvement and should be prepared to help others who wish assistance.
4. There is not a lot of time for these changes to be made if the world is to avoid some undesirable consequences.

To Begin. Time is too limited today to outline all the steps that would be required to launch such a large-scale effort, but it is important to begin. For the United States, I suggest as a first step that we set a national goal of 2.5 percent annual productivity improvement. Ask the new President — whoever that may be — to announce it in the spring of 1989.

Many government agencies and many firms in the private sector would need to be consulted and brought into the thinking, discussing, organizing, and planning process as to how the nation could work toward this goal — getting productivity explicitly considered in public policy formulation, improving productivity in government, improving productivity in firms and industries, and so on.

In the remainder of this chapter, I will focus on a very important area: productivity statistics, or the way we keep score.

Productivity Statistics. The United States has one of the best productivity statistics gathering and dissemination programs in the world. Even so, it needs improvement.

In 1979, a panel formed by the National Academy of Science did a comprehensive review of government data on productivity and came up with 23 recommendations. The main categories:

• Measurement of output (especially quality, health, education, regulations)
• Measurement of inputs (capital, labor, intermediate inputs, and multi-factor measures)
• Measurement of sources of change
• International comparisons of output and productivity
• Presentation and interpretation of productivity measures
• Inter-agency cooperation and coordination
• Inter-firm comparisons

The panel's chairman, Al Rees, pointed out that their work came uncomfortably close to reviewing the entire body of economic statistics collected by the federal government. I faced the same problem in this lecture, for if I were to look at all statistics that impact productivity, I would need to examine needs for improved statistics in savings, investment, R & D, education, trade, interest, price indexes, and many others. (This illustrates the pervasiveness of productivity as a central economic concept for nations.)

A report on the status on the panel's recommendations was prepared in 1983 for the White House Conference on Productivity. It showed much progress on many of the recommendations, and work continues.

It is not possible to comment on each recommendation, but I do want to indicate several items to which I think high priority should be given. This statement of needs neither overlooks nor is intended to disparage past accomplishments or ongoing progress. What it does mean is that we need to move forward even further and faster:

- *Quality* — improved measures of quality changes in products and services.
- *Services* — improved measures for the service sector.
- *Industries* — deeper and wider coverage of industries.
- *Total factor* — expand to two-digit standard industrial classification (SIC) code level.
- *SIC codes* — more frequent revisions in SIC codes to reflect more rapid shifts in the economy.
- *Revisions* — reduce magnitude of revisions.
- *Statistical enclave* — the organization of some body inside government to work toward coordinating data collection and data exchange in government.
- *Users* — involve users in design, analysis, and dissemination of data; not only train managers in statistics, but also train statisticians in management.
- *Forecasting* — improve the accuracy of forecasts of productivity because it is such a critical component of GNP growth. Every 1 percent increase in productivity adds about $32 billion to real GNP.

Though all these are important, I see the greatest need for expanded work in the international area.

Comparative Economic Statistics. The major gap in productivity statistics, in my opinion, is the international arena — sector and industry level and trend comparisons among nations. It is increasingly important for several reasons:

• *Developed nations.* Developed nations need relative productivity data if they are to stay ahead of hard charging challengers. No longer can they remain inward-focused, complacent about their lead, and stick with old industries, techniques, and ideas. Firms need such data to know when their productivity is declining relative to others — how fast, in what industries, and whether they are gaining or falling behind.

The populations of the developed nations are also aging fast. The OECD projects that by 2020 the United States will have 16 percent of its population 65 and older; Japan 21 percent; France 20 percent; U.K. 15 percent, and Germany a whopping 22 percent. The challenge will be to keep these nations adjusting, not resisting change, and having sufficient productivity to afford the higher pension and health costs of an older, non-working population.

• *Rapid change.* The need for timely knowledge about relative productivity differentials has always existed — England might not have met her economic fate had she seen such data in time, in the late 19th century.

Today, such information is not only still needed, it is needed rapidly. Enormous advances in transportation and communication and widespread education have collapsed time and geography and redistributed skills and technology at an incredibly fast rate. A two-year lag in productivity data could be fatal for some industries. For example, the day after the announcement of superconductivity, Japan's Ministry of Trade and Industry (MITI) called a meeting of business executives, scientists, and government officials to launch a scientific and commercial program to exploit the potential of superconductivity as fast as developments occur. Comparative advantage these days is about as fleeting as fame.

• *Centrally planned economies.* All together, the centrally planned economies (CPEs) of the world constitute almost 25 percent of world GNP — not an insignificant figure. However, political differences have, in the past, largely sealed off those nations from comparable data collection and analysis.

For example, CPEs do not use the two most familiar measures of national output, namely GDP and GNP. Instead, they call aggregated national income "net material product (NMP)," a term that connotes material output and those services deemed "productive."

Glasnost and *perestroika* are now opening a window for the CPEs to become part of the global economic community. If the world is to seize this opportunity to build a truly global economy, their data and relative productivities need to be integrated into the global economy.

Developing Nations (LDCs). It is clear that the differences in GNP per person across the globe are largely explained by differences in productivity, and the LDCs are evidence of that.

The GNP of China, the most populous nation on earth, is exceeded by the GNP of four relatively tiny western European nations — the United Kingdom, France, West Germany, and Italy. Pakistan, with a population close to 100 million, has about 15 times as many people as Switzerland, but a GNP about one-third as large. The explanation is lower relative productivity.

And it could get worse. The LDCs continue to expand their populations at a fast clip. While the LDC population growth rates have slowed a little to about 2 percent annually, that rate is still four times faster than the industrial market countries rate of 0.5 percent. Ben Wattenberg estimates that the fraction of total world population in the western community will be only 13 percent by 2010, dropping to 5 percent by 2085. By the year 2000, the developing nations of the world will constitute 80 percent of the world's population of an estimated 6.2 million people, and how they fare will impact world growth and world peace.

The LDCs of the world need not only productivity information as a guide to development, but also assistance on how to improve productivity. Because if they do not, the lower productivity of LDCs forces these nations to compete on the basis of protection, subsidies, low wages and profits, and a low standard of living — thus trapping an ever larger part of the world in unending relative poverty.

Finally, unless developed nations' productivity growth rates stay robust, the LDCs' markets will dry up and they will be effectively frozen at their levels of poverty, disease, and ignorance: an inhumanity and a danger. With large populations constituting a majority of the world — many with large debt levels and a growing gap between the have's and have-not's — the situation is a ticking economic time bomb.

What Data Do We Have Now? We now have comparative productivity data generated by national governments, the OECD, national productivity centers, the Asian Productivity Organization, the International Monetary Fund, the World Bank, the CIA, the United Nations, associations, consultants, newspapers and magazines, and others.

But what it all adds up to is pretty deficient, compared to what is needed. The main bases for comparisons now are:

- *GDP/capita*: Gross domestic products (GDP) divided by the entire population. Levels and growth rates are available for most nations. While a measure of national wealth, it is not a good productivity measure because GDP is divided by every man, woman, and child whether employed or not.
- *GDP/employee*: GDP divided by the employed labor force. A better productivity measure, but it does not account for the difference among nations in hours worked. Available in levels and trends for major nations and trend data for selected industries.
- *GDP/hour*: GDP divided by hours worked or paid. The best productivity measure, but generally not available internationally for comparisons, except for manufacturing productivity in advanced industrial nations, and even then only growth rates, not levels.
- *Currency conversions*: Market exchange rates are available for most all nations except CPEs. To attempt to improve comparability, "purchasing power parity" exchange rates are used for most major nations.

There are a number of reasons why such data have not been collected extensively to date:

- A belief that comparative data are not needed, especially when the world grew more slowly and economies were more isolated.
- Difficulties in obtaining data from some nations where such data either do not exist or are available only with long lags.
- Differing definitions, methods of estimating, and classification systems for the various components of productivity: base years, hours worked, capital, output, industries, etc.
- Nations not always on the same calendar year complicate the job of comparisons.
- Lack of language skills to read, write, or communicate with a multitude of nations make it difficult to gather and interpret data.
- Data secrecy, controlled markets, and artificial official exchange rates in centrally planned nations.
- Low interest (thus, low priority) up until now in comparative international statistics by politicians, government officials, businessmen, and many economists.
- Lack of funds to expand statistical work.

What Data Are Needed? The following is a list of what I think should be adopted as minimum goals of improving international productivity statistics. (Data are also needed for other relevant economic statistics such as savings, investment, R & D, and so forth):

- *Two key productivity indicators* — *GDP/employee and GDP/hour*: For nations, sectors, and industries, regarding both levels and growth rates.
- *Data standards*: A standardized system for recording or converting economic data for comparison purposes.
- *Timeliness*: Data not more than 12 months old across the world.
- *Currency conversion*: An improved and constantly updated system for converting currencies to a common denominator for comparisons ("purchasing power parities").
- *CPEs*: The conversion of centrally planned and mixed economies' data into comparative terms, even if imputation and estimation are required.

None of the above will be easy or swift. But few projects could be of as much importance, not only for the United States, but for the world. Even if the measures can't be precise or as neat as we would like, at least let's develop surrogates, proxies, estimates, and label them as such.

Though it may sound heretical to a purist, I agree with a teacher of mine who once said, "If it's worth doing, it's worth doing badly."

How To Begin. I suggest that the United States take a leadership role, initiated by the Census Bureau.

Let's seek simultaneously the involvement and participation of organizations in America and all over the world. As an example involve the U.S. Departments of Labor, Commerce, and State; OECD; national productivity centers; APO; consulting and accounting firms; and CPEs, perhaps through the Council for Mutual Economic Assistance (COMECON). The American Productivity Center would be glad to be a part of the effort.

The Census Bureau already has a network of thousands and experience in international coordination of data through its International Statistical Programs Center (ISPC), the Foreign Demographic Analysis Division (FDAD), and the International Demographic Data Center (IDDC). There are undoubtedly other units and individuals in Census, Labor, and Commerce who could form a cadre of expertise to initiate the effort.

Where Will the Funds Come From? This will cost money. While everyone acknowledges the importance of data for decision making, providing funds for statistics gets extremely low priority in the federal budget of the United States, and probably the same is true in most other nations.

Such funds are begrudgingly allocated, always in small increments and within traditional fields. To make it worse, budget cuts in the United States have impaired the overall statistical effort — statistical funding is one of the first to go. Funds for statistics do not have the sex appeal or political clout of new bridges, social security, and weapon systems.

Regardless, I recommend large-scale funding of an improved productivity (and other economic) statistics effort even in the face of large U.S. budget deficits. The funds are a necessity, an investment in the future of America — economically and militarily.

Economically, each 1-percent gain in productivity adds about 32 billion real dollars to the economy annually. Militarily, history repeatedly shows that when an economy declines, military power erodes. There is a significant correlation over time between economic strength and military strength. If there is no other way to secure funds, it would be a good investment in defense to cut the U.S. defense budget to fund this program.

Some short-term goals should be set for the first five-year period. But for the bulk of the effort, I would set the year 2000 as the goal for reaching all major milestones — that's only 12 years away.

Productivity: A Unifying Theme. What are the dangers if we don't do this? Stagnation, poverty, and war. History shows that when nations feel economically trapped, or great powers see early stages of decline, they often resort to war. If war is avoided by the major powers, then stagnation and poverty are likely to be the lot of a growing majority of the world's population. While in the past they had to — or were willing to — tolerate these disparities, such is not likely to be the case in the future.

I have four children, aged 8 to 28. And I want them to grow up in a win-win world, for themselves and for all the people on this globe. The rising tide could lift all boats, and even rescue those under water. If that is to happen, my strong belief is that the single greatest contributor will be a universal rise in productivity growth all over the globe. I would rather all of us work on a productivity gap than a missile gap.

It is toward that end that I call for a global focus on productivity improvement, beginning today. Let's call it "Productivity 2000."

3

Exploiting Technology to Regain Markets

Bobby Inman, Chairman, Westmark Industries

I spent 31 years of my life looking at the outside world. I was an avid user of technology throughout most of those 31 years. I've now had five and a half years to look intensely at my own country. The data base is still shallow, but the opinions are strongly held.

I have listened with growing fascination to what amounts to a public debate on the state of the U.S. economy and how we might deal with it. I watched those who were in public life searching for ways to describe the situation in the kind of simple terms that might capture electoral support. They use pat phrases like "level playing field" and others. You will learn as you go with me that one of our problems in trying to come to grips with the country is that we have a very complex set of issues to face. You have some marvelous speakers on this program to deal with specifics. I will deal in very large generalities. But I will also focus primarily on what I believe we need to do here in this country to regain our competitiveness and not what we need to do to other countries because of the difficulty we're finding in competing with them in the marketplace.

Role of Technology in U.S. Economic Development. Let me dwell first on the role of technology in developing this great economy. Our forefathers imported technology the first 100 years of our existence.

They used it with great effectiveness to span a continent and to put in place the infrastructure to permit the growth of what is still the world's largest economy. And you live very near the center of that. I was reminded by the marker driving up yesterday that not all that many miles away in Ogden, Utah, is the Golden Spike for the first linkage of a transcontinental rail system. That was the state-of-the-art technology in that time frame for moving goods and services. It was very near that same time frame, in the heart of the darkest days of the Republic (1862), when Congress, in its wisdom, enacted the Morrill Act, creating the land grant colleges and laying the foundation for creating technology in this country on a broad scale. That same Congress also passed the enabling legislation, creating the National Academy of Science, understanding early that a country that pushed the frontiers of science and actively used that science had the best prospect of building and sustaining an economy that would give an improving standard of living for all its citizens.

In 1984, a major study was done at Massachusetts Institute of Technology looking at the growth of the U.S. economy. It was their judgment that from 1865 to 1940, between 80 and 85 percent of the growth of the U.S. economy came from creating technology and applying it. Universities played a critical role in that early on. In the late 1800s, the state of the art in new technology frequently was focused on agriculture. And one of the best processes for technology transfer, the county agent, was put in place to directly deliver the fruits of that research to those who could use it in a timely way.

As that great economy was developed, we saw the creation of large corporations. We went through some interesting times of efforts to create monopolies, efforts to manipulate markets that helped accelerate our movement into recessions, occasional depressions, and market crashes. And we set about trying to regulate the growth of that economy, focusing on the reality that it was a domestic economy. You could essentially regulate it almost in its entirety simply by focusing on the sources of production and the flow of capital inside the country. You can trace the advent of major additional investment in research by those large corporations as they grew, and then, in this century, by the steady growth of national laboratories sponsored by the federal government. By 1940, we already had the largest base for pushing the frontiers of science, for creating new technology, that existed anywhere in the world.

Sense of Urgency to Commercialize New Technology. But if you look closely, you'll find that there was also no sense of urgency to move the fruits of that research into new products. Particularly in the larger established companies, you can chart pretty easily that with the great focus on the cost of production, the basic tenet was: Don't rush to introduce new technology that's going to run up the cost if your competitors aren't rushing to do it. Only in the small business sector did you see some sense of speed to turn new technology into workable products.

World War II fundamentally changed that. The sense of urgency was instilled by the need to produce not only weapons systems, but also substitute goods and services to fight the global conflict. And what you saw pretty quickly were collaborative efforts between industry, the academic sector, and government, with government as a catalyst, on a scale that we'd never seen and that the world had never seen. Out of it did indeed come the weapons for the war. But also out of it came the major impacts on a commercial economy, ranging all the way from synthetic fibers to the first large-scale computers.

1946 to 1961 was a period of enormous growth of this economy, untrampled by the damage that had been done by war to the economies in Western Europe and in Asia. We set out with great generosity to help rebuild those economies. We made a major investment in our talent pool. The GI Bill fundamentally changed access to baccalaureate education in this country. Along with it, a very forward-looking program from the government, led initially by the Office of Naval Research and its counterparts in the other services, and subsequently by other created organizations, such as the National Science Foundation and National Institutes of Health, provided major sources of grants for graduate studies, particularly in science and engineering. And by the mid-1950s we had opened our already sizeable lead to world predominance in talent needed to attack a whole range of problems to create new technology. But you can also chart in that same time frame some slackening of that sense of urgency about turning the fruits of research into products. You've got occasional surges from the government, such as the race to the moon through NASA, but they have become spasmodic, not a continued focus on timing.

Concern for Gaining Access to International Marketplace. 1960 is, for me, the watershed point for a variety of reasons. In 1960, international trade accounted for only 3 percent of our gross national product.

No major sector of industry had more than 10 percent of its revenues drawn from international trade. We were still essentially a domestic economy, and that's where growth was to be found. But we were beginning to worry about access to that international marketplace, the European Common Market. Our concern that we were going to be shut out of that market led us to focus on how we could guarantee long-term access to that market, as it grew and created, and perhaps began to close, its borders. We pioneered in such things as putting manufacturing facilities in those countries, particularly in Ireland, looking for the combination of lower-cost labor and the certainty that we would have production facilities inside the Common Market. We led in the creation of new organizations — General Agreement on Trade and Tariffs (GATT) and others — designed to lower trade barriers and to encourage the rapid growth of international trade. Of course, that was an enormous help to countries who looked to exports as the driving feature of their economic growth. We made very little change in our approach — either from government policy, within industry itself, or in the academic sector — in beginning to focus on what changes would be necessary if we were going to make sure we were competitive in that changing marketplace. In fact, if you look at the trends from 1961 on, you see a very different set of activities underway that served to make us less competitive, not more competitive, in that marketplace.

Forces that Reduce U.S. Competitiveness. Beginning in 1963, a focus on defense very sharply curtailed the availability of grants for graduate studies in science and engineering and the flow of equipment to universities. Under the new standard of, "Is it cost effective?" it was not cost effective to make investments unless you could very specifically tie those investments to a prospective future weapons system. That was a period when National Science Foundation (NSF) funding and National Institute of Health (NIH) funding were beginning to grow, but the race to the moon, NASA's effort, helped obscure how severe the impact was. If you want to document it, the date to begin with is 1968. The cutoff in 1963 shows up in 1968 with the beginning decline in U.S. graduate students in science and engineering. This audience knows better than most, seats didn't go vacant. Students came from all over the world to take those vacant seats, often with full scholarships for the finest technical education to be had in the world.

But it is the point in time at which, in relative terms, our lead in talent to create technology and to apply it began to decline relative to what was happening in the outside world. R & D expenditures began to decline.

From 1946 to the late 1960s, the federal government spent about 3 percent of its budget in R & D. Industry tended to track fairly close to that. As we began to come to grips with "guns and butter," paying the cost to Vietnam and not raising taxes, one of the areas of cut-back was in R & D. You can chart that by the early 1970s (the Office of Management & Budget did its calculations on how you got money early), the federal government's investment came down to about 2.2 percent. That pace continued throughout most of the 1970s. Industrial investment, in broad terms, followed exactly that same profile. So the interest in pushing the investment that would let you take evolving science and turn it into usable technology began to decline in real terms.

Unfortunately, in looking back at this history, one of the real problems was that the changes were gradual. There was no crisis to mobilize us, to wake us up to the fact that the world was changing and that our involvement in that world was changing, and we weren't working hard at how we adapted to that. We had a process of antitrust regulation and requirements on capital formation and capital flow that continued to look only at a domestic marketplace. We created a business culture that told us to be very cautious about dealing with competitors on any environment. Pricing was the clear area where you were certain to get into difficulty, but there was enough ambiguity that even pre-competitive collaboration was worrisome — and there are plenty of cases of corporations that got pulled into court and paid large fines, and even a few whose senior executives went to jail, that helped reinforce that culture to be very cautious about collaboration.

We also built a capital formation process that put the focus on minimizing risk. We required a long stand-off distance between the sources of capital and those who were going to undertake production. We required very cautious debt-to-equity ratios. That translated into higher interest rates, higher than those in competing countries. That, in turn, had its impact on business. In the established companies, it led toward a basic approach of being cautious in the pace at which you used new technology. Test markets, do some models, test the market again, take the result of that test marketing data to the lending institution, borrow the money to put that production line in process, and then put together a marketing strategy aimed at recovering cost as quickly as possible and paying down that expensive debt. This became the strategy rather than going out for a broader market share.

Japan Focused on Exploiting Technology. What was happening in the outside world? Well, let me turn to the example of Japan. Building an economy aimed at competing and exporting is critical to economic growth. Secondly, they were operating from an environment with a very shallow technology base, with the basic presumption that new technology would be available abroad, in the United States and Western Europe one year, two years, and maybe three years before it was available to Japanese companies. Therefore, the whole approach was aimed at the speed with which you turned the technology into products once you got it. Bank representatives were actually sitting on company boards of directors without a stand-off distance being required.

They were willing in Japan to make rapid decisions on going directly to the market, cutting back very sharply on that extensive phase of building test models and going out for test marketing. But they also added something else. We collectively laughed at those early Japanese products as they began to rebuild an economy shattered by war, and they understood the impact of quality. In the late 1960s, just as we were moving toward a strategy of a shorter life cycle, throw away, don't-bother-to-repair products, without much focus on quality, they were beginning to build quality into every aspect of what they were going to approach. That led them to a strategy of five times the number of engineers on the factory floor. They were focusing on both the quality and the speed with which the technology would get used. And because the interest rates were so much lower, companies didn't look at how they would service the debt immediately. The basic strategy was to go for market share. And once you had the established market share, then steadily adjust the price structure that let you service the debt that was nonetheless much less expensive to run.

I would argue that with those fundamentally different approaches to capital formation, and to the pace at which you use technology, you aren't going to get a level playing field simply by creating barriers to the flow of products, goods, and services. You may need the threat of barriers to make sure you get fair access to markets. It may be the only device you have. You may need to use some temporary protection for an industry that's in deep, difficult transition. But I will telegraph my views quickly. I do not believe it is in the public interest to protect an industry taking the investment and using it to move to an entirely different sector, such as from steel to oil.

Improved U.S. Productivity Needed. How, then, do we compete in this changing international marketplace? And, make no mistake, it is changing dramatically. Now, in the late 1980s, 12 percent of our GNP is drawn from international trade. It's not at all unusual to find 25 percent of the revenues in the industrial sector coming from international trade. In fact, some areas like machine tools or small appliances are already well past the 50-percent mark. We may even be recovering a little from that in machine tools.

We have no option but to adjust because we already are experiencing a declining standard of living in our failure to adjust. This marvelous economy has created an aggregate of about 8.8 million new jobs in the last six years. That's very remarkable for any economy. But look more closely at those numbers. The reality is that over those six years we actually created about 10.4 million new jobs in what we loosely call the service sector. And we lost 1.2 million jobs in manufacturing and 400,000 in mining. Of the 1.6 million jobs lost, the average weekly wage was $444. Of the 10.4 million new jobs created, the average weekly wage was $272. These figures are obscured substantially by the fact that, increasingly, where there are two adults in the family, both are working. Two incomes have helped sustain a standard of living.

You'll hear the argument that the only way the United States can adapt to this world is to accept a declining standard of living. I don't buy that. I think the real answer is (1) how we increase our productivity to sustain a favorable level of productivity and (2) how we attain the ability to sustain the quality that lets our goods and services be competitive in that international marketplace.

U.S. Product Quality and Understanding Foreign Culture. Let's break into three areas for discussion: Creating technology, applying it, and marketing it. I will have very little to say about the marketing side because I have no direct experience. But I have watched it for a long time. I'm persuaded that there are many critical factors, but I can identify two for you in looking out to that marketplace of the mid-1990s.

One is quality. We've got to perceive, as well as realize, that the quality of U.S. products matches that anywhere else in the world. The federal government has made a lot of effort over the last two and a half years to try to talk down the value of the dollar. They have been very successful with part of our trading partners. But most observers miss the reality that now, as the nature of our trading partners has shifted — the newly emerging countries in the Pacific with about 14 percent of the trade, Latin America or Mexico with 14 percent, Canada with 21 percent, the oil importing countries taking up another 8 to 9 percent — you're left with those traditional trading partners — Western Europe, 25 percent, and Japan, 17 percent. Those are the ones whose currencies change. For more than half of our trading partners, their currencies are pegged to the dollar and they continue to appreciate to the same two-and-a-half-year time frame. That's why we've not had that much impact on dealing with those markets, not because of the tax policies and discrimination.

The export/import balance still is unsatisfactory, and the only answer I can come up with is that the U.S. customer has proven willing to pay a higher price for imported products that they judge to be of better quality. So we're going to have to tackle that one both domestically and abroad if we are going to grab substantially increased market share.

The second one is the reality that in the growing market, particularly in the Third World, we're going to have to put a lot more effort into understanding the cultures of the countries where we want to market and in being able to market in the language of the country where we want to sell. Painful though it's going to be for us, if we really think we're going to be successful in the year 2000 in telling them all to speak English, we're going to be in for a very rude shock.

Maintaining U.S. Lead in Creating New Technology. We still have a clear lead in most areas in creating new technology. But there are a few areas where it's either close or we have already lost the edge. Usually we've lost the edge because of failure to invest, often for environmental reasons. Nuclear power generation technology comes to mind because of our own failure to invest as opposed to a continuous investment by the French and, to a slightly lesser degree, the

Japanese. In some cases they have collaborated with U.S. firms who have exported their activities so that the technology lead, if not already abroad, very soon will be found abroad in that sector. In most areas, however, we still have the lead. But in a declining pool of talent, we clearly have to insure that we move faster to build on the lead we have. We can't let it slide further. There are a whole variety of activities that need to be undertaken.

We need grants for graduate studies in science and engineering. Five and a half years ago, the conventional wisdom I used to hear was that you couldn't get bright U.S. youngsters to go on to graduate school. It's all industry's fault. Those starting salaries they paid were simply too attractive. If you get industry to lower the salaries, they might stay on. One of the inducements that got Microelectronics & Computer Technology Corporation to go to Texas was a commitment from the city of Austin of $750,000 a year for ten years in grant aid for graduate students in computer science and electrical engineering.

In May 1985, I had the pleasure of helping take part in the commencement ceremonies at the University of Texas at Austin awarding advanced degrees to those coming out of the computer science department, ranked number 10 in the country. Half of those getting their doctorates were from East Asia, and almost all of them were going back to pursue their careers there. In the entering class that fall, every vacant seat was filled by very high quality applicants from the United States, with more than 200 points higher on GRE scores than the entering class the year before. What was the difference? $18,000 a year as a study grant.

The answer is simple. It's the same answer we had in the 1940s and 1950s and forgot. Bright youngsters will go to graduate school on grants, but they won't continue to borrow money. If they borrowed money as undergraduates, most of them want to get out and start paying it off. And a viable program of grants will fill those seats and sustain the lead. But they've got to have equipment in those laboratories as well.

The R & D tax credit, enacted in 1981, clearly brought a significant increase in industry's investment in that creative cycle. But you get lots of arguments. The congressional budget office did their study saying that all industry did really was reclassify things into R & D from other areas. I'm perfectly prepared to stipulate that some of that took place. But the reality is still very clear that in 1982 in one of the deepest recessions of the postwar environment, the overall expenditure by industry in research went up — not down. That was the first time. I'm persuaded that the R & D tax credit was the major ingredient in causing that to occur.

Applying Technology. Government investment has gone up in research again since the early 1980s. That's good news, but there's also bad news attached to it, that concerns the application of technology. Critical to our long term success in the international marketplace is the speed with which emerging technology becomes available for exploitation. One of the most vital sectors of the U.S. economy is the small business sector and the speed with which the right innovators move to use new technology. The hazard for innovators is that a year or two later, the industry leader comes in with a different approach which becomes the standard. They learn very quickly that it's difficult to be in bed with elephants if the elephants roll over and take a different approach than the one you've taken.

Barriers to Commercializing Government-Funded Technology. Particularly worrisome to me, in looking at this problem from the private sector side, is the time frame that now applies before much of the technology funded by government becomes available for commercial exploitation. From the 1940s to the early 1960s, the defense procurement cycle was four to five years. The technology became available for commercial exploitation in a pretty timely way. We then set out to reform the defense procurement cycle. To make no mistakes, we created a cycle of 12 to 13 years, a perfect monstrosity. One of the costs to us as a country seeking to have no mistakes, all reinforced with a focus on waste, fraud, and abuse, is that most of the fruits of the research from that large investment are no longer available for commercial exploitation in a timely way.

I would argue that we could afford a lot of mistakes in the defense procurement cycle and still be ahead, net, as a country. We could put a ceiling of six years on that process and cut back on many of the things that have stretched it out, where what you're looking for is the earliest availability for broad commercial exploitation of the research coming out of that funding. What I'm hearing instead is, "Let's shift that research funding to a new civilian agency to manage its allocation in the government." Forgive me, but my 31 years of government experience leads me to be very skeptical of creating yet another new agency to parcel out that funding and to make the wise decisions of where it will do the most for the long-term growth of the economy.

Actions for Speeding the Commercialization of Technology. We clearly must take a focused look at how we can take technology to the marketplace faster. Government side packs policy to encourage it — by investing on the side of education and the work force to demonstrate it can be done. I give the government high marks for its decision to invest as 50-percent partners in Sematech for a concentrated effort to focus on process, in this case in the semiconductor industry. Sematech is a consortium created in 1987 by the semiconductor industry to restore U.S. competitiveness in computer chip manufacturing. The question remains, how can you move faster, with some concurrency, into taking that emerging technology into a high quality product through the application of automation?

The academic world must focus much more effort on technology transfer. How do we help facilitate the flow of technology to industry from the university laboratories? How do public universities get patent policy in place? Another approach is to get rid of bureaucracy. Again, the focus is on the timeliness with which the technology gets used.

On the private-sector side, I'm persuaded that there must be more collaboration in the pre-competitive phase in research, pushing the frontiers, making sure that you get the critical level of effort and sustain it long enough. You have to get a critical mass. You don't get it when it is uncertain whether funding will continue in a subsequent year. We already have several models that prove collaborative research will accelerate the creation of new technology. But we have no certainty yet that it will also result in the timely use of that technology.

Focus on Time, Cost, and Quality in Applying New Technology. On the industry side, I believe it's fundamental to bring about a focus on time and quality as well as cost. We've got to build in a process that asks from the beginning, "How do you deal with the cost of change, not just the cost of continuing production with existing technology?" Zero defects has to be a fundamental rule across the board. None of this will take place without a constant focus on the human element. For indeed, it is fundamental to prepare a work force that is ready to deal with the changes in environment, automated offices, automated service institutions, automated manufacturing, and ready to service them. I don't know what your experience is in getting your automobiles repaired, but I would say that I can give you *prima facie* evidence that new technology, even in U.S. products, is already substantially outstripping the ability to get service done confidently and quickly to sustain that level, even before we move to the next stage. So the overall competency of the work force must be improved.

The demographics are certain. Given the birthrates, we are going to see a very major difference in the structure of those entering the work force as early as the mid-1990s in some states. They are going to impact directly on Utah. In Florida, Texas, Colorado, New Mexico, Arizona, and California, before the turn of the century, more than half those entering the work force will be non-Caucasian. And how we draw them into this whole education cycle is going to have a lot to say about how competent that work force will be to deal with the world in the year 2000.

Ultimately, there have to be incentives all across the board to bring everybody's focus to time, quality, and cost if we are going to be competitive in that marketplace in the year 2000. If we don't adapt, we are certain to see a declining standard of living in this country. We are also likely to see a very dramatic impact on the world in which we live. Forgive me for a quick look back at where I spent 31 years of my life.

Peaceful World Depends on Alliance and Economic Growth. When I was an undergraduate in the late 1940s, one of my learned professors held forth that we had been very fortunate to get 20 years between World War I and World War II. In his judgment, we'd be even luckier if we got ten years between World War II and World War III. Well, we're celebrating 40 plus years without a global conflict. We've had some regional ones. We're going to continue to have a lot of regional ones. We've been pulled into a couple of those and on the edge of a couple of others. But we've stayed out of a global conflict. I'm persuaded that the alliances that we strung together in the late 1940s and early 1950s have been the key to keeping us out of that global conflict. If I'm even close to right, how we manage our own change to be competitive and then help the whole international economy grow is absolutely critical to sustaining those alliances because those alliance partners are our principal competitors in that international marketplace. We must adapt or we will not be the leaders but rather those who suffer from the changes that follow.

4

Managing in an Information-Rich World

Herbert Simon, Nobel Laureate, Carnegie-Mellon University

We often hear our society described, nowadays, as an "information" society. It is said that tangible products, like steel and wheat, have been replaced in the world's economy by information and by devices for displaying, transmitting, and manipulating information. There is a measure of truth in that description, although the death of manufacturing and agriculture has perhaps been exaggerated — the great bulk of the world's employed population is still engaged in cultivating plants and animals or manufacturing products made of wood, metal, fiber, and plastic.

Perhaps, then, it would be better to speak of an "information-rich" society, a society in which information is produced and flows at rates unprecedented in world history. Our society is surely information-rich in this sense. We are bombarded by information, engulfed in it. It pours out of newspapers, books, the television set, the telephone — to say nothing of our traditional human conversational partners, who are still a vital part of our personal communication system. I almost forgot to add the computer as one of our new information sources — in many ways, I will argue, the most important.

If Information Is Plentiful, What Is Scarce? Plentifulness and scarcity are relative terms. At Easter time, new rabbit pets appear in some homes, and then in some yards. And those rabbits tend to multiply, as rabbits do. Then we discover that wherever rabbits are plentiful, grass is scarce. A rabbit-rich society is also likely to be a grass-scarce society. The abundance of one resource causes a scarcity of another. What is scarce when information is plentiful? I think we all know the answer from personal experience: When information is plentiful, time to attend to it is scarce. Attention is the scarce factor in an information-rich society.

When Abraham Lincoln was a young man, he had access to very few books. It was worth his while to walk long distances to borrow books. (Remarkably, he also walked long distances to return them!) Time for reading was plentiful relative to the scarcity of good books. Fortunately, he found a few very good ones, and he studied them with great care. Nowadays we would be skeptical that someone could educate himself or herself, as Abraham Lincoln did, with a dozen books.

Because our basic attitudes are rooted in a culture where time could be plentiful, but information was scarce, we sometimes think that we must pay attention to information just because it is there — like the mountain-climber Mallory, who said that was why he climbed mountains: They were there. If the newspaper is delivered, we must read it (some academicians even think they must read the Sunday *New York Times*). If the telephone rings, we must answer it.

A Rational Information Strategy. In this information-rich world, it is instructive to ask oneself what would constitute a rational strategy toward information. Let's begin with the daily newspaper — whichever one you are addicted to. In the first place, most of what you find in today's newspaper was in yesterday's — some of the lead paragraphs perhaps excepted. The world does not change very much in one spin of the globe: Nicaragua, Afghanistan, Ireland, Sri Lanka, ax murders, Irangate were with us yesterday, are with us today, and will be with us tomorrow.

In the second place, most of the tiny incremental changes that take place from one day to another can be predicted. There will be one new political scandal, one new corporate takeover attempt, a few cases of aggravated assault, and so on. Of course, the names of the actors will change, but almost all of them are strangers to you anyway.

In the third place, how often it is efficient to update your information store depends on what use you are going to make of that information. What do you intend to do about Afghanistan? About ax murders? About corporate takeovers? And do you need to have today's or yesterday's news in order to do it?

Having carried out this exercise myself, I quickly concluded that I could dispense with the daily newspaper and turn to the weekly news magazines instead. Applying the same analysis to them, I progressed next to monthlies. Then I discovered a wonderful little book, *The World Almanac*, which reviews and updates the world's history annually. The savings of time and attention have been colossal.

But, you will object, important things do happen in the world from time to time: Presidents are elected; wars are declared. Certainly you need to know about those. Indeed you do, and if you go to lunch with a few friends each day, you will learn about them at lunch, at the very latest. As a bonus, you will acquire a reputation as a good listener.

I hope that you do not think I am prejudiced against newspapers. What I have said applies equally well to radio and television. All are dispensable, and when dispensed with, the time available for reading informative books is increased enormously.

Why do I exempt books? Because books (the right books!) contain information that is not as transitory and ephemeral as the information in periodical sources. If you want to understand contemporary China, the least efficient way is to take a brief trip to China, without knowledge of the language. The next least efficient is to read everything that is printed about China in any newspaper. The most efficient is to spend a much shorter period of time reading a few authoritative books on Chinese history, Chinese culture, and the contemporary Chinese government and economy. That is the cost-effective way to gain knowledge in an information-rich world.

Applying the Strategy to Management. The same analysis we apply to our personal information-ingesting habits can be applied to information-processing in business organizations. The fact that information can be created is not a sufficient reason for creating it, nor the fact that it can be distributed a sufficient reason for distributing it, nor the fact that it is available for reading a sufficient reason for reading it.

A few years ago, the State Department faced a problem in its communications between embassies around the world and Washington. Whenever a crisis occurred anywhere in the world, a great flood of messages flowed into Washington, not only from the embassy at the site of the crisis, but from all of the embassies in nations that were directly or indirectly affected by it — that is, almost all embassies. The teletypes in Washington could not handle the message load, and great backlogs developed in which were buried, with all the others, the few critical messages that really needed to get through.

Information processing experts were consulted. Their solution was to replace the teletypes with line printers that had adequate capacity to keep pace with the message flow. So the information flooded in — to be read by whom? The capacity bottleneck in the printers was simply replaced by a capacity bottleneck in the foreign service officers who were supposed to read their output. A typical outcome, you may say, of a technological fix that does not draw the boundaries of the system broadly enough.

This incident cannot be dismissed as an isolated example. Our capacities for duplicating information — by printing, photocopying, or distributing via a computer bulletin board — have exploded, while our capacities for absorbing information have not increased at all. The history of so-called "Management Information Systems" illustrates how costly this mismatch between sending and receiving capacities can be.

Management Information Systems (MIS) were hailed as opening a new era of informed management. What the first generation of these systems accomplished, for the most part, was to inundate managers' desks with irrelevant reports that they had neither the time nor the desire to study. As a result, MIS is in generally bad repute and has been replaced by new buzzwords like "Management Decision Aids." The change in label, if accompanied by a corresponding change in viewpoint, is a notable advance.

The first generation of MIS was designed mostly by experts in accounting and computing who observed that a great deal of information lies around in most companies — information about costs and revenues, about production and sales and inventories — and that the powerful new technology of computers could assemble this information into reports that analyzed it from every conceivable angle. How the reports could or would be used was little considered. The designers of the systems were simply not knowledgeable enough about what it is that managers do, what decisions they make, and what information would be relevant to these decisions.

If a corporate information system is to be useful for management, then its design must begin with an analysis of the jobs of managers. What decisions do managers, in different locations within the organization, in fact make or participate in making? What kinds of information would help them to make better decisions? When these questions are asked, and the jobs of managers are studied carefully, certain important facts about the decision-making process begin to emerge.

First, a great deal of the information that would aid decision making does not originate inside the company at all, but outside. It is information about customers, about competitors and the industry, about trends in the economy in the short and long runs, about developments in international economic affairs. It is especially true as we move towards the top of the executive ladder that the information managers need for their decisions is external information, information about the outside world, rather than internal information about the company.

Top executives do not simply look inward, managing company internal affairs; they are the principal "interfaces" of the company with the outside world, discovering the needs for change and innovation that arise from external opportunities and threats. A management information system for top management has to be based at least as much on information obtained from the outside as on information derived from company records. Organization units have to be created that can produce this information, or it has to be purchased.

Second, the bulk of the information that would aid decision making is not numerical information, but information written in natural language — the language of newspapers, trade journals, correspondence, and books. A computer system that is to aid managerial decision making cannot simply crunch numbers; it must be equally adept at processing words, extracting their meanings, filtering them, analyzing them.

In short, if managerial decision aids are to make good their promises, they must draw on the full resources of artificial intelligence to provide computer programs that (1) have access to information originating outside the company, (2) have sophisticated capabilities for filtering and analyzing such information, and (3) have natural-language capabilities as extensive and powerful as their numerical capabilities.

In its original forms, MIS showed how to produce information. It did not show how to absorb it. The challenge today is to produce systems that can analyze vast amounts of information with such sophistication that they need to output for human consumption only a small part of what they receive. A good rule of thumb for a computer system is that it should not be installed unless it inputs several orders of magnitude of information more than it outputs to its human users.

The idea of "filtered" or "analyzed" information creates concerns. How will we be sure that the system will give us access to the information that is really important? Won't we miss something? These concerns miss the point of my central argument: That as long as information is in long supply and attention is in short supply, we will necessarily "miss something." We are capable of absorbing only a trivial fraction of the information that is around. It is essential that we attend to the most important information and ignore the less important. Computer systems, properly programmed, can make that selection for us. Their selection will not be perfect, but it will be more effective than the hit-or-miss selection we can make ourselves or with only human help.

Artificial Intelligence and Experts. The practicality of introducing computers as intelligent assistants in selecting and analyzing information hinges on our current understanding of intelligence and our abilities to program computers to exhibit it. An assessment of these capabilities best begins with an account of what we know about human experts, and then proceeds to the design of expert systems for computers.

The problem-solving and decision-making processes of human experts have been studied intensively by psychologists for the past 30 years. From that study, important generalizations have emerged. We know that expertise is based on extensive knowledge. Typically, the expert has at least 50,000 "chunks" of knowledge about his or her special domain. This knowledge is organized in a particular way: It is "indexed" so that when the expert finds himself faced with a problem, he will notice cues in the situation that will make him recall the relevant knowledge he has stored. The number 50,000 does not seem so large when we remember that our natural-language vocabularies are larger than that.

We know also that it takes a long time to acquire this indexed memory — not less than ten years for world-class performance. In the nearly dozen fields of human performance that have been studied, the biographies of world-class experts show without exception a period of intense training and development over at least a decade. Not all experts are world-class, but the intensiveness of the training required reminds us of the immense investments in human experience we have in all of our business organizations.

The way in which the expert knowledge is organized explains why experts can solve many problems and respond to many situations "intuitively" — that is, very rapidly, and often without being able to specify the processes they have used to reach their answers. Intuition is no longer a mystery. It is simply the capacity to recognize familiar cues in the situations that arise, and to use these cues to retrieve information. It is not a special faculty, but the inevitable by-product of the acquisition of knowledge, and its storage in this form.

The numerous expert systems that have been built and are now being built as applications of artificial intelligence (AI) are based squarely on the understanding we have gained of human expertise. There are now many examples of expert systems that are capable of performing at a good professional level. Among the best known of these are medical diagnosis systems like Caduceus and Mycin.

Of more direct relevance to management are expert systems that can perform financial analysis. As long ago as 1960, Geoffrey Clarkson had built a system capable of making investment decisions for portfolios of trust funds. The system's decisions matched closely with those of a trust investment officer of a bank. More recently, Marinus Bouwman has shown how expert systems can diagnose the health of companies by automatic analysis of their financial statements — again, at a good professional level of quality.

The Future of Artificial Intelligence. We might ask what the boundaries are beyond which AI cannot penetrate. If there are such boundaries, it is not at all clear where they lie. Nor is it too profitable to ask where the present boundaries are, for they are moving rapidly. Hence, probably the most fruitful inquiry is to determine what are the most essential and the most promising directions of motion. (The most essential and the most promising need not be the same.)

Natural language. The processing of natural language by computer is a research direction that has both great importance and great promise. Its importance for communication between people and computers is obvious. The progress to date has been considerable. Today we have systems that can understand natural-language descriptions of problems and program themselves to try to solve the problems (UNDERSTAND). We have programs that can read physics problems, written in English, interpret these problems, convert the interpretations into algebra, and go to work on the solutions (ISAAC). We have programs that can analyze very simple stories sufficiently to determine the plot, the motivations of the characters, and so on.

All of these programs understand English, but only with severe restrictions on vocabulary and the domain of interpretation. We may say that we have a grasp of some of the principal mechanisms required for handling language, but have a long way to go to achieve the generality that characterizes human use of language.

Originality. Programs have now been written (DENDRAL, AM, BACON, and others) that can search for regularities in data, and thereby discover scientific laws. The BACON program, for example, has been able to (re)discover Kepler's Third Law of planetary motion, Ohm's Law of electrical currents, Black's Law of temperature equilibrium, and many others, by careful, highly selective induction from the original data. These programs, and others like them, provide a decisive answer to claims that programs cannot go beyond the skills of their programmers.

Learning. A variety of learning schemes for computers have been devised and are under study. One of these, adaptive production systems, allows the computer to learn a skill like solving algebra equations by examining worked-out examples of solutions — like those presented in standard textbooks. The adaptive production system analyzes each step in the solution, finds what action has been taken, detects a cue that can be used to recognize the relevance of the action (hence signal when it should be taken), and builds these insights into new instructions that can solve equations. Learning is an exceedingly active domain of research in artificial intelligence today.

Sensing and acting. Robotics, the construction of systems that can sense the situation in the real world around them and act to change that situation, have proved to be the most difficult challenge to AI research. The human eye and ear and the limbs whose actions they can guide have proved to be very sophisticated organs — much more sophisticated than the "new brain" that does our high-level thinking.

While steady progress is being made, we are much further from building computer sense organs that come close to matching their human counterparts than we are to building problem-solving components that can think like engineers, businessmen, or professors. We may be closer to automating the skills of a manager than the skills of a bulldozer driver.

Natural language, originality, learning, and robotics are some of the main areas of artificial intelligence research and progress today. As our capabilities in these areas grow, the applications of AI will grow correspondingly. In cooperation with people and computers, the division of labor will continue to change.

Artificial Intelligence and Cognitive Science. I have emphasized the use of computers to perform tasks requiring intelligence, thereby broadening the domains for the automation of skills. But computers have equal importance as tools for gaining a deeper understanding of, and thereby enhancing, human performance. The main body of intelligence in our society resides (and will for a long time continue to reside) not in computers but in human heads. We can improve our productivity by enlisting computer intelligence to augment human intelligence. But we may be able to improve it even more rapidly by improving the quality of human intelligence. There are several domains in which this might be done: Education, business decision making, and the formation of public society.

A large fraction of the human resources in our society are engaged in education. I am not referring to the teachers, but to the students. A third of our lives are spent in educating ourselves so that we can spend the next two-thirds productively. Yet, the theories that underlie the practice of education are primitive and shallow. They amount to little more than a theory of infection: If you spray people with lots of words, some of them may be catching.

As we begin to understand the nature of learning processes (as in the adaptive production systems I mentioned earlier), we should be able to improve our educational processes. Even a 20 percent increase in their efficiency could support an increase of 10 percent in lifespan working time. As our population ages, that 10 percent could become crucial to maintaining even our present levels of per capita productivity.

The improvement of managerial decision making, and the improvement of the quality of our public policy making, are other goals that research on human thinking may help us to attain. Today, we are faced with the worldwide problem of finding a sustainable source of energy that is compatible with a liveable environment. There is little use in solving just one facet of the problem (energy or environment) without solving both. We are going to need all of the resources of intelligence we can muster to find viable alternatives and to understand the global consequences of those we find.

But in dealing with the difficult problems that face us, we need not rely exclusively on either human intelligence or machine intelligence. The most promising direction is to harness them together — to design cooperative man-machine systems that can carry out analyses that neither component by itself could sustain. Computers today can share the work of thinking with us, and there is plenty of work — and will continue to be — for both of us.

Understanding Ourselves. To some people, the idea that we are learning how human beings think, that we are gaining an understanding of the workings of the human mind, is a little threatening. It threatens, in particular, the uniqueness of that mind — its separation from the rest of nature. In the same way, Copernicus threatened the uniqueness of our location in the universe, and Darwin threatened the uniqueness of our origins as a species.

Perhaps there is no threat at all. Perhaps uniqueness is not the touchstone of human worth. Today, we have seen our fragile planet as viewed from space. We have learned that humankind must live in peace on that planet. The task is not to show how we are unique and set apart from nature. The task is to show how we can live in harmony with, and as a part of, nature. The study of human thinking, the achievement of a deeper understanding of our minds as part of ourselves, can help us find that harmony.

5

The Work Ethic*

James Buchanan, Nobel Laureate, George Mason University

I am very pleased to visit Utah State again as a participant in the general Partners' Program. When initially invited, I was a little concerned about what I might talk on that would fit in at all in your general theme of the program at this setting, namely information, innovation, and technology. Most of my work would not fit that very well, but I thought that no matter how much innovation and technology advance we might have, there is still the problem of good old-fashioned hard work. So I suggested that I might talk on the work ethic and try to give you some of my thinking.

I started thinking on this last year when I was invited to give the commencement address at my own university, George Mason University in Fairfax, Virginia. I had never given a commencement address before. So I didn't know quite what I was going to do, and then I remembered something that had happened to me earlier that year. So I shall tell you the same autobiographical story.

I was down at my country place deep in the Virginia mountains over the Christmas holidays 1986-87 and the third and fourth of January 1987 were the two days of the NFL play-offs. There were four games on television, and I felt extremely guilty about being a couch potato for those four games. On the other hand, I wanted to watch the

---

* Based on a tape-recorded lecture.

games. I had this real guilt complex, and then I happened to remember that a few weeks before I had gone out there in the yard and picked up a lot of black walnuts that had dried out. But these walnuts hadn't been shelled yet, and if you know black walnuts, you know that shelling them is a pretty hard task. So I got a flatiron and a bowl and a nutpick and a hammer, and I sat there for those two days. I got to watch all those television games, but in the process I shelled several jars of black walnuts, which was no small feat. And I had genuinely assuaged my guilt complex. No longer did I feel guilty about watching television, because I was in fact doing something that was creating value at the same time I was watching television.

Why the Work Ethic? That made me start thinking about just why I had those guilt feelings in the first place. Why did I feel guilty about sitting there and watching television, and why did shelling those walnuts assuage those guilt feelings? Obviously I was imbued with the old-fashioned, sometimes called Puritan, work ethic. But what was this, why did I have this, and did it have any function? Or was this somehow a throwback to a genetic trait that had survival value at one time when we were still climbing around in trees and we needed to have that ethic in order to survive in a personal sense in that tribal setting? Was it the case that the ethic or constraint built into our psyche might no longer have any meaningful content and therefore no social function? Or, I said to myself, was there something still in this ethic? Was there economic content in it? Maybe, I said to myself, economists in particular, at least the group that I run with, had put Max Weber aside a little too quickly. Max Weber, you remember, early in this century wrote on the Protestant work ethic and the rise of capitalism. Maybe Max Weber had been put on the book shelf too quickly; maybe he did have something to say.

Paradox in Economic Theory. The more I thought about that the more I decided that there was a paradox in economic theory and so I developed what became a bit of a criticism of my fellow economists. If you look in chapter one of almost any elementary economics textbook or even in the quasi-journalistic presentations of economics you will always find examples of the value of being involved in a complex economic exchange network, the value of economic interdependence. I believe it was Milton Friedman in his little book, *Free to*

Choose, who early on uses the example that you can go out and buy a pencil for 25 cents. This pencil, if you had to make it all on your own, would take a year to make, if you could ever do it. The pencil is available for 25 cents despite that fact that the lumber may have come from British Columbia, the graphite may have come from Arkansas, the copper may have come from Chile, and the rubber may have come from Malaysia. The whole international network of economic interdependence has produced that pencil that you buy for 25 cents. Obviously, you are a lot better off by being a member of that general network than you would be had you been forced to do everything on your own.

So, clearly there are tremendous gains from specialization and widening of markets. Of course, economists have known this all the way back to Adam Smith in 1776 who talked about the specialization and division of labor and how the extent of the division of labor is limited by the extent of the market. So there is a general recognition in chapter one of that popularized economics textbook of the value of being a member of a large interdependent network of exchange, specialization, and production. Everybody will accept that, but if you shift forward about seventeen chapters in the standard textbook and look at chapter seventeen there is, in great detail, the theory of distribution under a competitive market system. It is a discussion about the marginal productivity theory of distribution, where the competitive market insofar as it works properly, will tend to pay input (capital, labor, or something else) owners in accordance with the value of the product that they generate. That is, the marginal productivity theory says that input owners will be paid in accordance with the value that they contribute to the market nexus, or to total economic value. The theory will go on a little further and say, if for all input owners all units of inputs are paid in accordance with the value of the product they contribute, then, under the proper conditions for the operations of a competitive economy, when all inputs are paid, that amount will totally exhaust the total products and there will be nothing left over. That characterizes the so-called competitive solution in the market place.

But there is something wrong with that. There is a contradiction between that and chapter one which says that we get tremendous gains from being a part of a complex, wide economic nexus and exchange nexus and at the same time we get paid the full value of the amount that we produce in competitive equilibrium. Because if the latter is true, if every input in the production process in an economy, if every unit of input does in fact secure the full value of the product that it contributes to the total value, then, if we withdraw that unit from the production exchange nexus, you would withdraw exactly the value that it has been getting as a wage or salary. So there would be no damage to owners of other inputs in the economy. There would be no real interdependence at that margin of adjustment. So that would seem to suggest that there is no advantage at all in being involved in the network in the first place. I would also suggest that an economy where everyone works less is not any more desirable than an economy where everyone works more. It seems to contradict that first position that we are all advantaged by working in a large economic exchange nexus. It seems to me that something has gone wrong in the logic. How could we possibly generate these rents that we get by being able to buy that pencil for 25 cents unless somehow we introduce something other than what is implied by the distribution theory?

Now, I am encouraged to think this rather simplistic approach may have something in it. My criticism fundamentally is of economics here, because I have tried it out with very sophisticated economic theorists. I get totally divergent answers. Some of them say, "Well, it's obviously all wrong." And others say immediately, "Oh, you're obviously right." So if they had said it's trivial then I would have been disappointed, or if they'd all said it's wrong I'd have been disappointed, but since some of them say it's right and some of them say it's wrong, maybe there's something in it.

Economic Content in the Work Ethic. Let me give you an example of what I am talking about. I will use an example that I will attribute to Bruce Ackerman, a professor of law at Yale, who wrote a book a few years ago called *Social Justice in the Liberal State*. Suppose you're floating around in a spaceship and you could land in different types of planets, or different types of economies. And suppose now you could land in Economy A or Economy B, and these two economies are identical except in one respect. They have the same number of persons, they have the same natural resource base and everything except in one respect. In Economy A, people work on an average of 40 hours a week, and in Economy B, people work on an average of 20 hours a week. Now assume that the person who's going to land knows that he himself is not going to be affected. He's not going to allow that to affect him. He just has to decide which of these two economies he would land and settle in. Would it be Economy A where everybody works 40 hours a week, or Economy B where on the average, people work 20 hours a week? Well, it seems obvious to me which he would choose. It seems obvious that he would choose to land in Economy A where people work on an average of 40 hours a week, for the very simple reason that he'd get a tremendously larger amount of consumer surplus. That would be the economy in which he could buy a pencil for 25 cents whereas in the other economy the pencil might cost him $2. And clearly he would land in that economy where the general work ethic prevails versus the one where the work ethic does not prevail. That led me to reinforce my view that, in fact, there is economic content in the work ethic. There's something more than simply a genetic trait there. There is economic content. Having the work ethic in a population does in fact add to the economic value that is produced and there is something in the Protestant ethic. To put this in technical economic terms, my proposition is that there are external economies that are not exploited in the market solution without the work ethic. What the work ethic does is internalize these external economies.

Now my proposition is not about metapreferences. It is not that somehow we would all like to see people have preferences for work. It is not about how you might instill habits of work, and how you might be better off in the long run and that sort of thing. It is not that type of problem. By saying that there is economic content in the work ethic, what I am really trying to say is that there are non-exploited gains that need ethical and moral constraints. That is to say, an ethical norm that treats work as praiseworthy and treats loafing as blameworthy increases the well-being of every one of us. In an interview with a Salt Lake City journalist yesterday, we were summarizing the content of what I'd be saying here today, and he said, "You know, once you mention it, I haven't heard the word loafing used lately." And it's too bad that we don't use the word "loafing" because loafing carries a pejorative impact when you talk about it. My argument is that an ethical norm that treats work as praiseworthy and loafing to be blameworthy, serves to, insofar as it's imbued in the population, increase the economic well-being of all of us who are involved in the economy. It internalizes this external effect.

Now there are technical economic problems here about how this can exist in a competitive equilibrium, but my point is that unless we have that, we will all be worse off. Therefore there are reciprocal gains to all of us from working, even though every one of us is on the margin of deciding on our own as to how much we want to work and how much we do not want to work. This goes along many dimensions. We could talk about a hours-of-work dimension, or a weeks-of-work dimension, or we could talk about a quality-of-work dimension. That's not directly germane to my problem. You can simplify and abstract my problem by thinking of this just as a quality of homogeneous work dimension, that is, just how many weeks a year you decide to work, and how many you decide not to work. My point is that we would all be better off if we all worked harder, despite the fact that the choice is made independently by each of us as to how much we work. If we just do this in a decentralized, individualistic way, there are probably gains to be made from a reciprocal agreement on all our parts to work a little harder if we didn't have this ethic. And that's what this ethic does. It constrains us. It makes us feel guilty when we don't work, and therefore improves our well-being generally.

Illustrations of Economic Value of Work Ethic. Let me give you an example where it obviously applies and I think that will be clear to you all. It is obvious that if you have taxes that are based on work, on income that you get from labor, and you use those taxes to provide public goods and benefits, then everybody enjoys. It's clear that if you worked less because they tax income from labor and don't tax income from leisure, so to discriminate against labor by taxing income from labor which is what our income tax system does, obviously, then you use that to provide public goods benefits which you get back. It is obvious in that case that everybody would be better off to work a little harder because everybody is then going to get a little more back from the fact that we are all working a little harder. It is clear in that case. You can work out the arithmetic quite simply. But I want to work it out even if we didn't have such taxation. It seems to me it is still true in a market-type arrangement. It is also obvious that you have that kind of effect if you have kind of a small team production where there is genuine interdependence amongst the members of the team, where they are complimentary to each other. But if that were true and limited to small groups, you would expect firms to be organized and organize themselves to capture those gains. But my point is really trying to extend this argument over the whole economy. That is, there is general interdependence of the economic nexus by way of a price system, and it does embody these external spillover benefits at the relevant margins that everybody makes. The competitive solution, if we didn't have the work ethic, would not exhaust all of the cooperative surplus that we might get. Otherwise we wouldn't get any rents, and this externality is a reciprocal one. That is, we could all do better by agreeing to work more. I couldn't do better by myself working more; I would benefit you that way, and not myself. But if we all agreed, we could move to a higher level of utility, each and every one of us.

Let me just give you a little example of that. Think of two frontier farmers. Think of Smith and Jones and think that initially they're self-subsistent and they both grow pigs and they both grow potatoes. Then they discover the advantage of specialization, and Smith says he will grow potatoes, and Jones says he will grow pigs. So then they specialize and then they trade. Jones grows potatoes and Smith grows pigs, and then Jones trades potatoes for pigs. They both end up with more potatoes and pigs than they did when they were separate in production. They've gained by entering the exchange nexus. Suppose they're roughly similar in how much they like to work. Suppose they end up working 200 days a year. Smith produces the potatoes and Jones produces the pigs. Then, for some unexplained reason, Smith decides to work 210 days a year. So he produces more potatoes. Obviously he is generating an external spill-over benefit on the other party to the exchange nexus. These spill-over benefits that exist at the margin of decision then, if they're exploited, can generate general reciprocal gains to both parties. So the point of all this is that there is economic value in the work ethic, and that if we didn't have the ethic we would not be achieving the full value of the cooperative surplus that we can achieve by being involved in an economic nexus.

Now, this ethical restraint could be possibly too strong under certain conditions. Maybe the Koreans and the Japanese may have too much of a work ethic, too much of a good thing. But maybe to the extent that our own culture has been losing the ethical constraint that deemed loafing to be blameworthy, maybe we have been reducing our economic value in a way that perhaps is damaging to all of us. I ended up that commencement address by saying that when you go out in the great world beyond and somebody says, "Well, why don't you take time to go out and smell the flowers?" just to remember that's it's you, not them, that is generating social value.

Adjustments for Women in Work Force. Now this made me think a little bit more about what has been happening to our own labor force in the post-war decades. As you know, the central characteristic of the post-war change in labor force participation has been the entry of women in the labor force. And the national income accountants, of course, reckon on the fact that as women enter the labor force, their earnings are accounted as income, but there is a failure to count the decline in the value of home production. So they say we should clearly include an offset for that. We also ought to take into account the fact that public goods production is way down because one of the most important of all public goods done by private people is women spending time with children. The national income accountants would say those two adjustments are corrections that really need to be made. But my argument here would say that there is adjustment on the other side that suggests that women's entering the labor force may have been much more beneficial than it would appear. Those two are negatives from the value of product that women produce. Home production is sacrificed and child rearing as a public good is also sacrificed. But my argument would suggest that by the fact that they have moved away from consumption for family purposes and to production for market purposes they have generated a surplus value that we have not reckoned in our national income accounts. Most of what I say here would obviously apply to savings also, quite apart from the work ethic, to have a saving ethic, and as you know, in our own situation now we have practically lost that all together. So in one sense, this is nothing more than a particularized application of something that I've said in almost every speech I've given for the last few years that touches on any periphery of this, namely that I think the Victorians had it right.

6

Competitiveness and the Union

Lynn Williams, President, United Steelworkers

Thank you for the opportunity to bring a labor union perspective to your proceedings. My responsibility is to hold your attention, which isn't always the easiest thing in the world. I've seen my share of glazed eyes while attempting to explain the distinctions among free trade, fair trade, comparative advantage, protectionism, Smoot-Hawley, and the like. The hard truth is that these words are as much a part of the labor lexicon these day as any we use in basic labor agreements. And I'm here to discuss with you their effects not only on members of labor unions, but on nearly all ordinary working people across the country.

Labor-Management Cooperation Benefits All Parties. I assume you already know the broad strokes of labor's views, considering that human resources and labor union functions are, in many cases, opposite sides of the same coin . . . human resource operations often having been created by managements in an attempt to blunt union organizing campaigns. Whatever merits the old way carried, today's volatile economic environment dictates — at the very least — an adjustment, with labor and management working together, addressing mutual concerns, striving for mutual goals, and enjoying mutual trust.

This is not a new position for the Steelworkers. We have been advocating this concept — which we traditionally called industrial democracy — for decades, pointing out along the way that it would be in the best interests of all involved to tap the least utilized resource a company possesses — its workers.

That thought is now being adopted, somewhat grudgingly to be sure, by some segments of the business community. The vogue term is "labor-management cooperation." This shift in attitude is more a reflection of the changing world economy than a trend toward egalitarianism. For whatever reason, and by whatever name, it is a move in the proper direction.

The United Steelworkers of America is an innovator in this area. Our experience shows that labor-management cooperation — with active, joint participation at all levels — can work to the best advantage of employers, employees, and their communities, generating jobs that pay living wages, and improving the economy. At the same time, any effort of this type can only be an adjunct to, *not* a substitute for, collective bargaining.

We have put the theory to the test in a number of instances, as, for example, in our contract with National Steel Corp., which has been cited by the U.S. Department of Labor as a model for others to emulate. Among other things, the National Steel contract provides for employment security, profit sharing, productivity bonuses and employee involvement in virtually the full decision-making process of the corporation, ranging from safety on the job to capital expenditures.

There have been concomitant improvements in productivity, product quality, and workplace safety, and an increase in resolving problems before they become grievances, without diminishing the integrity of the basic labor agreement.

We have found in our dealings with National Steel and other companies that these initiatives cannot succeed without trust and commitment — from both sides. Too often, mutual goals and benefits have been sacrificed to managerial prerogatives, particularly the long-held but increasingly invalid view that success comes only *when managers manage and workers work*. This *noblesse oblige* posture has deprived many companies of substantive contributions from their employees, and caused a deterioration in labor relations.

In the Steelworkers, as part of ongoing training, we recently shared our experiences and the ideas of consultants in the field with local union, management, and government representatives during a two-week seminar at the USWA's Education Center. The participation of steel company executives in this seminar was a unique event in the industry's history.

The potential benefits have not been lost on government. Pennsylvania Governor Bob Casey will soon unveil details of an Office of Labor-Management Cooperation, which the Steelworkers helped formulate. New York Governor Mario Cuomo has created an Industrial Cooperation Council, on which I am happy to serve. And Congress has established a National Economic Commission to explore a full range of items affecting our economy.

Actions for Promoting Well-Being of Workers. While improved labor-management relations are a worthy goal, they cannot by themselves improve the nation's worldwide competitive position, nor ease the related problems of chronic unemployment, poverty — among the working *and* non-working — and homelessness. To do so, we still must address the question of unfair trade, the effects of which have been felt here in Utah as elsewhere, most notably in the abandonment of Geneva Works by U.S. Steel. We also must change fiscal policies that inflate the real interest rate and make capital improvements unattractive and unfeasible. We must rewrite the formula that factors-in unemployment as a component of economic policy. And we must convince the federal government to engage in much-needed public works programs such as refurbishing the nation's infrastructure, so vital in the conduct of commerce.

The latter is a proposition that will pay for itself many times over in the long run. For example, a study of Pennsylvania's bridges, conducted at the University of Pittsburgh for the Steelworkers, projects *116,000 man-years of work* in the rehabilitation and replacement phase alone, with a multiplier effect in related service and supply industries — and tax payments — not to mention the improvements in efficiency that a modern bridge system would generate. The jobs that would be created would pay decent wages, enabling workers to be participants in and fuelers of the economy.

Apart from any other question, promoting the well-being of all American workers makes solid economic sense. The more people working and generating incomes, the more people there are purchasing goods and services and creating demand for more. It's a simple equation: *jobs* plus *jobs* equals *jobs*. As matters now stand, the economy loses hundreds of billions of dollars a year as a direct result of a lack of opportunity for meaningful employment.

The most astonishing aspect of the Administration's lassitude is its inability or refusal to recognize this basic fact of economic life. It's as true on Main Street as it is on Wall Street, where the chickens are coming home to roost, a statement I make with absolutely no pleasure whatever, despite the obvious temptation to do so. On Wall Street, for the past seven years, many have luxuriated in the rationalization of American industry. Rationalization — that's a euphemism for layoffs, and plant closings, and firings while inflating company stock prices. There's concern on Wall Street that Black Monday will result in up to 35,000 layoffs of brokerage house personnel. It's already begun at E.F. Hutton, where, last month, scores of employees were fired after the company was acquired by Shearson Lehman, many of them losing bonuses and severance pay.

We share in Wall Street's concern, because a half million of our members have suffered the same kind of blow. *Newsweek* magazine is saying that lessons of the crash have signalled the end of a decade of greed. I would hope that prediction is true, although the lessons exacted a heavy price — on Wall Street, and in mills, factories, and communities around the country.

Roadblocks to Economic Justice Removed but Many Remain. I've been a member of the Steelworkers since 1947 and privileged to serve as International President of the Union since 1983, a period of unparalleled turbulence in the steel industry. I must confess it's sometimes tempting to look nostalgically to those early, seemingly less complicated days. I will also say that, having lived through that period and having worked as an organizer and negotiator, the recollection is illusory. Times were difficult then, as they are today. American workers, for the most part, had no such things as health insurance, pension plans with government-guaranteed benefits, safety and health protection, or equal opportunity — either for jobs *or* promotions. Wage increases, when they occurred, were measured in pennies per hour.

Such illustrious labor leaders as my four predecessors — Philip Murray, David J. McDonal, I.W. Abel and Lloyd McBride — among many others in the labor movement, joined by progressive political

leaders, overcame an ingrained antipathy to workers and helped remove roadblocks to economic justice. It was not, as you may know, a
rose-covered path lacking in sacrifice. There was, and, regrettably,
continues to be, stubborn, unrelenting opposition, a fact millions of
American workers have learned in this decade. For them, the struggle
has come full circle. They are being forced to pay the price to meet objectives they did not set and to correct problems they did not create.

The Price of Corporate Greed. While it is true, by some measures,
that we have come a long way, it is *equally* true that we still have a long
road to travel, a road that has been littered with millions of shattered
dreams during the past seven years by the bottom-line mentality of
some segments of corporate America, with encouragement and support from the Reagan Administration. The term "bottom line" is just
another euphemism. The correct word is "greed," and this is what
greed has led to:

- *Greed* has given us mergers and acquisitions and takeovers and leveraged buyouts in which 500 *billion* dollars changed hands in the last
  three years alone. There were huge profits for the wheelers and
  dealers . . . huge fees for lawyers and bankers and brokers . . . and,
  inevitable, wholesale layoffs — but *few new products* and *few new
  jobs* of sufficient quality to contribute to the general well-being of
  the economy.
- *Greed* has given us a further shift in wealth so that fewer people now
  control more of the money.
- *Greed* has given us a proliferation in the number of corporate executives with million-dollar-plus incomes. According to *Business Week*
  magazine, there were four in 1981. There were 220 in 1986.

While the rich have been getting filthy rich, 7.2 million people
are unemployed . . . 1 million people are so discouraged they've given
up looking for jobs . . . 5.7 million people are working only part-time
because they can't find full-time jobs . . . 33 million people are living in
poverty. Moreover, there has been a decline in real wages for those
fortunate enough to still have a job.

All of this in the name of greed, with no consideration for the
value and benefits of a decent job with decent wages.

- Decent jobs with decent wages provide homes for the homeless —
  and there are 3 million homeless people in America.
- Decent jobs with decent wages help keep children in school — and

the school dropout rate ranges as high as 50 percent, with an estimated 23 million Americans considered to be functionally illiterate.
• Decent jobs with decent wages offer hope to single mothers — and
there are 10.5 million single mothers in the work force.

Unfair Foreign Competition. A principal cause of this suffering, in
steel as in many other industries, has been unfair foreign competition, aided and abetted by the Administration's position on trade,
which posits this scenario: A free market in a global economy unfet-
tered by nationalistic and political considerations will determine the
survival or demise of companies and industries based on their competitiveness. Additionally, this scenario looks to a *post-industrial*
American economy of services and high technology, described as
part of a natural economic progression in which each entity is self-
sufficient.

If these things were true, then the high-tech and service industries would not be under attack, as they are. The trade imbalances
with Japan and the Pacific Rim countries would not continue to
widen, as they have. Nor would there be a consensus, as there is,
that, absent any significant policy changes, the overall trade deficit
will not improve appreciably over the next four years.

There's little reality or logic to the free-traders' positions. The
facts demonstrate that the classic notion of free trade does not exist.
Even if it did, there is an ordered interdependency in our economy,
beginning with a healthy industrial base. It's one thing for an industry to shrink and employ fewer people. It's something else again to
say we can get along without that industry, or that its reduced employment prominence significantly diminishes its contribution to the
total economy.

The post-industrial economy theory is refuted by Stephen Cohen
and John Zysman, directors of the Berkeley Roundtable on the International Economy. They cite agriculture to buttress their point. Agriculture hasn't gone offshore — as many American manufacturers have
— nor has production suffered. The significant change has been
toward mechanization and automation. While direct employment in
agriculture is 3 million, there are support jobs — services — linked
to the farms, pushing agricultural employment as high as 8 million.
That coincides with the experience of the steel industry, where it is estimated that every job in a mill creates two to three jobs *outside* the mill.

Nationally, Cohen and Zysman say, *25 percent of the gross national product consists of services purchased by American manufacturers.* And they add, "If manufacturing goes, those service jobs go with it." They say further:

"We are not experiencing a transition to a post-industrial society, but from one kind of industrial society to another. Of course things have changed. The division of labor has become infinitely more elaborate."

But the key generator of wealth... remains mastery and control of production. Because the wealth and power of the United States is at stake, the post-industrial economy view is a radical and terribly risky policy guide. Their evidence tells us that mature industries not only can survive, they can prosper — as has occurred in Germany — and they can enhance our economy and our standard of living.

The status of American workers is further subsumed by representations that lower wages are the key to competing in a global economy. What that would lead to, of course — what it already has achieved — is a drastic reduction in the standard of living for millions of Americans. This kind of competition doesn't make sense in a global economy when it results in a lowered standard of living, a reliance on the lowest common denominator.

What is needed is a clear recognition that 18th century trade theories are not applicable to trade problems of the late 20th century. Professor John Culbertson puts it this way:

> ... the basic error of the free-trade doctrine is that it relates to an imaginary situation and an imaginary pattern of trade rather than to the real world and actual trade.
>
> I see the basic issue... as one of realism versus unrealism. Japan and many other countries have interpreted the workings of international trade realistically, and have shown admirable skill and efficiency in advancing their interests by designing policies that fit the realities of the world. The United States has interpreted international trade on the basis of an ideology-based delusion, and was thus led into a Quixotic crusade for "free trade" that is ruining its economy, sacrificing the interests of its workers, and setting world trade on a path that can only have an unhappy ending.

What we ought to be doing is finding ways to avoid this unhappy ending, instead of engaging in a destructive debate on *the merits of pulling the plug.* A debate limited to free trade versus protectionism is sterile.

Unfair Dumping and Subsidies Hurt Steel Industry. One element injected into this debate is competitiveness. It's a nice-sounding word, but what does it really mean? My office dictionary defines it as "inclined, desiring, or suited to compete;" to compete is "to strive for an objective," leading us into competition, described as an "effort... to secure business... by offering the most favorable terms."

Certainly we're inclined and desirous of competing, but are we suited? There's no question we have an objective, but can we offer the most favorable terms? The major portion of the answers rests with the Administration and the Congress and what they do about meaningful trade legislation, the budget deficit, and the trade deficit. Labor has done its share and then some, and it is willing to do more — despite the heavy price working people have paid already in job losses, wage and benefit reductions, and altered lifestyles. In the steel industry, as one example, our members accepted reductions of more than $2 billion in 1983. But Wheeling-Pittsburgh Steel wound up in bankruptcy.

In 1986, many of our members again were called upon for sacrifices, including $3.60 an hour at LTV. LTV is now in bankruptcy.

At the same time, there has been a sharp increase in productivity and quality. *The manhours required to produce a ton of steel in the United States are the lowest in the world.* Yet the specter of bankruptcy persists. Despite these productivity advances and cost reductions, direct imports eat up 22 percent of the U.S. steel market, because some foreign producers are dumping their product, or they are being subsidized by their governments, or their wages are as low as one-tenth what they are in this country — or any combination of these reasons. It follows, then, that the American steel industry can't compete on the basis of wages; it can't compete when foreign producers — as in England, France, and West Germany — are subsidized, and it can't compete when foreign-made steel is sold here for less than its cost of production.

We have had some help with voluntary restraint agreements (VRAs) with certain of the world's steel producers. These agreements are supposed to limit imports to 20.5 percent of the American market, a limit that has been exceeded each of the three years VRAs have been in existence. The current import penetration of 22 percent represents only finished or semi-finished steel products. When indirect imports are included — that is, steel used in such things as cars, appliances, or tools — the figure rises to 36 percent. The results for the steel industry — and its employees and their communities — have been devastating. Multi-billion dollar losses, bankruptcies, 30,000 lost jobs, wage and benefit reductions, retirement incomes placed in jeopardy, elimination of essential municipal services. All to little avail.

The persistent and pervasive consequences of this devastation prompted a fundamental change in our approach to collective bargaining in recent years, requiring us not only to insure the best interests of our members, but to attempt to save an industry. We have completed our negotiations. In the process, we have had a short strike and two long and bitter lockouts, based on principle and social conscience. We have made innovative strides in employment security and worker participation, and the industry seems to have stabilized, even if temporarily. We have also concluded that government must play a major role, because neither labor nor management alone, nor the two of us acting jointly, can cure problems created by unfair trade.

Labor Management Participation Teams. Government help notwithstanding, it is incumbent on labor and management to forge a new partnership to serve our mutual interests. In plain words, the companies should welcome our members' involvement. Give them a piece of the action. Utilize their skills and talents. We began this process with Labor Management Participation Teams in our 1980 contract. Some worked better than others. Some did not work at all. But they provided the foundation for quantum jumps in this area in our most recent bargaining. During these talks, in the several cases where it was essential, our members accepted wage and/or benefit reductions of varying degrees. In return, they received profit-sharing and stock ownership plans, productivity bonuses, unprecedented participation in the decision-making process of their companies, and language that puts strict limits on the contracting out of work and provides a substantial measure of employment security.

Our agreement with National Steel *guarantees* employment security and a minimum level of profit-sharing, even if the company fails to post a profit. National Steel employees who would otherwise be laid off are instead placed in an employment pool — with no reduction in pay. They are being assigned in one of several manners:

• To traditional jobs that otherwise would be contracted out, and to temporary vacancies that would be filled by overtime.

- To nontraditional jobs such as work redesign teams, training and re-training, customer service, statistical process, quality control, and technical problem-solving groups.

Profit-sharing and gain-sharing bonus plans are permitting National employees to more than recoup sacrifices they accepted in wages and cost of living allowances.

Cooperative Partnership Program. We also have a Cooperative Partnership Program in place at National Steel in which Union members have been participating in essentially all strategic decision-making, including:

- Capital investment, and short-and long-range business plans at the corporate level, and
- Scheduling, work assignments, safety questions, overtime, contracting out, and other quality of work life and organizational efficiency issues on the departmental level.

We've had a similar program at Wheeling-Pittsburgh Steel Corp. for more than two years. There have been disagreements, which is not surprising, but from all reports the system is working well. It has been endorsed by both our people and the company's. The mini-boards, as we call these teams at Wheeling-Pitt, have been identifying problems and generating efficient and cost-saving solutions, again including the retrieval of work from outside contractors. Their most recent success was the modernization of a galvanizing line, which has resulted in improved yield, productivity gains, and lower raw material costs. The conceptualization, design, construction, and installation all were done in-house at a savings of 60 percent on a job that in times past would have gone to an outside contractor.

We also have a Steelworker representative on the Wheeling- Pitt board of directors, which makes the commitment complete. And, let me emphasize, if there is no commitment on the part of management to make these programs work, then they will not work. We've seen both sides of that coin in successive management at Wheeling-Pitt. And we've seen the commitment to make the plan work at National.

Cooperation Pays Off but Obstacles Remain. While the National and Wheeling-Pitt developments have received the most public notice, they are not isolated occurrences. The Union's position throughout our negotiations — in steel and elsewhere — was twofold: To achieve employment security and to insure that any help to the companies by our members would be in the form of investments, not merely sacrifices. It's working out in steel, and it's working in copper.

On a relative basis, the copper industry was hurt more than the steel industry over the past seven years, both financially and in terms of employment. Two-thirds of the industry closed permanently, and employment was reduced from 36,000 to 12,000. Here in Utah, the Kennecott mine — which had been idled because of huge losses — is back in operation because workers agreed to lower wage and benefit levels, which had been the highest in the industry. The company, for its part, is proceeding with its commitment to invest $400 million in modernization. We have similar agreements with Inspiration and Magma in Arizona, where plans tied to the price of copper paid bonuses in the third quarter and will pay them again for the fourth quarter.

Although we have had some successes in our labor agreements, and manufacturing is making a comeback, I don't want to give you the impression we have reached nirvana. We have not. There still are employers unwilling to fulfill their end of the bargain. USX closed Geneva Works within days of our contract settlement a year ago, after leading us to believe it would not. We helped find a buyer, won retirement benefits for several hundred workers who chose to retire, and reached a collective managing agreement that helps the new company get underway. About 1,400 people are now working and by all accounts any difficulties associated with the reopening are *not* related to labor relations.

Elsewhere, we've been forced into unnecessary and expensive litigation through the grievance and arbitration procedure to settle disputes over the new language covering the contracting out of work, and we are now having to deal with the assigning of excessive overtime in lieu of recall of laid off workers. These are things that can only be handled in the context of our basic labor agreements, but they are resulting in the wasted time, money, and effort that could be put to much better uses elsewhere.

There also remain differences between unions and employers on the questions of wage levels, job conditions, and the distribution of profits. To assume that easy agreement is possible is to deny human nature. So we have to be realistic about what we can accomplish through cooperative endeavors. The situation is not advanced by skirting contract compliance, or by union avoidance efforts such as the "Committee for a Union-Free Environment" under the aegis of the National Association of Manufacturers.

Value of Employee Involvement Recognized. Despite the obstacles — both those that are built in and those that are created — increasing numbers of companies are coming to recognize the value of employee involvement. For those who are not, I offer these words from James Houghton, the chairman of Corning Glass:

> ... management must recognize that the worker, if allowed, can provide the most important impetus for improvement. On the surface, this sounds almost routine, especially among companies that pride themselves on progressive human-resources practices. There is evidence, however, to show that we're not moving quickly enough on worker involvement.

In a recent Gallup Poll on quality practices in American industry, workers were singled out as the primary source of quality problems by a majority of surveyed executives. This is pure bunk. If there is one thing our company and others like us have learned from our efforts to enhance quality, it is that the person on the job knows more about that job and how to improve it than anyone in the organization. For too long we managers have worn blinders when looking at our workers. We have underestimated their creativity and failed to tap their resourcefulness. They want to do a good job. They want to be an integral part of the quality process.

Managers who oppose the involvement of their employees are squandering valuable resources. They should welcome this participation. Instead of fighting with labor, and fighting against union organization, they can put their energies to much better use by *joining* labor in repulsing the assault we're facing from foreign competition.

Our first goal is passage of effective trade legislation to give American industry some short-term breathing room. The longer haul requires several layers of actions.

- There is a need for managing trade, which has been done for years in the European Common Market. The United States has been involved in managed trade agreements, such as the multifiber agreement and the American-Canadian auto pact. While they're not perfect, they have served a good purpose. We need to refine these practices, not turn our backs on them.

- We must attack the budget and trade deficits, bring interest rates to a realistic level, and make a commitment to raising capital by increasing production, rather than generating capital for its own sake as occurs in such things as mergers and acquisitions, where workers and their wages are the first victims.

We don't want to beggar our neighbors. We're not opposed to Third World development — far from it — but we must deal with it in some more integrated way, not exploit it as a source of cheap and disciplined labor. We need an economy in which the world is advancing, moving forward. If workers are put under the gun in country after country to see who can exploit them the most, that creates the kind of world that none of us wants. It isn't, then, just a matter of having an industrial economy or a service economy, or of managing trade decently or being competitive. We must have all of them to reconstitute and develop a fully rounded society.

Workers Willing To Be Partners. American workers are more than willing to become partners in this. But they refuse to be silent victims, to accept on their backs alone the consequences of failed governmental and management policies. They *will* continue to fight for what is right, not only for themselves, but for their friends, neighbors, and co-workers. There's nothing magical about what we seek:

- A decent job with a decent wage, so workers can provide for themselves and their families, and be the kind of consumers of goods and services upon which the nation's prosperity depends.
- A safe workplace, so they can enjoy the fruits of their labor without fear of illness, injury, incapacitation, or worse.
- A real voice in the decisions that affect them in their jobs.
- Employment security.
- Just and humane treatment for those whose jobs are unavoidably lost, including training and retraining for those who can re-enter the work force, and income security for those forced into retirement.

Retraining is one of the ways we have been trying to deal with structural unemployment in the steel industry, where more than 31,000 Steelworkers have gone through programs sponsored jointly by the Union and companies. Of that number, 21,000 have been placed in new jobs . . . the great majority of them in service industries at average wages of $6.50 to $7 an hour — an amount that makes it very difficult to support a family.

One striking example of this quandary occurred five years ago, following a visit to Pittsburgh by President Reagan. During a tour of a local college, he met a young Steelworker who had been out of a job for a year and was studying electronics. When the Steelworkers gave President Reagan a copy of his resume, the resultant publicity got him a job with Radio Shack. But he had to leave his new job when offered the opportunity to return to the mill because this new, high-tech job paid him only half the amount he was making in the mill, an amount on which he could not support himself and his family.

I don't mean to imply, nor should you infer, that we should abandon retraining. On the contrary, training and retraining — a commitment to educating our workers to take full advantage of the opportunities arising from changing demands in a changing economy — are vital to bringing about full employment and narrowing if not eliminating the wage gap. But this won't happen if American corporations keep seeking out the cheapest labor or pliable governments that will do their bidding, as they are now doing in places like Haiti and Mexico, then pulling up stakes and moving on when they've pumped the well dry.

Job Loss to Offshore Plants Causes Human Suffering. If we don't act, more and more corporations will go offshore, millions more workers will lose their jobs, our manufacturing capabilities will continue to fade, and our status as the world's leading economic power will ebb. I have attended scores of meetings such as this in recent years where the subject has been a variation on today's theme: How to put America back to work, and how to make America competitive in a global economy. I've heard and seen arguments on all sides of the question: Statistics and theories, charts and graphs, pleas for workers to become more cooperative with management, for managers to make employees feel they're part of the team, discourses on fair trade, free trade, dumping, protectionism, Smoot-Hawley, trade bills, Congressional action, and Presidential vetoes.

There's been merit to some of these arguments — some of which I've used myself — and there is a validity to making them, because we obviously need to draw the dimensions of the problem to arrive at a solution. But while we've been talking, the problem and the dimensions have been growing. So we need to raise other questions: Are we simply talking to ourselves? Have we become fiddlers on the economic balcony, consumed by the flames of our own rhetoric? There are some, suffering the pangs of an empty stomach, the finality of lost hope, overcome with despair, who would answer yes. We've all seen them, young and old, male and female, of different races and colors, and their numbers have been increasing. They are not merely entries on a ledger.

In Pittsburgh, across the street from the Steelworker headquarters, St. Mary's Catholic Church has been providing free lunches for years to the homeless and needy. At one time, not too long ago, the food line started forming about 11 am, usually populated by men, aged 40 or above. These days, they begin queuing up about 9:30 am, because the line is longer, swollen by younger people and women. The story is much the same at the Rainbow Kitchen in Homestead, Pennsylvania, which serves one meal a day, five days a week, to more than 100 people, among them pregnant women and children as young as three.

In Kansas, according to a report in the *New York Times*, hunger has become a constant among many farm families. A sociology professor quoted by the *Times* says, "Third World conditions have reached the Middle West." A farmer featured in the report told the *Times*, "The kids aren't getting enough to eat. There's times when my youngest says to me, 'Daddy, I'm hungry.'"

And *U.S. News & World Report* reported last week that there are 9 million working poor in this country — people with jobs that don't pay enough to support a family, jobs that don't provide health insurance — jobs that don't provide a living wage.

While farmers and their families go hungry in Kansas, while pregnant women eat at soup kitchens in Pennsylvania, we hear claims — truthful claims, no doubt — about record numbers of job holders, we read — until recently, at least — of fortunes being made every day on Wall Street, of aspirations for fancy cars and VCRs . . . paeans to Adam Smith and requiems for John Keynes.

It's time that less emphasis be placed on what is present in America's rec rooms and more thought given to what is absent from America's dining rooms. If we don't, then we'll keep hearing the plaintive words, "Daddy, I'm hungry."

7

Responding to the New Reality of Global Competition

John Young, President and CEO, Hewlett-Packard

Having to compete in the world environment is a new idea for most Americans. We have taken being competitive for granted during most of our nation's history. That can no longer be safely assumed.

Today I will start with an assessment of where we stand, and then I'm going to try to leap from global competition to information systems, if you can believe that. I'm not going to postulate information systems as the savior of our national competitiveness, but I think I can make a credible case for it playing an important role. In fact, a partnership between a lot of the academic work and a lot of the practitioners' work in companies might be the best way to bring about that renaissance.

Responding to Global Competition. I'd like to talk about responding to this reality of global competition. As I indicated, it's a subject that I have spent an awful lot of time on. I did chair this commission for President Reagan, and gave him our report in January of 1985, just about three years ago. I learned that the fate of many commission reports is to go directly to the Smithsonian without passing through either very many hands or heads.

I discovered that there's also a reason for that. There's no owner for a report like this. You don't clear out your desk and push this new idea to number one on your overall agenda. So I formed an organization, the Council on Competitiveness, to provide some continuing emphasis and that's what we're doing. We're looking for those windows of opportunity, particularly in the public policy area, where we can advance our competitiveness agenda. Incidentally, we just completed a project of assessing the competitive statements and postures of all 13 presidential candidates.

Let's start by reviewing the changing environment that causes us to have to rethink that taking for granted of our ability to compete. In 1960 we had less than 5 percent of our gross national product involved in any way in international commerce. That's up close to 25 percent today, and we are deeply linked by a whole variety of institutions with the world trading environment. World trade itself has grown dramatically, by a factor of seven, since 1970, faster growth than most nations' economies. So the international marketplace is a real area of opportunity.

There are new competitors. We mostly grew up in this country thinking about Europeans as our natural trade alliance. The facts are that by 1991 or 1992 we will do two times the trade with the Pacific Rim countries that we do with all of Europe. And that rate of increase is diverging at a very rapid rate. So we have to understand who these new competitors are. The so-called NICs — newly industrializing countries on the Pacific Rim — have made concerted efforts to nurture specific, high-growth industries. They have taken advantage of some national targeting strategies, things that are well understood by the Japanese, and have been perfected by the Japanese. These strategies include closing the home market, building a base of capability, assembling the technology in today's very mobile technology world, and then developing export markets.

These targeting strategies constitute new rules of competition to which governments — and other firms — have not yet responded. They work like a charm, and you do it with a very different cost base that lets you catapult your economy ahead in a dramatic way that has never quite been accomplished before: real GNP growth rates of 5, 6, 7, 8, 9, 10 percent per year.

With the growing trade of things like intellectual property, there are whole new rules of the road. Non-tariff barriers to trade have grown up at a dramatic rate, and despite four rounds of improving GATT — the Tokyo round, the Kennedy round, and others I'm sure you're familiar with — the real barriers to trade have grown, not decreased. A lot of that has to do with the character of trade. It's no longer just manufactured goods, it's intellectual property. The most important things we own fit on a roll of tape. Yet, you can buy that roll of tape for a floppy program with Lotus 1-2-3 on it at any vendor stall in Hong Kong for $1.50. That's the cost of the floppy. What's on it has no recognized value by a very large fraction of the trading world. These are all issues that are before us that we have to think about in considering what's going on.

Let's start with an agreement on what competition means. You have to get your mind out of what it means as a company and start thinking about a country because we're talking about a nation. Competitiveness is the degree to which a nation can, under open and fair market conditions, produce goods and services that meet the test of international markets while simultaneously maintaining or expanding the real incomes of its citizens.

That means not marking down your goods by cheapening your currency, like we are doing today to clear our inventories. The challenge is to meet that international competition under open and fair conditions, doing it in a way that enhances our standard of living.

Note that competitiveness isn't an end in itself. It's a means to an end, and the desired goal is a rising standard of living. For individual people, that means rising real wages. Those high wages don't come automatically, they must be earned in a world economy. For nations, a rising standard of living provides the means of achieving other national goals — at least any that require money from tax receipts.

Symptoms of Declining Competitiveness. We've got some symptoms that we are not doing as well as we might in meeting that competitiveness test. I distinguish symptoms from the real root causes. I'm going to talk about both, but first let's look at some of the symptoms:

1. Massive trade deficits
2. Declining rates of return in manufacturing
3. Loss of world market share in high tech
4. Stagnant real wages
5. Failure of the economy to create new jobs

A merchandise trade balance is an indicator, a symptom, it's not an end in itself. After all, Uganda had a positive trade balance last year but you wouldn't argue that was a total proxy for affluence in the world market. So this taken apart from everything else is just an indicator. It's one of several ingredients I think you have to look at. Yes, our trade balance has been exacerbated by the strong currencies in the 1980s. But you can see we began having our problems well over a decade ago. We had a positive trade balance every year this century until 1970. It began really changing over the 1970s and 1980s and even at times when the currency was cheap. So that's an issue.

Real returns on capital. What kind of pay-back do you get from investing in manufacturing assets? You can look at the industrial bond yields as a kind of a proxy for the market rate of return for that kind of not-too-risky a return, compared to equity returns, the investments, and real manufacturing assets. We can see again a long-term trend line of declining returns. In fact, in recent years you could have made as much money on passbook savings as you could have made by investing in American industrial assets. Again, this is not too persuasive a picture that we are in fact competing effectively as a nation.

Some people say, "Okay, big deal. Most of the stories you hear about industrial America, the so-called Rust Belt, don't matter. Those industries were last year's. High tech is what it's all about, and it is going to save us from this problem."

Well, if you define high technology simply as those industrial sectors that spend, on an average, more than 5 percent of sales on R & D, you will see that by world market share comparisons, in only three cases has our market share even stayed the same or grown. In most cases it's dramatically declined. In fact, if I looked at the statistics for 1986, the only year that we have complete, we see that the trade deficit with Japan for electronics is greater than it is for automobiles. There's a partnership between the technology and traditional manufacturers that's quite real.

One of the tests we said we had to meet was maintaining or increasing our real standard of living. A lot of people know in their hearts and in their pocketbooks that we, in fact, are not doing as well as we have done over a lot of years. We crested in the early 1970s and we are about 8 percent below that level today. That's why there are so many working spouses, two-family incomes, and other arrangements that have gone on to allow consumers to continue some of their historic growth patterns, which have happened for some different reasons than the output per hour really being improved.

Factors Determining Competitiveness. With some of these symptoms, then, let's move to the next step and see what these underlying problems are and see what policy choices there are in thinking about improving some of these activities.

First of all, we said trade policy was one of those underlying causes.

In theory, the way it works is this. It only works this way in the United States. The U.S. trade representative (USTR), Clayton Yeuter, negotiates trade policy, but the total enforcement mechanism is in the Department of Commerce. That sounds a little crazy, but it turns out it doesn't matter because they don't have the power anyway. All of the real key decisions are made by either the State Department, for reasons of political interest, or by the Department of Defense to enhance national security issues. Time and time again over our postwar history, we have traded away, subordinated, and otherwise given short shrift to our trade issues for other national policies.

That was great after the war when we had such an enormous influence in world policies. Today, that is no longer the case. We really have to have a very different understanding of, and enforcement of, our trading system.

There's a kind of blind response among so many in the current administration that free trade is the answer to every problem, which simply doesn't recognize the realities of life. There are so many non-market economies, so many mixed and planned economies, so many developing countries who use different rules than are covered by the rules of the road, that it simply doesn't map out the reality of today's world marketplace. The world's trading system has inadequate rules for trade in intellectual property, and there are as yet no remedies for many "non-tariff" or hidden trade barriers. The upcoming GATT round and many changes in this area are absolutely critical to maintain the integrity of the world trading system.

Likewise, the instability of world financial markets calls for better coordination of fiscal and monetary policy among the world's most active trading nations. Capital issues are fundamental. Cost of capital is an ingredient that grows across parts of our country. Our savings rate is abysmally low. It's the worst among all of our trading companies, and of course you can't invest what you don't save, and that means our cost of capital is high.

The Commission in Industrial Competitiveness assembled more than 30 economists to give testimony on our nation's cost of capital compared to our major trading partners. We got our greatest surprise: They agreed with each other! Now they didn't agree on how to compute it, but the answer was clear. Cost of capital is somewhere between two and four times as large in the United States as it is for our Japanese competitors. A very fundamental ingredient, savings rates, is much higher even in Germany. But if I add the newly industrializing countries' rates — Singapore's, Korea's, and so forth — you would find savings rates up in that 40-percent band. It's just a dramatic reinvestment climate.

These first two factors — trade policy and savings rates and capital costs — should motivate business leaders to get more actively involved in public policy issues, to which only government leaders can provide the solutions.

The currency ratios, a subject of very great debate and discussion in the newspapers of the United States is interesting to take a moment to talk about. I claimed at the outset of this section that these were the root causes, but I want to tell you that despite what many people think and say, I do not think that currencies are a cause. Currencies are a dependent variable. They're an outcome of many other activities. If we're incurring a trade deficit, we're paying for the goods that come in, let's say from Germany, in dollars. But if we're selling less to them, we're not generating as many marks as the Germans are paying us. So if you go home to Germany with this sack full of dollars, you cannot spend dollars in Germany. You've got to convert them into marks to have something that's useful to you. So there are more dollars to be converted into marks and you would see the dollar then tending to go down, not up.

That's the textbook scenario, but in reality it's going exactly backwards from what logic would tell you would happen. Why? I puzzled about that for months, and I finally discovered the answer. There are so many dollars in the world today. It is the international currency of exchange. If I went to New York this morning and today was a typical day in New York at the New York Fed that clears dollars, you would find that about $1 trillion will change hands in New York today. You compare that with our $4.5-trillion economy and you see that's a lot of dollars. It turns out that the financial transactions in dollars are about 50 times larger than the trade transactions.

If I take some actions that get the financial aggregates out of balance, the resulting transactions overwhelm trade. So what happened? The trade imbalance was going as we just described, but we currently created this giant fiscal deficit. We drove up the interest rates that had every portfolio manager around the world thinking in dollars, moving that money around to take advantage of these higher returns in dollars. So we've created this trade situation out of fundamentally a fiscal imbalance problem.

It's really important to understand the differences between the real root causes and some of these symptoms. No amount of trade bill activity, no amount of legislation aimed at that problem, is going to really solve the root cause. It's so important that our Congressmen understand that and we keep working to make that point.

Let me move to another factor in competitiveness — technology. Commercial technology. If you eliminate defense, we're being dramatically outspent by our competitors. And the growth rates are dramatic. Probably 75 percent of the U.S. productivity growth rate has been influenced by technology. You can probably get a sense of what's likely to happen.

Productivity is a fair competitiveness factor. This is probably the summary judgment. Yes, on an absolute level of output, we're still pretty good. But these are rates of change, and all of those competitors have dramatically better rates of change and are closing in at a very rapid rate. So our real wealth per person — our standard of living — fundamentally goes back to getting more output per person. You see a rather discouraging spot when you're even below the UK. I could have picked any period of time, and we could have gotten that same answer. We'll get the same answer no matter what.

White Collar Productivity. We're starting to head now more towards some other issues that end up at the management of information systems. When we look at the goods producing sector, we see that total output per worker from the mid-1970s to mid-1980s went up, for all workers, roughly 11 percent. If I take a look at only production workers, people whose job really is production, we see that despite a lot of criticisms about productivity, they haven't done that badly. They have a 20-percent increase in output per person. Let's take a look at another category of employers, roughly called knowledge workers — that is, people who work with information. That's roughly half of the jobs in the country. Here we find a rather interesting story. Their lack of productivity, or negative productivity growth rate, has in fact offset half of the growth from the real production workers.

The information sector has a much different job mix than the goods-producing sector, and output per worker in the information sector is so low — those service economy productivities are so bad — that it's really ruining America's productivity situation. This, mind you, is happening in spite of huge investments in high technology equipment.

The Public Sector Agenda. I think about competitiveness by thinking about a public sector agenda and a private sector agenda, because we are really partners in this country. Companies don't make trade policy. They don't set fiscal policy. They don't deal in monetary policy. They don't set the investment levels for technology and so forth. But how well that's done indelibly sets the framework within which competition takes place. If that is not done well, I don't care what kind of a genius manager you are, you're not going to win in today's world marketplace. So that's the public sector agenda. A lot of things we've been talking about have to do with that set of issues.

A Shared Agenda. We have a couple of areas in which we are real partners — education and technology. About half of the R & D dollars, $125 billion last year, are spent by the private sector and half by the federal government. It's a real partnership. Of course, a lot of that gets spent in universities and other educational institutions, which brings us to the other partnership — K through 12 as well as the university. That's public money. Yet for companies like Hewlett-Packard, one of our largest investments is in training and retraining employees. A young person entering the work force today is probably going to have five different careers. He and she will need to be retrained five times in their working lives. It's a very major investment to acquire and maintain those skills.

The Private Sector Agenda. For the private sector, being competitive is only their responsibility; no government can do it for them. If Government could, of course, the Concorde would be the world's most successful airplane, having been legislated into existence and supported. Of course, that is simply not the case. So the private sector has to do its job well.

That's all I'm going to say about public policies. It was more of a way of getting into this information idea, and I'm going to use our own company as a proxy for the private sector, not that it truly is, but it's one that I know enough about to credibly discuss. Some things we've been working on, particularly how information ties to a competitive renaissance in American private sector competitiveness, are quite relevant.

So let me just go on to some of the things we have been working on in our own company. This is about the same set of issues that our Commission identified that people ought to work on.

First, *increased international presence*. You just can't export things from Logan, Utah, when that's your only base of operation. You have to have a real international understanding, a presence in many countries. Many U.S. companies have not made that effort. Our Commission determined that about 25,000 more companies could export than do today. We are so horizon-bound as to not see the potential. For Hewlett-Packard, half of our business comes from outside the United States and we have major manufacturing and marketing locations in almost 50 countries around the world.

Second, *shortened product-development cycle*. With the mobility of technology today, time to market is everything. Mobilizing your resources to take advantage of flexible manufacturing and some of those other things that have been the issue for the last ten years — I think time to market is the issue for the next ten years. It's really incumbent on companies to understand the full implications of that. So reduced manufacturing costs, getting a team, fielding a team of employees, getting rid of those cultural barriers — all these are critically important issues. This includes simpler, easier-to-build design, total quality control, standardization and consolidation of key manufacturing processes, and closer relationships with suppliers.

Third, *focusing on real customer needs* sounds obvious, but it's honored in the breach many times. Customer needs should dictate strategy and structure. HP has just completed a major overhaul of its computer platform.

Finally, *using information systems to create this competitive advantage*. We're going to see in a little bit of detail how we have approached this problem. HP is running at about $10 billion this year. We are active in measurement and computational products and very active particularly in distributed computing. That business direction mirrors our own use of computers inside of HP. We have about $200 or

$300 billion dollars in expense for our business information systems. It is up 3.6 percent of sales; not an insignificant investment level. We run our company on about 850 of our HP 3000 computers, all networked together. We have 82,000 employees. And for the business needs, not engineering, but the business of Hewlett-Packard, we have about 65,000 terminals and personal computers for those 82,000 people. We have perhaps the most information-rich environment that I know of in any company, and we use it as a very real strategic asset in our business. It's a way of connecting people to the critical issues we are trying to improve in our company. Managing information is considered an integral part of running the business at HP. Our information strategy is set and managed by our Management Council — the company's key operational committee. Each functional area — manufacturing, R & D, marketing, and so forth — defines the information needs for its activities. This approach means that the applications and systems implemented really match the strategic needs of our business partners.

At HP we've identified which information flows need to be managed on a uniform, global basis and which ones can be adapted a bit more to meet local needs.

There are five global systems that gather information from HP's more than 375 sales and service offices and its more than 54 manufacturing facilities. The global systems are controlled from the corporate level. However, there are many other local or "shared" systems that have been adapted to suit the operational needs of different HP entities. To ensure that we can still gather data from these local systems and amalgamate it in a useful way, we've defined 30 different basic business codes. These are items that must be uniquely identified on a companywide basis — such as employee, customer, or part number. These codes enable us to centralize the information without centralizing the activity.

Using Information as a Strategic Resource. What kinds of issues have we pursued, given our agenda? First, the better execution of our business activities. Second, improving quality and productivity. Third, managing our assets. Fourth, tightening our supplier relationships. Fifth, shortening our product-development cycles. Finally, working across geographic and organizational boundaries.

This last one is an interesting one to think about, organization-ally, at least. Most of the real payoffs of CIM, computer integrated manufacturing, could be described as the automation of cooperation. What are some of the payoffs we've seen from our investments in information systems? Well, let me just list a few of those most easily quantified.

1. HP's sales in 1987 were $8.09 billion. If our inventory was still at that level of 20.5 percent, we would have had a total of $542 million in working capital tied up in inventory.
2. Similarly, we've reduced our accounts receivable by $146 million over the same time frame. We achieved this by using our distri-buted information systems to improve the accuracy of our order processing. Since we installed this system, we've cut our costs to process a dollar's worth of orders by two-thirds.
3. At the beginning of this decade, we began efforts to reduce our field failure rates to one-tenth of their 1979 levels, and we're well on our way toward achieving that goal.
    Our total quality control efforts deserve the credit, but information systems have played a key role. For example, we're able to provide our suppliers with very accurate quality data, and we've used it to help them reduce incoming defects by 90 percent since 1982.
4. Finally, we've provided our sales force with portable computers, which has enabled them to reduce time spent in meeting and infor-mation gathering and to spend more time with customers.

How did we achieve those results? Well, working on quality has been one of the major drivers. I set a goal for our company of cutting the failure rates of the hardware products we make by 10 to 1 over the decade of the 1980s. There's no question we're going to achieve that objective. And if you plotted out what that meant today we would be a factor of 6 better than in 1979, and that's exactly where we are. There's been a terrific pay-back in a variety of ways. Certainly cus-tomer satisfaction is a big intangible, but there's some very major tan-gible benefits of reduced costs. In analyzing our manufacturing costs it's not just the 1-percent warranty cost that we have that is affected by better quality. Around a third of total manufacturing costs are incurred because you do not do things right the first time. That's what's there to be gained.

Inventory savings are another. Most of your inventory is in place to fix failures. Inventory really is a stockpile to fix the mistakes. When you stop making mistakes, suddenly you don't need that inventory.

In fact, that turnover ratio is down significantly, it's a half a billion dollars in inventory we don't have. That is more than the total profit price of every computer at retail value we own in our company. Out of assets substitution alone, we have gotten back that total information systems investment just in inventory.

Things like accounts receivable savings simply prove that quality works in information as well as in products. Amazingly enough, you send a customer a bill that looks like what he ordered, they send you a check. But if you send them a bill that doesn't match what he thinks he ordered, they assign the newest clerk they hired to spend at least six weeks wrestling that problem.

Let's look at sales force productivity. We did a total quality control analysis of this process-oriented discipline. We found out that, by putting a portable computer in the hands of every salesman, we could change the way they work. We have increased the time in front of our customers by 35 percent measured data. That's a dramatic improvement in productivity.

Technical Barriers To Using Information. There are a lot of technical barriers to using information. HP's product strategies have been aimed at eliminating these technical barriers:

1. Slow support for standards
2. Hierarchical and proprietary networks
3. High cost of ownership for computers
4. Inability of PC users to access data located on corporate systems
5. A bewildering variety of "unfriendly" computer user interfaces

In short, HP understands what technical barriers have prevented people from using information as a competitive resource. I won't give you a marketing pitch, but I can assure you that our product strategies have the goal of eliminating those barriers. And I'm proud to say that the list is getting shorter every day.

Management Barriers. There are some further management barriers to using information. Information people started in that funny glass room that was temperature-controlled and had that 100-horsepower chiller out there to keep things from burning up. Computer gurus talked funny languages and they never got integrated into the fabric of the company. They weren't accepted as real strategic partners.

Consequently, operations people do not appreciate, in every case, what information they need or could better help what they do, and the information people are often isolated from the real strategy in the company. This kind of a separation presents a pretty serious problem.

There's also a narrow view of the strategic potential of information systems and their investment returns. I've heard CEO after CEO say, "How do we get our information systems costs down?" They don't ask how they can get the value up or what they can do to take advantage of their information resources. If you don't take a lot of care at looking at cause and effect relationships, you don't see those potential problems.

A third management barrier is the lack of companywide information flows. One even more cynical than usual CEO remarked to me the other day, "Why should I spend all this trouble getting my computers to talk to each other when our people don't talk to each other anyway?" Well, I think he had a point. In his case it may be hopeless, but it's a sad commentary on the kind of teamwork that it takes to win in that new global marketplace we're talking about. There is no room for the "them and us" or the half-hearted effort. It's got to be a dedicated team environment and you need to work across these boundaries. The organizational cultural barriers we need to change are very real.

A Vision of the Future. A vision has begun to emerge of technology that will make it possible for business and technical decision makers to gain access to useful information and to use it to competitively differentiate their firms.

- Computer customers will be able to choose from a wide variety of applications and systems provided by different vendors and to integrate them into a companywide network that makes it possible to exchange information.
- Computing technologies will become more specialized for particular functions such as database management, design automation, and so on. These specialized resources will be distributed on the network and available to a broad set of users.
- "Smart" networks will automatically select the computing resources on the network that are the most appropriate and available for a given task.
- Software tools (for instance, data reduction tools) will be available to search for the information, translate it into a usable form, and display it in a way that complements decision making. Artificial intelligence will play a role here.

- User interfaces will be intuitively simple and consistent across all applications, allowing the user to communicate with the system in a very natural way. Artificial intelligence "agents" will enable users to automate complex tasks.

My conclusion to all this is as follows: Tough competition is here to stay. This is not a one-time aberration of the Japanese suddenly showing up selling cars on our shores. The mobility of technology today is dramatic. It is not going down, it is going up, and you'll find increasing numbers of the world's countries with far lower cost bases than we with access to the most modern technical tools, manufacturing processes, and know-how that you can imagine.

We have a joint venture with Samsung Corporation, one of the very large corporations in Korea. On my first trip there some five years ago, I was touring their facilities. I saw them making television sets and sitting at PC monitors. I watched them ramp the VCR lines with all these control charts and all these processes — very sophisticated. I saw a lot of automated equipment. I asked these guys, "You're paying these people on a production line 40 cents an hour. How come all this automation?" They said it would be crazy to start a world business today depending on cheap labor. They need the quality; they need the repeatability. They need to do it right. I said, "Where do you get these control charts? Every one of these wave-solder machines has defect densities on how things are going. Boy, that's pretty elegant. I don't see that very often in the best plants anywhere." They said, "Yes we have to keep control." I asked where they had learned to do this. They said they took advantage of an anomaly in the Japanese social system. You know, they require all of their key people to retire at age 55. So they just went to Japan. They got all the retiring production managers and they brought them over here to Korea. And six months later, they were close behind the cutting edge of how it's done in the world today.

Productivity is absolutely the key to winning. You have to face the simple reality of that 40-cents-an-hour labor force. We have to earn our standard of living every day in the world marketplace, whether we like it or not. That is the reality of it. We do that by being better at what we do and having to regroup our forces and get our productivity turned around. A lot of our white collar workers, our knowledge workers, are at the core of our productivity problem. We could really solve a lot of the problem with better information management systems.

Some of the barriers to using information are technological. Vendors and academic institutions working with them really have to aim at eliminating those. But the most significant barriers I think are managerial. While academic institutions such as the business school here can have, I think, a major role through symposia such as this, I think a lot of us who run major businesses have to go back and take personal responsibility for re-examining our programs and making sure that we are preparing our companies to fully compete in the very changed world environment we find ourselves in today.

8

Challenge to America's Industrial Leadership*

Armand V. Feigenbaum, President, General Systems

It is a great pleasure to join with you in this opening plenary session of the Thirteenth Annual Productivity Seminar. I have come to know the importance of what you have been doing in the Partners Program at Utah State's College of Business, and I greatly respect what you have accomplished.

What I think brings all of us together is our sharing of three basic convictions, each of which I want to spend a few moments on. The first is that quality has become crucial to the industrial strength of the United States. Let me try to quantify this. Our data on customer preferences for the year 1987 indicate that eight out of ten buyers now make quality equal to or more important than price in their purchase decisions. Only three to four customers out of ten thought this way and bought this way in the year 1979. This 100-percent increase in buyer emphasis on quality in less than a decade is perhaps the most rapidly exploding marketplace trend in American business history.

The second conviction is that while American industry has made substantial quality gains, accomplishing the full job of international quality leadership still is a long way ahead. I spend a great deal of my time offshore in connection with our General Systems Company business, in the countries which are America's major trading partners. I find that the prevailing judgment is that a strong foreign manufacturer with a quality strategy can't help but succeed in the U.S. market today — whether the dollar goes up or down. What's behind this are three widely held beliefs:

1. Some American companies have already given quality their best shot and haven't pulled it off.
2. Those who have won't stick with it when the quick fixes don't get spectacular results.
3. American trade policy is like a log floating down a river carrying thousands of ants, each of which thinks it's steering — a policy whose ambiguity minimizes long-term foreign concern about any genuine barriers to American market entry.

The Commerce Department estimates that nearly three-quarters of all the products manufactured in the United States are now targets for strong import competition; our own studies as we work throughout the world indicate that nearly all of American non-defense manufactured products will have import vulnerability by the early part of the decade of the 1990s. This means that to protect its position in the U.S. market, an American company must be able to design, build, and sell its major domestic product lines today with the potential also for supremacy in the international marketplace — even though there isn't yet much import competition or interest in exporting. Murphy's Law, internationalized, says that if an American company *can* get foreign competition today, it *will* get it. Operating in international quality leadership terms is the only way for a business to grow with Murphy rather than be eroded by him.

This leads to the third conviction, which is that accelerating our rate of quality improvement is the single most important competitive task facing all of us. In today's American market, when a customer is satisfied with quality he tells eight people; when he's dissatisfied, he tells 22. That is the hard arithmetic of quality's effect on sales growth in the American marketplace. Moreover, quality leadership can give companies a five-cents-on-the-dollar competitive advantage, as much as ten cents in some cases. For many companies, this can be the best opportunity for improved profitability and return on investment, and one that our experience shows will pay off early, with a sustained and growing return.

The acceleration of quality improvement is as important in American service operations as in products. In some service processes, only one work product out of ten goes through error-free. While much of the widely publicized increase in service employment has come about through market growth, some has been created by these do-the-job-over quality problems. They are a principal reason for the minimal productivity increase in services.

While it is not yet widely apparent, without significant quality improvement, some American service operations have the same vulnerability to foreign competition that affected manufacturing long ago. Our experience in the quality processes of financial service companies is an example. A telecommunications satellite is indifferent to whether the service operations of a financial institution or of a data processing organization are located in Frankfurt, Tokyo, London, Paris, or New York, so long as the operations are quality-effective. The industry is now moving toward this kind of quality-driven consolidation.

In my judgment, we have great capacity for achieving these necessary quality results in the United States. Several American industries continue to set the world quality leadership example — consumer-household durables, electrical equipment, diesel engines, aircraft, computer electronics, and agricultural equipment are just a few in my experience. Moreover, the total quality control improvement rate we've been able to achieve recently for some pace-setting American products has been much better than in my experience with some comparable foreign products.

Weakness in the U.S. Quality Program. Why then have so many American products been overwhelmed by foreign competitors? And why does there still seem to be so little serious attention to quality in the high profile programs and statements on America's competitiveness coming from both Washington and the top business community — even though clearly our challenge is to recognize that America's industrial strength is dependent on America's quality competitiveness? The reason is, sadly, that in some companies quality programs are still widely thought of as a sugar pill to help the organization swallow the really important improvement ingredients of technology and automation and financial restructuring. This sugar pill mixes fireworks displays of top management quality interest together with some corrective action projects, but without any managerial foundations that get at improving the basic business work processes which are really important to quality leadership.

In these companies, there can be a dozen different quality problem-solving systems, none of which are fully effective because they are inevitably blocked at somebody's department wall. So additional task forces are formed to create still more quality-improvement schemes. Veteran employees are likely to view them as just more quality crusades that will die and be buried without autopsy like the seven or eight other crusades they have already seen come and go. Because there's no ingrained commitment to quality, 30 percent of all resolved customer complaints leave a dissatisfied customer. It's too high a cost for producer, merchant, and buyer to pay — a cost that continues to mount because of the network of troubleshooters required to keep the constant stream of buyer corrective actions on some sort of track.

Leverage through Quality and Automation. There is a staggering difference between this and the effective actions of the companies that are the quality leaders I have mentioned. The approach of these companies is that quality is today's most powerful corporate leverage point for achieving both customer satisfaction and lower costs. Automation was once thought to give that leverage but current experience shows that without a quality foundation, automation merely generates more bad products quicker than before.

There is a fundamental managerial difference between basing quality results on robots as compared with basing it on people-based organization-wide programs. This difference recognizes that the continually upward moving buyer demand for quality is the result of fundamental economic changes in American businesses and basic social changes in American homes.

The automobile industry is a major example of the volatility of these quality trends. It is still not too widely known that in the late 1970s, for example, several hundred thousand Japanese cars were sitting in unsold inventory on American docks when the Iranian oil crisis and the consumer price explosion simultaneously hit the market. Suddenly, the Japanese inventory evaporated and the Japanese were rewarded for persisting in their quality strategy.

In 1987, the situation has once again changed. Recent data showed a very large inventory of unsold Japanese cars in the United States, up significantly from the previous year. American car buyers who had been partial exclusively to Japanese products are now actively shopping American cars again. This can be due as much to the renewed emphasis on quality of American manufacturers as to the higher prices of the Japanese products generated by the strong yen. Future corporate results in this automobile market will almost certainly continue to be governed by these trends in quality. The recognized objective for some car manufacturers is that by the early 1990s, companies must offer essentially perfect automobiles with the features that buyers really want, produced at one-third less cost. It is clear that those companies which meet this target — whether American, Japanese, European, or Korean — will be the ones to survive, perhaps even succeed, in the U.S. car market. What is equally clear is that a major acceleration in the existing quality improvement rate of some automobile and automobile supply companies is required if they are to achieve this.

The automobile industry is just an example of the changes that are sweeping across almost all other American markets. Summarizing these changes very simply, the life-styles of consumers and the work processes of companies now depend almost completely upon the reliable, predictable operation of products and services with little tolerance for the time and cost of any failures — something very different from the past.

Seven Bench Marks for Building Companywide Program. Think about today's demand on the washer and dryer of a large young family every Monday morning; on the new car that serves as the family bus 14 hours a day, seven days a week; on the telecommunications network that is a company's only data source; and, indeed, on the weapons system on which the life of a young airman, sailor, or soldier may depend. The no-easy-backup products and services we buy today explain quality's major influence on sales and market share. They also explain why the old "we'll always fix it for you" policy of many companies, while honorable and important, is a horse-and-buggy, after-sales service approach — a failure-driven policy instead of one reflecting quality leadership. Quality is, in its essence, a way of managing an organization today, a way of managing that goes way beyond knowing all the right buzzwords. It means knowing how to lead companywide programs which build on seven basic bench marks:

1. That quality is not a technical or department function but is instead a systemic process that extends throughout the company.

2. That quality must be organized to recognize that while it is every-body's job in the company, it will become nobody's job unless this company quality process is correctly structured to support both quality work of individuals as well as quality teamwork among departments. This is indeed the worst understood and implemented of the seven characteristics.
3. That the quality improvement emphasis must take place in marketing, in development and engineering, in manufacturing, and particularly in services — not merely in production for the factory workers only.
4. That quality must be perceived in this process to be what the buyer wants and needs to satisfy his requirements for use — not what the company needs to satisfy its requirements for marketing and production efficiency.
5. That modern quality improvement requires the application of new technology, ranging from quality design techniques to computer-aided quality management measurement and control, and is not a matter of periodic quality fireworks displays or of dusting off a few traditional quality control techniques.
6. That widespread quality improvement is achieved only through help and participation from all the men and women in the company — not from just a few specialists.
7. That all of this comes about when the company has established a clear, customer-oriented quality management system throughout the organization, one that people understand, believe in, and want to be part of.

This is Total Quality Control for the 1990s, as we practice it in the General Systems Company in our projects with companies in Europe and the world over, building upon the 35 years of application experience we have had throughout the world since we first originated what is sometimes called TQC.

Implementing this doesn't depend on geography or national cultural difference because quality has no nationality. What makes this work is a clear customer-oriented management process and work process throughout the organization — one that people understand, believe in, and are a part of.

Company Readiness for Structuring Quality Programs. What is the readiness among companies to succeed in structuring this genuine total quality improvement? There is a very wide variation.

While there are many fine examples of American companies with excellent quality programs, the quality programs of some other companies have traveled at best only 15 to 20 percent of the hard road to meeting the quality demands of today. In these companies, quality is still not a boardroom interest, still is thought of as primarily a technical job operating at secondary levels of the organization. Quality is still not a mainline activity in development and engineering, where innovation is thought of as the basic drumbeat for technology, and quality work a much less challenging task. Nor is quality a mainline activity in the finance communities of these companies — even though accounting miscodes and billing mistakes can create more customer ill will than product returns. Nor is it mainline in marketing — where quality is thought of as what you have to sell to the customer even though the engineers and production people may not be doing it right. In these companies, high quality is still thought of as gold plating requiring higher cost — even though experience clearly shows that higher quality means lower cost; that quality and cost are partners, not adversaries; a sum, not a difference.

It takes relentless, consistent, and disciplined management leadership and methodology to convert all of this to a company quality program that matches the competitive strength of today's strongly quality-leveraged companies. We know from our General Systems experience in installing such total quality systems throughout the world that its implementation incorporates three primary areas into the practice of modern company management.

The first of these is to directly improve the quality process itself. To be successful in achieving quality leadership today, management must personally address the quality process or system in its own organization — to identify how it is presently operating, to determine the specific needs for strengthening its effectiveness on the hard road to quality excellence, and to lead in systematically accomplishing and maintaining these improvements.

This quality excellence-driven approach is a managerial task fundamentally different from the widely used approach that might be described as quality failure-driven, which merely sets in motion — within the existing and traditional quality process, strong or weak — one project after another to fix up quality problems, sometimes within some kind of overall improvement program which the organization recognizes is temporary. The hope here has been that, as a byproduct of their necessary purpose of providing specific quality corrective actions, these individual quality projects will also somehow bring about the repair and modernization of the quality process itself. Experience clearly shows that this does not succeed.

The reason is that an inadequate quality process is likely ultimately to reject or to limit the application of the statistical controls and customer measurements and vendor cooperation steps initiated by the projects, which gradually die and are buried without autopsy. This is why quality reviews, statistics, and other necessary techniques do not sustain themselves or take permanent root in some companies and seem to require continual renewal and re-emphasis. The achievement of quality excellence is thus a far more demanding managerial task than emphasis only on some individual projects. The history of barriers between departments and the concept of quality as control and policing rather than prevention and self-steering remains deep and strong in many organizations, and is changed only by direct rather than indirect management time, attention, and leadership in the institutionalizing of a strong, modern, and fully oriented quality achievement process throughout sales, production, and technology in the company.

The second primary area of managerial attention is to make quality improvement a basic and continuing habit that is relentlessly pursued within the organization. The managerial purpose is to ingrain into the day-by-day detailed work of the company the actions which recognize that quality is a rapidly upward moving target in today's market and that quality programs must be organized to recognize this. Traditional quality programs have instead been directed to the objective of establishing what was thought to be the single right quality level for a part and product and then directing all effort to meeting and maintaining that level — with improvements in the level only periodically examined. The management practice today, in contrast, must be oriented to the approach that when this so-called "right" quality level has been attained, progressive improvement must continue to more and more upgraded quality levels for the appropriate parts and materials as a way of life in the operating practice throughout the organization, because this is what customers will demand and what international competition will call for.

For example, the more successful a product becomes, the higher the quality levels it must be programmed to achieve if it is to grow profitably. A 1-percent failure rate for a major integrated circuit-based consumer product with a production rate of 50,000 units a year places

500 failing units in the hands of customers. A tenfold sales and production increase to 500,000 units with the same 1-percent failure rate places 5,000 failing units in customers' hands. This is equivalent, in the actual number of dissatisfied buyers, to what would have been the highly unacceptable failure rate of 10 percent at the earlier production rate.

Without a strong quality improvement program, the company's success in achieving this higher volume could be a time bomb. The products that represent a high risk of customer dissatisfaction are not necessarily those with high failure rate percentages but instead those with high exposure to a large total number of dissatisfied customers. That's why, more than ever, the only way to compete with quality is with more quality.

The third primary managerial area is to establish the principle that quality and cost are complementary, not conflicting, objectives in today's company management decision-making. For many years, the managements of some companies routinely received recommendations from members of their organization that a choice had to be made between quality and cost — the so-called trade-off decision — because better quality inevitably would somehow cost more and would make production more difficult. Experience throughout the world has shown that this simply is not true. The reason is that good quality fundamentally leads to good resource utilization — of the work force, equipment, and materials — and consequently means good productivity and very low quality costs in the organization. Modern management must make clear throughout the company that what is expected is both quality and cost control — not one to the detriment of the other. The management thus does not give the old myth that good quality is in some way more expensive the opportunity to become a self-fulfilling prophecy within the company.

Some of the world's most successful products are now managed on this basis of the quality and cost partnership. Let me use the example of large consumer durables in the American market — such as household refrigerators which were one of our very early total quality installations. These household refrigerators are sold for several hundred dollars — a price that has not significantly increased in several years in spite of some inflation in the economy. They are produced at the rate of several million units per year. These products are subject to heavy stress by all family members, from children to grandmothers, 365 days a year for at least the 10 years that are a typical ownership cycle. Because of relentless quality improvement in what was one of the very early total quality installations, the products of the largest manufacturing companies in the consumer durable industry now require little customer service and have an extremely low failure rate — requiring a very low maintenance cost for the buyer — and very, very low quality cost for the manufacturer. There is sufficient confidence in the quality and cost of these products that, in this year of 1988, these manufacturers now sell some refrigerator models on the basis that the buyer will receive a full return of all of his purchase money after months of use if he is not completely satisfied. With the refrigerator's already fine reputation, this very strong additional confidence in its quality represents a formidable challenge to any foreign manufacturer. The business principle is that the way to compete with quality is with more quality.

We have extremely strong resources in the United States for this kind of competitive quality leadership — whether in household durables or across a very wide range of other American products.

Renewing U.S. Industrial Leadership. Re-igniting the explosion of our quality growth means the restoration of quality to a primary role in American management from the secondary role it has fallen into in some companies. It means the redirection of technology investments toward quality. It means the reemphasis of the quality-mindedness of the American worker. It means broadening quality improvement from production. It means genuine effectiveness in development, in finance, and in marketing, and it means the creation of a much greater role for our universities in providing strong educational support for our competitive objectives — particularly our business schools in which quality has, up to now, too often been a footnote at best.

Customer-oriented product leadership was developed in the United States and many American companies still excel in it. The application of technology to productivity and quality achievement characterized the industrialization of the United States from the 1920s onward. We are very strong in quality engineering and manufacturing engineering. Both are now crying out to be used.

The United States has the full potential to renew its industrial leadership, as more and more American managers return to personal leadership of strong and effective quality programs. This is not only in our national interest, but in the long run, in the interest of people throughout the world.

Certainly, also, this pursuit of excellence leads to a greatness of spirit and action — adding a new and higher level of satisfaction to the work of all of us who are dedicated to continuing quality improvement for sound economic growth and higher standards of living both now and in the future of what is likely to be the demanding quality decade of the 1990s.

Building World Market Share through Quality and Pricing. So far, I have emphasized that quality leadership has become a central factor in economic strength as we approach the increasingly competitive decade of the 1990s. I would now like to discuss what international experience throughout the world indicates are key steps through which upper management should direct its competitive strategies to assure this quality leadership in both American markets as well as in world markets. Indeed, the clear business principle today is that a company must have international quality leadership if it is to retain quality leadership in its traditional American markets.

Let me begin by making clear that many of the world's most successful companies are achieving this result through building their market share growth around a deceptively simple business competitive strategy that fits the economic environment of the 1990s. This strategy, as we develop it in our General Systems programs, is a combination of competition in its highly visible and traditional form — that is, product versus product — together with a perhaps less visible but equally potent competition involving companies' effectiveness in quality management.

This has been the essence of Japanese export and acquisition strategy for a quarter century as well as that of some major American companies. The objective is to create market share through excellent quality and aggressive pricing which, while built around discounts, nonetheless provides profitability because of costs that are lower and quality that is higher than the competition realizes. The Japanese describe this as the business approach that is invisible to the West, although, happily, we have also applied it in some American firms.

It continues to be a very effective type of blind-siding competitive strategy for both Japanese and American firms. This is because some traditional managers remain highly oriented to the visible side of product competition — the steel, the iron, the circuitry, the silicon — which was the approach many of us used in the earlier years of our experience. It is where you try to understand the competitor's cost and quality by counting and analyzing the parts, which is no longer a good indicator. The key to competitively high product quality and deep cost reductions today is in the effectiveness and quality of the systematic internal work processes that produce the steel and iron.

Traditional management has been highly oriented to product competition. Indeed, at the very highest levels, the graduate business schools have taught it thoroughly in their emphasis on marketing and finance, and some engineering schools have been similarly oriented. Technology investments and developments have become heavily product-directed and business and cost measurements have been highly product-line oriented. So far as it goes, this is all to the good — a business strength.

Until recently, however, quality and productivity were thought of as essentially specialist activities that belonged to some technical corner of the organization.

In many traditional companies general management planning and reporting are accepted as routine in such areas as finance, production, and marketing. But devoting such personal top-level executive attention to quality and productivity still raises eyebrows in many quarters, still raises questions in some boardrooms as to whether it represents proper application of executive time.

Hence, many American managers, highly skilled in competition among products, have been far less familiar with personally leading the new and all-important form of competition involving quality leadership. There can thus be a tendency to reach for straws, a lack of personal quality know-how, and an unsureness about investing at levels that are routine in product terms, in the new quality programs that are needed if their companies are to remain competitive in national markets — let alone world markets.

Three Problem Areas in Managing Quality. This lack of sureness of touch has led to what I call the three basic problem areas of traditional management quality attention. The first of the problems caused by lack of managerial know-how is that it has encouraged superficial quality programs in some companies. This includes such programs as periodic fireworks displays of top-level quality attention through management speech-making, but with very little follow-up emphasis; or dusting off a few traditional quality control techniques and calling this the company quality program; or emphasizing off-line programs of technical projects and motivational techniques located at very low levels of organization and receiving very little operational support. These programs tend to be based on sloganeering, superficial change, and single-sentence improvement formulas instead of the necessary emphasis upon consistent on-line implementation of the specifics of quality achievement throughout the organization, using all the modern methods needed to get the job done.

These superficial programs inevitably wither and dry up when touched by heavy production demands or economic fluctuations or budgetary pressures. This is why long-service employees in some organizations will tell you that they are now going through the seventh or eighth quality improvement crusade in their careers. These employees want to know what is solid and different about the 1988 program that will really make it stick.

Second, lack of managerial know-how has led some companies to think it possible to deal with competitive quality vulnerability by sending some local production abroad for later sale here, thus fighting engineering and manufacturing wars in foreign plants where quality and productivity are already competitively strong. While sometimes it may be necessary, this is again a partial solution which avoids the fact that the wrong production is likely to be sent abroad. It is likely to include the very components and products that should be improved locally to build the foundation for future competitiveness. Having someone else fight your quality and productivity wars starts an irreversible downward competitive cycle, as the product experience of several industries will tell you.

The third problem is that we have sometimes approached quality programs as being primarily for factory workers and for mass production. This has completely missed the reality that the white collar and service areas are also crucial (and often overlooked) areas for modern quality and productivity attention. It has missed the fact that both middle management in production and much of the development and engineering community require far more quality know-how help than they have received. It has missed the crucial point that one-of-a-kind development and manufactured products have had even more success in applying total quality control improvement programs over the years than have the more visible mass production products.

First Step: Make Quality Leadership a Goal. By comparison, the great business quality strength achieved by many successful exporting companies — whether the company operates in Japan, Europe, the United States, or Latin America — is the result of personal management skill and emphasis upon hard and unrelenting work in what General Systems calls the three fundamental areas of implementing total quality control. I think of them as the hard road to quality excellence, and I would now like to discuss this quite specifically.

The first step on the hard road to quality excellence is the major business decision to make quality leadership in the domestic and export marketplace a basic strategic goal of the firm. Unless management clearly defines specific quality results in quantitative terms, rather than through vague generalities, and then budgets the specific resources for manpower, machines, and systems to meet these priorities, the quality results are not going to come about for the firm in its export markets.

Quality leadership today means a policy commitment to the engineering, production, and sale of products that consistently and with very low failure rates will perform correctly for buyers when first purchased and that with reasonable maintenance will continue to perform with very high reliability and safety over the product life.

Let me make clear that modern quality leadership is much more than product service or technical assistance. It makes heavier demand on an organization than the traditional policies of customer quality satisfaction that have primarily meant that product service and technical assistance from the firm will be readily available to customers. Because it is so important, let me repeat what I said earlier. The traditional assurance that a company "will always fix a product so that it will work again for the buyer" is honorable and important. However, it represents a policy of customer service based on product problems. The modern customer instead wants his product to work well for a long time without requiring any technical assistance.

Moreover, because it is so important, let me repeat another point — quality is an upward moving target in competitive markets, and quality programs must be correspondingly dynamic. Let me give an example from our experience that shows why this is so important and how quality must be managed in dynamic competitive terms.

General Systems Company divides consumer-product development into four stages of a product maturity cycle, each with a different marketing and engineering product quality approach to assure customer satisfaction.

Let's discuss the product maturity cycle of a television set. In the first stage of maturity the quality of the sets was dominated by *innovation*, which sold the product. Rough quality edges like unclear and wavy pictures, incessant static, and intermittent operation hardly deterred the consumer.

As market acceptance increased, the television set entered the second stage — *conspicuous consumption*. The tube was placed inside a handsome piece of furniture and became a console as well as a television set. Appearance was now a big factor in the consumer's perception of quality.

By the time the third stage was reached, television had become part of the consumer's lifestyle. This is the *function* stage. The whole family uses the set for entertainment and news. Quality — consistent product performance — determines the purchase decision.

The product enters the fourth stage of maturation when virtually everyone owns one and it becomes taken for granted. This is the *commodity* stage. Reliability and product economy are now essential to quality acceptance.

Those television products that were handled as if the product were still in the appearance state were doomed to failure in the international marketplace. They were faced with internationally distributed products targeted to a successful company quality strategy which had dynamically been moved ahead to a function and commodity oriented quality approach. This is where the consumers wanted to be. It was precisely this type of strategic management/quality decision that helped some international television product companies and their smaller supplier firms build major market share.

My second example has to do with a very popular electronics growth product, the small computer. In one part of this small international computer market — the highest selling computer peripheral product — the dominant product with the lion's share of market penetration sold at an average price of $4,000. After-sale costs over the product life added another $3,250 — including $2,500 for maintenance and service which was 35 percent of the life-cycle cost for this product.

One traditional way to manage the quality strategy of a competitive company would be to engineer a product with comparable features and market it at a lower price. In this case, management of the competitive firm decided instead to bring out a product priced higher, at $5,000, but engineered and produced to have after-sales costs (including only $500 for service) of 7 percent of life-cycle cost for the product and one-fifth of the other product's service cost. Despite its higher selling price, product sales result of the new product are excellent. They are running four times greater than those of its competitor and they continue to grow and dominate the market. The reason? The quality has been moved upward to meet the customer demand rather than being permitted to remain at the earlier level.

The basic principle is that, for product success, it is necessary today to have a carefully organized quality strategy that fits the existing market situation and to have the quality management and technology to implement it in depth effectively.

Second Step: Companywide Implementation. Hence, the second step on the road to quality excellence demands that implementation of the necessary actions take place throughout the company, not just in the quality control department. Data show that 80 to 90 percent of quality problems requiring improvement are beyond the scope of the inspection and testing actions of traditional quality and reliability departments — effective and conscientious though they may be. This has caused corporate management to rethink, and frequently to fully restructure, quality management operations.

In the Far Eastern, American, European, and Latin American firms with successful quality programs, these quality implementation actions have been made part of the mainstream company actions throughout marketing, engineering, production and service in the firm, as well as in the quality departments and in general management itself. They are quality disciplines, if you will, to be applied by each function.

This is one dimension of the reason I felt impelled to develop Total Quality Control as a structure of managerial and engineering technology to provide a practical, operational foundation for guiding a company systematically through implementation of a modern quality program. In effect, quality is itself systematically managed and systems engineered just as firms in earlier times learned to systematically manage their engineering, production, and sales.

How deeply such implementation penetrates is attested by the new relationship it makes between quality and productivity. There exists today in many companies what our General Systems engineers call a "hidden plant" — both in the factory and in the office — sometimes amounting to 15 percent to as much as 40 percent of total productive capacity. This is the capacity that exists because of either the making of errors or the correcting of these errors.

This "hidden plant" is, in part, the direct result of the traditional industrial rationalization approach that I call *factory-efficiency based* — where productivity was conceived primarily as "more product and service output per unit of resource input."

This traditional approach creates very deep business quality problems because it includes as satisfactory production output such contributors to the "hidden plant" as products that can't be sold because they have defects, or that have to be recalled because they are unreliable or unsafe, or that have to be returned for product service too frequently. There is no greater waste of resources for companies and nations.

To correct this in General Systems, we today are using a new approach that I call quality-efficiency based. In productivity terms, we are changing the old "more product output per unit of resource input" to the new measurement of "more salable, good quality output per unit of input."

This approach recognizes that in today's international marketplace a poor quality product is of negative business value to the company that offers it, no matter how "productively efficient" the production process may have measured in the traditional sense. It is more good product that is the meaningful national and international measure of productivity today.

The result of this change in productivity approach and measurement is very significant. We find that many production operations throughout the world that were reported to their managements to be as high as 90-percent productively efficient are, in fact, at least one-third lower in true productive efficiency — approximately 60-percent productively efficient — when evaluated by more accurate and realistic productivity measurements in quality-efficiency terms.

This one-third and more productivity deficiency has demonstrated to many companies that one of the true causes of the persistent upward trends in their costs and expenses in recent years and their inability to be internationally competitive lies in their using only the traditional factory-efficiency industrial rationalization approaches rather than the new total quality-efficiency approaches.

The quality improvement contribution is very important to solve this problem today. In several of our General Systems operations, a significant proportion of the entire new company productivity increases, required in order to close the deficiency in productivity that exists for many companies, are now targeted and budgeted to come from the quality improvement contribution of modern quality programs, and they are being achieved by these programs which now return productive efficiency to a true 90 percent or more.

Third Step: Commitment and Training. This brings me to the third step on the hard road to quality excellence — continuous commitment, motivation, education, and measurement throughout the organization.

There are two requirements that make quality education and training effective for an organization. The first is that they have to be specifically job-related. Generalized, philosophic training simply has not gotten the job done. What will help the general manager is understanding quality strategic planning and how to manage total quality. What will help the design engineer is training in know-how to perform, for example, the quality-parameter design, an approach in which thousands of American and Japanese engineers have been trained for a number of years. What will help the manufacturing engineer is to know how to perform process-capability evaluations. This know-how, moreover, may help motivate his quality interests.

This leads to the second requirement for quality educational effectiveness, which is that it must be operated as an integral part of the total quality system rather than as an overlay that is hoped somehow to evangelize the organization on its own. The principle is that knowledge is power only when it can be used. To put the matter somewhat differently, our total quality system is the necessary foundation on which training and new approaches such as computer quality aids can operate effectively — it does not work the other way. This integration is the most important key to education's effectiveness. It succeeds only when management achieves widespread employee understanding and genuine acceptance of quality-oriented operating conditions throughout the organization — the quality work rules and disciplines that we call total quality system procedures. For example, product design reviews are organized to use such quality-education contributions as parameter-design results and process-capability demonstrations.

A primary goal of this is to assure positive managerial attitudes which are the keys to success for some organizations. A major task remains to develop these attitudes, the organization's quality culture if you will, required for a positive approach. The need for this is great at all levels of the organization, including the professional, because due to deficiencies in our educational programs, many in this present management and engineering generation — to put the matter bluntly — have not been conditioned to think of industry and business in primary terms of quality. Economics textbooks have usually dealt with technology leadership, price, production, and sales demand as the principal determinants of economic activity, with quality often touched on as of more incidental business interest. The more superficial forms of what has been called business strategic planning can all too likely automatically emphasize product function and features, and to treat specific customer quality use requirements only in a general non-quantitative way — thereby locking companies out of genuine modern quality leadership before product design has even begun.

The important function of research, development, and engineering is a particular example of the importance of establishing the correct quality mentality. As one of the important steps to establish today's product quality requirements with the required degree of realism, it is necessary that development and design engineers themselves talk and work directly with customers and users of the product. This is one of the strengths of smaller firms and is fundamentally different from the traditional tendency of some larger companies — and of some engineers themselves — that the engineer remain in his office and laboratory and be insulated by the company organization from contact with the users of the products. Today, direct discussion with customers and users has become an organized and ongoing engineering activity in the development of genuinely customer-oriented product specification, and in the testing of products in the quality programs of an increasing number of strong companies. The laboratory test and the professional test engineer — while important — are no longer enough, and research and engineering thinking must be oriented to recognize this.

ROI as Motivation. So much for these steps in the establishment of total quality control — strategic quality leadership, companywide implementation, and commitment and training. There is a strong economic reason to move in this direction. The motivator exists in the excellent industrial and business results that have come from a genuine quality leadership policy in the international marketplace.

This begins in terms of the ROI, the return on investment, which for industry is an extremely important economic indicator.

Our experience demonstrates that the returns on investment from strong total quality programs in major firms throughout the world today are excellent. They have consistently exceeded the industry ROI pattern shown from most other customary capital investments. This has been a tremendous business benefit for these companies of which some of their competitors are largely unaware.

To repeat what I said earlier, the essence of the business management principle is that today, quality and cost are a sum, not a difference — partners, not adversaries. This is very different from the myth during much of the 20th century that higher quality means gold plating and somehow makes development and production more difficult and more costly.

There are three principal reasons for this outstanding economic return on investment. The first has to do with improvements in quality costs. We have been measuring in our General Systems data base the effects of quality costs on the income of firms since we first developed the quality cost measurement approach more than 30 years ago. This includes the full costs of assurance — quality improvement programs, inspection control, and so forth — plus the full costs of the failure of this assurance — customer returns, rework, and so on — all systematically structured within the financial and accounting system of the concern. These data for 1987 show that the true costs of quality through many major manufacturing and service companies average from 15 to 20 percent of sales.

The data also show that the quality costs of companies which have had long-term systematic total quality emphasis were from one-half to two-thirds of this average because they improved the prevention effectiveness of assurance, were able to minimize inspection control and greatly reduced the costs of failure.

When you compare quality cost as a percentage of total sales for recent years you find a significant cost savings trend over a two- to three-year period resulting from the quality leadership programs of the firms. This means that we have avoided continual cost increases that would have characterized the continuation of quality practices that no longer meet present market requirements. Such quality cost reductions have become a principal reason for the cost advantage certain major international companies enjoy in today's world marketplace. These cost reductions have also enhanced positive cash flow as well as profitability for the firm.

The second reason for the excellent economic results from total quality programs is productivity improvement. There is today no more effective way to improve productivity than for quality programs to convert the "hidden plant" to productive use. A significant proportion of the productivity increases of key international firms is now being achieved by quality programs.

The third reason is that higher sales result in today's market from the achievement of lower levels of quality failure and service costs. There is now clear evidence of the positive correlation between market share and market quality. Sales growth that favors products with high quality and low quality costs is becoming characteristic of the international marketplace. These results emphasize why the very strong new relationship between competitive world leadership and total quality control has emerged as an enormously powerful new influence on the management, engineering, and marketing policies of firms — both large and small.

Conclusion. The power, innovation, and continuity of strong total quality programs are thus becoming a major competitive strength for American business growth. The key is, in my experience, that the company has a systematic foundation so that quality is itself managed and systems engineered and motivated throughout the organization with the same thoroughness and depth that the product itself is managed, engineered, produced, and sold.

Certainly the favorable effect upon business growth of such total quality policies has many examples in American companies, whose strong businesses speak for themselves today. Leadership in this matter is one of the principal jobs of the manager in a company that intends to succeed in today's intensely competitive business environment.

This decade of the 1990s may well be described by companies and nations that maintain business strength as their "Decade of Total Quality Control Emphasis."

9

The Reckoning: Made in America or Japan

David Halberstam, Pulitzer Prize Winner

This lecture is not about me and my generation. It's about yours. It's about you. When I grew up in the 1940s in a small mill town in northwest Connecticut, we thought that we competed for jobs with the great metropolis of Tarrington, 25,000 people and 9 miles away. You will not compete with the people in the next town or in the next state. You are going to compete with the children of Osaka, Tokyo, Seoul, and Coala Lumpeur. It's a different world, less sentimental, harsher.

End of Easy Affluence in America. My book, *The Reckoning*, is really not a book about automobiles at all. It is a book about the end of the American century, the end of the easy affluence, as we have known it for much of the last 40 years. It is a very hard time. It is not going to necessarily get easier just by wanting it to get easier, or by complaining.

I have been made nervous by the Gephardt campaign. I don't want to go into particular politicians here, but there was a sleaze factor to it. I thought that it was sending out precisely the wrong signal — the American baby signal — you have a right to feel that you are being cheated; we are the victims. I had a feeling that people who were cheering Gephardt were the people who don't insist that their own children do any homework, don't care about what they are doing in school, and don't pay any attention to schools. They are the same people who vote against any tax referendum that would send more money to education and to better education. They do that and then they go off and curse the Japanese for being better. There is a price out there and we had better pay it.

America's Attitude toward Education. You can strip away almost every other factor in the coming competition between the United States and East Asia, and it comes down to education — primacy of education, value by the society, value by the government, and value by the family. It is a moment not unlike Sputnik, except we are not treating it like Sputnik. We need somebody in a campaign to use what Theodore Roosevelt called "the bully pulpit," to explain to the American people just what is happening and why. But even the change in the government will not change the equation if we do not change our cultural attitude towards education. I am pleased to be in one of the parts of America where there is a sense of the importance of education, as in Utah. But as long as in most American small towns throughout the country the average male child who gets good marks is regarded as something of a nerd, unless he is Bill Bradley, we are going to lose, because that is where the very core of the competition is.

I recently sat with a group of students at Hyrum College in a small town in Ohio. They were trying to ask what had gone wrong. I said, "Well, you all came from regional high schools. What did your average student classmate do in the way of homework?" They thought and the answer came back, "Thirty minutes." I said, "There's your answer." It is not a world where that is going to be accepted anymore.

Koreans call the Japanese the "lazy Asians." At exam time in Korea, the lines to the library start at 4 am. Korean students in many schools double brown bag it because the teachers are graded on how many students they can advance to the next level of education. I don't want American kids to be drones, or drudges, but there is an acceptable minimum level that we are not anywhere near in terms of use of the human brain. In the new economy, the application of the human brain is a form of economic power.

It is a societal thing. It's not that there is bad labor, or bad management, or bad this or that. In the immortal words of John Kennedy, who when asked to explain what had gone wrong at the time of the Bay of Pigs, who was at fault, said, "There is enough to go around for all of us." Even now when we are deep into this crisis, the particular profession that I am a part of, the media, and in the most important part of the mass circulatory system, network television, networks do an unacceptable job. The true invisible men and women of network television are their correspondents in Tokyo. It should be a great story. It isn't. It is a great story for print, but in television a weak story with good photos will beat out a good story with weak photos. And since Roger Smith did not go over and fire a bomb at Toyota car and Lee Iacocca did not go over and picket the Nissan factory, it's not film, and as it's not film, it's not on television, and as it's not on television, it's not part of the national debate.

So it is a difficult time. The Japanese are good. They are getting better, despite all the slogans you will hear from various advertising people about how America has come back. We have only incrementally begun to attack the problem.

Challenge to America's Industrial Production. Robert Anderson of Rockwell recently said on a scale of one to ten, America a few years ago, in its industrial production, was a one. It has now mightily moved itself up to a five. The first stage of the Japanese challenge was in industrial production — cameras and cars. The second stage is taking place now, and it is in high financial services. The Japanese have been Puritans, and Calvinists, and have saved more; they are ready to spend, and they will spend here. That is a very mixed blessing, if we are as we are now, constantly without policy.

What is true is that we have gotten better, but so have the Japanese. We have constantly underestimated the Japanese. A whole series of myths have fallen. First, that they could do something small like cameras, but they couldn't do something big like steel. Then they could do steel, but they couldn't do autos. Then they could do little autos, but not big autos. The launch of the Honda Acura is the most successful launch of a middle-sized car in recent years. The latest myth is that they are a nation with a Xerox mentality. That is, they can take what we invent and apply it a little better. I think a nation that believes that will go to the graveyard. They are good. They are pouring out scientists and engineers at a per capita 2:1 ratio. Their own scientific plant is getting better. They may do it communally rather than individually. It is a great mistake to believe that we can rest on laurels that are no longer there, and that somehow we will be rescued.

What is really true, the toughest secret headline, the headline you haven't seen, is that the Japanese in the last two years have absorbed a quantum shock in their currency evaluation from roughly 240 to 140, and they've kept coming. They are process driven. They have made their processes better. As American production becomes cheaper, they will come here to do it. I must tell you that in the early days of doing my book I would go out to Detroit and go into the offices of the very powerful men in Detroit, when the yen was at 240, and they would say, "The whole problem is this currency thing. If we could only get it down to 200, we'd clean their clock." It is at 140 and no one is doing any clock cleaning. It is much more than currency evaluation. It is a whole attitude. It is a covenant. It is priorities. It is education. We had best be more careful.

New Economic Age Replaces Age of American Hegemony. What is true about the Japanese and East Asians is that they have brought in a new economic age. The old age in which America flowered for so much of this century, the American century, or the oil century, was an age in which economic richness was in no small part measured by size, soil, mineral development, and a positive economic system. The Japanese, coming from a rocky little island with no natural resources to speak of, have inaugurated an age in which economic power comes from the maximization of the human brain. That is a powerful idea. It has happened in the last 25 to 30 years. They planned this "miracle by design," as my colleague Frank Gibney calls it. They figured it out. They looked at us, studied us, took parts that worked for us and would work for them, and built their own model. In the past, a nation without resources was supposed to be weak. They turned their lack of resources into an asset by becoming the low-cost purchaser throughout the world.

Secretary of State Schultz, in his poignant statement at the time of the Iran-Contra hearing, said a very interesting thing. He said that, at one time, a nation was rich in the area of communications by having a lot of copper under the soil. But it doesn't matter now. There is a new definition of richness, because we live in an age of fiber optics. Think of it; it's a whole new world.

If one age is beginning, another one is ending. If I can serve you well today I will try to define the age that is just ending. It is really the post-World War II age. World War II brought us kicking and screaming to the zenith of our power. We were probably more economically powerful before the war than we realized. Our economic system was stronger than our political awareness of it. Then in that war, protected by two oceans in an age when weaponry could not cross over an ocean, we became stronger as others became weaker. When the war was over, we stood rich in a world that was poor, ally and adversary. Britain was a victor, but exhausted by two wars, about to lose its colonies. France was a victor, but humiliated in the second World War, about to fight two colonial wars. Germany, defeated, probably lost 20 million people and was divided with its market cut in half. The Soviet Union, a victor, but ravaged, probably lost 25 million people and had an economic system that demonstratively does not work. And Japan was not only defeated and ravaged, but actually was almost psychically defeated, as if a god had failed in its own vision of itself. In that moment when we were rich and everyone else was poor, I think we mistook a historical accident and perceived it to be a permanent condition. That is over.

The age of American hegemony is over. No one is ever going to be that rich again. We are going to have to adapt to the limits of our power, the limits of our resources, and be wiser and more careful. That is not necessarily a bad thing. It is a bad thing if we do not realize it. It is a bad thing if we are not wise about it. We will still be rich and powerful if we are careful.

Lee Iacocca, when he is complaining about the Japanese, likes to use the phrase "the even playing field." It is true that the playing field in some ways is not even, particularly when the yen was too soft. Certainly Japan is an exclusionary society, and it is very frustrating to export there. It is exhausting and difficult. But in the larger sense, for the first time since World War II, the playing field is even. There are other people out there who are good, and dynamic, and have systems that work. They are sometimes different from ours. Their capital formation may be different. We no longer automatically set the standards. That is okay in some ways. But we ought not to be careless, and we ought to know what we are doing and why, and we ought not to think that when it doesn't work out well, we are being cheated.

I should point out also that the Japanese challenge is merely the first. There are others to come; Korea, Malaysia, and other nations out there that are hungrier, more ambitious, and desperate for the dignity of a middle class life. That is no small thing. We had an ascending nation here in the 1920s and 1930s when people who had been without dignity in their economic life began to get jobs that offered them, for the first time, a roof, decent food, and a sense that they could pass on to their children an education, protection, and some measure of security. We have had that for about 40, 50, or 60 years. Other parts of the world are now getting it, and it is about the most potent octane you can imagine: The sense that no matter what sacrifice you are making in your lifetime, you can see your children live better than your parents. This is the beginning of a new international order. There is going to be far more competition. The slices of profit are going to be smaller because there are going to be more people in the middle class.

Impact of New International Order on U.S. Someone once said to me, "Mr. Halberstam, doesn't that mean that the nature of the lifestyle here in America will change?" I said, "It already has." When I graduated from college in the mid-1950s, even in as poorly paying a profession as journalism, you could be middle class on one income. That is not true in most of urban America now. If you want to be a good, certifiable, card-carrying yuppie, you and your spouse both have to have good jobs. I mean we have to work harder to stand still. That is the difference.

I should point out, lest anyone think it is going to be easy, that the learning curve in an age of high technology gets quicker and quicker. Let me give you just briefly the example of the auto industry. When the Japanese came here in 1958 with their clumsy, underpowered tanks disguised as cars, or cars disguised as tanks, they made every mistake in the book. They had a dealer network that was largely incompetent. If you had once sold a used car, you could probably get a Nissan dealership. They had no advertising budget, and their cars in no way were geared to the American demand. It took them nine years to get good, and they got good, very good.

Now comes the launch of Hyundai. From day one, they have a dealer network where millionaire dealers are fighting to get in. Their television is done by the same people who brought you the light beer commercials from Miller. Their product has instant credibility, reliability, and efficiency. They did it from the start. That is what I mean by the learning curve getting shorter.

Before I go on, I should say that there are many things about the Japanese that are very difficult and frustrating. It is an exclusionary society. It really does believe that free trade is a one-way street. A colleague of mine, Donald Richy, a writer, refers to it as the "electronic tribe" which I think is a very good phrase, because it catches at once the ultramodernity of it, in almost a tribal nature. They do not open their markets. They do keep products out. Nakasoni meets Reagan. They shake hands. An announcement is made about barriers coming down, and nothing happens. They lobby here, but we cannot lightly lobby there. They are bewildering negotiators by our standards. And yet, they have worked harder, saved more, expected less. They have been better Calvinists, better Puritans. In manufacturing, where they have excelled in contrast to us, they are more the true children of the original Henry Ford. We want to know who has done this to us. Unlike Mr. Gephardt's commercials, I say it is we ourselves. What Mr. Gephardt does not tell you is that even if the Japanese opened up all markets, in the unlikely event that they took our beef, citrus, some of our high biotechnology stuff, and our tobacco, it would only affect the trade balance about 20 percent. So we really have to look at ourselves to understand what has happened.

U.S. Emphasized Finance, Not Manufacturing. That period of enormous affluence spawned our largest companies and industries into de facto monopolies. As that happened, the government was sitting there making sure no one went out of business. It was all about economies of scale. Big was better. Power passed within the company from the creative people — the designers, the engineers, the manufacturing men — to the financial cadre, conservators, who believed that you could make money without risk in stagnant companies. Probably the best single quote in the book was one from George Romney when in 1950 he was trying to break up General Motors and he said quite prophetically, "There is nothing more vulnerable than entrenched success." At those meetings the creative people were beaten down again and again by the financial people who wanted to just do what they did last year, and make a little bit more money while doing it. No one ever said, "What is a better car? What is better for the customer? Is this the best we can do? In the long run, won't we be better if we just make a better product?" What they were really doing was taking quality out. Nobody was speaking for the customer.

There is an anecdote I tell about the perception of what you are in business for, and who your customers are. In the early 1970s, Lynn Townsend, then the head of Chrysler, was at a dinner party with

Jean Borgnie, a Ford designer. Borgnie said, "Lynn, I am worried about the quality of our cars." And Townsend said, "Jean, don't worry about quality." Jean said, "What do you mean?" Lynn responded, "Jean, the only thing people care about is their splits, that is, their stock splits." That was it. The real customers were not people buying the cars. The real customers were the stockholders. You can get in trouble with a philosophy like that. You won't get in trouble immediately, but someday, someone is going to come along who is going to do things right.

Our system was preoccupied with finance, the Japanese with manufacturing. We took manufacturing, which had been a great American strength, for granted. Our manufacturing men became a backwater, second-class citizens. They got cut up in meetings. They weren't represented on the boards. Japanese boards of directors were filled with people who had actually run a manufacturing line. Ours were filled with the children of the Harvard business and law schools. That is a quantum change. The Japanese, backed to the wall at the end of the war with a reputation for shoddy, dinky goods, seized upon our statistical quality control people, like Edwards Deming, and made them gurus. They didn't just make slogans. You could actually stop the line if it wasn't good enough.

What Makes the Japanese System Work? One of the things that I think is a myth is the quality of Japanese managers. I don't think their managers are better than ours. In fact, I think our managers, if they had the fabled Iacocca-level playing field, would be better. What works for the Japanese is a system, an idea, a covenant, a culture of adversity. In that adversity, a rocky little island, there is a covenant on the part of the average person to be a part, to accept authority, a covenant on the part of the person at the top of the matrix to be respectful of those below him. They have a capitalism different from ours, a state-guided, communal capitalism. The people at the top don't make that much, and the people at the bottom don't make too little. There are a number of component parts that are terribly important. First, they probably have the best blue-collar workers in the world, not just in attitude, but in preparation, based upon a ninth or tenth grade education. You can ask almost anybody who has dealt with both American and Japanese workers, and one of the great differences will be in the ability to deal with a complicated mathematical manual and thus, with quality. That is an important part, and it goes right back to education.

Second, there are the high number of practical engineers they use flooding the factory floor, making endless tiny little improvements, here, here, and here. These are not brilliant, just little improvements. We have been taking our engineers and putting them in this high abstract position. They have put them on the factory floor and they, therefore, have been able to design for quality, as we were not. They have been good. Don Lennox, a former Ford executive, once told me that he went there in the late 1970s and it was a revelation. He thought he was going to see some great technological thing that they had that we didn't have. Not at all. He just saw all the tiny little things they had done, and continued doing it, until one day it was a quantum breakthrough. There was a big, big difference. They caught up and passed us in manufacturing. This is something to be wary of. We were once better in technology than they were, they were in effect at a technological disadvantage. That is not true anymore. They now are technologically more advanced in their process than we are. So one should not underestimate the challenge.

Third, there is a close, almost incestuous, relationship between the banks and the companies. You can hardly tell where one begins and the other ends. This allows their managers, unlike our managers, who are torn by quarterly reports in an equity driven economy, to think long range. This allows them to build quality and not worry about the immediate gratifications. It's a reat advantage. One of the things this country really has to do, if it is going to match East Asia in quality, is to change and adjust our capital formation.

Fourth, the leadership of their high bureaucracy, MITI, the Ministry of Trade and Industry, and the Ministry of Finance, guides Japan's limited resources into the areas where it can do the most good.

Their success has been built on manufacturing, education, and being careful. I want to emphasize again, and again, the importance of education. It is critical. It is how a family in Japan and in East Asia defines itself. It is the hope of an ordinary family. It is vested in the children, particularly in the males. Maybe it is the size of our bountiful land, maybe there has been so much wealth here that's come by so easily, that education has become somewhat secondary here. We do not see education as being the key to a better life. Or at least most Americans don't. We have got to change that. You can see that with the East Asians even when they come to America. In areas where the school system doesn't seem to be terribly good, suddenly there is the new East Asian community, or new Asian community, and they are suddenly showing up with merit scholars.

Fallacy of Protectionism. Protectionism is not going to get us anywhere. It can't be done. We have a historical role, a political role, as leader of the free world. It is a role that will be adjusted, but it is a role nonetheless. We cannot be a political leader of a segment of the world and economically isolationist. It doesn't work. What is really true is if we become protectionists, then we really legitimize the weakness. Then we almost withdraw from the battlefield. We become the largest retirement community in the world. We either compete, and have the confidence that we can, or we get out.

Protectionism doesn't work. There is a very good word, reciprocity. We have the right to ask that. We have the right to ask of the Japanese that whatever they can do here, we can do there, and be tough about it. They are very tough coming here. I think they understand toughness in negotiations. They may not like it, they may complain, but anybody who has ever dealt with the Japanese knows that they are formidable and relentless negotiators, and therefore we can be relentless too. But we need them. We need their energy. We have carried this particular international burden for a very long time. We need their scientific talent. We need their financial successes. We need to harness that together and make use of it. We are tired. They have things they do better than we. We have things we do better than they.

It is an awkward relationship. We have historically had as allies people from whom we have descended and with whom we are culturally similar. We have historic links and languages with them. The Japanese are a mirror reverse of us. It's hard on them. It's hard on us. But it can be done. There are a lot of things that we can do.

We can elevate the importance of trade, which we have taken for granted, by making it virtually at the same high level as national security. We can dramatically increase incentives for manufacturing. I think we need to stop some of the manipulation that goes on in Wall Street such as the leveraging of money, which is almost anti-productive. We can greatly increase the size of scholarships for scientific students in our great universities. We have the best high educational plant in the world. The danger is, as they say about MIT, that one-third of the students are Japanese, one-third are Jewish, and one-third are foreign. We can change our capital formation and we can begin to look at ourselves more honestly. Where are we? Why have things gone wrong? What do we need to do? Why are other people doing things that we used to do better than anybody? Why are they doing it better? What can we do?

We need less sloganeering and more truth. If I were doing a report card on the future of America to indicate what it would take to be a great power in 40 years, it would show that in many ways we're rather well prepared. In agriculture, which is going to be important, we are probably the best in the world. In mineral resources, which will be less important than now, but for an industrial society, it is better to have minerals than not to have them, we are rather blessed. We have a diverse and potentially varied economy. We have the best venture capital system in the world, and that is quite wonderful. We have young talented Americans betting on themselves. We have the best higher educational system in the world. We have a diverse and potentially talented people. They represent an ethnic complexity that the Japanese don't have to deal with, but in the long range, I believe that is a strength if we deal with it right, rather than a weakness.

What are our weaknesses? Well, there are really only two, I think. One is the declining secondary school system. A federal report — I think it was the Carnegie report — said that if a foreign power wanted to weaken the United States, it would give us nothing but the school system we already have. The idea that you can be a great nation without a first-rate school system, without a priority in education, is ludicrous. The second weakness is the coming together of people's expectations after 40 years of limitless affluence, to more limited, or somewhat limited circumstances. It is the degree to which we can now begin to see the world as it is, and what we need to do, and how life will be different, and how we can be more disciplined, and more careful, and how we can do that with some measure of equity of sacrifice, how we adjust to different circumstances — that is really going to be the supreme test of our political system in the next ten or 15 years.

10

Merger Strategies and Goals

Richard Bierly, Senior Corporate Vice President, Unisys

I am impressed with Utah State's Partners Program. You are very fortunate because it is not something done in a lot of places. For those of you interested in learning more about personnel management, I hope I can contribute by telling you about the Unisys merger and some of the things that went into it — perhaps then you'll follow our company as time goes on. There's no right or wrong about how mergers are done. We did what we thought necessary for our corporation, and I hope this Unisys story adds to your knowledge and can help you.

Merger Background and Purpose. The first thing that is important to keep in mind is that the purpose of our merger was to create something new, bigger, and better than what we were before. A lot of mergers are not done for that purpose. Companies go together because they intend to strengthen the balance sheet, use the assets in some other way. That was not the purpose of our merger. It was to create something bigger and better. I was a part of that, not as a consultant, not as someone who spent a few days or a few weeks working on it, but someone who was a principal in it and had a job to do while going through what was a very unusual experience. I think most of my colleagues in the company would agree that it was a very unusual experience.

We operate in a very unusual marketplace in the computer business. I spent some time with a class and I asked them how many of them had heard of Unisys, what it was, what it was shaped from or came from. There were a good number of young people that hadn't heard about it. But they all knew about IBM. IBM is a wonderful company and a very major vendor in our computer business. For decades, IBM has dominated the information systems marketplace. In 1985, the IBM share of the mainframe market equaled 76 percent. Burroughs' share was 6 percent. The Sperry share was approximately 4 percent. If you think about that, there aren't very many companies or industries where a single vendor dominates to that degree. In 1985, the value of worldwide computer shipments by U.S.-based manufacturers was approximately $66 billion. Of that amount, IBM shipped 41 percent, DEC 7.9 percent, Burroughs 3.6 percent, and Sperry 2.5 percent.

Burroughs and Sperry felt the same way, that we often had a better solution, better answers to customers' problems, more effective applications, but we lost business because of the fear factor. Customers said, "Yes, that looks pretty good, but you're smaller. We're not sure you're around for the duration." Think about it. The fact that two companies, both of which are $5 billion companies, would have customers question whether they'd be around to be worth the investment they would make in the company's applications. It drove our chairman, Mr. Blumenthal, crazy — the fact that we would lose business and lose customers because they didn't think we had a viable long term future. Customers needed reassurance. The message was clear to us that in order for us to compete over the long haul, we had to have more resources to convince our customers that they had to stay with us. That's particularly true in the computer business where high tech is moving so fast and the costs are so high.

This is the size of the companies combined. Burroughs Company, with a little under $5 billion, and Sperry Company, with close to $6 billion, totalled a little over $10 billion. In Burroughs, we had just over 56,000 employees, Sperry had 65,000, and combined there were about 122,000.

There were some differences in the two companies, but there were more similarities. There was a heavier emphasis in Sperry on defense business, more emphasis on commercial business in Burroughs. There was some difference in the customer size and emphasis. But both companies operated on a full range of computing systems on a worldwide basis. Both companies had similar histories, having been pioneers in developing electronic computers.

The history of Sperry and of Burroughs was quite similar. They were old, established companies. Burroughs was 100 years old two years ago. Sperry was 75 years old last year. Both had large and loyal user bases. Sperry's computer business grew out of a machine called ENIAC. The ENIAC was the first large scale digital electronic, multipurpose computer and was developed at the Moore School of Engineering at the University of Pennsylvania in the mid-1940s. John Mauchly and Eckert designed and supervised building ENIAC with funding from the Army. Eckert and Mauchly left the University of Pennsylvania and founded a private computer corporation in 1948. That company floundered and in 1950 was sold to Remington-Rand. At Remington-Rand, Eckert and Mauchly were instrumental in building UNIVAC, which was the first commercially successful computer. This was actually before IBM got into the computer business. In 1955, Sperry acquired Remington-Rand. Eckert became a Sperry vice president, was the director of research, and supervised building the first solid-state transistor computer.

In the late 1940s and early 1950s, a Professor Ferris was a director of research at the University of Pennsylvania. He had monitored the development of ENIAC and was an early pioneer in computer technology. In 1950, Burroughs retained Professor Ferris and other people from the University to assist on the conversion of its products to the computers. Ferris was largely responsible for establishing Burroughs' development facilities at Paoli, Pennsylvania, just west of Philadelphia, and was no doubt a primary factor in the early concentration of Burroughs manufacturing sites in the Philadelphia area. Sperry had more of a high-tech origin and Burroughs was more in the mechanical and electro-mechanical.

Merger Negotiations. The merger goal was to build a company for the long term by creating a critical mass necessary to compete worldwide with the likes of IBM, Japan, DEC, and others. The objectives were to reinforce core strength through advanced technology, provide more resources for systems software development, enlarge the customer base, maximize cost savings through procurement efficiencies, economies of scale, commonality of infrastructure, efficient use of plant and equipment capacity, common engineering requirements, and concentrated R & D. That was our goal, and it's worth bearing in mind as we talk about the subject because it's different than the goal of a lot of other mergers.

In the summer of 1985, an offer of $65 a share was made to the Sperry board and management. It failed. One of the reasons it failed was it had very poor financial press and business press. The financial community injected a fear factor into it. People misunderstood the potential benefits. There was speculation about seeing failure similar to the previous computer industry acquisitions when Honeywell bought GE and Sperry acquired RCA some time ago. Those computing company mergers resulted in both companies eliminating the architecture of the company that was acquired. Most customers of those companies ended up either spending a fortune to convert or, in many cases, moving to another vendor. There was some reference to that as we talked about our first offer.

After that offer was rejected, Sperry did some things that had actually made them even more attractive. It sold the Sperry New Holland Farm Equipment business, put its balance sheet in good order, and undertook third-party financing of receivables. Sperry also initiated "poison pill" defenses, the primary one being large and potentially expensive — golden parachutes (bonuses) for 136 top executives. These were three-year and, in some cases, five-year parachutes that could be very easily activated. They would result in a potential payment of over $80 million if they were all activated and the loss of some important talent to this new company. Additionally the Sperry board had a staggered three-year term. This had been in place several years before the merger, but if we couldn't get together with the board and had to go to what would be called a hostile takeover, they could have resisted and fought and there would have been a lot of wasted energy, time, and money. We really didn't want to do that. Our chairman was convinced as he considered the options for the future that this merger was the right thing to do. If we didn't execute the merger or find a partner large enough to give us the clout we were looking for, we would continue to lose market share and probably so would Sperry. We really had an uncertain future.

So remembering the initial effort to negotiate a friendly merger, because of Sperry's hesitancy and because of the investors' lack of understanding, the decision was made to make a more compelling offer to Sperry, management and the board, and to go to the shareholders only if necessary with what we labeled a friendly "bearhug." We also took steps to have a better explanation for all concerned, especially the financial press. That better preparation for the press paid off. The offer was made in May of 1986 and after 22 days of hard negotiation with Sperry management and the board, an agreement was reached. Both boards approved the merger agreement in May, the stockholders on September 16, 1987, and the price then was $76.50 a share. This time the press was favorable and friendly to the point of ecstasy. *Fortune* referred to the merger as a surprisingly sexy computer marriage. The *Wall Street Journal* reported, "the Sperry/Burroughs merger wins praise, the union born of inspiration, not desperation." A business reporter described it as computerland's biggest merger ever. The $4.8 billion union of Burroughs and Sperry has been much disparaged, but matchmaker Michael Blumenthal is making it work with a huge cost savings and deft handling of executive egos. The happy couple's only worry: IBM.

Putting Two Firms Together. We wanted to work quickly on dealing with our customers. Both Sperry and Burroughs customers were worried that their investment in applications was going to be wasted and they'd be faced with a costly conversion. Our philosophy from the beginning was that we were going to maintain two different architectures. As our chairman has frequently stated, it's easier for one well-managed company to manage two architectures than it is for two companies to manage separate ones.

As we got into it, experience showed us that the complement of Burroughs and Sperry products, services, and lines of business was greater than we even thought. The various product lines, technologies, geographic presences, and business positions support each other across a very broad spectrum providing synergy. Reassurance was further given to our customers by creating an office of customer communications. We had a small staff put together who immediately went to work on explaining to all of our major customers our commitment to the two core computer operating systems and establishing clearly defined lines of business so that our customers who might have been on the fence saw no reason from our behavior to look to another vendor.

So we made the deal, and the people and the press seemed to like it. Where do we go from here? How to proceed? How to make it come together? We knew why mergers failed. They failed because you have the wrong partner, you paid the wrong price, the deal is made at the wrong time, or companies are put together the wrong way. We commented from time to time that our chairman and a handful of people worked on most of the planning for the merger offer and pulled it off and then they gave us the job to make it happen. They sat back and said they'd done their part and it was up to us to do the rest. We knew we'd accomplished three of the four. We had a good partner, we had the right price, and we knew it was the right timing. The biggest and continuing challenge was putting these companies together. This is the area where the theory and planning meant the reality of human involvement and reaction, both inside and outside the company.

An active rumor mill compounds concerns, so we had to deal with the human element with great care. One of the first things we did back in July was to hire two psychologists who were experts, who had read, studied, and written about the merger syndrome — Professor Mitchell Lee Marks, of the California School of Professional Psychology, and Professor Philip Mervis of the Center for Applied Social Science at Boston University. These chaps had studied together, had written on merger syndrome and associated stress and uncertainty. They became known affectionately as the M & M boys. Their role was to act as a sounding board for concerned executives of both companies, Burroughs and Sperry, because there were concerns on both sides. They were confidential confidants for people who needed someone to talk to or had a problem to air, and morale auditors to help guide us in the continuing integration of personnel. There was a lot of concern and uncertainty.

The Sperry people had to confront a number of issues. They had an uncertain future. They had fear and job insecurity. Who will be my boss, being bought by another company? How will my record be established? I've worked 10 or 20 years developing credibility and sponsors. What happens with all new management? Will I be pushed aside? Will my life be made unpleasant so that I want to leave? Should I quit, be super active, or do as little as possible?

The Burroughs executives had to confront similar issues. We tried to avoid a winner/loser syndrome by the way we talked and behaved.

They had their own uncertainty about the future. Mr. Blumenthal was so dedicated to making certain that the Sperry people understood we weren't going to have a winner/ loser mentality that we had some Burroughs people in Detroit wondering who bought whom. So we had to deal with attitudes on both sides of the ledger.

These are natural reactions, we learned from our M & M boys, to the massive changes that introduce discontinuities into the personal lives of more than 120,000 people, especially where the potential for personal benefit is decidedly unclear. So we developed some ground rules on how we were going to proceed, some principles that we used as a bench mark for all decisions and actions that we took. I mentioned we constantly worked on making sure it was clear that no one had a winner/loser mentality. The merger would only work if it was a partnership. So we reinforced time and time again that this was a partnership between two companies creating something new.

We said that jobs would go to the people who were the best qualified, regardless of which company the person came from. We didn't put all the good jobs in the hands of the Burroughs people. We selected people based on their qualifications as best they could be determined and what we thought they could do. This was an attractive ideal, as you can imagine, an idea with broad appeal and once it was seen that we really meant it, it meant an awful lot to our integration effort. Right now three of the four commercial line of business presidents are former Sperry. Five of the 14 domestic regional marketing heads are from Sperry. Thirteen of the 17 European-African marketing heads are from the Sperry Corporation. So we thought we practiced what we preached as we put our organization together.

Selecting Company Name: Unisys. We talked about unity. We saw a need for creating a new identity to rally people from both companies. So we announced that neither Sperry nor Burroughs would survive. We created a new identity and a new name. We eliminated the counterproductive identification of individuals with each or either of the former names. We had a clever idea. All employees were invited to help select the new company name. We had 32,000 entries, far more than we ever dreamed. Unisys turned out to be one of those entries. We had a cash prize of $5,000 for the first person to submit the name that was selected. The name Unisys was derived from three words: united, information, and systems, so I'm told.

The name Unisys helped set the stage for the involvement of both sets of employees. That is, we symbolically created something new and you can see it when people answer the phone or talk to each other; they identify themselves after a very short few weeks as members of Unisys. People talk about Unisys like it's always been their company. We really think that was one of the smartest things we did.

We adopted a philosophy of dispatch, the operating method "When in doubt, do it now." We recognized that delay lends fuel to uncertainty. All this helped focus the attention of our people on the common competitive threat to both the former companies in the ways they would fit in to address the challenge. We kept harping on the fact that Unisys has a greater capability to compete, the power of two. I'm sure you've seen that theme in the commercials. Now is the time. We didn't miss a beat, by the way, quarter to quarter, despite all the reorganization we went through.

It's in this area that some people say we made some errors. Some people internally say they feel we moved too fast on some things. But when you sit back and talk about that in retrospect, it's hard to determine what we would have done differently. What would we have not done if we could do it all over again, in terms of things that we worked our way through?

Merger Coordinating Committee Back in June of 1986, we formed a merger coordinating committee. This was formed to carry out the company integration planning. There were six integration objectives:

1. Develop a new organization
2. Worldwide marketing integration
3. Non-core business review
4. Operations consolidation
5. Products technology integration
6. Improved financial performance

Senior executives from both companies had formed MCC, as we called it. It was a central control point and umpire. (Many of the MCC executives became the Unisys executives, but when this was first established only one person knew for sure what his job was — and that was the chairman.) This commissioned 13 different task forces. Each one of those was co-chaired by a person from each company, Burroughs and Sperry. They went through the whole array of things that had to be looked at and came up with recommended action plans to this MCC in September of 1986, when it was eliminated.

We hired Booz-Allen to help support the MCC. They were also a neutral party, took a look at our timing, our plans, helped us prioritize, and acted as a catalyst as we thought our way through. Because everybody had a vested interest, as hard as you tried to be objective, it was useful to have a disinterested third party helping you look at the objective issues being dealt with.

At our first meeting in September, when these task forces were going to report to the MCC, someone had a great idea and suggested to Mike that we create the Sperry/Burroughs hat with the old logos for both companies. Mike had about 30 of them made up and all the brass in the Plaza Hotel in New York City reviewing these task force presentations were wearing baseball caps. We talk about putting on our corporate hat. When the presenters would come in, there we were, sitting around with our baseball caps on. They were thrown two or three of these and told to "put on their corporate hats." Then we had our final planning meeting in December and we had our Unisys hat. They're all now part of our company memorabilia. It was that kind of thing that helped us focus on and concentrate on thinking about these issues from the standpoint of this new corporate perspective.

Good Communications Reduce Rumors. We launched communications programs. Even before the offer was accepted by Sperry we were communicating and having meetings with people. We communicated throughout that whole period in the summertime — task force assignments, decisionmaking timetables, anything we could do to keep people informed so they would not speculate and create rumors that would create a problem as we went into this.

There was a vigorous external PR campaign aimed at the trade journals and financial press. This campaign recognized that what is broadcast publicly about Unisys has an impact on employee thinking and morale. Our CEO stayed very involved as an operating executive on this. He met with internal and external audiences. He toured the country and in the first few weeks met with clusters of Sperry management, talking about his vision for this new company. This visible, hands-on involvement of the CEO and other executives was a positive sign to both companies and our active leadership that we had a clear vision of our future potential, and that we had a specific mission to exploit that potential.

Benefits of this involvement were many. It demonstrated commitment to partnership; key executives got to know each other and learn to work together. The input from both sides helped to insure that the best from both worlds would be chosen. Potential problems and opportunities could be identified early.

Merger stress can hit at every tier in the company. All employees went through some sort of stress as a result of this activity. We took the sting out of that by making sure that all people at all levels understood their new mission by maintaining levels of participation up and down the corporation, keeping levels of tension under control, and acknowledging achievement. We put together a package, with the help of our M & M boys, with which we trained human resource representatives on the concepts of merger syndrome and organization building.

New Culture Evolved. We're evolving a new philosophy and culture. People ask me about how we can bring the two cultures together. I'm not sure you can talk your way through a new culture. You behave your way through a new culture. But we had to focus on what we wanted to become. We wanted to work as a team, the customer comes first, we back the innovator, we honor high ethical standards, and we practice quality in everything we do.

Under this umbrella, HR priorities are to produce an environment in Unisys where people feel it's a good place to work, they're paid competitively, and career opportunities are fair. We are establishing an environment that encourages employee involvement, where we work as a team, and where the working environment demonstrates respect and concern for people. We won't become anything by talking alone. Employees, customers, and investors will be impressed by the results of what we do, not what we say. I believe our management team at every level accepts that challenge.

Unisys After One Year. Unisys one year later is a reorganized company from top to bottom. The field units worldwide have been integrated and in many cases now operate out of the same building. The plants and labs are now under common leadership in management. We organized all of the U.S. commercial marketing under one head. We organized all of defense business under one head. We have realized benefits more than we had anticipated, such as large synergies and operating savings in procurement, research and development, engineering, plant capacity utilization, manufacturing, and distribution. We have an attractive position in defense systems, about one-fourth of our Unisys revenue.

Our divestment program was a major success. We raised in excess of $1.8 billion dollars, which exceeded our target by over $300 million. We sold the Sperry microwave operation to Honeywell and Sperry marine instruments to Newport News Shipbuilding. We sold parts of the Burroughs Memorex subsidiary. We achieved our debt target fully 12 months before the original deadline. The debt to capital ratio has been reduced from 55 percent one year ago to just under 35 percent in November of 1987. Our credit rating improved. In October of 1987, Standard and Poors upgraded Unisys from BBB to A-. In the second quarter, Moody's Investor Service upgraded Unisys from B to A3. That's important for our future if we need to borrow again.

We were faced with plant closings and layoffs, which were part of the consolidations we had to experience. Before the merger, both companies had 122,000 people, as I said before. Our current head count is 93,000. But our reductions were accomplished by various methods, the largest one being the divestitures as companies were sold. They amounted to 19,000 people. We had an early voluntary retirement program in all of our facilities, and about 2,000 people left under that. We reduced another 2,500 simply by not replacing under attrition. We then had layoffs of about 5,500. Even there we tried to do that in the best way we could. We made every effort to place the people within the company and in some areas we were successful in doing that. We had two printed circuit manufacturing facilities, one in Egan, Minnesota, one in Rancho Bernardo, California, and we closed Egan and moved people from there to Rancho Bernardo. We had more than generous severance plans for the people who were terminated. We extended their benefits coverage longer than the policy called for. We paid up to one week's pay for job search and job training related to the job search. We offered professional out-placement assistance for all people laid off, which cost us a little over $2.3 million.

In the communities where we had to close facilities, we tried to be as thoughtful and helpful as we could. In Bristol, Tennessee, where we closed a facility, we provided cash donations to offset the loss of the tax base to the community. We donated land to the community, which they could then use as an industrial park. We loaned personnel to the Chamber of Commerce to help in their efforts to attract people to that industrial park. In Liege, Belgium, where we had a facility we no longer needed, we found a buyer that was able to purchase the facility and save 400 of the 500 jobs that were in that facility.

To date, we haven't lost a major customer due to this merger. That's largely due to the earlier stated support to both architectures, and Mr. Blumenthal's visits and personal reassurance of those major customers. We know we've gotten some new business that we wouldn't have gotten without the added clout and the size of the organization. Two of these were $450 million accounts for radar-based, weather detection systems, and a $50 million account with the Bank of Hong Kong and Shanghai, and they told us without the combination of the talents they wouldn't have bought the business from us.

We've had great employee support. We've had an absence of critical mail, horror stories, and sour grapes. We've had a below average number of employee-initiated law suits come out of the merger. We've had a willingness of Sperry people to stay on and no overall major attrition problem in the company. We conducted an employee opinion survey in August, and the results were good and satisfying to us. There was no significant difference in the attitudes of both Sperry and Burroughs people. We were pleased to see that, no polarizing of attitudes on the part of people who were in this new company. Eighty percent of the people said that they felt we had the resources to be more competitive in the future. They bought into this vision that we are a stronger company. They were, of course, interested in knowing how they fit in as individuals, which is the right kind of question. We did have a disproportionate number of neutral answers on our survey questionnaire, which suggests to me a "wait-and-see" attitude about what the future will bring, and frankly, I consider that a remarkably sensible position for people to take.

The annual report is not out yet. I was trying this morning to get my hands on the *Wall Street Journal* because Mike was interviewed by them the other day, and the only person who can announce results ahead of official results is the chairman. So I wanted to make sure I quoted the chairman. He said he thought we'd be operating between $8 to $9 earnings per share in 1987, and all the experts laughed at him. With our stock split, he did say to them we'd be somewhere between $2.67 to $3 per share. So that means we're going to come in meeting our financial targets throughout all this for 1987. So while we went through all this turmoil and all this restructuring we still continue to service our customers and run the business that allowed us to come right on target for 1987.

What's Ahead. So what's ahead? We're continuing to build and strengthen our organization. Meritocracy has to apply to systems and programs as well as people. Our key objective is to have company-wide policies and procedures and systems that support our other programs. That's easier said than done, because two multi-billion dollar corporations have deeply entrenched the differing ways to do many common tasks. In some ways this second year is going to be more difficult, because we have to make tough decisions about how we're going to operate. That means someone's ox is going to get gored as we make these decisions. Communications is as important now as it was in the beginning of the merger, but now middle managers have the task of communicating and executing this vision, this mission, and how things should get done in the future. I'm a lot wiser, proud of our accomplishments, proud of the human resource role that was played in all this, proud of the sophistication of all of our people throughout all of this. I'm glad that I had the experience, but I'm not entirely certain that I'm looking forward to doing it again right away.

11

New Skills and Productivity

Ray Marshall, Professor, University of Texas

I have been asked to talk about new skills in productivity. This is a terribly important subject. There is debate going on about it, because one of the most important things we need to discover is what kind of work force we need in order to be a world class economy and maintain our standard of living. Part of the debate is over the question of whether or not all of the major social, economic, and other trends will require more skills or fewer skills and whether the technology is deskilling or whether it will require more skills and higher levels and different kinds of education.

More or Fewer Skills Required? If you examine this debate you would find that it is inconclusive. You can pay your money and take your pick. You get studies that show that technology is displacing skills. There are two things that you have to look at. One is the effect of trends on particular occupations. The second main concern is what's happening to the occupational mix. There are more highly skilled occupations being created. My own view is that you will never resolve this question and, for reasons that I'll indicate, you really ought not to spend a lot of time with it.

In the first place, there are serious measurement and analytical problems that make it very difficult to know what a skill is. You get a fair amount of circularity: Do people have high incomes because they've got the skills, or do they have the skills because they've got the incomes? It's clear that high incomes and high levels of schooling tend to be strongly correlated. So I don't see how you untangle that. We're also dealing with a fairly dynamic, rapidly changing problem. As somebody recently said to me, trying to do school reform is like trying to work on a train going a hundred miles an hour, because it's a dynamic and moving process. It doesn't really make a lot of difference for us to talk about what has happened in the past since the future is not going to be much like the past.

Educational Institutions Resist Change. This is why many of the so-called reform reports on education miss the point. The basic point is that we've never had the kind of education system that we need to have in order to be world class and competitive in this rapidly changing world.

It's also clear that technology has different effects through time. When you first introduce a technology, for example, the skill requirements apparently are very much higher than they are when it becomes standardized. As you go through a process, a lot of skills are required at the beginning. However, when a technology gets standardized, it permits the recombination of skills into more complete jobs.

My view is that we need to pay much more attention to skills. We do not have across-the-board world class learning systems. However, our higher education systems are still competitive. We export about $6 billion a year in higher education services, net. Our best institutions of higher education are the best in the world. It's not necessarily because those institutions themselves are efficient; they resist change too much. Like General Motors in 1965, they do pretty well because they're rich. But because they don't have to be as competitive as they will have to be in this kind of world that we're moving into, higher eduction institutions must become more efficient.

It's also fairly important to recognize that you can get an overeducated work force. In India, for example, they have unemployed doctors. So you've got to pay some attention to the match between the people in your learning systems and the demand for what they can do. It's quite possible that you can get too many people trained in the wrong things. Therefore, we need better counseling and information and projection systems.

Theories for Organizing Work Affect Skilling. Another very important point is that whether we get skilling or deskilling depends on management philosophies and theories used for organizing work. Many of the people who talk about deskilling and the need for fewer skills believe that traditional so-called "scientific management" systems in the United States will predominate. That is to say that when technology is introduced it will be done in a way that will deskill. What Frederick Taylor had in mind was to transfer skills from workers to management and machines, to fix the jobs so that the dumbest sorts of people could do them. Workers would become appendages to machines. Management would gain control of the work that way.

Now I thought Frederick Taylor had kind of died out. Taylor's management system is like the school system: It's not necessarily that it was wrong for its time, but it does seem to be wrong for the kind of world we're in today. I thought that "scientific management" was losing out until doing research on my 1987 book, *Unheard Voices: Labor and Economic Policy in a Competitive World*, which I commend to your attention and my profit. Then I ran across an editorial in *Iron Age* which said that the thing that kept Frederick Taylor's dream from coming true was that you never really could completely deskill a lot of the jobs; they couldn't really figure out what a lot of these machinists were doing. They were all doing different things and having similar outputs, so that suggested that there may not be one best way to do it. And what they concluded was that there were certain kinds of intellectual skills that could not be transferred either to the machine or to management. But, this editorial said, now that we have numerically controlled machines, Frederick Taylor's dream can finally come true; you can even transfer intellectual skills to the machine. People who take that view believe that we're headed toward deskilling.

Schooling Does Not Equal Education. Now let me define some terms, before I talk about what seems to me to be why we need to pay a lot more attention to skills and why the "scientific management" view is wrong. We need in the first place to be clear what we mean by skills and education. A lot of terms are used as synonymous when they're not. Some people will use the following logic, which I see in editorials all the time. They say everybody knows that the performance of American students on exams is lower than the performance of students in other countries. Our students usually rank in the bottom half of international tests on math and science and, therefore, this proves that our work force is inferior to the work force in other countries. Well, that's not the case. Nobody knows what the quality of our work force is.

You certainly cannot get at the quality of our work force by looking at schooling. Why? A lot of learning goes on outside of school; decidedly, from an economic perspective, most of the important learning goes on outside of school. So it's important to recognize that schooling does not equal education.

If schooling equaled education you couldn't find what I found when I had responsibility for the Job Corps. About 20 percent of the high school graduates coming into the Job Corps were illiterate. They had 12 years of schooling but they certainly didn't have 12 years of education.

We need to concentrate on education, not schooling. In fact, one of my concerns about America is that we value schooling, but not education; we don't pay enough attention to intellectual activity, as opposed to just attending school, and other important learning systems. We're learning more about this all the time. One learning system is the family and early childhood development. In fact, some of the most interesting work being done on learning these days shows how important the first three years of life are to performance as an adult, not to just performance in school. The kind of nurturing and learning young children get makes a lot of difference, and people are surprised that they can learn a lot when they are very young. A lot of my colleagues believe they can predict high school dropouts almost from birth data; being underweight, having poor health, having a mother with limited education greatly increases the probability of being a dropout. The most important predictors of educational achievement are the education and income of the parents.

Furthermore, a lot of learning occurs on the job. People don't realize the extent to which jobs have become learning systems. Many corporations are more like graduate schools than they are factories. American companies spend $210 billion on education and training; $30 billion of that on formal education. There are about 18 American companies that award degrees. And many of them are doing much more interesting research on learning than in many colleges and universities. Why? They have found that one of the highest yielding investments they make is in human capital. As Ted Schultz indicated when he received the Nobel Prize, the return to human capital is higher than the return to physical capital. Therefore companies are starting to make those kinds of investments in their people.

The other point about the quality of the work force is that a lot of learning goes on while American workers are using the world's most advanced technology. The fact that we still have a substantial technological lead means that workers learn while interacting with machines. In fact, there is some interesting research about "humanware," or the interaction between the workers and machines. After all, a lot of the capital technology results from the transfer of skills and knowledge to the machines. That interaction, therefore, produces constant improvements, causing American workers to learn a lot. It can therefore be argued, in absence of better measures, that we have the highest quality work force in the world, because the best measure of the quality of one's work force is productivity. And we have the highest average level of productivity in the world. But what we have to be worried about is that we're rapidly losing that lead.

Concurrent Trends Impacting Required Skills. Now, it's also important to recognize that human capital is not the same as education. It also includes the knowledge, skills, and health of the work force. Another major preliminary point is the need to realize that we're not really dealing with single line trends, we're dealing with a matrix. There are a whole lot of things going on at the same time that determine what kind of skills we need to have in order to be a world-class economy and maintain our standard of living. Since the most powerful of these trends are all coming together at the same time, they will cause people to reach the wrong conclusion if they just look at one of them.

The first one is the increased international competition as a result of the globalization of the American economy. This means that everybody faces a lot more competition than they did 10 or 15 years ago. The whole environment is becoming a lot more competitive and deregulated. In fact, the whole question of deregulation combines with internationalization. When deregulation came about, internationalization had already deregulated financial markets so our political system simply recognized that. The big forces at work in this change were technology and international competition. Another main trend is, therefore, technology. Technology by itself does not have an independent life, but once you combine technology with intensified international competition you get a different system.

The third set of universal imperatives is related to demographic and labor market changes, especially the increased labor force participation of women, which is interrelated with technology, which determines what kinds of jobs are likely to become women's jobs. Technology determines how much time women have to work in the work force. In fact, the most important labor market development of this century is the increased labor force participation of women. No longer ago than 1950, 70 percent of American households were headed by men whose income was the sole source of income. Today less than 10 percent of American households are headed by men whose income is the sole source of income. Labor market tensions therefore result from the assumption that women are temporary peripheral participants in the work force where the reality is that women are permanent, integral, important participants in the work force.

Another important demographic development is the fact that the United States is becoming increasingly a minority country. The declining group in our society is white males. In fact, white males are becoming a declining group throughout the world, mainly because of age. The median age of Anglos is about 33; Hispanics, 23; Asians and blacks, 26. That means, of course, that most of the increase in the work force and population well into the next century will be women and minorities. In the year 2015, there will be roughly 91 million minority people in the United States. They will be, at that time, about 34 percent of the population, and probably 40 percent of the work force. In June 1985 they were 17 percent of the population. And that means, of course, that the kind of education and learning opportunities minorities get will have a lot to do with the quality of the work force in the United States.

Being Competitive versus Maintaining Living Standard. One of the problems with a lot of this debate is that it ignores a very important reality, and that is that while we've got these powerful trends, we don't necessarily have to yield to them. We must keep this in mind in trying to answer the question of what kind of work force or skills we need. You tell me the whereas's and I'll give you the therefore's; you tell me what kind of country you want to be, what kind of state you want to be, and then I'll tell you what kind of work force you need. I believe that the prevailing standard ought to be: Do you want to be competitive in internationalized markets? If you do, how do you define that?

Now, if you define competitiveness as being willing to cut your wages and income enough to beat the international competition, then there's no problem. That's what we've been doing. And if you ignore standards of living and wages, then we don't have a competitiveness problem.

On the other hand, if you believe that we ought to try to maintain and improve our standard of living and try to continue to be a world class player, in terms of defending and projecting our values in the world, the therefore's are very different. I believe we ought to try to be world class players, and we therefore ought to try to be competitive. And that carries some therefore's about the quality of the necessary work force to accomplish these objectives.

Let's think that through very specifically. What do you mean by being competitive in order to maintain that relatively high standard of living, and for the United States to be a world class player? Well, it's easy to specify the general conditions of competitiveness. It means you produce a quality product at competitive costs. In order to do that, you've got to attend to about four different propositions. First, you have to be concerned about productivity. But you have to be concerned about more than productivity if you want to be competitive. You have to be concerned about efficiency as well. And that's a different concept. Productivity is a physical concept. It means physical output per unit of input. For example, in no major industry is Korea more productive than the United States. But in a lot of industries Korea is more efficient than the United States. Why? Well, their wage costs are much lower than their productivity differential. Their wage differential is about six to one, and their productivity differential is about four to one, so they can therefore produce some things at a lower cost than we do, even though they're very inefficient in terms of productivity. Now that is an extremely important point to keep in mind, because you can only compete generally in two ways. You can become a lot more productive, or you can take a lower income. Therefore we have to decide what we want to do.

In addition to that, one of the big surprises to Americans is the third item on our list, and that's quality or excellence, if we're talking about learning systems. And quality is very closely related to productivity. I worked with a number of American companies on improving productivity, and they were surprised to learn how important quality was to productivity. The typical American approach has been that quality costs you more. What W. Edwards Deming and other people taught the Japanese is that quality costs you less. Therefore if you really want to be world class and productive, you will give heavy attention to quality. This should not have been a surprise, because quality determines the morale of a work force, market shares, and one's ability to make incremental improvements. Doing it right the first time costs much less than trying to undo mistakes. Quality is therefore very important. The chairman of the board of General Motors said to me in 1979 that what had happened was what he feared most; "Made in America" had become synonymous with an inferior product. We have changed places with Japan. There used to be a time when "Made in Japan" was a mark of an inferior product. But that's been completely turned around. Why is that so important? It's important because it's not hard to change your cost disadvantage, but it's very hard to change your reputation for producing an inferior product. It takes you a long time to do it. So you have to pay attention to quality.

The fourth one of these main items that you have to be concerned about if you want to be competitive is flexibility, ability to adjust to change, take advantage of opportunities, get out of things where you have no competitive advantage, and get into things where you do have an advantage.

Elements of Competition: Wage Levels. Now those are the general conditions. What do you have to do specifically? Well, you can compete, as I've said, in two main ways. These are the elements of competition. First, you can try to compete according to wages. If we try to compete according to wages, we'll lose, because we are a high wage country, even though we are no longer the highest wage country. We're now about eleventh or twelfth; by some accounts the Japanese wages are higher than ours. But we're still a relatively high wage country. And we're competing with people whose wages are a good bit lower than ours, who are willing to work a good bit harder, and who are developing very high quality work forces. By some reckonings, the Korean work force has a better education level than the American work force. One of the Carnegie projects looked at results from a VCR plant near Seoul, Korea, in about 1984. They found that those workers were relatively well educated. In fact, IBM's chief scientist, who chaired that Carnegie Task Force, said that IBM's best educated workers in the world were in Korea. Those workers worked 12 hours a day, 7 days a week with 2 days off a year, and they made $3000 a year. Now if we're going to try to compete with wages, we are going to lose it. Therefore, in my view, we ought not to even try; that is not the kind of competition I would like to see us win.

The fortunate thing about our options is that wages are becoming a less important element in international competition. Technology is causing the capital-cost/labor-cost ratio to rise. Therefore wages are becoming a smaller part of the total. That's the reason we are repatriating a lot of industries that had gone offshore. Information technology provides some real advantages to being in the market where products are produced. Of course, wages were never the main element in the competition for big ticket items like automobiles and capital goods. Performance and quality tend to be much more important in these items, which also have higher capital costs relative to labor costs.

Now, let's be very specific about that. How do you get a world class technology? Let's first define technology. The way economists ordinarily use that word is not just capital equipment. Technology means the way you do things. Because after all, capital equipment is simply knowledge and skill transferred to the machine. A management system, the way you organize the work, is also a technology. In fact, one of the greatest innovations in post-World War II is the realization that a management system is in fact a technology and can go through the same process of development. That is to say, at first you introduce an innovative management system, organization, and then it gets well understood, and you refine it and it gets standardized, just like capital equipment. And once it gets standardized, it can be exported. And therefore, anybody can do it.

One of the reasons many Pacific Rim and Third World countries have come on so strong is that they can exploit those management systems. We have no across-the-board advantage in management systems. Some of our management systems are world class; some are not. This Tayloristic system is not. Oligopolistic pricing is not. The American automobile industry does not have a world class management system, although it's trying to get it, and trying hard. If you want to see the extent to which they do not have it, I commend your attention to the NUMMI plant in Fremont, California, which General Motors couldn't make competitive; they had high turnover, poor workmanship, high absenteeism, and great difficulty in managing those United Automobile workers. Toyota came along and entered into a joint venture with General Motors. They did not, like General Motors is doing in its other operations, plan to automate, because they already knew what General Motors learned after it spent $60 billion trying to become more competitive. That is, if you don't pay attention to the management system before you introduce the technology, you'll simply pile up scrap faster, to quote Roger Smith, the chairman of General Motors. So, Toyota took essentially the same technology GM had and recalled all those UAW members that GM couldn't manage. In fact, it made a deal with UAW to help recall those workers and put the system in place. What did Toyota change? Mainly the management. They did away with General Motors' management system. How? First, they simplified jobs, to three main job classifications. People were given greater flexibility, mobility, and job security so they had a motive to improve productivity. NUMMI did away with the idea that only management is responsible for quality, and therefore people couldn't say, "That's not my job." In NUMMI's new system, everybody was responsible for quality. Workers had an obligation to stop the line and close the plant if they saw some shoddy product coming by. They no longer have just a wage system. Part of the workers' pay was a bonus that depended on how well that company performed.

The consequence of that should be a tremendous shock to the American automobile industry, because the NUMMI plant has become one of the most productive automobile plants in the United States, whereas General Motors' more automated plants are not as productive. The Ford plants are doing well with their Employee Involvement System, not because Ford was smarter than General Motors; they just didn't have the $60 billion to spend on automating. Therefore they did the right thing, which was to pay attention to their workers, strengthen their Employee Involvement System, and then gradually automate with employee involvement. So a manufacturing system is an important technology.

Now, to go back to the whereas's, if you want to be a world class player and have a high standard of living, what do you have to do? You must have leading-edge technologies, including the management system and the equipment, because once technology gets standardized and can be exported, you have no unique advantage at all; wages then become the determinate of efficiency, and therefore of competitiveness. So if you don't want to compete according to wages, you must have leading-edge technologies.

Employee Participation. It's not hard to tick off what a world class management system requires. First, it must be participative. And if we haven't learned anything else from Fred Taylor's system, whatever advantage it might have had at the time, it is obsolete for today. You have to make the assumption that they made at NUMMI and at most well-managed companies, and that is that workers understand their work better than anybody else. If you'll put them in the right kind of system, they will work hard to improve quality. It's not surprising that a participative system can allow you to have much higher productivity.

Take Care of the Worker. Second, a world class system must give heavy weight to workers. That's part of what Deming taught the Japanese. He said that American companies have got it all wrong. The first thing they take care of is the stockholders, then customers, and then workers. If you ask Deming how to do it, he would say, first you take care of your workers, then your customers, and then your stockholders. Why? Stockholders and customers are going to make out very well only if you have a quality work force, and only if you pay attention to quality and productivity and all the rest of it. It's almost counterintuitive, but it is a reality that many companies that concentrate mainly on profits make the lowest profits. And many of those companies that concentrate on service and quality make the highest profits. It's because maximizing profits is not the main thing that compels world class companies.

Job Security. Third, the system must emphasize job security for workers. Why? Because this is coupled with another main attribute of world class companies; they give heavy attention to education and training. They're more like postgraduate schools than factories of the 19th century. The learning and finding out more about learning is very profitable. Whoever comes up with efficient learning technology will get very rich, because learning is one of the most important pursuits, and especially technology that could overcome the serious educational deficiencies in our work force, like mathematics. Now, if you're going to make heavy investment in workers, you want to keep them. You don't want to have high turnover, and therefore you provide job security.

Career Development. Fourth, you must concentrate on careers and not jobs. That's what's wrong with this old business about deskilling, which asks, "How much skill do you need to do that entry level job?" Well, if you're a good manager, that's not what you look at when you hire somebody. You say, what kind of growth can that person have, what kind of learning process can they go through? So, more is required than just the ability to do a particular job. Some economists talk about overeducated Americans. Well, they might be, and maybe people get more history degrees than they need. In India they've got too many doctors relative to the number they can profitably employ. But I don't believe that we've got overeducated people, and you cannot say, just because you have more skill than the minimum needed to put bolt number 35 on a rear left wheel, that you're therefore overeducated for that job. The question is, what kind of career development can you have?

Decentralize Technology. The fifth basic requirement for a competitive system is that the capital equipment will not be centralized in engineering departments and management, but will be decentralized to the work place. The most efficient use of most information technology is at the work place, and for a variety of reasons. One is you've got to debug it. The other thing that we're learning is that every piece of equipment is idiosyncratic. You therefore have to get the feel of it. You have to have the synergistic and symbiotic relationship between those workers and those machines in order to detect problems, in order to make improvements in those technologies. If you don't have the people on the job with command of the technology, a minor problem can become a major problem, because machines don't have judgment. They can't see the process messing up. One of the advantages of this technology is that it makes it possible to have short runs, and to customize. If you customize you must have people who can pay attention to the customer and pay attention to how the work is going, and therefore prevent defects. If you have short runs, you're not going to be able to recoup your losses by amortizing a large number of units over high fixed costs. All of this, therefore, puts a premium on people and technology at the point of production.

Incentive System. The final thing that you need for a world class management system is an incentive system that achieves what you want. I can't stress that too much. It's amazing how many of our institutions have no explicit incentive systems. There seems to be no understanding of the nature of implicit and explicit incentive systems, and therefore people are always surprised with the outcomes. You get what you pay for, what you reward, and that ordinarily is what you measure. If you don't want to reward it, don't measure it. You can't be like universities, a prime example of a perverse incentive system. They say they want you to be a good teacher. My experience is that if you win a teaching award it might not cause you too much damage, but it's not going to do you a lot of good either, because what they want is not what they say they want. They want publications and research, and they don't pay a lot of attention to teaching. Therefore they don't get it. If you don't reward it, you're not likely to get it. Our school systems are the same way. Many of our public school systems face obsolescence for the same reason that General Motors was obsolete. They're geared to a different era than the one we are in now. It's not surprising, when you look at our incentive system. *Public Agenda* reported a couple of years ago that only 9 percent of the American workers saw a connection between improving productivity and their personal welfare. Fifty-three percent of them said their managers weren't interested in productivity. Ninety-three percent of the Japanese workers said they saw some connection. Why? Well, improving productivity did improve their welfare! They had a bonus system that depended on company performance. One of the fears of American workers is that if they become more productive, they will lose their jobs! They can and have lost their jobs when they improved productivity. One, therefore, must pay particular attention to incentive systems. Now what does all this have to say about skills? If we want to be world class we must have people who can deal with change and learn, handle responsibility, help manage (if we are going to have a participative system), and help with quality control.

Required Worker Characteristics. All of this means the following: First, you need to have people who can learn, and that is very important. We don't do much systematic instruction in colleges, universities, and even in schools. We need to have people who know how to analyze information, because most of these workers are going to be information workers. Workers also need to be able to deal with abstractions, which is a problem for a lot of Americans. We have been a pragmatic people. We've learned mainly by observation. Much of what you need to know today cannot be seen. You can't see why light is coming into this room. You have to know something about the theory of electricity. You can't see what's happening on a megachip. If we are going to be at the leading edge of technology before it gets standardized, we have to be creative. Creativity is, by definition, an abstraction; it is that which can only be seen in the mind's eye.

Assembly line people do routine work. They are told to put the blue wire to the blue wire and the red wire to the red wire, but they are not asked to figure out why this thing is not working and what needs to be done to make it work. It's predictable that in the future people will be paid more according to what they know, not just what they do, so the knowledge to be able to do the right thing is terribly important.

We have got to be able to deal with ambiguity, which is another place where we have not done a good job. We always have to look in the back of the book to find the answer. Well, in life there's no back of the book, and a lot of times, no answers. So you have to do the best you can. I used to tell my staff that perfection was not one of their options. We must, therefore, figure out what is the best thing that we can do with the information we have at the time. That is what you really must teach students. People also have to be able to communicate with precision. The importance of mathematics is partly the habit of thought that you acquire, and partly the substantive use that you make of it. People are going to have to handle authority, if I am correct in assuming that future viable enterprises must have more participative work forces. I believe that strongly. This means we must have people who can handle authority. That requires different skills than working all by yourself.

Reforming Public Policy Making. Now, people will quickly say, "What does all of this have to say about school reform?" School reform is a necessary but insufficient condition for a world class economy. We need to reform the schools; we need to adopt the same kind of management systems in schools as in other enterprises. You can go down the list and recognize that those things need to be done in the schools. You could say, then, is school reform sufficient? We have people who say that learning systems aren't going to solve the problem. I agree with that, but you're not going to deal with any of the rest of these problems if we have second or third class schools. If people come into on-the-job learning systems with inadequate preparation, they are going to have trouble.

So I believe fully that one of our most competitive disadvantages is not our schools or our private management systems. It is our public policy. Our public policy puts American producers at a bigger disadvantage than any of the rest of these things. Our policies cause us to have high cost money and uncertainty. The net after-tax cost of money in Japan between 1974 and 1984 according to Data Research, Inc. was virtually zero. In the United States it was 5.3 percent, because we have a high interest rate policy. If industry is increasing by capital incentives, that puts us at a serious disadvantage.

There are few policy surprises to Japanese business, because they help make the policies. They don't follow our practices where somebody makes the policy and surprises you with it. You know we have a lot of professionals trying to figure out what the Federal Reserve is going to do. In a democracy that strikes me as a strange way to do business. There are no surprises like that in the Japanese system. If you want to test that proposition I'll put the following question to you: What good does it do you to be an American businessperson? What do you get that Japanese (or any other foreign businessperson) working in this country wouldn't also have? Now unless you know an awful lot about the intricacies of defense procurement, you can't tell me anything. And yet, you get a lot of trouble, you get a lot of uncertainty, lack of consensus regulation, and the rest. Reforming our learning systems will not solve the problem.

Conclusion. People sometimes say, "But do we really have to have a world class learning system?" Can't we just have some educated elites? That is one of the attitudes that stand in the way of developing a world class educational system. There are several sub-attitudes that cause great trouble. The first is what we believe causes educational achievement. American mothers have been tested and they are likely to believe it's innate ability. If you ask Japanese mothers what causes educational achievement, they say, "hard work," which is the right answer. There's hardly a more elitist idea than that educational achievement is the result of innate ability.

The second attitudinal problem is that we are mainly concerned about schooling, not education. We also view education and learning systems as costs, not investments, in spite of all the evidence about their high yield.

Finally, we believe we can get by with this kind of educated elite and not have education be pervasive. The reason this is so important is that people are either going to be assets or liabilities. One of the things that Ted Schultz demonstrated is that educated, trained, healthy, motivated people are an almost unlimited asset. The reverse of that is also the case; uneducated, unmotivated, untrained, unhealthy people can be serious liabilities. If you restate the proposition, the single most important thing we need to do, if we're going to be competitive world class players, is to make much heavier investments in our people and create world class systems within which they can work, learn, and think.

12

Cost Containment

Carl Reichardt, CEO, Wells Fargo Bank

Utah has special historical significance for Wells Fargo. Wells Fargo arrived in this state in 1865, with an office in Salt Lake City. Those were the days when Wells Fargo was not only a bank; it was also an express company and operated a network of stagecoach lines.

Utah was one of the few places outside our home state of California where we offered both banking and express services. One of our proudest traditions was chronicled in a pioneer Utah newspaper in 1868, which commented on the dependability of the company's stagecoach operations. The paper reported, "We were informed that the stage was due at three o'clock. The hands of the clock had no sooner indicated the hour of three, than the stage drew up to the door, punctual to the minute."

We use our history very actively in our marketing programs at Wells Fargo, and one of our current slogans is: "We deliver — on time, every time." Well, at least we try.

Where Is Banking Headed? I was asked to talk with you today about cost containment, something which has become a Wells Fargo hallmark and which influences virtually all of our actions. But, in a sense, cost containment is a "catch-all" phrase that relates to a whole lot of other business issues, such as productivity and competitiveness that are much on people's minds today. So I would like to discuss the issues facing banking and finance in a broader sense.

As all of you well know, the last several years have not been dull for banking in America. Banking is in the throes of a major shake-up and shake-out. The 20th century philosopher, Yogi Berra, who was also known as a catcher for the New York Yankees, once said, "If you don't know where you're going, you might end up someplace else." I'm afraid we sometimes look like an industry that doesn't know where it's headed.

We've had to deal with crisis and upheaval, ranging from Third World debt to the largest number of bank failures in the last 50 years. We have often generated unflattering headlines. We have shown little unity as an industry.

As a result of the recent debacle in the stock market, however, we have been joined in the tank by other segments of the financial industry — brokerages and investment bankers, to name two. And compared to the fiasco on Wall Street, banking suddenly looks like a paragon of stability.

Any crisis as dramatic as the stock market crash always results in agonizing reappraisals and a lot of finger pointing. The following are some headlines generated by the crash. Try to figure out who did what to whom.

- "Market Volatility: Who is the Culprit?"
- "Overseas Decline is the Culprit."
- "Program Trading Played Role in Plunge, SEC Chief Says."
- "In the Aftermath of Crash, Many Ask if SEC Chief Is Up to His New Post."
- "The Market to Washington: Wake Up."
- "A Free Market Failure."
- "Too Many Regulators Spoil the Markets."

The wild gyrations in the stock market that followed the so-called "meltdown" on October 19 have caused some concern that the economy is unraveling, just as it did in 1929. I, for one, do not subscribe to that theory.

Yet a crisis such as this almost always leads to over-reaction and hand-wringing. We have already had calls for overhauling the market and imposing stricter rules and regulations. As the latest issue of *Fortune* magazine points out, we now need to be wary of regulators who may want to fix too much. The urge to regulate and re-regulate is always strong.

Many of the banking industry's problems stem, at least in part, from the fact that we are adjusting to a deregulated environment. As a result of deregulation, we are undergoing a very significant restructuring, which will change the nature of banking and determine who the key players are likely to be in the future.

Bank Restructuring. What's happening to us, as an industry, is not unique. A recent article in *Business Week* described the restructuring process that is affecting U.S. business as a whole. As a result, companies in many industries are taking a new, tougher approach to business in their efforts to improve efficiency, productivity and competitiveness at home and overseas.

Cost-containment is one of their strategies. They're cutting costs to the bone, selling marginal businesses, closing inefficient operations, and reducing staff. But they've also become innovators in product development, marketing, and distribution.

Banking is following the same road. Most of us have recognized we must become more efficient and productive to survive in today's harsh and competitive environment. A recent report by the American Bankers Association illustrates the upheaval in our industry.

- The number of unprofitable banks in the U.S. rose from 750 in 1981 to 2,700 in 1986.
- In 1975, banks had nearly 40 percent of the market for financial assets but, by the end of 1985, market share had fallen to 32 percent.
- Between 1980 and 1985, commercial banks' annual growth rate for assets was around 8 percent, the lowest for all financial institutions. (Highest was mutual funds with about 32 percent annual growth in assets.)

Acquisition of Crocker. It was these trends and our efforts to deal with them that led to Wells Fargo's cost cutting efforts a few years ago and, eventually, to our acquisition of Crocker National Corporation in 1986. That acquisition truly was an exercise in cost rationalization.

We recognized, when we looked at Wells Fargo and Crocker, that both banks had similar operations, goals, and strategies. By combining the two banks and eliminating a wide range of redundant or overlapping operations, enormous economies of scale could be achieved. We realized that if we could operate the two banks as efficiently as we had run Wells Fargo alone, a lot of money could be saved and, in the process, greater earnings generated.

Since the acquisition, we have successfully consolidated overlapping branches, and reduced the number of offices from 621 to 442. We have combined automated teller machine networks and data processing systems, centralized many operations, and sold off or closed business lines which did not fit in with our strategies. We have done this with a minimal loss of business in our targeted markets. Our core deposits, for example, total around $30 billion, just as they did at the time of the acquisition. Our expense reduction goal at the time of the acquisition was to cut some $240 million annually from the combined company's expenses within two years. We are on target to realize this savings by the end of 1987.

To give you some idea of what expense control can mean in the banking industry, let's look at one measure of cost efficiency — the ratio of non-interest expense to average assets. Before the acquisition, we were running at a number of 3.30 percent. We were just about the lowest-cost producer in our marketplace. After the Crocker acquisition, that number went to 3.64 percent — 34 basis points higher. If you assume that each basis point represents nine cents a share after taxes, multiply those 34 basis points by nine cents, and you can see the sort of leverage that is involved in expense control in such an acquisition. At the end of the third quarter of this year, we had that ratio down to 3.42 percent. We have made good progress, but we still have a way to go.

Sick Banks and Savings and Loans. The tremendous restructuring taking place in banking involves far more than acquisitions and mergers. Banks are being allowed to fail if they cannot adapt to this tough world of deregulation. There have been 156 bank failures so far this year, compared to 138 for all of 1986. As a result of the failures over the past several years, the industry is purging itself of weaker elements. Not all sickly banks are being padlocked, however. Some of them are being patched together and preserved by unusual, dramatic rescues.

Look, for instance at the plan put together by former Chicago banker Bob Abboud, to take over failing First City Bancorp in Texas. As part of the rescue effort, Abboud's group is pulling together $500 million, and $970 million will be tossed into the rescue pot by the Federal Deposit Insurance Corporation (FDIC).

The restructuring of banking is also bound to be affected by a proposal from the Federal Reserve Board that would allow bank holding companies to acquire healthy savings and loans associations. We used to be permitted only to look at the real "sickos." The new rule is aimed at encouraging banks to inject new capital and new management into the troubled savings and loan industry. The thrift industry could use a lot of both.

The Federal Savings and Loan Insurance Corporation (FSLIC) is almost in as bad shape as some of the thrifts it insures. The agency has chalked up operating losses of $1.3 billion by taking control of failing savings and loans and allowing them to continue to operate.

What's worse, the General Accounting Office in Washington has reported that 45 institutions taken over by the FSLIC are now in poorer shape than when the agency began taking them over in mid-1985. The FSLIC is seeking to raise $11 billion in new capital. Unfortunately, about 20 percent of the nation's 3,100 savings and loans are basket cases, and the head of the FSLIC has said that the new capital still won't be enough to solve the problems of the savings and loan industry. So, until the market crises of recent weeks, banking and thrifts were the sick sisters of the larger financial services industry.

Adding to Reserve for Third World Loans. An overriding issue for major banks continues to be Third World debt — one of the most persistent and serious problems we have had to face. There had been some wishful thinking that perhaps over time the problem of Third World debt would magically go away. But last February, when Brazil suspended interest payments on $67 billion of medium- and long-term commercial bank debt, that hope was pretty well shattered.

As you know, in the second quarter major American banks, including Wells Fargo, made large special additions to their loan loss reserves. In effect, we have acknowledged that a substantial amount of Third World debt may well be uncollectible. Over all, the 13,000 banks insured by the Federal Deposit Insurance Corporation added a total of $21.2 billion to reserves for bad loans in the second quarter. This resulted in a second quarter loss totaling $10.6 billion for the U.S. banking industry — the worst industry performance in well over half a century. The second quarter industry loss wiped out a record first quarter income of $5.3 billion, which was posted even though banks had added more than $4 billion to their loan loss reserves for that quarter.

Third World debt problems will not go away soon. But in the five years since the magnitude of a possible disaster became apparent, there has been an on-going effort by all sides to solve the problem rationally. And that five years has bought the banks time to strengthen their reserves.

Hopeful Signs. Some recent statistics in the *American Banker* indicate banks are showing tentative signs of being on the mend. According to the publication, the median bank had net chargeoffs of 0.30 percent of loans and leases in the first half of this year, down from 0.35 percent in the first half of 1986. Non-performing loans dropped to a median of 2.18 percent of loans and leases in the first half of 1987 from 2.36 percent last year. Finally, average loss reserves rose to 1.34 percent of loans and leases form 1.23 percent, a significant strengthening in our ability to deal with problem loans.

It's not pleasant to have to set aside huge amounts of money to cover potentially bad loans, but the action by the banks has had some positive results. The favorable reaction generated by the increased loan loss reserves helped drive up the market value of the nation's largest banks in the second quarter.

According to another survey by the *American Banker*, the 50 banks with the largest market capitalizations increased their aggregate value by 2.7 percent, to more than $100 billion in the second quarter, compared with a value of just under $98 billion at the end of the first quarter of 1987. So there are some improving signals amid all the turmoil. If the restructuring process rids the industry of its walking wounded, so much better for the industry and the customers it serves.

As the restructuring continues, I think banks will have to face the fact that keeping costs under control is a never-ending process. We will constantly have to find new ways of improving productivity and efficiency. As far as I am concerned, this means getting back to basics and sticking with what you do best. Even Wall Street firms are now picking up the cry. Just last week, a former Dean Witter executive said of the brokerage industry, "I see a return to basics, in exposure and products." The president of the Securities Industry Association said of his industry, "There will be a greater evaluation of profitability. Firms will say to themselves, 'Should I really be in this business?'"

It's a shame we all have to re-learn these lessons every generation or two — usually with a crisis as the impetus. But the lesson seems to be hitting home once again. I think this can only benefit American business and industry. Banks and other firms which survive the current turmoil will be stronger and better managed institutions. They will know where they are going, and will not, as Yogi Berra would say, end up "some place else."

PART II

Human Dimensions
of Productivity

13

Constraints and Opportunities Faced by Women Managers

Mylle Bell, Director of Corporate Planning, BellSouth

I appreciate the opportunity to take part in this seminar. Judging from this year's agenda as well as those of past years, Utah State University must surely be unequalled in your thorough treatment of human resource issues. I'm honored to share the podium with so many distinguished business and academic leaders.

My topic is the constraints and opportunities faced by women managers in today's business environment. When preparing my remarks, I asked my corporate research staff to do a literature search on the topic of women in business. They brought me quite a pile of articles, dozens of them, going back over several years. Some were from general business periodicals, like *Business Week* and *Fortune*. Some came from women's magazines. Others were in specialized publications on management, marketing, and various other business disciplines. After plowing through most of these articles, I came away with two impressions.

First, there isn't much of a consensus about how well — or poorly — women managers are faring in the business world. In fact, I found that the same statistic — the percentage of all management made up of women — had been used in support of both sides of the argument. On the one hand, women aren't progressing fast enough in corporate America, and on the other hand, we're doing very well, thank you.

My second main impression from my reading was that the question of business opportunities for women is too often viewed mainly in the context of male attitudes. The good will, or lack of it, on the part of male executives is assumed to be the dominant influence on advancement prospects for talented women.

Well, I'm not so sure. I want to talk about several other factors that I am convinced are at least as important, and becoming more important all the time.

As a preface, let me tell you briefly about my personal experience as a woman in business. I've never felt discriminated against in a business setting because I was a woman, at BellSouth, and doing business all over the world as president of BellSouth International. Nor was I at GE, before my BellSouth days. (By the way, one of my jobs at GE was running a plant that built locomotives. Some people argue that heavy industry is one of the last hold-outs against female management. I've got news for them. Those locomotives were about as heavy as anything gets.)

I don't mean to deny that prejudiced attitudes toward women managers are out there. But it has been my good fortune not to be damaged by them. I believe strongly that the experience that I've had is closer to the modern-day norm than are the stereotyped images, male or female, still hanging on from a bygone era.

I see three major influences at work. That is, three major influences are increasing the opportunities for women to enter management ranks and advance as high as talent and drive allow. The full force of these three influences has not yet been felt, not by a long shot.

First, we exist in a tumultuous business environment characterized by rapid and often unpredictable changes. Second, certain demographic trends will manifest themselves between now and the early years of the 21st century. And third, pervasive changes are occurring in the nature of work itself, and especially in the roles of managers.

Business Environment Creates Opportunities for Women. Let me expand on each of these for just a few minutes and describe the impact I see them having on women in the workplace.

A combination of elements — technology, the emergence of a global economy, gyrations in the financial markets, explosive growth of the service sector, regulatory upheaval, takeovers and corporate restructuring — are all part of the dizzying swirl that characterizes much of today's business climate. And it seems to me that as the swirl gets bigger and faster, women tend to rise higher.

This very point was made in a piece last summer in *Fortune*. The article laid out a strong case that women move highest and suffer fewer gender-related obstacles in fast-paced industries where the rules are changing or have never been written at all. There are a number of excellent examples; computers, financial services, telecommunications. In fact, the industry I know best — telecommunications — illustrates the point perfectly.

The divestiture of the Bell System was one of the most far-reaching events in the history of commercial enterprise. Almost all the ingredients of that "swirl" I mentioned were present — deregulation, a revolution in technology, the creation virtually overnight of huge new corporate entities, a marketplace that was fast becoming global in scope. From a gigantic and slow-to-change monopoly, American telecommunications has transferred itself in four years into one of the country's most dynamic and innovative industries. The old Bell System gave way to a completely restructured and reoriented AT&T, plus seven telecommunication holding companies with the muscle and heft to compete in any market, not to mention the entrepreneurial opportunities all this activity created for aggressive niche players.

To meet the challenges of this demanding environment, companies like BellSouth, AT&T, US West, GTE, and others have eagerly rewarded talent, desire, and commitment, whatever the source, of either gender, of any race, color, or creed. Last June, *Business Week* ran a list of "Fifty Women to Watch," which really nails down this point. Many of the companies for which these top executives work are technology-oriented — computers, telecommunications, biotechnology, and information systems. A large number are in banking and financial services, which also have been subject to enormous change in recent years. And still others are corporations that, for a variety of specific reasons, are in the process of remaking themselves from within, RJR/Nabisco, Navistar, and Allegis, for example.

The message is clear: dynamic, fast-paced business environments create the best opportunities for capable woman.

Demographic Trends Shape Opportunities for Women. The second influence I want to discuss is demographic trends. For the past two decades in the United States, the female work force has grown rapidly, both in absolute number and as a percentage of all workers. The rate of increase is slowing down now, because a "max-out" level is close at hand.

Today about 55 percent of American women participate in the labor force, up from 33 percent in 1948. Participation should keep rising to a cap of between 58 and 60 percent, probably near the end of the century. So the main influx of women into the workplace has already happened, leading to something of a steady-state condition in which the presence of women in large numbers, and at all levels within a company, will no longer be at all remarkable.

This slow-down of women coming into the labor pool coincides with a general decline in the growth of the American work force, stemming from the maturing of the Baby Boom. From 1966 through 1986, the work force in this country grew an average of 2 percent per year, a tremendous rate of increase. But in the two decades ahead of us, the work force should grow by no more than 75 percent a year. Coupled with severe problems in American education, which unfortunately time doesn't permit me to go into, this trend will create serious worker and manager shortages, and thus will open up the doors of opportunity wider than ever for skilled and ambitious women.

There's one more demographic factor at work which should be mentioned. I'm not an actuary, but it's not hard to figure out that a progressively aging population will mean relatively more retirees. Even with later mandatory retirements, the work force will shrink more rapidly than we are used to. Some countries are already grappling with this problem. In Finland and Sweden, where population growth is virtually nil, the government has taken some interesting steps. Part of their answer has been to actively encourage women to enter the work force, or to keep working, after starting a family. Finland, for instance, guarantees up to six months of maternity leave at 90-percent salary. The Swedish government also furnishes day care and requires that a mother receive a full day's pay for no more than six hours of work until the child reaches eight years of age.

I don't offer these policies as recommendations, but rather as an example of how responses to changing demographics are shaping opportunities for working women elsewhere in the world.

Changing Work and Roles of Women Managers. The last influence I'll mention is the changing nature of work and the changing role of the manager. Several of the conditions I cited earlier as causing a tumultuous business environment are also placing significant new skill demands on managers. Among these are information technologies and the evolution of a global economy. Interestingly, these two very different circumstances call for many of the same workplace capabilities: the ability to analyze and synthesize, creative skills, adaptability to constant change, openness to new ideas, and, as BellSouth's Chairman, John Clendenin, says, "the ability to turn information into insight."

As managers, women must demonstrate special skills that dovetail with these demands of the modern workplace. Consensus building is one of the most important of these skills. Autocratic, highly structured corporate environments do not promote top performance in today's business climate. An accelerating trend in large companies is problem-solving by task force, bringing together a temporary team to deal with a specific, finite situation. To be effective, the task force approach means that the group must willingly move to a common ground from which to take action, in other words, consensus building.

Women managers also are adept at encouraging worker participation, another skill that meshes well with contemporary workplace realities. Some companies seeking to change their corporate culture, Navistar, for example, have promoted women managers for this very reason — to break out of a rigid, hierarchical mentality and get people engaged in more than doing a repetitive job.

So these are the three primary influences: the business environment, demographics, and the changing nature of work and management. Together, they are molding new opportunities for women in business that no remnants of outdated attitudes can hold back.

One final comment about all that literature I spent so much time reading — there seems to me to be an excessive amount of paper and ink devoted to who will be the first female CEO of a major company, and when it will happen. When the day comes, it will be front-page news, as it should be. But in the meantime, the more important news is the growing cadre of qualified candidates, the even larger group of rising women managers behind them, and the across-the-board gains women have made in every type of industry and profession.

Today some 36 percent of American executives and managers are women, a 50-percent gain in the past 10 years. Since 1970, women practicing law have quadrupled, architects and computer scientists have doubled, and doctors have increased by 80 percent. And we haven't even talked about women entrepreneurs. One of every three businesses is started by a woman. These numbers will climb as the three factors I've mentioned develop more momentum.

Conclusion: More Opportunities than Constraints. If it occurs to you that I've talked more about opportunities than constraints, you're right. I honestly see more opportunities. The constraints I see are the delicate balancing of career and family, and some residual resistance to female leadership. As we've seen, there are powerful forces at work to mitigate the latter. And, albeit slowly, many companies are moving toward creative solutions to accommodate the family responsibilities of women employees, management and non-management alike. The value of excellent management talent is too great to do otherwise. By the time students here at Utah State are hitting their career stride, I suspect that a seminar such as this one may no longer need to treat the subject of women managers as a special topic.

14

Women in Management: View from Adolph Coors Company

Rosa M. Bunn, Director of Community Affairs, Adolph Coors

I noticed in some of the publicity for this seminar that speakers in the previous four years have included famous economists, pundits, and prognosticators. I probably don't fit the mold of any of these, but I am very pleased to be here because this topic of women in management is very near and dear to my heart. Like you, I also appreciate the importance of education and of examining issues. My responsibilities at Coors include education programs designed to improve employee economic awareness and quality of life. I think it is a tribute and a benefit to all of you that the student-driven Partners Program here at Utah State is a model for other efforts to expand the horizons of students and business leaders.

Changing Industry's Impact on Women. I have 20 years of experience with Coors, a closely held company in a male-dominated — almost macho — industry, which qualifies me to speak on this topic. In my two decades with Coors, I have worked in such diverse areas as human resources, ceramics manufacturing, and public relations. Most of these years have been spent in management roles and working for men. Although I have faced numerous constraints and challenges along the way, the opportunities have also been great.

When I gave up my role as full-time mother and homemaker 20 years ago, I had no idea what I was getting myself into. In 1967, I re-entered the business world not because I was pursuing a career, but because we were broke and needed the money. Back then, there was no women's movement and few female role models in business. Adolph Coors Company was a small regional brewer distributing one brand of all-natural beer in a handful of western states, including Utah. Today, Coors is the nation's fourth largest brewer, selling six brands in markets that stretch from coast to coast and to Canada and Japan.

The beer industry was and is a male-dominated industry but, in recent years, women have been infiltrating the upper and lower echelons. As our economy has moved from an industrial society to an information and service society, the brewing industry has also changed. This has created more opportunities in information-related areas, such as public relations, sales, marketing, law, purchasing, and real estate. Right now, women make up 21 percent of the work force at Coors, the highest in the industry. In the future, we will see many more women managers not only in the information-related areas, but also in production. For example, one of my daughters is a production manager at Coors.

Challenges Facing Women Executives. I'm sure that you are all familiar with the challenges that many women have faced trying to break into management, and especially into the executive suite. Some of these constraints have come from the business world, while others come from women themselves. Not too long ago, women were excluded from management by questionable stereotypes and the "good-ol'-boy" network. Back then, it was widely accepted that women were unstable, indecisive, temperamental, and manipulative and were not good team players because they had never played football. Being from Denver, I know how important football can be, but let's be serious. Along with these stereotypes, the good-ol'-boy networks that excluded women and minorities have faded in most industries.

Meanwhile, some women have helped to create their own barriers to the executive suite. We have, in a sense, held ourselves back by our choice of priorities. Many of us have chosen to raise a family or support our husband's career full-time. Often, this decision is made when men are making important career moves. Then, we usually must start over again upon re-entering the work force. Other women who stayed in the business world accepted lower wages in exchange for flexible or shorter hours, limited travel, or other compensation. In other words, the traditional family structure constitutes a career setback for many women. These are choices that women frequently make willingly, although many elements of society encourage us to make them. I have often said that I would have been a vice president by now if only I had a supportive little housewife at home to help me.

Significant Gains by Women in Management. In spite of these constraints, there are growing numbers of opportunities out there. Women are entering management — and even upper management — in record numbers. A third of all management positions are now held by women. Gains are especially noticeable in the fast-growing information and service industries. For example, approximately 44 percent of the officials and 53 percent of the professionals employed by the nation's 14,000 banks in 1985 were women, according to the American Bankers Association. That is up from 26 percent of officials and 32 percent of professionals a decade earlier.

Although women hold less than 5 percent of the highest-ranking executive positions, some industries are showing greater numbers of women at the top. For example, more than one-fifth of companies in the health services (at 23 percent) and social services (at 21 percent) industries are run by women. Male attitudes toward women are improving, too, with much greater acceptance of women bosses today than only 20 years ago.

Many women not willing to wait to work their way up the corporate ladder have found that the quickest way to the top is to own their own businesses. There are now 3.5 million female entrepreneurs in the United States. This number represents more than a quarter (27 percent) of all businesses in the nation.

These gains will continue as more women continue to enter the labor force and place a higher priority on their careers. The U.S. Bureau of Labor Statistics estimates that 59 percent of all women will be working by the year 1995, up from 34 percent in 1959. As these women gain experience, a larger number will reach the top levels of management.

Female Skills and Free Market Economy. Some of you may be surprised to learn that our free market economy is also working to help women overcome work bias. Companies have discovered that selecting only male candidates for leadership roles mean ignoring about half of the best talent available. Over half of all college degrees now go to women, and businesses that do not take advantage of this vast resource are finding that they cannot compete against those businesses that do actively recruit women.

Equally important, as our economy comes to be based more and more on information and services, the management skills that women have traditionally possessed will become increasingly valuable. The traits that in the past were discounted as feminine weaknesses — such as sympathy, creativity, sensitivity and flexibility — will become more valuable. In this new economy, the emphasis will be on getting the best out of people.

I'm sure you would agree that, even today, men and women are generally raised and socialized differently. Women are usually taught to be more concerned with people and with feelings. They rely on intuition more. I also found from my own experiences raising four children that motherhood teaches some skills that are valuable in business — including the arts of compromise, conciliation, and listening, not to mention efficiency and time management. As anyone who has raised children knows, motherhood is also good training for crisis management. All of these abilities will become more important in the future, bringing more management opportunities for women.

Women Must Have Can-Do Attitude. What does it take for an individual woman to get ahead in business, to enter the ranks of management? More and more, it will take the same things it takes a man. For the most part, I think that being a woman will be a factor only if you want it to be. Whether you are male or female, there will always be individuals that present challenges to you. Like everyone else, you have to find a way to deal with these individuals. If, on the other hand, you start out thinking, "I'm a woman and this is going to be difficult," then it will be difficult.

Many people debate the topic of whether Americans are truly born equal. Whether we are talking about women, men, you, or me, the literal answer must be, "No." Our nation's founding fathers meant that we are all born with equal opportunity. They were not referring to skills or assets. We can make the most of our brief time on this earth by concentrating on the opportunities presented us, rather than the constraints. Many of our limits are self-imposed. We must cast off these limits and get going. Over the years, I have just thought about what I wanted to accomplish, went after that, and not worried about being a woman. I don't think that being a woman has hindered me. My advice to women, when they ask me if it's tough to break into management, has always been that it's tough for anybody who doesn't put his or her mind to it. However, if you set goals and objectives, have at least average intelligence, and have the stamina to work hard, you can be whatever you want to be.

Need for Role Model and Plan. One thing that I have found important is to have a mentor or role model. Most successful individuals have known someone, a very special someone, or perhaps several individuals who have helped to change the very direction of their lives. Personally, I have had several of these special people in my life, as have most other women and men. They can teach us many of the things we need to survive in the business world, whether you are in a small or large company. You need someone to help you who has actually been there, and then you must be willing to learn from this person to grow professionally. By the way, you won't find this type of education in a text book.

Beyond that, I think it is very important to have a plan to help you get where you want to go. Here's a simple plan that will work for anyone, man or woman. I call it the three keys to success:

First, form a clear vision or picture of exactly what you want to accomplish. This is the same thing as setting a clear goal. Be as specific as possible. Just like a ship with no rudder, we will drift aimlessly unless we establish a direction. Be sure to set specific deadlines for your goals. Decide where you want to be and when.

Once your goals are clear, you should write them down. This helps them to crystallize in your mind and remain clear. It also helps you to remember them.

Second, believe that you can and will succeed. In other words, keep a positive attitude. Form the habit of believing in yourself and your ability to reach your goals. By filling your mind with the positive, you leave no room for the negative. Many believe that, by controlling our thoughts, we can control our destiny. Henry Ford once observed, "Whether you believe you *can* do a thing or believe you *cannot*, you are right."

Third, begin now and stay with it. This is the most difficult step, but it is also the most important, since this is where you get results. Once you have your objective, and you truly believe that you can reach it, it is time for action. The most thoughtfully planned and worthy goals are useless if no action is taken to reach them. To be successful, you must keep in mind that "success is a marathon, not a sprint."

In conclusion, I urge you to use these three keys to start you on your way toward reaching your goals. Have a plan and enlist the help of others who have been there. Although challenges will still arise, stay with your plan. By keeping your goals clearly in mind, by shutting out negative thoughts, and by persisting, obstacles merely become minor detours on your road to success!

15

Successful Women at Transamerica

Patricia J. Blair, Corporate Personnel, Transamerica

I'd like to talk about successful women at Transamerica and use the commonplace apple and orange comparison to opportunities and constraints affecting women managers at Transamerica and any other environment.

"Ah," you tactfully say to yourself. "She's been too long in California." But, aren't we at this conference to acquire "tools" to help us become more effective individual performers and, ultimately, more effective managers? That's how the apple/orange idea popped into, or should I say, "grew" in my mind. As with men and women — both are similar in overall size and shape, yet attractively different at a single glance. Both are good for us and can be adapted easily to various uses. They can even be mixed together — each retaining its own distinctive uniqueness, but enhancing the end product. Both are easily transported, stored, prepared, and utilized. The orange may take more time and a bit more preparation but that does not affect its value or multi-purpose usefulness. Both are readily found in the marketplace and similarly marketed, but are taken for granted by consumers. Consumers are often biased toward one or the other, a bias which may prevent them from enjoying or appreciating the ultimate benefits gained through experience with both. This analogy suggests that to become successful, we have to overcome learned or assumed biases about people, too.

At Transamerica, the skills, traits, education, and experience proven most successful are those most closely matching our culture. We have a highly educated staff with specialized experience. Educational backgrounds and experience in specific industries and disciplines provide a common "language" and put people on more equal footing. At best, this "language" can give an inside track, at worst, it places an individual on the track and that sure can't hurt.

Before moving on, let me immediately offer one valuable tool. Read David Peoples' book *Presentations Plus*. Mr. Peoples, of IBM, states that by becoming merely a good presenter in a world of poor presenters, you will become too valuable to keep in your present job at your present pay! Think about it. Presentation skills are orange pips and apple seeds: that is, an essential part of the whole.

Now, a word or two concerning constraints in general. In very broad terms, constraints may be increased or minimized by your career choices, by the size of the company, its culture, its history, and its population mix. Any or all of these factors can either provide or inhibit opportunities. Therefore, it pays to put serious up-front time into research before you select a field of interest, accept a new job, or change companies.

Impact of Structure and Culture on Career Opportunities. Corporate structure and culture are key elements which substantially impact career pathing and future potential. Transamerica Corporation, for example, is very positive toward raising women upward, but because the corporation itself is small — less than 100 employees — opportunities are fewer than in a larger company, such as Transamerica Occidental, one of our larger subsidiaries with a population nearer 5,000. Our chairman and chief executive officer has a wife and several daughters who are politically conscious and active in business and cultural affairs — all of whom have sound general education backgrounds. As a result, our CEO is more open to and involved in supporting women and providing avenues of growth. He has gained a comfort level in working with women and has developed respect for their intelligence, talent, leadership, and work ethic.

Folks in our company generally do the job first and the title and rewards come later. That is true for both men and women. That process can take months or years. Once an official promotion occurs, the "proving yourself" process begins again. Management expectations automatically escalate, even if you have been doing the job. In addition, an individual may come into a job with a certain established reputation in one area (computer skills, for instance). Credibility does not necessarily follow over into the new area. Management keeps testing, evaluating, and increasing the level of acceptable performance.

At this stage I'd like to draw my parallel to Murphy's Law which is, "Managements' expectation is that it will take you 1 percent to 10 percent of the time it actually does take to do a project, and they don't want to hear justifications or excuses."

Success Depends on Goals and Achievements. What does success look like? Success is a fluid concept reshaping and reforming itself from many perspectives. Success may be defined differently by self, family, peers, management and measured by achievements, status, or rewards. Success depends upon our personal goals linked to our achievements. Identifying the steps necessary to guarantee doing the right things to achieve success must tie in with personal goals, establishing checkpoints along the way. The only person ultimately responsible for your own career is you.

Peer groups, not unexpectedly, tend to define success by more visible, tangible signals — titles, office versus non-office, various perks, and status symbols. Management may view success more selfishly (or should I say narrowly). Bottomline, are we doing what it takes to make management look good? If we are on target, the tangible rewards should follow. As you know, the trick can be to correctly identify the target.

How Success Is Viewed by Women Managers. Given that success, like beauty, is in the eye of the beholder, what does it take at Transamerica? I mentioned earlier that our CEO has about the same comfort level in dealing with women as with men because of exposure, education, and positive experiences over time. He has learned to value the differences between men and women while appreciating the similarities which contribute to successful business operations.

Preparing for today, I chatted with several Transamerica women at different levels of management for their insights and viewpoints. The following are highlights of what these women had to say.

In addition to talking management's language, it is essential that women play the game as good sports — as men would. What does that mean? Well, the obvious points are no tears, no "that isn't fair," no pouting, or hostility showing if things go wrong, or simply don't go your way. The less obvious point is that even the most enlightened male managers still unconsciously assume that men will do whatever it takes — working nights, weekends, giving up vacations, free time — while women still have to prove that they will (if, of course, they choose to follow that path. Many cannot or will not).

It is necessary to do so for success at Transamerica for any position over the manager level and the higher you aspire, the greater the time demands. Moving ahead demands flexibility, resiliency, and tenacity accompanied by a good sense of humor (to pull you through all the situations that require the other qualities). Education is highly valued. Graduate degrees are considered important for upward mobility past the manager level.

The differences they perceive between women in line versus staff jobs are noted in the following table:

LINE	STAFF
• Still take longer to get ahead, even with more enlightened management.	• More visible, more easily seen.
• Management still tends to look differently at women.	• Move up more easily.
• Harder work — more a function than a role.	• May be more financially limiting as well as offering narrower career paths.
• Skills often quite different.	
• Takes longer to build trust and credibility.	
• More volatile arena — part of being in the right place at the right time.	

Table 15.1 Women in Line vs. Staff Positions

My apple and orange analogy is not limited to the differences between men and women, but also applies within the sexes. Each of us has our own distinct style, our own "copyrighted" personality which leads me to my last two points on success.

The first is simply — develop your own style. It sounds simple but can be tricky in the face of management push or, worse, wrath. But it is so very important.

- Have personal convictions and stick to your guns.
- Be true to yourself and you will build trust and credibility even if management doesn't agree with you all the time.
- But, choose your convictions and your guns wisely and carefully!
- Be an individual with strengths and convictions within your team. Team members may play equally, but they have different jobs. Even if you are a pain in the tutu at times, if you believe in something, stick to it.

The second point, probably even more important than your style, is that only you can manage your own career and your own experiences. Set goals. Establish checkpoints, then practice. Try to improve. Ask yourself, "How can I do it better next time?" Before starting a project, or when you've been boxed heavily on the ears and nose because it wasn't what they wanted, ask questions of yourself and others so you can do a better job and give them what they want next time.

Practice...
- Practice writing proposals.
- Practice making speeches.
- Practice leading meetings.
- Practice chairing committees.
- Practice becoming a leader.
- Practice becoming successful.

Because... men do tend to practice while many women seem to assume they can do something and not consider the importance of practicing. Thus they are often caught unprepared; caught short in the comparison between men and women.

Profiles of Successful Women. As I earlier remarked, Transamerica has been a good company for providing opportunities for women with a corporate population of under 100. We have:

- One woman senior vice president reporting directly to the CEO.
- Two women vice presidents: one in legal, one in risk management (she began as secretary to a vice president 10 years ago).
- Six women directors in various departments. (Several of whom began in non-management jobs.)

- Ten women managers. (Most of whom have been promoted upward from within the corporation.)

I have worked my way through three Transamerica subsidiaries to the corporation over a period of 22 years in spite of once answering an incoming call from the president of my subsidiary by saying "Transamerica *copulation*" and later, at another subsidiary, destroying (or at least seriously damaging) a relationship between an important field sales vice president and his companion by inquiring of her how she had enjoyed the recent trip to San Francisco with the manager. She smiled sweetly at me and between clenched teeth said, "I have not been to San Francisco in three years." Gulp!

You may be interested in the general profiles of these successful women at Transamerica Corporation:

Vice Presidents and Directors
- Average age is 43 for vice presidents and 39 for directors.
- Education level is up to post-graduate often with specialized credential (such as CPA).
- Tend to be very assertive, very individualistic. Each has her own style of dress which is not necessarily the "dress for success" look (except on board meeting or special high-level meeting days!).
- Often put job before personal lives.
- Technically outstanding in their fields.
- Expect equal treatment.
- Time with Transamerica — three to 25 years.

Managers
- Average age is 40 (oldest 58, youngest 30).
- Education level is undergraduate degrees for most but not all managers. Graduate degrees for some.
- Frequently put job before personal lives but depends upon department and personal goals.

That briefly touches upon structure and culture and their role in career path opportunities, gives you some thoughts about defining success and the importance of goal setting and career managing, how success is viewed at Transamerica through the eyes of its women managers, rounded off with profiles of some of those women.

I'd like to close by reinforcing these two points (or perhaps I should say four points):

1. Practice. Practice. Practice.
2. Find your own style.

Moving from the prosaic to the provocative a moment — remember if you are an orange by nature, training, education, and inclination, you cannot try to become an apple and still remain credible, effective, respected, and above all true to yourself.

And, keep in mind that working toward success might be likened to sex. The preliminaries may prove titillating and the achievement may be satisfying, but unless you have properly planned and prepared yourself, the result may be an unexpected surprise.

16

How Ford's HR Staff Supports Strategic Planning

Raymond H. Johnson, Corporate Employee Development,
Ford Motor Company

I would like to talk about the role of human resources in strategic planning from a corporate, worldwide perspective. I will begin by sharing some interesting facts about Ford Motor Company. Then I will discuss Ford's strategic issues and how the Employee Development Strategy and Planning Office is helping to address those issues. I will conclude my remarks with some implications for the future role of human resources in strategic planning.

First, a few interesting facts about Ford. Did you know that:

- Ford is the second-largest car and truck producer in the world.
- Ford is the second-largest finance company in the world.
- Ford is the second-largest glass company in the United States.
- Ford is the third-largest tractor producer in the world.
- Ford is the seventh-largest U.S. savings and loan.
- Ford is the eighth-largest U.S. steel company.
- Comparing 1979 with 1986, Ford Motor Company, worldwide, sold about the same number of cars, trucks, and tractors, yet earned about three times as much. Net income was $1.17 billion in 1979 and $3.3 billion in 1986.
- As another example of Ford's improving efficiencies, the company's net income in 1986 was up 31 percent from the previous year, but worldwide vehicle sales increased by only 6 percent.

- Ford has reduced its operating costs by about $5 billion since 1979. The break-even point has been reduced by about 40 percent in the North American automotive business since 1980, and by about 20 percent worldwide.
- Quality of Ford Motor Company's 1987 cars is 60 percent better than the 1980 models, continuing a trend that has spanned seven straight years.
- Surveys show that Ford customer satisfaction has improved nearly 11 percent since 1980 from a 6.6 to a 7.3 rating (on a scale of 1 to 10). This reflects improved quality, enhanced value, and a commitment by our dealers to quality customer care after the sale.
- Ford's worldwide productivity (measured in vehicles per employee) was up 46 percent between 1981 and 1986. Over the same period, Toyota's productivity declined 13 percent, Nissan's declined 10 percent, and Honda's improved 4 percent.
- Ford's 1986 profit-sharing payout ($370 million) is believed to be a record for a U.S. company in a single year. The total payout by Ford from 1983 to 1986 ($1.02 billion) also is believed to be a U.S. record and promises to be even better in 1987.
- Ford Motor Credit Company completed its twelfth consecutive year of record profits in 1986, with net income of $611 million. Ford Credit's profits have grown by an average of more than 25 percent annually for the past six years.
- The company's share of the U.S. car and truck market reached 21.2 percent in 1986, up 1.5 points from 19.7 percent in 1981.

In summary, Ford seems to be doing well. However, few executives are complacent about this progress. The order of the day is continuous improvement to prepare ourselves for the increasing challenges ahead. Let's turn now to Ford's corporate strategy, the foundation upon which present and future success depends.

Some Definitions of Strategic Planning Terms. Let me share a few definitions and examples of strategic planning terms used at Ford. This will reduce misunderstanding as I describe Ford's strategic plans.

In case you're wondering, I'm not spilling the beans when I talk about Ford's strategy. What I am about to tell you is already public information. I'm sharing it now as a context for describing the role of human resources in its development and implementation.

Ford's strategies and operating business plans emphasize continued improvements in the fundamentals of our business, building on the lessons learned during the difficult times of the early 1980s

---

DEFINITIONS

Vision is a statement that describes what management wants the company or operation to be. [Example: Ford's *vision* is to be a low-cost producer of the highest quality products and services that provide the best customer value.]

Mission is a statement of the principal activities of a business or an organization. [Example: Ford's *mission* is to be a worldwide leader in automotive and related products and services and in newer industries, such as aerospace, electronics, and financial services.]

Values are the basic motivators for business conduct. [Example: Ford's basic *values* are people, products, and profits.]

Guiding principles are a code of conduct that tells us how to behave toward our customers, our dealers, and our suppliers.

Objectives are specific statements that identify the achievement required to support the mission. Objectives should be specific and measureable, whenever possible, and lead to action.

Strategic direction is the policy and strategy committee's direction on operating concepts — applicable to all businesses.

Operating strategies are approved operating concepts that establish priorities for plans and resource allocation — applicable to the company or an operation.

Plans are actions to implement operating strategies and achieve objectives, including identification or the results of the actions.

Ford's guiding principles are:

- Quality comes first.
- Customers are the focus of everything we do
- Continuous improvement is essential to our success
- Employee involvement is our way of life.
- Dealers and suppliers are our partners.
- Integrity is never compromised.
- Best-in-class quality ratings in major markets.
- Nine percent after-tax return on assets.
- Employee involvement and teamwork at all levels.
- Total quality excellence.
- Cost competitiveness.
- Customer-driven.
- Technology.
- To serve the Asia-Pacific markets, small cars will be sourced from Mazda.
- 1987 budget.
- NAAO product cycle plan.

Table 16.1 Strategic Planning Terms

and the successes of recent years. Above all, we learned the importance of three fundamentals in our business:

1. *The customer is always right.* We are determined to make Ford a customer-driven company, wherever we do business. In our view, the Ford people who work most directly with the customer have a special voice in the products and services we sell. Because, in the end, either Ford is customer-driven, or its products are not.

2. *The way to satisfy our customers is by offering them value for their money* — value they perceive to be best in class. That means making quality the number-one priority and controlling costs so we can provide excellent products and services at competitive prices.

   Quality — Quality is an ethic for us in everything we do — not just product, but all aspects of our business where we are seeking continuous improvement. Ford's quality is better now than our domestic competition's, and our goal is to be better than all of our competition.

   Competitive costs — We have restructured our business to make tremendous progress in cost. However, we still are not fully competitive with the world's most efficient volume producers — the Japanese. Closing that cost gap is perhaps our most pressing challenge — but we intend to do it through new ways to design, manufacture, and sell products. And we are mindful that our competition is not standing still. Again, attention in detail to the basics is important — so that we employ the most efficient ways to conduct our business.

   Product — We are absolutely committed to design, manufacture, and sell superb, "no-excuse" products that respond to what our customers want. We call this a "customer-driven" approach. We have an advanced technology commitment to function, comfort, and value-for-money. Our goal is recognized leadership as builders of cars that respond to customers' needs — whether it be a car with outstanding six-passenger comfort, a car with excellent performance and handling, or a fuel-efficient basic "in-town" car. Whatever the customer's need, we strive to provide the vehicle attributes that will satisfy that need.

3. *We want to take good care of our people.* That's a simple statement, but it packs a complex punch. We call it "people-centered management" — making Employee Involvement a way of life, treating one another with respect, removing artificial barriers, working together as a team to attain common goals. People are our most important resource. We've provided a more supportive environment to capture their good ideas, but we have much further to go. We are convinced that people make the difference between success and failure. We intend to use new and innovative ways to employ and compensate

people, so that their real strength — creative minds working on complex challenges — can be fully realized and rewarded.

These fundamentals are linked together in a continuous chain. Caring about Ford people leads directly to quality and excellence and efficiency in everything we do. And that leads to better products and services and lower costs. And that means customer satisfaction.

Guiding Principles. We've made our fundamentals part of the formal framework that guides our actions. We've written them down in a statement of our Mission, Values, and Guiding Principles:

- Quality comes first — to achieve customer satisfaction, the quality of our products and services is our number-one priority.
- Customers are the focus of everything we do — our work is done with our customers in mind, providing better products and services than our competition. We will strive to continue to be a full-line producer — to satisfy the gamut of customer wants.
- Continuous improvement is essential to our success — we strive for excellence in everything we do: in our products, in their safety and value — and in our services, our human relations, our competitiveness, and our profitability.
- Employee Involvement is our way of life — we are a team. We treat each other with trust and respect.
- Dealers and suppliers are our partners — the Company maintains mutually beneficial relationships with dealers, suppliers, and our other business associates.
- Integrity is never compromised — the conduct of our Company worldwide must continue to be pursued in a manner that is socially responsible and commands respect for its integrity and for its positive contributions to our society. Our doors are open to men and women alike without discrimination and without regard to ethnic origin or personal beliefs.

Strategies. To ensure a clear focus on the future direction of the company, Ford has developed a Corporate Vision as the underpinning of its strategic planning. This overview vision is to be a low-cost producer of the highest quality products and services which provide the best customer value. In order to move this vision, consistent with Mission, Values, and Guiding Principles, the company has adopted the following strategies for the future:

- To build the best quality vehicles in the world and have our customers know it.

- To be customer-driven — internally and externally — know their wants and needs, respond with products and services more quickly than our competition.
- To reduce costs without compromising key objectives.
- To optimize the company's global resources.
- To form alliances to supplement internal resources.
- To develop new sources of earnings designed to improve the stability of profits and sustain growth.

Taking all of these elements together, we are building for the future in the way and at the pace that is correct for Ford. We are taking the steps necessary to broaden and strengthen the company.

How HR Staff Supports Strategic Issues. I would like to focus on the role the Employee Development Strategy and Planning Office has played over the years in supporting corporate strategic issues. It's important to remember that all of the Company's strategic issues have one common denominator — they all depend on the capacities, competencies, and commitment of our people.

So what has the Employee Development Strategy and Planning Office done to support the company's vision, mission statement, and strategic direction? The mission of this office is to improve organizational and individual effectiveness worldwide by expanding human capacities and upgrading business processes through the application of cognitive and behavioral science knowledge, concepts, and techniques. The functions involved in carrying out this mission include: (1) strategy formulation, or conceptualization, (2) research and analysis, (3) consultation, (4) communication, and (5) education and training. What follows are examples of major activities that illustrate the role and impact of our office on corporate strategic planning.

Participative management and employee involvement. The most important activity was the development of participative management and Employee Involvement as a human resources strategy in support of the company's most pressing strategic issue — improved quality. In 1979, we were instrumental in developing a policy letter that sanctioned employee involvement. Essentially it says:

> It is the policy of the Company to encourage and enable all employees to become involved in and contribute to the success of the Company. A work climate should be created and maintained in which employees, at all levels, can achieve individual goals and work satisfaction by directing their talents and energies toward clearly defined company goals.

The concept was also sanctioned in a letter of understanding with the United Auto Workers (UAW).

Thus, the company and the UAW began a journey toward a participative culture. Over the years, with the support of the UAW, management, and employees, EI has grown and evolved to become a significant part of our culture. Today, key executives at Ford credit EI with much of the improvement in quality we have enjoyed.

1984 mission statement. In November 1984, the Board of Directors approved and Mr. Henry Ford II introduced a statement of Mission, Values, and Guiding Principles to the top 400 executives in Ford. We call it the Mission Statement. The statement was developed because the environment in which Ford does business is changing dramatically and because forces pull us in many directions as we face complex business problems around the world. The statement described what the company stands for and what our priorities are, and reflects the kind of company we must be in order to succeed in the future.

The Mission Statement is the foundation for all of the company's strategic planning. Our role, sanctioned by the chairman and president, was to develop a strategy for communicating the mission statement to Ford employees at every level worldwide. We established a task force of key line and staff executives to guide the effort. We established a meeting process for discussing the mission statement and for examining its implications for day-to-day operations. These meetings started with executive vice presidents and cascaded downward. A booklet describing the Mission Statement is available for those interested.

Employee opinion surveys. Another important role we play in support of development and implementation of strategic planning is conducting periodic employee opinion surveys. Here are some examples.

Every two to three years, we conduct surveys of salaried employees to track morale, to gage the impact of human resource policies and programs, and to surface any issues that need attention. In a way, these surveys serve a strategic function because we are able to compare our results with those of other *Fortune* 500 companies in the Mayflower Group (a national survey consortium). These surveys are strategic because results are presented to the Policy and Strategy Committee (the top 12 executives in Ford). These executives frequently refer to the results of the survey in their decision-making process.

Another example involves a survey of the top 400 executives in Ford worldwide regarding critical elements for a human resources strategy. These executives will be attending the Ford Worldwide Management meeting in Tucson later this month to deal with a number of strategic issues, one of which is called the "human resources issue." Here's their assignment:

> All of the company's strategic issues (quality improvement, customer satisfaction, cost reduction, and so forth) have one common denominator — they all depend on the capacities, competencies, and commitment of our people. Although marked progress has been made in changing our corporate culture to capitalize on our human resources through the empowerment of our people, the strategic issue, now and into the future, is how to create and sustain a "right"-sized, flexible work force with the capacities, competencies, and commitment (including the technical and managerial leadership) that gives us a competitive edge in a turbulent, uncertain world marketplace. Results of the executive survey will be used to guide the discussion of this cross-functional executive group and to enhance the likelihood of line management acceptance of the resulting human resources strategy.

Process improvement. Process Improvement is derived from the company's Mission, Values, and Guiding Principles — encompassing the concepts of customer satisfaction, quality, continuous improvement, and employee involvement. It is a powerful tool to realize business objectives and implement business strategies. By optimizing processes, the company can improve quality and timing and reduce costs.

Process Improvement is simultaneously a concept, a methodology, and an ongoing program. The concept of Process Improvement is that a business is a network of interdependent processes, rather than a set of organizations, functions, or products. A process is a group of related work tasks that transforms resources (people, capital, material) into output (products, services, information) while adding value. Processes are by definition dynamic, not static. Improving processes is a key means of achieving business objectives — increasing their added value through higher efficiency of resource use (lower costs) and better effectiveness of output (improved quality and customer satisfaction). Some estimates say improvements in processes could account for as much as two-thirds of our cost reduction opportunities. Process Improvement is particularly useful to approaching processes that cross organizational and functional lines — typically the areas most difficult to address and those most in need of improvement.

The methodology of Process Improvement is a systematic, structured means of defining, analyzing, and improving business processes. It provides individuals, teams, and larger groups with a common approach, tool kit, and vocabulary for effective improvement of processes.

The ongoing program for Process Improvement aims to establish widespread use of the concepts and methodology at all levels of the company through education programs and management participation. Our office serves on a management committee established by the office of the chief executive. The committee is chartered to develop and recommend a strategy and plan that would result in the use of Process Improvement as an integral part of the day-to-day work at Ford. Our forte is to provide expertise on the human resources dimensions of process improvement, as well as on the technical and training dimensions.

Forming corporate alliances. A major strategic direction for the company is to form alliances to supplement internal resources. What we have learned as a company is that the human resources dimension is critically important to the success of associations. Because we are relatively new to this game, we're still learning about the process and specific human resource elements that need to be managed. Presently, our Corporate Strategy staff, responsible for developing business associations, has commissioned a Human Resources task force to further define what needs to be managed from a people perspective. We're going to see a lot more activity in developing business associations in the future, and HR can make a significant contribution to progress on this strategic issue.

Employee development process model. Our office developed an employee development process model to guide career-long training, education, and development starting with recruitment and selection through preparation for retirement. The training and education element of the model is a process that starts with an existing resource — either a new or existing employee — and provides development along five basic tracks which results in an enhanced resource through training for excellence. Our five basic tracks include:

1. Core company values, policies, practices, and guidelines.
2. General business, technical, and strategic skills.
3. Professional/functional knowledge and skills.

4. Community, governmental, and societal involvement and knowledge.
5. Individually-motivated personal development.

These five basic tracks are all within the context of a need to integrate with our basic business functions an understanding that employee development is the responsibility of the entire organization.

Leadership education and development program. Another activity with strategic implications is just getting off the ground. Called the Leadership Education and Development Program, it is targeted at developing the leadership competencies of mid-level managers (staff supervisors and department managers at a plant). The program is to be supportive of company strategic direction (for instance, best in class quality, concept to customer, centers of excellence, and so on) and integrated with other company programs (like the Executive Development Center, existing functional development programs, Quality Education Development Center, and the Management Development Program).

The program will provide support for participant transition from a functional ("chimney") perspective to a cross-functional process perspective that enhances a team-building approach to the business. The program content is grounded in our core business and integrates an understanding and analysis of our business systems and processes. The program incorporates subject matter, content knowledge, and skills and abilities required to provide effective leadership in the business. The program will include developmental activities that focus on current "real" operational issues suggested by senior operating management in addition to formal classroom education. The end product should be a more competent mid-level management, improved selection for upper management positions, and long-term organizational improvement.

HR's Future Role in Strategic Planning. I've outlined Ford's corporate strategic plan and related to it examples of what the Employee Development Strategy and Planning Office has been doing to support the company's strategic direction. True, my functional area is only a part of the Human Resources function. Nevertheless, our experience suggests opportunities to strengthen the role of this HR function in strategic planning.

First, as Human Resource professionals, we need to understand the business and its strategic issues. In effect, we have to be more than just HR professionals; we need to think like business men and women.

Second, HR professionals need to adopt more of a systems perspective than perhaps we have in the past. We need to better identify where our HR systems impact and support corporate strategic issues. At the same time, we also need to apply the principles of Process Improvement to improving the interface and connections among the various subsystems of Human Resources.

Third, Human Resources needs to demonstrate its competence in strategic planning and implementation. We need to clearly specify the value-added benefit of the HR function in formulating and implementing business strategy. We need to be able to surface the Human Resources implications of strategic alternatives and provide options for handling HR issues that are directly related to strategic planning issues.

As some authors note, too often strategic planning has had little input from Human Resources because line management has had little confidence in HR's contribution. And often that input, when it is requested, is limited to succession planning and management development for key executives. We need to break this pattern by thinking more broadly and demonstrating that Human Resources input does make a difference in accomplishing strategic plans. In short, we need to evolve the role of Human Resources from an administrative role to a consultative one in running the business.

17

HR's Impact in Strategic Planning at Xerox

Douglas Reid, Senior Vice President of Human Resources, Xerox

Xerox has been around for a long time. It was formed originally as the Haloid Company, which produced commercial photographic papers. In 1946, management came across the xerographic process, which had been invented by a gentleman by the name of Chester Carlson 50 years ago in 1938. The company had leveled off in terms of its revenue and they needed a new product to get the growth of the company going. So for 13 years they put everything they had into the development of this process of xerography and introduced it as a commercial application in the marketplace with the first plain paper copier in 1960. We enjoyed explosive growth because for most of that time period we had the market to ourselves. We then got into a phase of what I call domestic or friendly competition. It was friendly in that the competition was on the dimensions of service and reliability of the equipment rather than price.

Then the Japanese landed in our marketplace, just as they did in the auto industry. So we went from a culture where "if spending money and adding people could solve the problem, you did not have a problem" to a culture where cost became paramount. We had to go through a significant culture change and are still going through that change.

Our business is best known for the copiers, duplicators (we call it reprographics), and systems. That's about $11 billion on a worldwide basis, but we, like the Ford Motor Company and many other companies, are also in the financial services business. That's a $4.5 billion business in 1987 with about 12,000 employees. Interestingly enough, it produces half our profit with 12,000 employees as compared with the business equipment side with over 100,000 employees. That has all kinds of interesting human resource implications.

HR Philosophy. What we try to do in personnel at Xerox is the classic responsibility — uphold the human resource philosophy. But the opportunity to be a much more important contributor to the success of the business is what we call maximizing productivity and satisfaction through development of human resource strategies, policies, practices, and programs. Our job is to increase the productivity of the human resource element at Xerox.

Underneath the human resource philosophy, we are absolutely convinced that personnel can make a difference in terms of managing the business and enhancing employee commitment. We hold our personnel people accountable for business decisions that impact people. It's not enough to say, "I'm a staff person. I made the recommendation to someone else." That is unacceptable in our environment. With all the legislation that exists today in many countries of the world and certainly the United States, we have a responsibility to insure that our practices are consistent with the laws of the land. Leadership through quality, like at Ford, is a key element for enhancing our productivity.

Under the "maximizing employee productivity and satisfaction" business objectives, we now are a partner in the business strategy development and certainly the implementation. We feel very strongly that we have a job to advocate new ways of enhancing employee commitment and thereby employee productivity, and, of course, for detailing and helping line management implement the strategies and policies and establish measures of performance. This is so that important objectives of human resources can be measured, like any other business objective.

HR Staff Gains Acceptance by Line. In terms of the human resource strategic plan, we've been working at this a long time, starting in 1978. It's only in the last three years that I think it's really starting to help the business make a difference. It started as a functional plan. What are we going to do in compensation? What are we going to do in training? What are we going to do in affirmative action? Quite frankly, it was happenstance if it happened to have any correlation with our major business objectives. So we started a process where, again, the key human resource people had a responsibility to learn what was going on in business. What were the business objectives and how could human resources help achieve those business objectives?

Initially we had resistance from senior management. The attitude was that human resource staff people don't understand the business. "We'll let you know when you can help. You can react to the decisions we've made." We had to fight for the right to sit at the general manager's table. We were helped in two ways at Xerox. One, we certainly leveraged the unfortunate experience of many companies in the United States who got involved in affirmative action suits. I'm sure you're well aware that in some cases those were $20 million to $40 million settlements. So management may not have been convinced previously that they should listen to us, but when those dollars and cents figures were put in front of them, they said okay.

The second way that we were able to win acceptance as a participant in strategic discussions concerned training and staffing. In our particular case, as we diversified from our copier base, which remains a cornerstone of our business equipment, to systems, we were not involved in the initial development of that strategy. When they were ready to implement it, they said, "Okay, help us." We pointed out that you do not convert people that can sell stand-alone pieces of office equipment, like copiers, into systems sales people by sending them to a one-week sales training course. We had to learn the hard way that you need entirely different skills. Also the training, instead of one or two weeks or a month, can require a year and a half. We had some difficulties initially in the systems marketplace because the human resource people did not have the proper skills. By pointing that out to top management and saying, "Get us involved in the early stages of your business strategies so we can point out these important elements." So it was a struggle, but we're there now.

Key HR Objectives. In terms of our environment, of the major issues that the human resource people are focusing on in order to help the corporation achieve its business objectives, cost is number one. In the business equipment business, the labor cost is 50 percent of our expense base, so we spend a lot of time making sure that our compensation levels and benefit levels are appropriate.

As a corporation, we have made a major sustained commitment to achieving affirmative action goals. In addition, our key human resource objectives are employee communications, labor cost competitiveness, and work force preparedness. These planks exist in our various operating divisions, business plans, and strategic plans. Now, there will be additional personnel or human resource objectives depending on the nature of the business, but what the plan is all about is regardless of where you work in Xerox, whether its financial services, or Europe or Canada or the United States, we expect the general manager with the assistance of his human resource colleagues to be addressing these issues. Indeed we inspect his plans during operations reviews and ask for progress against these elements.

Labor Cost Competitiveness. Moving into the cost area, we're addressing that in a variety of ways. Perhaps the one aspect that we had not emphasized enough was the whole area of compensation communications. We hadn't told people the facts, which were that they are well paid. We had not looked at putting benefits together with compensation, which is anywhere from 20 to 40 percent of base salary in terms of its cost impact. So now once a year we tell employees, "Your salary is $50,000, and your benefits are another $30,000, so in effect the company is paying you a total of $80,000 a year." That has helped people come to grips with the fact that we're slowing down our rate of salary increases. We were repositioning our compensation in the marketplace from being the highest payer in the United States to being competitive in the office equipment industry. As we explained that through our compensation communications efforts, people have a much better understanding. Entry level hiring by college recruiting is a less expensive form of bringing people in than bringing in experienced people so we're putting more emphasis on that.

Employee Communications. I've referred to employee communications in the compensation area. If you want your employees to be committed to helping you achieve your business objectives, you must explain to them what your mission is, much like Ford is doing, and how well you're doing against your plans. You have to open up the books and tell them where you're making money and tell them where you're losing money. We do this with every employee in the company, from the production worker on up. We do this on a sustained basis through a variety of media.

The management focus program is when our senior management, during the first quarter, goes around on a world-wide basis and explains to all employees how we did against our previous year's objectives, where we missed, what we're going to do to correct those deficiencies, and what our 1988 objectives are. Then we expect managers to carry this forward on a quarterly basis at a minimum so that every employee knows how well we're doing against our business objectives. This is a powerful tool, but it has to be done on a sustained basis and you have to involve all employees.

Management of Work Processes. The next major area we call management of work processes, or making the organization more efficient. I won't hit the quality or employee involvement, because we're exactly where Ford is. Employee involvement is an extremely powerful tool. We have trained 100,000 employees in the last five years with a minimum of four or five days training in employee involvement practices. It is making a key difference in our business.

HR Initiatives. Some of the human resource initiatives include new approaches to work, eliminating levels of management, throwing out span-of-control guideline books so that in some cases we have a manager with 50 people reporting to him, while in other cases, we have no manager in a stand-alone manufacturing operation. In some cases a team manages the business and depending on which stage of the production cycle it's in, a particular person will take over the leadership. These are still experiments, but they are encouraging in terms of their earlier results. We expect the human resource people to identify these new opportunities and convince line management and operations by saying, "Let me work with you to give this a try, because I think we can increase our output and hopefully the satisfaction of our employees at the same time."

Work Force Preparedness. Another major area of emphasis is this whole area of work force preparedness or training. It has several elements. We have to do a much better job of forecasting what kind of skills we're going to need in the future and make sure our intake at the recruiting level, at the college level, is responsive to those needs. Even more importantly, we need to build training programs for existing employees whose skills may no longer be appropriate for the new business needs and retrain them. This is a major commitment.

In our particular business, mechanical engineers are no longer in high demand. We have a lot of mechanical engineers and even some electrical engineers, because basically our product was a mechanical, electrical product. Now that we're moving into electronics, we are taking a lot of these civil engineers and turning them into software specialists or electronic engineers. One program places these people in school full time for 11 months. The example I'm referring to is in Rochester, New York, in conjunction with a local university. It's a very expensive program to convert these people, but this is one of the things that we feel is important in enhancing the commitment of our employees to the changes necessary in the business. We demonstrate to them that if they are willing to make the commitment to go to school and work hard then we'll continue to pay them at full pay while they're doing that. So the whole area of training in every element of the business has taken on increased importance. We expect the personnel function to lead that.

Affirmative Action. The last major plank, which is no longer limited to the United States as it has been, is the whole area of affirmative action. We've been at this on a serious basis for 20 years and are reasonably satisfied with our current situation. Some 50 percent of our sales force in the United States, which numbers 6,000 to 7,000 people, are either women or minorities. Fifteen percent of our managers above the first level of management are minorities and 30 percent of our managers are women. The way we made that happen is the way you make most things happen in business. You set a target, hold managers accountable for achieving that target, and reward them accordingly. That's what we did starting 18 years ago and it has paid off. But we are continuing to monitor that and we will not take the emphasis off until every level of management and every function has achieved what we call a balanced work force. We're well on our way to achieving that objective.

Summary. I did not articulate our business objectives and strategies but, as was pointed out earlier, you must have that before you can have any meaningful human resource strategies. We have those; they're in place. The strategies are now supporting those business objectives.

The rate of change that we've all read about is incredible. I guess Tom Peters' latest book, *Thriving on Chaos*, makes the point. This is going to be a way of life, probably forever. Until recently, at least at Xerox with all the changes we were making and with all the tough actions we were taking, a large number of people and managers still said, "This will go away. All things pass. It's like a recession. It's going to be tough for awhile, but we can go back to the good old ways." Well, the good old ways in our company are gone forever. So you have to help people cope and deal with this rate of change.

Ten years ago in global economics our Japanese competitors had a 50-percent cost advantage, and that had all kinds of implications in how we manage our business. With the appreciation in value of the yen, that's disappeared. But now the Japanese are building them right in the United States, whether it's motorcycles or autos or office copiers. In the meantime, Mexico has a wage rate of $3 a day and you can train people there to do good work. That has all kinds of implications for manufacturing in the United States, and you've got to deal with that from a human resource point of view.

That's what we mean by the human resource strategic planning process at Xerox. Those are some of the major issues that we're focusing on. Having been with Xerox for 25 years, mostly in the human resource function, I've seen a real transition from where we had a reactive staff support activity, reactive to what top management wanted, to now where we are a partner at the general management table. We are expected to make a significant contribution to helping the business achieve its objectives.

18

Compensation Strategies of John Hancock

Kathleen Dole, Executive Consultant, John Hancock Insurance

Pay for performance is a perennial issue in compensation circles and at John Hancock. Our environment at John Hancock has been changing a great deal in recent years and continues to change and those changes have certainly affected our pay for performance.

To put my remarks in context, let me tell you just a little about John Hancock. We are a very large life insurance company — in fact the sixth largest in the country. Our business mission is to be a full-scale financial services provider. In that arena, we are a very small company. As we have been seeking to make the transition to diversified financial services, we have been taking a hard look at our business style, our values, and our culture and made the decision that these things need to change if we are to be successful. In the compensation area, one of the first things we looked at was how we've been paying people and what return we've been getting for our salary dollar. Without labelling them, I think we've identified three broad pay issues we currently need to deal with.

Issue 1: Pay for Non-Performance. The first issue is *pay for non-performance*. The life insurance business has historically been conservative and slow to change. We now need to move in new directions more quickly and less cautiously than we have in the past. To do this,

209

we find we need to attract and reward different kinds of employees and, at the same time, stimulate new behavior in our career employees. As we became aware of this a couple of years ago, one of the first things we looked at was how we were dealing with poor performers.

Talk about pay for performance is sometimes symptomatic of the belief that there are people who are getting paid for non-performance. At John Hancock, we have found that rank-and-file employees are quick to recognize the co-worker who isn't pulling his share of the load and resent the company for permitting it to happen. It is doubly expensive to the company because we are paying for the non-productive employee and negatively affecting the morale and production of those who would otherwise be good performers. The extent of their awareness was brought home to us a couple of years ago when an attitude survey revealed that a majority of our employees felt that the company was carrying incompetent people on the payroll. Our long-standing paternalistic style of management had fostered a tradition in which employees were rarely fired and, even then, more often for gross misconduct than gross incompetence.

Since that survey, faced with an increasingly competitive business environment, we are getting tougher with poor performers. As a starting point, we have been steadily refining our performance management program to get a handle on what constitutes average, above average, and exceptional performance at John Hancock. Firings are still relatively rare but they do happen and occasionally at fairly high levels. In addition, since 1984, the company has sponsored two "Golden Handshake" programs and a special voluntary severance package as ways to accelerate the reduction of the work force. While these programs have not targeted poor performers, they have provided marginal long-service performers with an opportunity to leave with pension benefits or generous financial settlements.

Issue 2: Exceptional Pay for Exceptional Performance. Although dealing with poor performers may be difficult and even painful, providing adequate rewards for the exceptionally good ones is even tougher. Another clear message we received from that attitude survey was that employees not only wanted us to get rid of the incompetent people, they wanted to see really premium pay for those with exceptional performance. Many of the managers with whom I talk agree with this idea but have found it hard to put into practice.

Again, a strong performance management program is essential. To be effective, a performance appraisal program has to be carefully tailored to your business needs, conscientiously administered, and well and widely communicated so that managers and employees truly buy into it. Few performance appraisal programs live up to these standards although at John Hancock, it is not for want of trying. We are currently implementing Phase II of our third performance appraisal plan in seven years.

Another pre-requisite to delivering exceptional pay for exceptional performance is management development: Managers need to be better prepared to set and communicate performance standards, make discriminating performance judgments, and deliver the kind of pay that goes with them. At John Hancock, compensation administration has recently gotten out of the business of producing rules and charts and begun focusing energy on delivering management development and compensation training programs which aim to produce a greater skill and comfort level with administering pay.

A third roadblock to delivering exceptional pay for exceptional performance is the cost of doing so. Many companies feel they simply cannot afford to pay fair and competitive wages to all employees plus a meaningful premium to the exceptional ones. Proponents of strong performance-based salary programs argue that competitive companies, like professional athletic teams, cannot afford not to pay megabucks to their superstars. But, like the cases of some highly paid athletes, the employer's cost is an enduring one and the exceptional performance may not be. Furthermore, once this exceptional treatment is administered, it seems to take repeated doses just to maintain loyalty and avoid demoralization. And that is one reason, I think, for the new focus on incentive pay.

Issue 3: Incentive Pay for Performance Results. John Hancock's recent efforts to expand its use of incentive compensation are what I believe prompted Utah State University to invite our participation in this conference. As applied to most John Hancock executive and middle-management plans the term "incentive" isn't quite descriptive since its literal meaning is "inciting to action or effort." My observation has been that those who work hard will work hard with or without an incentive plan; and those who don't, won't. As evidence, I can only tell you that one of the best performing companies in the life insurance industry is the only one of the top 15 which has no incentive plans of any kind.

So why incentive plans for executives? The real benefits we hope to get from our incentive plans are qualitative — not more work, but better work.

As you may have guessed by now, John Hancock is trying to change its corporate culture. Our industry is also in transition as what used to be distinct insurance, banking, and finance industries gradually blur together as financial services providers. In short, we have a lot of new messages to deliver.

Incentive Plan Tied to Goals. Like any other business, we've been announcing goals for years but it is only recently that we have begun to talk in terms of an integrated long-term strategy in which the annual incentive plan goals are intermediate steps. We hope that presenting the goals this way will make the point that the company is extremely serious about them.

In spite of the remote quality of the annual goals in the past, performance against them has been driving the executive incentive plan since its inception in 1971. Unfortunately, there has been no obvious correlation between an individual's contribution to corporate results and his or her award, which has generally seemed to be based on a discretionary judgment of his or her attitude, appearance, and attendance.

Incentive Aid in Changing Management Behavior. Another objective we have for our incentive plan is to change management behavior by providing performance road maps. A high proportion of our executives have spent their entire careers at John Hancock and enjoyed a good deal of success doing things a certain way. The old adage, "If it works, don't fix it," is often heard. With the best intentions, some executives have been trying to achieve goals in the new business climate and work culture with tried and true, but no longer effective, work approaches. It was an outside consultant who tipped us off to the fact that while we had been very good at the conceptional aspects of strategic planning, we've been negligent at translating them into operational objectives for our managers. We are trying to use annual incentive plan goals to make that translation.

Incentives Promote Esprit de Corps. Another thing we are hoping to accomplish with incentive plans is the regeneration of *esprit de corps*. The standards of the so-called "me" generation have been blamed for the disappearance of company spirit and that may have something to do with it, but I think the real culprit is the way in which business life has evolved over the past 20 to 25 years. At John Hancock, the last 20 years have brought business diversity, which in turn has brought a diversity among the people we employ and physical dispersion not only outside the Boston area but now in several different locations in Boston.

Recently, I participated in developing a brief nostalgic presentation for a meeting of the company's senior officers. The presentation concluded with the distribution of sheet music and an invitation to sing the John Hancock company song, which dates from 1927. The recording of the song was clearly enjoyed but nobody sang along. I'm afraid that a company song will never again be a useful way to rouse the corporate troops (unless, of course, we can get Bruce Springsteen to write us one).

Incentive plans built around the growth and profitability of a business unit and in which all contributors have the opportunity to share can help to generate some cooperative spirit and enthusiasm — the feeling that "we're all in this together."

John Hancock has witnessed just how well these plans can work for this purpose in our subsidiary companies, many of which have been home-grown scratch operations and have been quite successful. Even those which have been less successful seem to share a camaraderie and "pull together" ethic.

So, we're trying to replicate the work climate in the subsidiaries of the parent company's profit centers. One element of that effort is the tailoring of incentive plan design and reward to profit center performance goals so that employees can regard the results for their business unit as something in which they have ownership.

Incentives Generate Loyalty. In somewhat the same vein, we also hope to establish and maintain company/employee loyalties through incentive plans. Like *esprit de corps*, loyalty is sort of an old-fashioned concept. Until a few years ago, there was a tremendous amount of reciprocal loyalty between John Hancock and its employees.

Today, loyalty based on the benevolent parent/dependent child relationship is gone. A new loyalty based on mutual well-being will have to take its place if employees are going to continue to build business careers and the company is going to pursue its ambitious business goals for the future. Employee incentive arrangements which create the fact or semblance of a vested interest in the corporation may be an important part not only in keeping them, but in keeping them interested.

Incentives and the Aging Work Force. As the baby boomers become middle-aged business people, the tremendous opportunities they enjoyed in their early careers are starting to dry up. At John Hancock, the work force demographics we've all heard so much about plus our recent "Golden Handshake" programs have produced a huge work force of young to middle-aged executives.

In the general population, 62 percent of our employees are now between 26 and 45, which means that many individuals have moved up very quickly but will enjoy fewer promotions in the future. Even our current president will have ended his career advancement opportunities in two years at the age of 52 when he succeeds as chairman. Very soon, there are going to be too many people all dressed up to move with no place to go.

Lateral opportunities, with meaningful incentives for making them, may be one answer to this problem. John Hancock has had an executive rotation program for several years in which executives with good performance records and perceived versatility have been moved into totally new operational environments. While a rotation opportunity has been considered a privilege, they also feel the change should be accompanied by premium compensation, or at least the opportunity for it. It will probably not be possible to enhance base salary enough to maintain a sane pay structure and satisfy these expectations; incentive plans, on the other hand, can do the job and will probably have to.

Outlook. What I see in our future is a proliferation of special incentive plans for all levels of employees. I also predict the unbundling of corporate plans in favor of plans tailored to the needs of the business units and, with that, some simplification of them. In combination with the improving reliability and credibility of our financial measures, I think these trends will mean that John Hancock employees will begin to truly believe they are getting paid appropriately for their performance.

And more than anything else, I see several years of constant change and experimentation ahead of us.

19

Union Carbide's 1987 Benefit Plan Initiatives*

Roger Wolff, Director of Corporate Benefits, Union Carbide

During 1987, Union Carbide Corporation implemented several significant changes to its benefits program to enhance cost effectiveness, while increasing value, flexibility, and options for our employees. These activities included:

- Plan redesign, new plan design, and cost shifting or sharing
- Introduction of new plans or redesigned plans offering new benefits and new options at minimal cost to the company
- Improving the quality of service
- Increasing understanding and appreciation of the value of the plans through better communication
- Taking advantage of tax provisions for employee benefit wherever possible

Before detailing these changes, it might be useful to briefly relate the financial environment in which Union Carbide has operated its businesses in the past three years.

Union Carbide is dramatically changed today from the $9 billion company of 1984. We saw that year end with the Bhopal tragedy, and we're still striving for a just, reasonable settlement for the victims.

In August 1985 we began a major restructuring program and later that year successfully fought off a hostile takeover attempt by

GAF. To accomplish that, an exchange offer to benefit our shareholders was implemented that entailed substantial borrowing and necessitated the sale of our $2 billion consumer products businesses.

In 1986, we completed our restructuring program involving several major divestments, and began a recapitalization program to ease our debt burden and give us greater freedom in operating our businesses.

Today, Union Carbide is a $7 billion company that is simpler and more sharply focused. We've substantially reduced our debt, overhead, and layers of management, and our businesses are doing well and moving swiftly through an era of renewal.

Review Benefit Plans for Cost Savings and Quality. It was in the financial environment of early 1986 that we began to review our benefit plans in an effort to reduce costs or increase cost effectiveness. Union Carbide's benefit plans package is not much different from what most of corporate America offers. We have a defined benefit pension plan, savings, and 401(K) plans, medical plans, dental plan, life, disability, and your typical vacation and holiday pay practices.

We first looked at our pension plan, an expensive benefit plan but a key one. We looked at a number of possibilities. We looked at switching from a final pay plan to other forms of pension plans in connection with some improvements in the defined contribution savings and 401(K) plans. But frankly, in the final analysis, we felt that this was going to be counter-productive to the long-term interests of the business.

In 1985, we had reverted $500 million of surplus assets from our pension fund. We had left, however, almost an equal amount of surplus in the pension fund. So, when we looked at whether or not to do a major revision of our pension plan, we saw that we really didn't have to from a cost standpoint because we had minimal funding requirements looking over the next three to four years.

We also were concerned that, given what the employees had gone through — the divestitures, the threat of takeover, loss of jobs, and so forth — that this was one bullet that we just didn't feel was worth biting with regard to our employees and the interest of the business long-term. We did, however, target primarily the medical plan or plans, and I'll get to that in a minute.

What we were looking for in 1987 was a net reduction in the cost of benefit plans packages as a percent of payroll. But we wanted at the same time to maximize the value of existing plans and to create new plan options and new opportunities where we could to improve employee perception of value without incurring any additional cost.

We also wanted to increase the quality of service. As you all know, you can have a very good benefit plan, but if the employee's experience with it is negative because the service isn't there, you get employees perceiving that a plan doesn't have the value that's commensurate with the cost that the company is incurring for that plan. So we increased the quality of service from our providers, our service organizations, and our in-house operation.

As far as cost control is concerned, we were looking at new plan design, at redesign with some cost shifting, cost sharing and tax effectiveness — tax effectiveness not only for the company, but where we could for the employee as well.

Medical plans received the most attention. Historically, we had local hospital, medical, surgical plans, and local major medical plans, local in the sense that it might be one plant or all facilities in a state, but that we did not have an overall national plan for all of our employees.

New National Comprehensive Medical Plan. In 1986 we decided to consolidate all local plans into one national comprehensive medical plan effective January 1, 1987. To do that, we obviously had to convince our employees and our unions that this was the right thing to do. As you would perhaps expect given the financial situation that we were in at the time, we were quite up front. We said we've got to cut and control costs. We told them why. We told them how much we expected we could cut, and they understood. In fact, the employees were going to pick up part of the cost. Many of our unions voluntarily signed on to the new plan mid-contract. Others elected to wait until the next negotiations. But, we have a few of our unionized locations still outstanding that we haven't signed. Overall, we've gotten about 90 percent of all employees now covered under this plan.

The plan is self-insured. We use an administrative services-only contract with a third party for claims payment. The cost reduction target was at least 10 percent of our projected costs. We wanted to do that in a way that the employees would, in their view, see the new plan as not being punitive but rather as being realistic — one that had a design they could live with and that delivered a high quality service. The cost sharing that we've insisted on may not look like much and it may not be as much as we'd like it to be, but it's 15 percent for the active employees and their dependents, and early retirees pay 30 percent for themselves and their dependents.

With regard to the plan's design, it is a standard comprehensive medical plan except for 100-percent coverage after deductible for hospitalization. Many companies have designs very similar to it. We use the pre-tax employee contributions for their share, thereby taking some of the sting out of it. We do have a first-dollar deductible of $200 per individual and $500 per family. However, we provide coverage for those expenses which we believe are critical elements of the plan, namely, outpatient pre-admission testing, additional surgical opinions, outpatient surgery, and the first $300 of diagnostic lab tests and X-rays. We have an 80/20 co-pay and stop-loss at $1,200 per individual and $3,000 per family. As an additional incentive, if the employee does not comply with the rules, the plan may pay as low as 50 percent rather than 80 percent.

Switch from Short-Term to Retirement Savings. I'd like to turn to another example of cost-effective benefit plans. As opposed to the medical plans, this is an example of where we were actually trying to reduce cost and, at the same time, accomplish a couple of other objectives.

We felt it was necessary to educate our employees on the impact of tax reform, on their savings and 401(K) plans, and we piggybacked on that opportunity by trying to persuade our employees to switch from our short-term savings plan — which is a plan that pays out every two years — to long-term savings either in the after-tax long-term plan or the pre-tax 401(K) plan. In other words, we tried to get them out of short-term savings and into retirement savings.

We also wanted to persuade our employees to become Union Carbide shareholders. We did not have a substantial percentage of employees who were purchasing and holding stock within the savings program. The participation was only about 8 percent. We wanted to offer maximum flexibility and options to the actives and the retirees under these plans without incurring any significant increase in cost.

What did we do? First, we reduced the eligibility requirement for the long-term plans. We had been requiring three years of service to be eligible for the long-term plans, but only one year of service to be eligible for the short-term plan. The result was that people would get into the short-term plan and never get out.

So, we moved up the eligibility for long-term plans from three years to one and increased the company match to 30 percent at the first year only for those employees who went into the long-term savings plan. We left it at 10 percent at the first year for those who opted to go into short-term savings. We also provided greater accessibility for the employee to his or her long-term savings.

One of the problems is that when an employee puts his money into savings, he wants to know he can have access in some form to his money. Otherwise, he won't put it in. As a result, we instituted a loan program, a hardship withdrawal provision, and more liberal withdrawal provisions with regard to the long-term savings.

In addition, we expanded the retiree settlement options. We permit our retirees to remain in the plan on a deferred account basis until age 70. We introduced period-certain installment options, whereby the employee can elect the period over which he wants to take monthly payments of his savings plan accounts — whether it's 10 or 20 years after retirement. We have done what we could within the IRS limits on partial withdrawals, both pre-retirement and post-retirement, while at the same time trying to protect the retiree against loss of lump sum distribution treatment on the balance.

We introduced a 10-percent discount stock purchase option as part of the savings plan. We also increased the ability of the employee to switch investments virtually daily, so that he can move from equity to stock to fixed income.

Our results have been quite gratifying. We've gotten 50 percent of our short-term savers into long-term savings in a space of six months. Our retiree accounts already represent 30 percent of the total assets in the Fixed Income Fund. These are people who want to leave their money in the plan rather than take a lump sum distribution immediately on retirement. Twenty percent of participants now buy stock, whereas before it was only 8 percent. So we feel that with modest changes that did not incur any substantial expense, we accomplished a number of objectives.

New Group Universal Life Program. In another effort to introduce some additional plans and options, and again with the ground rule not to incur additional cost to the company, we introduced two new plans. First, we introduced a Group Universal Life program effective December 1, 1987. It allows the employee — at his option — to buy additional insurance at up to five times his base pay in addition to the two times pay he already has under the basic life insurance program. He can buy spouse and dependent children insurance as well as an optional accidental death benefit. In addition, there is a cash accumulation fund for the employee and/or his spouse, in which by lump sum or payroll deductions he can make contributions to develop a tax deferred buildup. We also offer a loan provision.

The insurance company we used for this program provided the up-front development money for the general expenses of start-up. The only expense we had in all this was the on-going expense of the payroll deduction and deduction changes that occur from time to time.

New Health and Dependent Day Care. The second plan we made available to our employees, which Congress almost shot down again on the eve of implementation, was the health and dependent day-care reimbursement program. Here again, it's only for those people who know they have unreimbursed medical expenses, dental expenses, eyeglasses, and so forth, or childcare expenses. Here is a way to use a pre-tax salary deferral.

We used the same administrative services organization as we did for our medical plan. The cost to the company is offset by the saving on FICA and forfeitures. If there is any forfeiture money left over that is not needed to cover the cost, then we will credit it back on an equal basis to all employees who participated that year toward their accounts in the following year. The annual deductions we used at present — within the limits — are health care at $3,000 and dependent care at $5,000.

Conclusion. We accomplished what we set out to do. Several significant changes were implemented to Union Carbide's benefits program to enhance cost-effectiveness, while increasing value, flexibility, and options as perceived by our employees. Plan redesign, new plan design, and cost shifting or sharing were the means by which we achieved our goals. We believe we have improved the quality of service, increased understanding and appreciation of the value of the plans through better communication, and have taken advantage of tax provisions for the benefit of the employee wherever possible.

20

Cost Effective Benefit Programs

Harold Loeb, Senior Vice President, Hay Huggins

We have reached a point in the history of benefits compensation when nearly everyone believes costs must be contained. But, even though the "fringe binge" may be over, there has been a great deal of change in the benefits area. There has been at least one significant piece of benefits legislation in each of the last six years. We have seen dramatic changes in medical plan design as well as other medical cost containment developments. We have seen employers make their benefit programs more flexible and orient them toward employee preferences. Finally, we have seen the explosive growth of the 401 (K) plan in the last few years.

To further complicate matters, benefits specialists must be more technically sophisticated than ever in order to keep abreast of regulations and trends. At the same time, benefits are increasingly being evaluated as part of total compensation rather than as separate and insulated components. As a result, the benefits professional must evaluate benefits from a strategic standpoint.

Ironically, it is the very complexity of benefits programs that provides the opportunity to solve the problem. Making benefits flexible so that they provide employees with more choice and adapt better to employee lifestyles is an ingenious way to improve employee satisfaction while holding the cost line. The choice and variation themselves are worth something to the employee, even though there is comparable or lower cost to the employer.

Employee Attitudes Toward Benefit Plans. The creativity and inventiveness of benefits plan designers have not gone unrewarded. Our employee attitude data, compiled by Hay's Research for Management Group, show not only that most employees are satisfied with their benefits, but they are just as satisfied as they were in the era of rapidly increasing packages. The following conclusions can be drawn from a decade of surveying employee attitudes:

- Work values, most notably loyalty and commitment, are in decline.
- There is a significant decrease in perceived job security at all levels of employment.
- An overall pessimism about chances for advancement is underscored by a decline in middle managers' perceptions of their growth opportunity.
- A decrease in pay satisfaction is worsened by a failure of employers to convince employees that there is a link between their pay increases and their performance.
- And yet, there is a continued high level of satisfaction with employee benefits programs.

Why in this era of diminished commitment at all levels of the organization, at a time of benefit reductions and employee cost-sharing arrangements in such areas as health insurance, does employee satisfaction with benefits continue to remain high?

Either knowingly or unknowingly, benefits plan designers have accomplished the following:

- Balanced necessary benefit reductions with give-backs in areas highly valued by employees.
- Designed benefit programs that have anticipated employee reaction to plan changes.
- Implemented programs which coincided with our employees' increased desire to participate in benefits decisions.
- Managed to design benefits packages that emphasize both cost control and employee satisfaction.

As a result, 62 percent of the employees in our database have a favorable attitude about their benefits programs in general. But the world is changing, values are changing, tax laws are changing, and employee benefits needs are changing. A company's ability to keep employee benefits at the appropriate level and in the appropriate mix is becoming severely strained. To maximize their benefits and minimize employee backlash in the face of change, employers must know more than just how employees feel about benefits in general. They must have more specific information.

Not surprisingly, more employees show a favorable attitude toward capital accumulation programs, such as thrift/savings plans, 401(K)s, and profit-sharing plans, than any other benefit. Not only do they see cash going into a fund, they also see the company match that is generally present and, in the case of 401(K)s, a healthy tax break. There is also a high level of employee understanding and involvement with these plans. Least appreciated, that is, receiving the fewest favorable ratings, are defined benefit pension plans. The low rating of pensions is probably less an expression of employee dislike than a statement about lack of understanding and concern about adequacy of retirement income.

Management may be surprised to see that there is very little correlation between what employers spend on a particular benefit program and the level of employee satisfaction with that benefit. The ever popular capital accumulation plans, for example, provide a high return on benefit investment. It is far less expensive than medical and dental plans at mid- and lower-level salaries and cheaper at all levels than pension benefits. But as we have seen, the appreciation level for these plans is the highest of all individual benefits.

Benefits Cost Containment Dilemma. What does the benefits expert do with all of this attitude information? The attitude data that we have seen provides a starting point and a direction, but we need more — more even than specific preferences of our own employees in relation to these national norms.

Occasionally, we can help companies limit their benefit plans and, through the right presentation or communication, provide employees with the same or higher level of satisfaction. Usually though, benefits cost containment is paid for in employee dissatisfaction.

We call this problem the "Benefits Design Dilemma" — how to achieve cost control without unacceptable losses in employee acceptance. In our experience, organizations approach this dilemma in one of three ways. The first group ignores the employee problem altogether. They reason that it is an unfortunate, undesirable effect of necessary business decisions. Since benefits are a form of largess in the first place, the giver is entitled to limit or even reduce the gift.

Most organizations, however, are in a second, more ambitious group that communicates with employees to find the least unacceptable change in the plan. Through focus groups of employees, through surveys and interviews, the companies study what employees like and value, what no-cost changes would make the benefits plan more attractive, and what cost containment measures would be least disliked.

The third group takes this communication intensive approach one step further and introduces formal benefit tradeoff analysis, a technique in which employee preferences for plan options are linked mathematically to their cost.

Benefit Tradeoff Analysis. Benefit tradeoff analysis is a formal quantified approach to a process that most benefits planners already follow. If the goal of the redesign is to contain costs, then the objective of the design project is to maximize the expected savings — cor strained, of course, by employee response. Tradeoff analysis not only calculates the expected yield on several alternative combinations of design changes, but also quantifies the expected gain of loss of satisfaction. Thus the method lets us find the least unpopular design changes that will yield any targeted amount of savings or, conversely, the most popular design changes for additional expenditures.

Tradeoff analysis facilitates subtle comparisons that would be hard to make without computational models. It can help to forecast enrollment rates for new voluntary plans and options, one of the trickier aspects of redesigning a benefits program.

The tradeoff analysis proceeds in a step-by-step fashion. In the first step, the organization sets its plan objectives, that is, to lower costs, to maintain costs but increase satisfaction, and so on. It also states the policies and constraints that would make certain redesigns not worth exploring.

Next the planners develop design options. This step results in an array of the realistic options that a firm might want to evaluate, such as the one shown in Table 20.1. Note that among these six benefit features, there are almost 1,000 combinations of plan provisions that could be established. Questioning employees on all these combinations would be impractical, if not impossible.

Levels

Benefit Feature	Existing Plan	Redesign Options
Pension — % Final Year Salary	60%	52.5%, 40%
401 (k)	None	25%, 50%
Child Care Assistance (Monthly)	None	$100, $150
Floating Holidays	None	1 Day, 3 Days
Dental Insurance	Fixed	100%, 80%, 50%
Major Medical Deductible	$100	$175, $225

Table 20.1. Levels of Coverage/Cost Within Features

The next stage, then, is to derive some manageable set of alternatives and employee preferences. In the approach we have used, called conjoint analysis, the myriad of alternatives are transcribed onto a set of six to ten cards. On one card, we may keep the pension income and dental insurance benefits the same, introduce a 401(K) savings plan, child care assistance program, and floating holiday schedule, but increase the major medical plan deductible. On another card, we may keep the floating holidays, dental insurance, and major medical deductibles the same, while reducing the pension plan income and introducing a child care assistance program.

Groups of employees sort a small set of cards into a range from "most likely to be accepted" to "least likely to be accepted." By tabulating the rankings, the analyst can then derive a satisfaction loss for each of the components. Finally the cost factor and satisfaction gain or loss are integrated, allowing the planners to select the most cost-effective options.

Case Study of Health Plan Redesign. This process can be illustrated by a small case study. The firm, with 5,000 non-union employees, was seeing profitability gains ended by its rising bills for health insurance coverage. In the previous three years, its insurance premiums had soared 75 percent, and now its carrier was asking for a 20-percent increase for the coming year. The company now felt that it had no choice but to reassess the makeup of its health care plan and identify potential cost reductions. From the outset, the company was determined that health costs be contained in the least disruptive and least distasteful manner possible.

The key questions for the plan sponsor to address were:

- Where do we want to be?
- How do we get there?
- How will our employees react?
- How can we integrate both employer and employee needs?

In order to answer these questions, we needed to probe deeper and ask perhaps the same questions in a slightly different way:

- What are the financial objectives?
- What are the benefit plan design options?
- What changes are employees most or least willing to accept?
- How can the company maximize cost control and employee satisfaction with benefits?

With a net 10-percent reduction in premium as the target, a redesign team drew up a list of potential reductions to the existing health care plan.

Benefit	Plan	Options
Employee Contribution for Dependent Coverage	$5	$10, $25
Major Medical Deductible	$100	$150, $200
Surgical Coinsurance	100%	90%, 80%
Hospital Deductible	None	$100, $200
Hospital Coinsurance	100%	95%, 90%
Hospital Pre-Certification	Not Required	Required

Table 20.2 Health Plan Redesign: Potential Plan Reductions

Table 20.2 shows the options under consideration for the company's health plan: the full range of ways in which the cost of health care can be shifted to the employee. In this typical case, all the options represent a real or potential financial loss to the employee. At the same time, the company elected to examine certain potential plan improvements. They felt that if these could be introduced for a small cost but with high employee satisfaction, then some of the takeaways would not affect employee morale as greatly.

Fifteen percent of the work force, representing random samplings of selected employee groups, participated in half-hour sessions to sort the possibilities according to preference. These preference data yielded computations of "satisfaction loss" (expressed as a percentage) for each of the potential reductions. Similarly, "satisfaction gains" were identified for the suggested plan improvements.

An analysis of the satisfaction loss for two of the options is revealed. Notice that (1) raising the hospital deductible from $0 to $200 results in a satisfaction loss of 11.4 percent and reduces the premium by 3.4 percent and (2) dropping the hospital coinsurance from 100 to 90 percent results in a nearly 19 percent loss in employee satisfaction, while saving only 3 percent on the premium. Therefore, raising the hospital deductible results in less satisfaction loss and a much larger savings on the premium. The construct that emerges from all of this is what we call "satisfaction-loss-per-dollar-saved" as illustrated in Table 20.3.

This is a very powerful method to make informed decisions that could not be made nearly so well with informal methods. By looking for the lowest satisfaction loss per dollar saved, the planners are able to identify a package of actions that will reduce premiums by 12.3 percent, certain that the least amount of satisfaction loss resulted. This method can be used just for plan reductions, improvements, or both; or just for options written into one plan, for example between medical and pension benefits.

The 12.3 percent of premium savings that could be realized by making the four indicated changes was more than the company was targeting to save; therefore, certain of the benefits plan improvements could also be introduced at this time. Three plan improvements could be made at a total cost of 1.4 percent of premium. Therefore, the employer could elect to introduce the four cost-saving changes and

Benefit	Change (From/To)	Satisfaction Loss	Employer Savings (% of Premium)	Satisfaction Loss per $ Saved	Cumulative Savings (% of Premium)
Pre-certification	Not required/ Required*	11.4%*	4.0%*	2.85*	4.0%
Hospital	None/$100	5.7%	1.7%	3.35	
Deductible	None/$200*	11.4%*	3.4%*	3.35*	7.4%
Major Med.	$100/$150*	11.4%	2.5%*	4.56*	9.9%
Deductible	$100/$200	32.9%	5.0%	6.58	
Dependent	$5/$10*	14.3%*	2.4%*	5.96*	12.3%
Coverage	$5/$15	31.4%	4.7%	6.68	
Hospital	100%/95%	18.6%	3.0%	6.20	
Coinsurance	100%/90%	41.4%	6.0%	6.90	
Surgical	100%/90%	27.1%	1.0%	27.10	
Coinsurance	100%/80%	50.0%	2.0%	25.00	

* Option Selected

Table 20.3 Plan Reductions

the three plan improvements for a net savings of approximately 11 percent of the premium.

In the case just presented, that is exactly what the employer elected to do. Its 1986 projected health insurance premium was $8.5 million dollars. The planned savings from the four benefit reductions saved the company over $1 million, while the planned improvements cost slightly more than $100,000. The redesigned plan then cost approximately $7.5 million, with a 10.9-percent savings on the premium.

Because the company solicited employee input and gave preference data equal weight in the decision-making process, management was better equipped to handle the never-easy task of selling a planned reduction to its workers. The explanation it could now use is as follows:

> In the past five years, medical costs have far out-paced salaries and revenues. We had no choice; we had to make changes to contain costs in our health care plan. We did not want to redesign the plan in an arbitrary way or secretive fashion. Instead, we wanted to find a way to

make reductions we knew would be least disruptive and most acceptable to you, the users of the plan. So we solicited your input and here is the new plan structured around the changes you indicated would be least troublesome. We're confident you'll still find this to be a generous and useful healthcare plan. We know too that it is now a more reasonable plan from a cost-standpoint for the company.

Benefits tradeoff analysis has been shown to work effectively in real corporate settings. This fact has elevated this new approach from a merely interesting idea to an integral component of the process by which benefit plans can be changed.

21

Employee Driven Productivity

Neal Orkin, Professor, Drexel University

Since 1970, no fewer than five federal productivity units (a Center, a Council, an Office, and two Commissions) have been established without any significant increase in American innovation. In fact, one may conclude from the following table that innovation in the United States in the last decade has suffered tremendously as a result of both deindustrialization and the loss of patenting activity to foreign nationals, especially the West Germans and Japanese. Are these foreign engineers and scientists more creative than their American counterparts, or are they merely better stimulated through a reward scheme?

In America, most employees who may be expected to produce a technical product must, as a condition of employment, sign a contract under which they undertake to transfer any rights to inventions over to the employer. In return, the employee is entitled to no remuneration. Any reward he may receive, ranging from a pen set or plaque to a bonus of a few hundred dollars, is at the largess of the employer. Many American engineers see the monetary fruits of their inventions being granted to management as large bonuses. Hence it is no surprise to find an engineer's main aspiration to advance into a managerial position. Without the skills of a technological work force, management would have nothing to market. This was aptly stated by Dennis Chamot of the AFL-CIO:

It is clear that the most elaborate and efficient development team, management structure, and marketing group cannot bring forth new products without those who begin the entire process, the inventors. (Testimony before the subcommittee on Courts, Civil Liberties, and the Administration of Justice of the committee on the Judiciary, House of Representatives, 97th Congress, Second Session, on HR 4732 and HR 6635, 29 July 1982, p. 37-38.)

U.S. patents per million population issued to U.S. citizens and corporations
1970: 255
1980: 169

U.S. patents issued per $ Billion of GNP in constant 1972 $$
1972: 53.7
1980: 25.8

Percentage U.S. patents issued to foreign applicants
1970: 25
1985: 44

Number of foreign corporations of the top ten receiving U.S. patents
1973: 1
1983: 7

U.S. merchandise balance of trade deficit
1983: $69.4 Billion
1987: $171 Billion

Table 21.1 U.S. Innovation

Antithesis. Our structure of a reward system for employee inventors is antithetical to that employed in Western Europe and Japan. Statutes in these nations generally mandate that an employee receive royalties from the profits resulting from his or her invention. These laws tend to divide inventions into two categories: *free*, or non-work related inventions which belong to the employee; and *service*, or work-related inventions which are subject to the royalty. The West German statute of 1957 is perhaps the most comprehensive and "workable" of the Western European laws. Guidelines based on such factors as the employee's job, and the amount of supervision and suggestion derived from the employer, are used to compute royalties, which vary typically from 2 to 7 percent of the resulting profits. When negotiations between the parties fail, the dispute is brought before an arbitration board. Because of good labor relations, however, the law works so well that only 1,100 cases were arbitrated during the law's first 17 years of existence. This must be viewed in the context of approximately 60,000 patent applications from German employees resulting in only 80 to 100 arbitrations per year.

During a visit to the West German Patent Office in Munich in November 1985, I was fortunate to meet Dr. Gernot Kaube, the head of the West German arbitration board. Although he voiced some minor complaints about the law, his most serious criticism concerned a lack of education among engineers and attorneys practicing before the board. He spoke of one case in which an inventor was dissatisfied with the 24 million DM (approximately $12,000,000) granted him by the employer; he unsuccessfully argued for an additional 4 million DM.

The Japanese situation is similar; however, compliance on the part of the corporation is voluntary. Arbitration panels within the corporation settle disputes. Direct invention royalties are less than $10,000, but must be viewed in the context of other Japanese employment practices such as salary increases and promotions for creative individuals.

Since 1970, attempts to enact a U.S. law similar to the West German statute have continually failed due to corporate lobbying and a lack of effort by engineers — who themselves are subject to the pressures of an employment situation that discourages "boat rocking." The last such effort — HR 3285 of the 98th Congress — led to hearings at which I was the only witness to testify in its favor. As part of HR 6286, the "Patent Law Amendments Act of 1984," Congress approved $250,000 to establish a commission to study employee inventors. (This amount was reduced from $1,000,000 initially approved by the House of Representatives.) President Reagan signed this bill into law, but with some reservations, portions of which appear below:

> I am disappointed that the Congress chose to include in this bill a new national Commission on Innovation and Productivity. This Commission would be established to study the productivity of inventors employed by private companies and, more generally, to make recommendations for changes in U.S. laws to better foster innovation and productivity. Employed inventors have contributed greatly to our country's competitiveness in high technology areas. Nevertheless, I believe that the private sector, rather than the federal government, is best able to decide

on methods to stimulate increased productivity on the part of employed inventors. My administration will oppose any appropriation for the National Commission on Innovation and Productivity authorized by HR 6286.

As of the date at which this article went to press, no monies have been allocated for this commission, nor does there appear to be any interest on Congress's part to do so, even with its "born again" interest in competitiveness.

To further encourage U.S. innovation, Congress enacted the Economic Recovery Tax Act of 1981. Aside from granting virtual corporate immunity from tax payments, resulting in huge federal deficits, this Act also allowed companies a 25-percent tax credit for increases in research and development expenditures. (The Tax Reform Act of 1986 reduced this to 20 percent and strengthened the definition of research and exploration.) For example, a company whose R & D expenditures were $1 million in 1983 could deduct $2 million from its 1983 taxes and get a tax credit of $250,000 for 1983. The results of the R & D tax credit were that "creative accounting" allowed for half of all firms claiming this credit to be non-manufacturing: fast-food restaurants, stockbrokers, movie producers, homebuilders, hair dressers, and banks. One might claim that a credit should be allowed to produce a "better hamburger." However, this so-called "better hamburger" will not bring sufficient monies into the country so as to enhance global competitiveness and reduce the merchandise trade deficit. Moreover, a tax advantage to an employer provides absolutely no benefit to the source of an innovation — the employee.

"Orkinomics." In the December 1982 issue of the *European Intellectual Property Review* I first conceptualized the doctrine of "Orkinomics" — a formulation of royalties and tax incentives to stimulate innovation. Very simply, Orkinomics regards three parties as essential to the innovative process:

• Employee
• Employer
• Employee Innovator(s)

The innovator could be likened to someone who makes the raw invention commercially successful, perhaps someone or a group that devises a non-patentable means to mass-produce an invention cheaply.

These three parties should all be rewarded for their creative efforts through royalties that may be tax free or subject to a tax credit for a limited time period, as follows:

- Income Tax Incentives and Royalties for Employees: Allow a portion of the employee's patent royalty to be tax free; for example, if the employee receives a $10,000 royalty, $2,000 would not be taxed.
- Income Tax Incentives for Employers: Allow a tax credit in excess of the employee's and innovator's royalty; for example, if the employer pays a $10,000 royalty to an employee, the company could deduct $12,000 from its income tax.
- Bonuses and Tax Incentives for Innovators: Make the employer (either voluntarily or compulsorily) pay a bonus to innovator(s) that would receive a tax credit similar to the inventor's.

Whereas the present R & D tax credit rewards only employers for highly speculative research as defined very broadly under the tax code, Orkinomics would reward the sources of the innovation, and only for those concepts that are commercially successful.

Reflections from a Legitimate Son of Schumpeter. Most modern economists, whether Keynesian or neo-classical, have basically regarded innovation as lying outside or separate from the economic system. The one exception is the late Austrian economist Joseph A. Schumpeter, who used Karl Marx's theories to disprove Marx. Schumpeter, who later taught at Harvard, contended that Marx asked the right questions, but provided the wrong answers. For example, profit, Schumpeter contended, was not a "surplus value" stolen from the workers, but should be viewed as the source of new jobs and income, thus allowing new innovations that increase profit and productivity to serve an economic function. He theorized that, by continuous innovation, capitalism would creatively destroy itself ("creative destruction," as he called it), and that from these innovations new industries would spring from old ones. One could either view this as the steel industry losing ground to high technology or the steel industry being made more productive by new process innovations.

In his later years (1940-1950) he became a political economist, but few seemed to be listening when he first defined in his greatest work, *Capitalism, Socialism, and Democracy,* the entrepreneur/innovator:

We have seen that the function of entrepreneurs is to reform or revolutionize the pattern of production by exploiting an invention or, more generally, an untried technological possibility for producing a new commodity or producing an old one in a new way, by opening up a new source of supply of materials or a new outlet for products, by reorganizing an industry and so on...

To undertake such new things is difficult and constitutes a distinct economic function, because they lie outside the routine tasks that everybody understands. To act with confidence beyond the range of familiar beacons and to overcome that resistance requires aptitudes present in only a small fraction of the population and that define the entrepreneurial type as well as function. This function does not essentially consist in either inventing anything or otherwise creating conditions the enterprise exploits. It consists in getting things done.

Perhaps Schumpeter was less king to the modern corporate executive whom America's businesses reward so highly:

> We have seen that, normally, the modern businessman, whether entrepreneur or mere managing administrator, is of the executive type. From the logic of his position he acquires something of the psychology of the salaried employee working in a bureaucratic organization. Whether a stockholder or not, his will to fight and to hold on is not and cannot be what it was with the man who knew ownership and its responsibilities in the full-blooded sense of those words. His system of values and his conception of duty undergo a profound change. Mere stockholders of course have ceased to count at all — quite independently of the clipping of their share by a regulating and taxing state. Thus the modern corporation, although the product of the capitalist process, socializes the bourgeois mind; it relentlessly narrows the scope of capitalist motivation; not only that, it will eventually kill its roots.

Schumpeter had also professed to three desires: to be the world's greatest economist, to be the world's greatest horseman, and, lastly, to be Vienna's greatest lover. Thus, since this author agrees with Schumpeter that the innovator is more important to the creative processes than the modern executive, he has, in effect, confirmed that he is one of the great Austrian's legitimate "economic progeny."

Some refinements must be made so that Orkinomics is more workable. The duration of the tax benefits must be such that the government would provide sufficient incentives to rekindle the fires of innovation without serious detriment to the federal treasury. In addition, the tax benefits should be allowed at a point in time in which the invention/innovation is a commercial success; if they are granted in the early life of a patent, perhaps no one would benefit from them. The most difficult issue that should be addressed is how to structure a legislative definition for the "innovator." In a nation such as Sweden in which engineering unions harmoniously bargain collectively on a large scale with employers, joint committees could be established to ensure that the proper individuals receive bonuses for innovations. In the United States, some legislative formula would have to be enacted to prevent internal corporate politics from granting bonuses solely to high-level management personnel. The author is presently studying this issue and he hopes to collect more information on this subject from individuals familiar with the proven West German legislation.

Conclusions. The United States Congress now has a choice. It can further study competitiveness, the trade deficit, and protectionism and conclude that legislation and tariffs are necessary to stop foreigners from stealing our technology or trading unfairly. If it does this it misses the root cause of our problem: the lack of stimuli to those who create technology — our scientists and engineers. One only need read Dennis Chamot's comment made earlier to perceive this.

The other choice is politically more difficult, but it must be made. Congress must cease denigration of our technological talent by allowing corporate employers to treat both employees and their inventions as property subject to a 19th-century attitude of *laissez faire*. If it adopts employee inventor legislation with the accompanying Orkinomic tax and innovator incentives, it will be to the benefit of all parties. Corporations will have more new products to sell worldwide, and employees will reap the advantages of gaining financial rewards for their creativity.

22

Internal Decision to Excel: Secrets of Super Achievers*

Charles Garfield, President, Peak Performance

As a novice computer programmer in 1967, I was part of the Grumman Aerospace team assigned to design and build the Apollo 11 mission's Lunar Module (LM) — the first manned craft to land on the moon. Something extraordinary began to happen as the work got under way. Thousands of ordinary men and women who had been competent workers — project managers, secretaries, technicians — suddenly became super-achievers, doing the best work of their lives.

Within 18 months, our section moved its performance rating from the bottom 50 percent to the top 15 percent. "Want to know why we're doing so well?" our manager asked me. He pointed to the pale moon barely visible in the eastern sky. "People have been dreaming about going there for thousands of years. And *we're* going to do it."

I wanted to learn more about what motivates people to superior effort, so I became a clinical psychologist. For a while, I worked with seriously ill cancer patients. Although their situations were far more complex than the average job could ever be, the long-term survivors — like my earlier colleagues at Grumman — spoke of a powerful mission that inspired them. One patient, a concert pianist, told me that he was drawing on physical, mental, and emotional resources he

* © 1986 by Garfield Enterprises. Reprinted with permission from William Morrow & Co. and *Reader's Digest*.

hadn't known he had. "Staying alive these days," he said, "is much more difficult than playing Mozart or Chopin. Staying alive has become my peak performance."

From seeing accomplishments in sports, as well as in other fields, I was soon convinced that the drive to excel comes primarily from within. Was it possible, I wondered, to discover ways of bringing peak performance under *voluntary* control, of *initiating* action leading to exceptional achievement? I was determined to find out.

In the past 18 years of studying high achievers, I have learned they are not superhumans, nor do they share a singular talent or winning strategy. What they do have in common is an uncanny knack for increasing the odds in their favor through simple techniques that almost anyone can cultivate.

Envision a Mission. Peak performers want more than merely to win the next game. They see all the way to the championship. They have a long-range goal that inspires commitment and action.

Thomas Watson, Sr., was 40 years old when he became general manager of a little firm that made meat slicers, time clocks, and primitive tabulators called punch-card machines. He recognized the potential of a machine for processing and storing information — a computer — a decade before its first commercial use. To match his mission, he soon renamed his little company International Business Machines Corporation. When asked toward the end of his life at what point he envisioned IBM becoming so big, he answered, "Right at the beginning."

In establishing a mission, the peak performer asks: "What do I like to do? What am I really good at?" He or she is less concerned with competence in everything than with specific strengths that can be marshalled toward a specific goal. Nobody ever commented that the great violinist Jascha Heifetz probably couldn't play the trumpet very well. The key is not to be an Einstein, but rather to be a more productive version of yourself.

Be Results Oriented. Workaholics are addicted to activity; super achievers are committed to results. They work toward goals that contribute to their mission. In their mind's eye they see the end they want and the actions leading to it.

Jim Gray was a telephone company lineman who wanted to be a maintenance supervisor. But he had no seniority and little hope of advancement. To signal his superiors that he existed, he focused all his energy on being the best craftsman on his crew: "All I had to show them was that Jim Gray and good work were synonymous."

The higher-ups noticed. They knew that even if Jim was working in a manhole no one else would enter, the work would still be perfect — because Jim had done it. He was moved from installations to maintenance, then accepted a transfer to booming Southern California, where he was asked to train new technicians. He was soon made a maintenance supervisor, his longtime dream.

Peak performers do not swell on the discouraging gap between where they are and where they want to be. Like Jim, they set intermediate goals in line with their primary aim or mission — what a partner at a major accounting firm calls "dreams with deadlines."

Tap Your Internal Resources. Psychologist Abraham Maslow believed that there is a tendency in *everyone* toward "self-actualization." He referred to "capacities clamoring to be used," a restlessness for self-development, accomplishment, and esteem. One's full potential emerges not just by adding skills, but by first unlocking the door to internal resources waiting to be tapped.

In 1953 many experts thought the four-minute mile was physiologically impossible. But Roger Bannister had internal resources that kept him from tripping over the so-called evidence; he was determined to see for himself. In 1954, with a time of 3:59.4, Bannister broke more than a world record. He broke through a self-limiting attitude. After his feat, runners throughout the world started recording sub-four-minute miles regularly.

By tapping internal resources, peak performers also see possibilities that would escape the rest of us. One day in 1984, headed for San Francisco, I drove up to a tollbooth. I heard loud rock music. Inside, the booth attendant was dancing.

"What are you doing?" I asked.

"I'm having a party," he said. "At 8:30 every morning, live people enter those other toll-booths. At 4:30 pm, they reemerge and go home. For eight hours, their brains are on hold. But I'm going to be a dancer someday, and this is my training."

The dancing toll-taker had been given the same working conditions as had all the other toll-takers. Yet he had a mission and the will to use the conditions of his job to support it.

Enlist Team Spirit. High-level achievement — especially in competitive situations within an organization — can be magnified by getting others to contribute their hidden abilities to your own performance.

A foreman at a Southern California thermodynamics plant explained why a unit of technicians who check temperatures and pressures on his plant's delicate equipment — a routine and repetitive job — have the lowest turnover rate in the company and a superb performance record. He pointed to the green surgical smocks they wore. "They are from my son, a cardiovascular surgeon," he said. "I told my men: 'We take care of these pipes the way a doctor takes care of your heart. There won't be any breakdowns in this plant as long as *we* are working on its arteries.'" With a mixture of humor and pride, they address each other as "Doctor."

Many U.S. companies are emerging as peak performers because they make employees feel like partners in a joint enterprise. When such workers are offered more autonomy and responsibility, along with opportunities for self-development, a rise in output, quality, and satisfaction usually results.

Fran Tarkenton was one of football's outstanding quarterbacks over his 17-year sports career. Then he founded his own management consulting firm specializing in training and productivity programs. In a football huddle, Tarkenton sometimes let linemen suggest plays because, he says, "They were closer to the action than the head coach on the sidelines was." His team experience on the gridiron, he adds, was more important to the success of his business career than was his formal business-administration education.

Treat Setbacks as Steppingstones. On their flights between the earth and the moon, the Apollo ships were off course more than 90 percent of the time. The crew repeatedly had to correct the trajectory. And you know what? Being off course all that time didn't matter. On course does not mean perfect. It means that even when things don't go perfectly, you are headed in the right direction. In a study of 90 leaders in business, politics, sports, and the arts, many spoke of "false starts" but never of "failure." Disappointments spur greater resolve, growth, or change.

Moreover, no matter how rough things get, super-achievers always feel there are other avenues they can explore. They always have another idea to test.

By the time Tom Fatjo was 36, he had turned $500 and a used garbage truck into the country's biggest solid-waste-disposal company. But he also realized what stress was doing to his health. He took up jogging, then began participating in races. Within a year his energy had returned, and he sold his company to finance construction of a conference center and health spa for executives in Houston. Next, he developed Living Well, Inc., a national company providing health and fitness facilities and services to both corporations and the public.

My own mission — an ongoing investigation into what makes peak performers click and tick — has led to an inescapable conclusion: What these super-achievers do is not abnormal, but normal. They are, for the most part, ordinary people who have become extraordinary by cultivating what the German writer Goethe called "the genius, power, and magic" that exist in all of us.

23

Total Employee Involvement

Norman Bodek, President, Productivity Press

Total employee involvement (TEI) is a simple and brilliant strategy. So why aren't we implementing it? How many of us have participative programs in our companies?

The phrase "participative program," does not refer to our picking up our paycheck every week. In one sense, we all do participate. We come to work and we work very hard. We use our bodies, our minds, and our emotions. We use what we have, but that's not what I mean by participation. There is something unique I want to describe, some quality that I think is missing in American management that I have seen elsewhere in the world.

One way to define "employee involvement" is to say that everyone is involved in continuous improvement.

Continuous improvement, in my opinion, is the key to Japan's success. I went there looking for a miracle but I couldn't find one. I couldn't find a new machine, a new device, or some innovation that was much more clever than the machines, devices, and innovations we have in America. What I did see was continuous improvement, a process that made today different from yesterday.

How do we install a mechanism in our organizations to help us focus on continuous improvement? We cannot rest on yesterday's success or even on today's — because tomorrow we must come up with a new idea — that is continuous improvement.

In 1960, it took seven Japanese to do what one American could do. Today, it's probably one to one. Actually, the Japanese are ahead of us in manufacturing productivity. How did they improve their production ratio 700 percent in the last 28 years? If we accept as true that in 28 years they reduced the ratio from seven to one, can you imagine what it will be like 20 years from now? If we are aware of what they do and implement similar strategies, we can remain competitive by raising our productivity rate. If we don't, however, we will be watching from the station as the train goes by.

What is TEI? Let me describe "total employee involvement" (TEI) again: It involves everybody in learning and continuous improvement.

Now, let's ask ourselves some questions about production work today. Of those of us who are manufacturing-oriented, how many actually have worked on the assembly line? How many would love to do what they did on that line for the rest of their lives? If they would not, there is something missing.

Well, it's up to us to eliminate the aspect we don't like in the work we ask others to do.

A number of years ago, I visited a U.S. automotive plant where I saw a man putting fuel into the brake lining of every other car. I watched him for a while and was amazed at how slowly he moved. Finally I asked the guide, "How long has he done that work?" The guide said, "I don't know, but we had one man in the plant who did nothing but put tires on the line for 43 years." He would pick up a tire and put it on a hook, and it would be taken on the line. That was his life. You can imagine the excitement of getting up in the morning to go to the plant and put tires on a hook!

So where do we look for enjoyment in our lives? What do we consider its essence to be? Probably in our leisure time. However, the work environment we have created for people in America is a problem. The factories we have created do not reflect the image of the Divine. We are created in God's image . . . but look at the work we do! We see it as an evil necessary for survival. Well, it does not have to be like that, Dr. Shigeo Shingo would tell you. I encourage you to read his chapter in this book because he is one of the most brilliant men in the world today. In appreciation of his contribution to manufacturing excellence, Utah State University granted him an honorary doctorate degree on June 4, 1988. Make it a point to know who he is!

Making Work Exciting. Let's go back to the plant scenario: We're talking about employee involvement, about how to get people to become creatively involved in changing their environment. Let's think of one idea to improve our companies right now. It doesn't have to be a big idea, it can be very simple. How many thought of an idea to improve their own work? I expected us to produce ideas mostly for other people. I didn't think we would have ideas for ourselves to implement. But that's what we mean when we talk about TEI. It is a system for organizational change, it is a system that improves people's working conditions.

All the factories that require the kind of work you don't want to do must change. Since many of us here are involved in creating and maintaining these job classifications and are, therefore, responsible for the current conditions, I'm not going to ask that we change them. Rather, I'm going to ask that we go back and establish a system that encourages our workers to become more involved in their work and allows them to make changes. Let them improve the environment for themselves. That's what I mean by TEI, what is so unique about Japanese industry.

Most work done in America is repetitive and boring. People don't wake up in the morning excited about their work. We have to change that if we want to ensure our economic survival into the twenty-first century, and the only way for us to do that is to allow everybody to become involved in continuously improving our work processes and environments.

Two weeks ago, I visited a plant in Chicago — and it was a terrible place. It was clean and smelled nice, there was no grease on the floor, the walls were beautiful, the people were paid very well — and yet, it was a terrible place.

Here's an example of what I am talking about. I watched a woman working at a blister-pack machine. She was taking four units of her product and positioning them on a board. Then she put this board on the blistering machine to be wrapped in plastic. Next, she took a blade and cut the pack into four pieces. Finally, she picked up the four products and put them in a box.

I watched her walk to where the items were stored, pick up the four she needed, and return. Then, she put them down because she had grabbed four of them and picked them up again one at a time, and placed them on the board. When this was done, she stood back and looked around. Then she pressed a button and the plastic came down to do the blistering. After that, she slowly walked over to where the blade was kept (I have no idea why it was kept in a different location), and carried the wrapped pieces to the box one at a time. She moved very slowly during the entire process.

I think it would kill me if I had to do her job day in and day out. I was afraid to ask how long she had been doing it. There was no industrial engineering at this plant, no concern for human engineering.

Knowing the Score. One major thing was missing: The worker didn't know the score. She had no idea how many units to complete per hour or per minute, or how to do her work better. A few times the boss came by and said, "Hey, Mary, please speed it up. I need a few more to ship tomorrow," trying to encourage her a little bit. She'd answer, "I'm working as hard as I can! You don't know what I do every day! If you want to do it better, go ahead!"

Most people working in our plants don't know the score. Basketball, baseball, and football are great sports, but can you imagine watching a baseball game where there is no score? There's nothing up there to tell you the inning, the runs, nothing to tell you how many strikes or how many balls. You might watch for ten minutes, but then you would get up and do something else. Well, the problem at work is that we don't communicate the score.

We want people to be responsible for their own improvement and see the score on improvements. People want to see the score about everything that's important to them. We have to learn to give them the score. What's the productivity rate today? Does everybody in the plant know whether we're behind or ahead of schedule? The manager might know; but does everybody on the plant floor know? No, because had we told them, we would have generated some excitement on that floor. There's no reason why we shouldn't apply the rules of baseball in the factory or office and maintain a scoreboard. It would help everybody become more enthusiastic about their work.

Generating Ideas. I discovered an idea method in Japan called the "Teian system." Like most of the ideas I observed in Japan, it was born in this country. Whenever I talk about Japan, people appear resentful. They don't want to hear about Japan any more. Instead, they want to hear what is right with America, that we're a wonderful country, a wonderful people. Of course we are! But other countries generate good ideas, too. There is a lot we can learn from other people. But, somehow, Americans resent non-American ideas. Well, you'll be happy to know that this idea was born here.

In 1898 Eastman Kodak developed the suggestion system. I'm not sure exactly when it arrived in Japan, probably around 1950. You know, when the Japanese study American management, they study it very carefully. They really studied Dr. Deming, and because they put into practice what they learned, they achieved a manufacturing quality that is envied worldwide. They also studied our suggestion system, thinking it had to be valuable since Americans were using it. They discovered that the American suggestion system had a problem: We give a monetary reward to the person making the suggestion. Because it is a lot of money, we spend too much time evaluating ideas and don't make enough awards. As a result, only a few ideas are submitted. By contrast, the Japanese pay less per idea but make awards promptly and receive many suggestions per employees.

How many companies get more than one idea per year from their employees? Toyota gets 50 ideas per worker per year. Canon gets 70 per worker per year. Panasonic gets 100 per worker per year. Panasonic is getting two ideas in writing per worker per week.

Talking about employee involvement, we mean only one thing — people releasing their own creative energy. People involved in solving their own problems to improve the quality of their work.

Japanese Working Habits. Recently, I was returning from Japan by plane. A man from NEC sat next to me. He told me he had been with the company for four years. I asked him how much vacation time he gets. He said, "I get 15 days a year." So, after four years, he had 60 days. I asked him how many of those days he had actually taken, and he said, "I haven't taken a vacation since joining this company." I asked him how long his work day was. He said, "I get to work at 8 am and go home at 9 pm or 10 pm. Also, I work every other Saturday."

Shocking, isn't it? I asked, "Are you the only one working that hard in your company?" He answered, "No, everybody in my group does it." There were 27 people in his group. I wouldn't want to run the American company competing with NEC!

We could say that it is unfair of the Japanese to work that hard, but that won't solve our problem. If we want to compete internationally, we must play their game and also work 60 to 70 hours a week. If we don't, we'll become second-class citizens in the world. We used to be the world's richest country, but we no longer are. You know who is buying whom. I haven't seen anything in the newspaper in the last two years about an American company buying a Japanese company. But I haven't seen a single week go by without a Japanese, British, or German company buying an American company. We are such a wonderful country, the world loves us so much that everybody is buying us. Isn't that wonderful for us? I don't think so.

You see, I'm my own boss. I don't mind having myself for a boss and I speak my own language at the office. I love the Japanese — my whole business is related to Japanese management. I am very impressed with their success and hard work but I can't speak their language and I wouldn't want a Japanese boss unless he promptly helped me learn Japanese so I could communicate with him. I recommend that everybody learn Japanese.

How many of us have a Japanese boss? Today, there may be only a few who do. But wait until next year. I guarantee that by then it will be at least 10 to 15 percent. If I asked the same question in California, what answer do you think I'd get? Maybe 50 percent. What about Hawaii? I don't even know if they still speak English in Hawaii.

That's what we are talking about: A system to generate ideas from our employees, to get them really involved. It's simple and brilliant, but we are not doing it. I don't know why. How can we eliminate the obstacles?

TEI Goals. Let me tell you some of the goals of the system. One is to make continuous improvement a habit for everybody. You want to get everybody involved because involvement is creativity, and if people are not coming up with ideas, they are not involved. They are just doing things mechanically. And we know that America is a nation with originality, a nation of creative people. Japan is a nation of copiers. Does everybody agree? We have all been brainwashed. Japan is a nation of copiers, and we are a nation of creative people. Yet we have described our own factories as being places where we would not want to work. We're a little confused about this idea of copying. Of course we all copy, copy each other. It is how we learn as children, we copy our parents. And if we are fortunate, the creative spark comes through.

What I am suggesting is a method that allows everybody to be creative. Creative energy is everywhere and within everyone. If we went back 10,000 years, what do you think this meeting would look like? What would our lives be like? No electricity, no automobiles, no printing presses, and so on, all the inventions that have come from someone's creative energy — the same energy that's available to each of us. As managers, our job is to bring out this creative energy in the people who work for us.

Our next goal is to improve skills. This can be achieved by continuously encouraging people to generate ideas to improve their own skill level. Another goal, of course, is to have more satisfied customers and happier workers. Increased productivity and quality are other attainable goals.

If I had a vacuum cleaner plant with 300 employees in the United States and was getting one idea per year per worker, that would give me 300 ideas to improve my plant. Matsushita gets 100 ideas per worker. They also have 300 employees at this particular plant, meaning that they're getting 30,000 improvement ideas this year. How can my vacuum cleaner plant compete with that?

Let's look at some of these ideas. One worker, by lengthening a platform, reduced a job from two people to one. Another idea, a top bar, prevented defects from occurring on a line. A third idea stopped workers from bending over too far, giving the work station more stability. Each idea either made a job easier or improved quality and productivity.

The TEI system engenders both a sense of achievement and better service, and ultimately, TEI encourages our companies to become world class.

Becoming World Class Companies. Who among us really feel that they belong to a world class company? Larry White probably does. He is plant manager at Omark. Dan Bills from Granville Phillips is another one. Some of us might be getting close, but I haven't seen too many world class companies in the United States.

A world class company responds to the needs of their clients when they arise, at the right price, with top quality, and at the lowest possible cost.

World competition will increasingly require the creative participation of every single worker. We can no longer waste our most precious asset — our people — in boring, repetitive tasks. Every single worker must become involved in continuous improvement. We must develop total employee involvement in our companies and start a process that allows workers to tap into their own creative energy to create a better work environment for themselves and for the rest of us.

24

Upgrading Workforce Ethics at General Dynamics*

Kent Druyvesteyn, Director of Ethics, General Dynamics

On May 21, 1985, Secretary of the Navy, John F. Lehman, sent a three-page letter to David S. Lewis, then Chairman of the Board and CEO of General Dynamics. Citing several ongoing investigations which he said "call into question the integrity and responsibility of the corporation," Lehman informed Lewis that he was directing Navy contracting officers to hold off further processing of contracts with the Electric Boat and Pomona divisions pending accomplishment of certain management changes by General Dynamics.

Three of the management changes Secretary Lehman called for concerned overhead billing issues. The fourth was "to establish and enforce a rigorous code of ethics for all General Dynamics officers and employees with mandatory sanctions for violation." At a news briefing soon after this letter was issued, Secretary Lehman was asked by the media: "Which do you think is the most important step that General Dynamics needs to take right now?" Lehman answered: "Well, I think the code of ethics, because I think that the others are merely manifestations of an approach, an attitude, that has pervaded their doing business with the government. It isn't the problem of one or two individuals doing the wrong things. It is a pervasive record of corporate policy that we want changed."

* This chapter is based on two documents published by General Dynamics entitled "General Dynamics Standards of Business Ethics and Conduct" and "The Ethics Program 1985/1986." © 1988 by General Dynamics. All rights reserved.

An effort was begun immediately within the company to respond to the Secretary's challenge. A large group of different individuals assisted in the effort and the Ethics Resource Center, a non-profit organization in Washington, DC, was contacted for advice. On June 6, the board of directors was briefed on emerging plans and a General Dynamics code of conduct that was already in written form was extensively revised and enlarged. The first draft of this revision was ready for review and comment by June 17, and the corporation made clear to the Navy that the response to Lehman's directive concerning ethics would be comprehensive. In a letter to Walter T. Skallerup, Jr., General Counsel of the Navy, the company emphasized that the ultimate goal was "to ensure that *all* of our employees understand where we stand on this issue and understand how to apply our Standards of Business Ethics and Conduct in their daily business activities."

Early in August 1985, the Navy responded affirmatively to the efforts undertaken by the corporation and lifted the suspension. On August 13, the inauguration of the General Dynamics Ethics Program was announced by a corporate executive memorandum. "In the final analysis," the memorandum read, "the integrity of the corporation rests on the integrity of its individual employees" who over the years "have proven to be, with few exceptions, honorable people with well ingrained standards of conduct." The memorandum reminded everyone, however, that "our business is becoming increasingly more complex, as we are more and more often being faced with business situations where the honorable straight-forward course of action is not always obvious." All employees were called upon to become fully knowledgeable and fully prepared to comply with the General Dynamics Standards of Business Ethics and Conduct.

Code, Aim, and Organization. So began the General Dynamics Ethics Program. The centerpiece of the program is the General Dynamics Standards of Business Ethics and Conduct popularly known as the "Blue Book" because of its blue cover (see appendix at end of chapter). The booklet sets forth the general responsibilities of the company, supervisors, and all employees for upholding the Standards. It describes the Ethics Program organization and tells where to go for help and information when questions or concerns arise about the application of the Standards. Most important, the Standards booklet gives practical guidelines to follow in daily business conduct and lists mandatory sanctions that will result from failure to comply with the code.

The primary aim of the Ethics Program is to integrate and maintain the Standards in the daily business affairs of the corporation. Beyond this, the Ethics Program aims at supporting the broad corporate objective (spelled out in the 1985 Annual Report) of "achieving in our administrative performance the same high level of excellence which we have historically achieved in engineering and manufacturing," thereby enhancing public trust in the company.

The organization of the Ethics Program begins with the Board Committee on Corporate Responsibility. The committee has broad oversight responsibility for company programs and policies in relation to employees, customers, suppliers, shareholders, and community. The committee consists entirely of outside directors. Besides the Ethics Program, it has responsibility for other matters such as equal employment opportunity, employee rights, safety and health standards, product and plant safety, environmental issues, and community relations.

In addition to the Board Committee, a Corporate Ethics Steering Group, made up of the heads of major functional departments within the corporation, has responsibility for providing corporate-wide policy guidance and general administrative direction for the Ethics Program. Similar groups at some of the divisions provide division-wide direction for the program. Company attorneys, at both the Corporate Office and at each division, support the Ethics Program with legal counsel concerning the laws, regulations, and government rules that lie behind the specific guidelines for conduct found in the Standards booklet. Corporate and division counsels also play important roles in investigations concerning violations of the Standards.

At the Corporate Office, and at each division, subsidiary, and major location, there are Ethics Program Directors who are responsible on a day-by-day basis for assisting management in the implementation and maintenance of the Ethics Program. The Ethics Program Directors provide advice to employees with questions about applying the Standards and are responsible for screening allegations concerning possible Standards violations. Many directors maintain hotlines.

General Dynamics is a corporation where leadership is most visible and effectively exercised through line management. Line management has been particularly important in the implementation of the Ethics Program and integration of the Standards. Line management defines expectations and sets the example. Ethical conduct depends on alertness and information. It is not a product of a specialized skill and requires no expert knowledge of philosophy, theology, psychology, law, or other academic disciplines. It depends heavily on commitment. "You gotta wanna," as the phrase goes, and in the area of employee attitude, management — up and down the line — has a special responsibility for setting an example. Functional departments, especially Human Resources, Legal, Security, and Internal Audit, also play an important supporting role. In the midst of all of this, the role of the Ethics Program Director is to assist management in its leadership role and to assist employees generally in their understanding and application of Standards to daily business conduct.

To achieve the primary aim of integrating and maintaining the Standards in the corporation's daily business affairs, the Ethics Program has implemented certain key initiatives to stimulate awareness, increase knowledge, and heighten commitment concerning the Standards. As much as possible, these initiatives depend for their implementation on existing structures, practices, and channels of communication. This approach, of using the strengths of the existing organization, has proven both practical and highly effective.

Distributing and Acknowledging Standards. It is one thing to publish a conduct code with mandatory sanctions for all employees. It is another matter to make every employee aware of its purpose, knowledgeable of its contents, and committed to its integration in daily business affairs. The latter is a test of sincerity, resolve, and sense of responsibility. The addition of mandatory sanctions required a whole new level of responsibility for communicating with all employees about the purpose and meaning of the Standards.

Starting at the top of the organization, the distribution of the Standards cascaded down through the corporation following management lines. Top company officials met first to receive the Standards booklet and discuss its role in daily company affairs. These officials then held a meeting of the individuals who reported to them and repeated the process of distribution and discussion. This process continued down through the organization, finally reaching first-line supervision and their direct reports. At each session issued, attendees were asked to sign an Acknowledgement Card which said they had received and read the Standards and understood that they represented company policy.

The task of distributing the Standards worldwide was divided into two phases. Phase I involved all exempt salaried employees, of which there were about 38,000 at the time the initial distribution took place. The process for this group took a month to complete and, in the end, only two individuals, for personal reasons, refused to sign the Acknowledgement Card. Refusal to sign the card during the initial distribution was not cause for dismissal.

The distribution process did generate a great deal of discussion, some of it emotional. In the best of times, talk of ethics and personal conduct elicits a wide variety of emotions, from anger and rage to anxiety and guilt. Seldom is someone delighted to talk about ethics (unless it's someone else's). But given the climate of negative public opinion surrounding the inauguration of our Ethics Program, felt even by employees in social settings and by children of employees at school, it is understandable that the distribution was sometimes accompanied by emotional responses.

Phase II involved all hourly employees of which there were approximately 65,000 at the time, most members of trade unions. In fact, when Phase II was begun in October 1985, hourly workers were represented by some 30 different unions and were covered by one of more than 90 separate collective bargaining agreements. In order to conduct this distribution, international union leaders were contacted. While some took a neutral position, none opposed distribution. Not all locals followed suit.

Phase II was largely completed by the end of 1985. There were some notable exceptions. At Land Systems Division, the major union was on strike and distribution was deferred until the strike was settled. At Material Service and Marblehead Lime, both commercial operations, local union membership expressed strong opposition to the distribution and it was not attempted.

Around the corporation, there were some negative reactions to the distribution. Some opposition was motivated by concern that the mandatory sanctions linked to the Standards abrogated existing discipline procedures under the applicable collective bargaining agreement. Assurances had to be given that this was not the case. Some was motivated by a mistaken belief that the Standards required union members to "rat" on their union brothers. Some opposition grew from a perceived indictment of the individual's personal ethics. "There is nothing wrong with my ethics," it was said. Related to this was the belief expressed by some employees that they had few or no discretionary decisions to make and, therefore, did not need the Standards. It was the "boss" in the front office or in St. Louis who needed the Standards and who had gotten the company in trouble in the first place. In the end, excluding Land Systems, acknowledgement cards were received from 99.7 percent of all hourly employees in the defense divisions. In the commercial companies, excluding Material Service and Marblehead Lime, 87.1 percent of all hourly employees signed the Acknowledgement Card. Again, signing was not a condition for continued employment.

Phases I and II covered distribution of the Standards to all current employees. New employees are covered at the time they are hired and it is company policy that signing the Acknowledgement Card is a condition of employment. The agreement signed by consultants with the company requires that the consultant adhere to the Standards. In 1986, some 115 such agreements were signed. In 1986, active suppliers received the Standards booklet and were asked to comply. In all, some 62,000 received the standards booklet together with a letter giving the General Dynamics hotline on which to report possible violations.

Corporate Policies and Procedures. One significant means of supporting and integrating the Standards into the daily affairs of the organization is through the policies and procedures that govern daily decisionmaking and conduct. At General Dynamics these are called Corporate Policies and Procedures (CPPs). While the Standards are broad, general statements of what conduct is and is not acceptable, the CPPs give detailed directions for acting in specific situations. At General Dynamics, CPPs are issued at the corporate level and are implemented through division- or subsidiary-level documents called Standard Practices (SP).

When the Standards booklet was first issued in August 1985, all existing CPPs were reviewed to assure they were congruent with and adequately supported the Standards. Where no relevant CPPs were found, new ones were written and issued. These CPPs describe in detail how the Standards are to be applied in specific business situations. For example, CPP 23-106 (Conflicts of Interest — Meals, Refreshments, Gifts, and other Items of Value to Customers) focuses on potential conflicts of interest in customer relations and tells what is and what is not acceptable in the giving of gifts, gratuities, and other items of value to customers. Another policy,

CPP 23-107 (Conflicts of Interest — Meals, Refreshments, Gifts, and other Items of Value from Suppliers) provides directions for avoiding both the fact or appearance of conflicts of interest in relationships with suppliers. All new or revised policies or procedures are now reviewed to include an appropriate reference to the Ethics Program.

Awareness Building and Training. Distributing the Standards to all employees in person created considerable awareness of the Ethics program and its importance to the corporation. How to deepen that awareness, increase knowledge, and strengthen commitment were the challenges of the Ethics Awareness Workshops that followed.

The training, like the distribution of the Standards, began at the top of the corporation and flowed downward. The effort to train all employees was divided into three rounds. Round I, for corporate officers, was held on January 6-7, 1986. Included in this session were the president, executive vice presidents, and all division general managers and subsidiary presidents. The session was led by the chairman and CEO. Round II followed at each of the divisions and subsidiaries, attended by all those reporting directly to the general manager or president responsible for leading the session. Round II began on January 28, 1986, and concluded on April 17. There were 16 such sessions, each attended by 25 or 30 individuals.

Round III, for all other employees, was divided into four modules. Module I was for direct reports to staff members of the general managers or presidents. Module II was for all other supervisory personnel including first-line supervisors. Module III was for all other salaried employees including professional and managerial. Module IV was for all hourly employees. Round III began April 1 and was virtually completed for the entire corporation by the end of 1986. On December 31, fewer than 1,800 employees of more than 100,000 still needed to be reached with a workshop.

The sessions varied in length depending on the company level involved. Round I sessions took about 15 hours and Round II sessions a full, ten-hour day. Round III sessions ranged from eight down to two hours. The number of participants also varied although, except for Module IV at some locations, most sessions had no more than 30 participants.

All sessions, regardless of level or length, followed a similar format. Each was led by a "boss" or "session leader" who opened with a "why we are here" statement. This was followed by showing a film called "Your Values — Our Values." Then came an issues identification/issues resolution exercise. Each session closed with information on the Ethics Program Director, the hotline, and how to get help with questions or concerns. This basic framework was enlarged in higher level workshops to include one or two case studies. In some Module IV sessions which had more than 30 participants, issues were identified and resolved in advance through focus groups and reported on to the session.

Almost all training was done by General Dynamics personnel. For Round I and II sessions, outside facilitators were used to conduct the cases and lead the issue identification discussions. Round III sessions used individuals from training or line managers who had been specially prepared through a train-the-trainer program. In all, some 750 people from around the corporation were prepared through the train-the-trainer program to conduct ethics training sessions. This was, without doubt, one of the great success stories of the workshop program.

Several desired outcomes guided the development of the training program based on a desire to build awareness, knowledge, and commitment in relation to the Standards. The workshops aimed at enabling employees to identify situations, issues, or dilemmas of an ethical nature in their own workplaces. Another aim was to call attention to the applicable standards, rules, regulations, or practices that applied, and to understand better the role that personal, corporate, and public expectations play in daily decisionmaking. A third aim was to teach some simple tests, rules of thumb, or key questions for easy use in making choices about matters of conduct. Still another aim was to insure that everyone in the session knew where to go for help when they had a question or concern they were unable to resolve themselves. Finally, the workshops aimed to demonstrate a commitment to the Standards through the example of session leaders.

From these desired outcomes, and based on discussions with top management in Rounds I and II workshops, a set of specifications emerged for constructing Round III workshops. Like Rounds I and II, Round III was top-down, line-driven, line-led, and, as much as possible, line-delivered. Many questions and doubts initially surrounded the notion of "line-delivered." A train-the-trainer program was developed and "line-delivered" turned out to be a brilliant success.

Round III's format was participative, stressing personal involvement and a team approach to the identification and resolution of questions and problems. This was accomplished through a workshop format transformed into focus groups as the training program reached Module IV and sessions larger than 30 were held. A careful record was kept of everyone who attended in order to assure accurate billing of training time and to certify completion of the training goal of reaching all employees, at all levels, at all locations worldwide. Finally, the outcomes, in terms of awareness, knowledge, and commitment were meant to be measurable.

The actual planning of the training program unfolded as follows: A group of individuals at Corporate Headquarters together with an outside consultant developed and helped deliver Round I. The decision to proceed to Round II was determined by Round I participants, and its delivery was accomplished using a number of individuals assembled by the same outside consultant used in planning Round I. Each division or subsidiary designated a lead trainer, who attended the Round II workshop with the Ethics Program Director. These individuals were directly responsible for the training flowdown at each location. Round III, Modules I to III were piloted at the Pomona Division with participation by a number of other lead trainers and Ethics Program Directors. In the meantime, a train-the-trainer program was developed using an outside firm to produce the materials. Each division or subsidiary designated their own managers to be trained and actually did the training. Module IV was piloted at the Electric Boat Division. All planning efforts and materials were flexible, adaptable, and stressed local initiative in delivery.

A minimum of materials was provided to conduct each session. The film "Your Values — Our Values" was developed and produced inside the corporation and featured General Dynamics employees. Some divisions adapted the film to their training sessions by featuring their own employees where appropriate. (Incidentally, the film won a Certificate of Merit in the 1986 Visual Communicators Department of the Year competition.) Two cases were used at higher level workshops, one of which was specifically developed for General Dynamics use. The Standards booklet was used for the issues identification exercise. A card was distributed at many sessions that provided a brief checklist to follow in resolving ethical dilemmas and gave the name and telephone number of the Ethics Program Director.

For remote locations or instances where only one person needed to be trained, a self-paced Ethics Awareness training instructional package was developed at the Space Systems Division and Corporate Headquarters.

While the Ethics Awareness training was taking place, several other large-scale, corporate-wide training efforts were under way involving subjects related to the Standards of Business Ethics and Conduct. These included Labor Recording training directed at some 88,000 employees, New Business Funds training directed at about 3,300 employees, and Overhead Expense Reporting training directed at 30,000 employees. Labor Recording training was more than 96-percent complete by the end of 1986. The other two training programs were completed in 1986.

Two-Way Communications and Hotlines. A critical ingredient in implementing the Ethics Program involves establishing special channels for employees to raise questions or seek advice about the meaning and application of the Standards. These channels must also serve employees who voice concerns or make actual allegations concerning violations of the Standards. To be effective, these channels of communication must be readily available, responsive, protective of the identity of the user and anyone else the user might identify, and offer reasonable assurance that anyone using these channels will suffer no reprisal. Employees are counseled first to raise their questions or concerns directly with other employees who might be involved, or with their supervisor. If neither approach is appropriate or they fail to work, employees are urged to contact the Ethics Program Director or the legal counsel's office. Several means are available for contacting the Ethics Program Directors. The company has established 29 hotlines around the corporation including a toll-free 800 number to the Corporate Office. The hotlines are answered only by Ethics Program Directors. When they are not in their offices, a 24-hour answering machine takes the call and offers the caller an opportunity to leave a number.

The hotlines were installed in December 1985. Posters were placed in prominent positions throughout the company. Stories about the Ethics Program Directors and the hotlines have appeared in the monthly corporate-wide employee news publication, *General Dynamics World*, to help maintain awareness. Monthly reports on communication activity are made to the Board Committee on Corporate Responsibility. These reports make clear that more than two-thirds of all communications — of which there were 3,646 in 1986 — ask questions or seek advice. These are usually handled immediately. The rest of the contacts raise concerns or make allegations. The Ethics Program Directors screen all contacts and classify them by degree of seriousness beginning with Priority I, which involve possible illegal activities or activities that could have a grave impact on the company's reputation. Priority II contacts do not involve apparent illegalities but nevertheless could prove embarrassing to the company if they were public knowledge. Priority III contacts usually involve information or suggestions. Only about 10 percent of all contacts are of Priority I or II.

The most common contact involves interpersonal relations: supervisor and subordinate, peer-to-peer, or company policy or practice and employee. The concern is almost always expressed in terms of fairness, and these contacts are generally worked through the appropriate line managers or the Human Resources function. The second most frequent contact involves labor-charging procedures. If these contacts are about the proper procedure for recording time, they are worked through the Labor Help Line. If they involve possible mischarging, they are worked through the company's legal counsel following the guidelines set forth in CPP 23-103 (Investigations and Sanctions). Others frequently called on to advise the Ethics Program Director or assist in fact-finding or investigation include Security and Internal Audit.

All investigations are carried out following the guidelines established in CPP 23-103. This policy describes a three-step process that aims at protecting the individuals involved and the company. Decisions regarding violations and appropriate sanctions are made by management. In 1986, based on allegations raised through Ethics Program Directors, over 100 sanctions were imposed ranging from warning to discharge and referral for criminal prosecution.

Recognition and Rewards. Another way of incorporating the Ethics Program into the organization is through the mechanisms by which performance is rewarded. As 1986 drew to a close, an initiative was undertaken to recognize all individuals who played significant roles in the planning and facilitation of the Ethics Awareness Workshops. About 750 individuals corporate-wide have been identified. While each received a special certificate designating them as Ethics Program Fellows, some received Extraordinary Achievement Awards for unusually exceptional contributions.

Review and Planning. Is the Ethics Program effective? Do the Standards make a difference? These are important questions that need answering if the program is to be systematically improved and if the use of scarce resources to implement it are to be properly accounted for. Several different means of measuring the program's effectiveness were tried in 1986. These included a corporate-wide employee survey and an Internal Audit verification of the Ethics Program. Both were conducted late in the year. These efforts indicate that the Ethics Program has been firmly established, that it has created a high degree of awareness and knowledge of the Standards, and that it has led to change in how the daily business of the corporation is conducted and how the company is perceived by employees. The results of these various efforts will be incorporated into the plans for the Ethics Program in 1987.

Appendix

General Dynamics' Standards of Business Ethics and Conduct

Our Mission. General Dynamics is a company of talented, dedicated, and resourceful people who share a responsibility to provide the highest quality products for the benefit of the United States and the Free World.

General Dynamics develops, produces, and supports innovative, reliable, and highly sophisticated systems and diverse military and commercial products to keep our nation technologically strong in every environment from undersea to outer space. These programs consistently evolve as the foundation for the next generation of technical advancements.

As a leading engineering-based manufacturer, we bring together a wide variety of technical and business concepts to provide cost-efficient production programs which uniquely satisfy our customers' challenging requirements.

Our Commitments. There are five key relationships in the business of General Dynamics. These relationships involve customers, suppliers, fellow employees, shareholders, and the communities in which we operate. All employees participate in one way or another in these key relationships. The following commitments serve as broad ideals for shaping these relationships.

- To our customers we will be attentive and strive to maximize the value, quality, and operability of General Dynamics products and services within the requirements of our contracts.
- To our suppliers we will be the best customer we can be and will emphasize both fair competition and long-lasting relationships.
- To each other, as employees, we will treat one another fairly and with the dignity and respect due all human beings.

- To our shareholders we will pursue our growth and earnings objectives while always keeping ethical standards at the forefront of our activities.
- To the many communities of which we are a member, and to society as a whole, we will act as responsible and responsive corporate citizens and in a moral, ethical, and beneficial manner.

Our Values. In order to fulfill these commitments, it is important for all employees to be:

- Dedicated and loyal to our company and to our country
- Law-abiding
- Honest and trustworthy
- Responsible and reliable
- Truthful and accurate
- Fair and cooperative
- Economical in utilizing company and customer resources

Our Responsibilities. Under these Standards, the company is responsible for:

- Implementing the Ethics Program.
- Distributing the General Dynamics Standards of Business Ethics and Conduct contained in this booklet to all employees.
- Providing all employees with clear guidelines on matters of everyday business conduct.
- Making sure through established educational and training programs that all employees are aware of and understand the Standards.
- Providing continuing counsel on company rules and regulations to any employee who seeks it.
- Maintaining working conditions at all locations supportive of employee responsibilities under these Standards.
- Enforcing compliance with the Standards.
- Recognizing employees who make an exemplary effort to implement and uphold the Standards.

Supervisors. Under these Standards, all levels of supervision have a special responsibility for the implementation of the Standards of Business Ethics and Conduct and will be measured in their performance for:

- Assuring that all current and new employees under their supervision receive a copy of the Standards of Business Ethics and Conduct and are trained in its meaning and application.
- Reviewing the knowledge and understanding of this booklet by employees under their supervision and ensuring that "refresher" programs are provided as necessary.

- Stressing to all employees in word and deed the need for a continuing commitment to the Standards.
- Demonstrating their own commitment by conducting themselves and managing their departments and the activities of all employees under their supervision in accordance with the Standards.
- Maintaining a workplace environment that encourages frank and open communication, free of the fear of reprisal, concerning the upholding of the Standards.

All employees. Under these Standards, all employees, regardless of rank or station, are responsible for:

- Reviewing regularly their knowledge and understanding of the Standards.
- Upholding the Standards and the policies, procedures, and practices that support them as demonstrated by their daily business conduct.
- Contributing to a workplace environment that is conducive to the maintenance of the Standards in daily business activities.
- Seeking help when the proper course of action is unclear or unknown.
- Remaining alert and sensitive to situations which could result in actions by any employee that are illegal, unethical, in violation of the Standards or the policies and procedures that support the Standards, or otherwise improper.
- Counseling fellow employees when it appears they may be in danger of violating the Standards or company policies and procedures.
- Reporting violations of the Standards to those to whom responsibility for discipline has been assigned.

Specific ethical responsibilities of employees should be clearly defined by the company in education and training programs. Any employee still in doubt about his or her responsibilities should feel free to seek additional counsel from his or her supervisor or any Ethics Program Director.

Our Standards. "A conflict between the private interests and the official responsibilities of a person in a position of trust."

As employees we should all consider ourselves as persons in positions of trust and conduct ourselves accordingly. We must be particularly sensitive to the many situations, on and off the job, where a conflict of interest or even a perception of such a conflict could originate. Such conflicts could involve customers, suppliers, present or prospective employees, shareholders, or members of the communities in which we operate.

Gifts, Gratuities, and Entertainment to Customers. As a company, our continuing objective is to provide our customers with the highest quality product at the best possible price.

It is a serious violation of our Standards for any employee to seek a competitive advantage through the use of gifts, gratuities, entertainment, or other favors. Under no circumstance may we offer or give any item of value to a customer or a customer's representative in an effort to influence a contract award or other favorable customer action. It is General Dynamics' policy to compete solely on the merits of its products and services.

In some foreign countries, customs require the exchange of gifts. In cases where it is desirable to meet such a requirement, the company will provide the gift; any gifts received will become company property.

Inside Information. In no instance may we as employees ever use or share inside information, which is not otherwise available to the general public, for any manner of personal gain as might be realized, for example, through trading in the stock of our company or any other company.

Outside Interests. A conflict with the interests of General Dynamics can arise when an employee holds a material investment interest in or is an official, director or employee of another enterprise, particularly if that enterprise is a supplier of products or services to the company. While such circumstances are not automatically prohibited, they are not desirable and must not be entered into or exist without prior written disclosure to and approval by the company.

Former Government Employees. The company has clear written policies and procedures which govern the conditions of employment of former U.S. Government employees and which will affect the duties they perform as employees of General Dynamics.

It is absolutely essential that the company and any such employee abide strictly by the letter and spirit of these policies and procedures to preclude the fact or perception of illegality or impropriety.

Selling and marketing. As employees, we should remember these key points in connection with sales or marketing of our products and services:

- If at any time, it becomes clear that the company must engage in unethical or illegal activity to win a contract, that business will not be pursued further.
- It is our responsibility as employees to understand the requirements of the customer and do the very best we can to satisfy those requirements by submitting realistic proposals on performance, cost, and schedule.
- We must make certain that the company's contractual obligations are clearly defined.
- All information we provide relative to General Dynamics products or services should be clear and accurate.

Antitrust. The antitrust laws of the United States and other countries are extremely important.

A wide range of transactions or practices are prohibited under those laws. No agreement or understanding may be made with competitors to fix or control prices, to allocate products, markets, or territories, to boycott certain customers or suppliers, or to refrain from or limit the manufacture, sale, or production of any product.

The provisions of the antitrust statutes apply to both formal and informal communications. Employees involved in trade association activities or in other situations allowing for less formal communication among competitors, customers, or suppliers must be especially alert to the requirements of the law.

Anyone in doubt as to the application of the antitrust laws in the United States or overseas should immediately consult a company attorney.

Pricing, billing, and contracting. Employees who are involved in any way in the pricing, billing, or contracting functions have a special responsibility to:

- Understand and adhere to all applicable procurement regulations and relevant company policies and procedures with regard to all aspects of the sale of General Dynamics products or services.
- Ensure that cost accounting standards and principles of cost allowability as well as relevant company policies and procedures are properly and consistently followed.
- Establish prices for company products and services that are fair and reflect their cost, the technology involved, the difficulty of overall performance, the market conditions, and all other relevant factors. In our pricing negotiations with the U.S. Government, we must at all times adhere to the provisions of the Truth in Negotiations Act and relevant company policies and procedures. Our prices should be clear, accurate, and presented so as to be fully understood by the customer.
- Accurately reflect, in all invoices to customers and others, the product sold or services rendered, the true sales price, and terms of sale. Payments received in excess of amounts billed must be promptly refunded or customer accounts credited, as appropriate.

Timecard reporting. Timely and accurate completion of timecards company policies and procedures is essential. We must ensure that no cost is allocated to a government contract which is unallowable, contrary to the contract or related regulations, or otherwise improper. All employees shall report only the true and actual number of hours worked by them. Shifting of costs to inappropriate contracts is strictly prohibited. Reporting of hours not worked, but for which pay is received, must also be true and accurate.

Suppliers and consultants. Whenever possible, materials, supplies, equipment, consulting, and other services should be procured from qualified suppliers at the lowest cost, keeping in mind the requirements for quality, performance, and the vendor's ability to meet delivery schedules.

As a company and as individual employees, we will always employ the highest ethical business practices in source selection, negotiation, determination of awards, and the administration of all purchasing activities. Whenever feasible, we will encourage, establish, and maintain competition and will at all times comply with applicable government regulations and contractual requirements as well as company policies and procedures.

Except for items that are clearly promotional in nature, mass produced, trivial in value, and not intended to evoke any form of reciprocation, employees of General Dynamics may not accept gifts, entertainment, or anything else of value from current or potential suppliers of goods or services from consultants to the company. Solicitation of any item, regardless of value, is expressly prohibited.

Quality and testing. It is our responsibility as a company to ensure that our products are designed and manufactured to meet the appropriate inspection, test, and quality criteria of our customers, to perform the testing necessary to meet these criteria, and to provide the necessary documentation in support of this testing. The inspection and testing documentation must be complete, accurate, and truthful. As employees we are all expected to be aware of and exercise this responsibility, as our jobs require.

Expense reports. Business expenses properly incurred in performing company business must be documented promptly with accuracy and completeness on expense reports.

In the filing of expense reports, employees must distinguish between personal expenses and business travel expenses, business conference expenses, and business entertainment expenses.

Employees using company funds for such expenses should indicate where, in their judgment, certain costs are or might be unallowable or inappropriate charges against government contracts.

Company and customer resources. The ability of General Dynamics to meet the broad commitments to customers, suppliers, employees, shareholders, and communities depends on efficiently utilizing company and customer resources. These resources include technology, data, buildings, land, equipment, cash, and the time and talent of employees.

As employees we may not make improper use of company or customer resources nor permit others to do so.

This particularly prohibits the payment of bribes, kickbacks or illegal payments of cash or other gifts in any form and in any amounts.

Other examples of improper use include unauthorized appropriation, possession or personal use of company or customer assets, technology and patents, software, computer, communication and copying equipment, or office supplies. Also forbidden is the unauthorized possession, use, alteration, destruction or disclosure of company sensitive data.

Technology and Information. The backbone of General Dynamics as a competitive business is our ability to develop and use high technology in day-to-day operations. Failure to maintain control of our technological edge could cause us irreparable harm. As employees, we are all responsible for guarding our technology against unauthorized disclosure. This applies not only to government classified information, but also to proprietary and private data developed or purchased by us or entrusted to us by customers or suppliers. These restrictions apply whether the information is in written or electronic form or is simply known by us as employees.

Cash and Bank Accounts. All cash and bank account transactions must be handled so as to avoid any question of bribery, kickbacks, other illegal or improper payments or any suspicion of impropriety whatsoever. All cash transactions must be recorded in the company's books of account.

All accounts of company funds shall be established and maintained in the name of General Dynamics or one of its subsidiaries, with the exception of petty cash accounts. All transactions and accounts involving company funds shall be clearly and accurately identified in General Dynamics' books and records. All cash received by the company shall be promptly recorded on its books and deposited in a General Dynamics bank account. No funds shall be maintained in the form of cash, except to the limited extent reasonably required for normal business operations.

Security. General Dynamics is a major contractor with the Department of Defense. We, as employees, have a special obligation to comply with those government regulations and laws, as well as with relevant company policies and procedures, which protect our nation's security and safeguard our nation's defense secrets.

The effectiveness of national and industrial security is heavily dependent on those individuals who have access to classified information. As employees, security is an integral part of our jobs, whether or not we work directly with such information.

Employees possessing a valid security clearance and requiring access to specific classified information will ensure that such information, in whatever form it exists, is handled strictly in accordance with the procedures set forth by the Department of Defense for safeguarding classified information.

We should not seek access to, accept, or retain any classified materials for which we have no need or to which we are not entitled.

The unauthorized possession of classified documents or classified information in any form, or failure to properly safeguard such information, violates these Standards, can endanger the security of the United States, and is punishable under the Espionage Laws and Federal Criminal Statutes.

Political contributions. Federal law and many state laws prohibit contributions by the corporation to political parties or candidates. Where prohibited by law, therefore, no company funds or other assets are to be contributed or loaned, directly or indirectly, to any political party or for the campaign of any person for political office, or expended in support of or in opposition to such party or person.

Where corporate political contributions are legal in connection with state, local, or foreign elections, such contributions shall be made only from funds allocated for such a purpose by authorization of the board of directors.

The company encourages all of us as employees to participate on an individual basis in political activities on our own time and in our own way.

Environmental actions. As a company and as employees, we must exercise good judgment with regard to the environmental aspects of our use of buildings and real estate, our manufacturing processes, and our products themselves. All necessary action must be taken to eliminate the generation, discharge, and disposal of hazardous materials. We must comply fully with all federal, state, and local environmental protection laws.

Safety and health. As a company and as individual employees we are responsible for maintaining a safe and healthful work environment. We must comply fully with all federal, state, and local health and safety laws and regulations.

International Business. Special care must be taken to identify and accommodate the differences between international markets and those in the United States.

As a company operating internationally, we encounter laws which may vary widely from those in the United States. These laws may on occasion conflict with one another. Local customs and practices with regard to business and social dealings may also vary from country to country. Our policy is to comply with all laws which apply in the countries where we do business. The laws of the United States and the countries in which General Dynamics does business must be obeyed. Furthermore, in countries where common business practices might be less restrictive than those outlined in the Standards, we will follow the Standards outlined in this booklet.

The Foreign Corrupt Practices Act and other U.S. laws prohibit the payment of any money or anything of value to a foreign official, foreign political party (or official thereof), or any candidate for foreign political office for purposes of obtaining, retaining, or directing of business. As a company and as employees, we must strictly abide by these laws. Any violations or any solicitations to violate must be reported immediately.

The Foreign Corrupt Practices Act, although silent on the subject, is said not to prohibit so called "facilitating payments," such as payments for expediting shipments through customs or placing a transoceanic telephone call, securing required permits, or obtaining adequate police protection — transactions which simply facilitate the proper performance of duties. While company policy does not prohibit such payments, employees are to seek advice in advance from company legal counsel in cases where facilitating payments may be involved. Any such facilitating payments must be properly accounted for in the company's records.

Proper use of the ethics program. An important aim of the Ethics Program is to provide guidance to all employees on matters of ethics and business conduct. The Ethics Program is available to answer questions, give advice, address concerns, and investigate allegations related to the meaning and application of the Standards of Business Ethics and Conduct.

Unfortunately such a program is subject to abuse. From time to time, in the name of "Ethics," an employee may attempt to harm or slander another employee through false accusations, malicious rumors, or other irresponsible actions. Such attempts, if proven, will be subject to discipline.

Again, from time to time, an employee who exercises responsibility for upholding the Standards may be threatened with reprisal by other employees including management. Such reprisal is not only against company policy, but, in some instances, is also a violation of the law. Reprisal, if proven, will be subject to commensurate discipline.

Acknowledgement. As a condition of employment, all new employees are asked to sign an Acknowledgement Card which states:

I have received and read the Second Edition of the General Dynamics Standards of Business Ethics and Conduct. I understand that these Standards represent the policies of General Dynamics.

All current employees are also asked to sign an Acknowledgement Card each time the Standards are revised and redistributed.

One copy of the card is to be retained by the employee. The other copy is placed in the employee's permanent personnel file.

All standard consultant agreements include a clause requiring adherence to the Standards as a condition of the agreement.

All active suppliers receive an annual solicitation to help support the Standards in business relationships between them and General Dynamics.

Help and Information. The company has designated personnel to assist employees in resolving questions involving ethics and conduct. As employees, we should not hesitate to avail ourselves of the help.

Supervisors. An employee with a need for help or information regarding these Standards is encouraged to take up that need with his or her immediate supervisor. If there is reason why asking the immediate supervisor is inappropriate, the employee should seek the help of the Ethics Program Director or a company attorney.

Ethics program directors. Ethics Program Directors have been designated for each of the various company locations and are available for employee counseling and assistance with regard to these Standards. The Ethics Program Directors may be reached by way of regular telephone, hotline, letter, or personal visit. Inquiries will be treated with courtesy and discretion.

Company attorneys. Company attorneys of General Dynamics are available to employees and management for assistance and information with regard to these Standards and for the issuance of interpretative opinions.

Discipline and Mandatory Sanctions. The Standards in this booklet are important to the company and must be taken seriously by all of us as employees. Accordingly, violations of these Standards will not be tolerated and, in accordance with company regulations and applicable collective bargaining agreements, will result in one or more of the following sanctions, as appropriate:

- A warning
- A reprimand (will be noted in individual's permanent personnel record)
- Probation
- Demotion
- Temporary suspension
- Discharge
- Required reimbursement of losses or damages
- Referral for criminal prosecution or civil action

Summary. It is the objective of the company and each of us as employees to operate according to the highest possible standards. We have a serious responsibility to ensure that our personal conduct is above reproach and, difficult as it may be at times, we also have obligations regarding the conduct of those who work around us. In cases where we are aware of violations of the Standards in this booklet, we should make that situation known to our supervisor or to an Ethics Program Director.

The Standards will be enforced at all levels fairly and without prejudice. Consistent with our obligations under the law, and within the enforcement processes established herein, the company will keep confidential the identity of employees about or against whom allegations of violations are brought, unless or until it has been determined that a violation has occurred. Similarly, the company will take all reasonable steps to keep confidential the identity of anyone reporting a possible violation.

25

Creativity at Bonneville International

Jean Bishop, Bonneville International

Yes, at Bonneville International Corporation, because we are engaged in the commercial broadcast and media communications business, we must be concerned with creativity. In fact, creativity is the name of the game for us. In our business, we live or die depending upon our creativity. We must present our on-air product/programming in a creative way — a way that will appeal to our target audience — those people we want to influence to listen to us.

Programming a radio station is a real art form as is producing a TV program or commercial. For instance in radio, the program director must design the format (the mix of music, news public affairs, commercials, and so on) that will compose the station's overall sound. Then the right people have to be selected to project the feelings and convey the image prescribed by the format.

Bonneville must promote its on-air product in a creative way. Our promotion must be packaged in a way that will encourage people to:

1. Start listening to us if they aren't presently a listener.
2. Keep listening to us if they are a listener.

We want to make them feel that our station has what they want to listen to and that they make a good choice when they listen to us.

Determining the right format and promoting it effectively is a real challenge in all of the markets where we do business. For instance, in both New York City and in Los Angeles, we compete in a market that has over 80 other radio stations! Obviously, our creativity is paying off, since our stations are consistently rated as one of the top in their market.

We are heavily involved in research. It is important for us to know what our audience's values are, what is important to them, what they think about, how they spend their time and money, what their predominant lifestyle is. We are constantly conducting focus groups and obtaining survey data and we use psychographics. We do some research internally but specialists do most of it for us — Magid, Lee Stowell, Yankelvich, and so forth. This data is analyzed in depth in many different and creative ways to assist in assuring us that we are meeting our audience's needs.

In broadcasting, we are fortunate to have regular feedback available that tells us how we are doing. There are the Nielson ratings for television and Arbitron and Birch ratings for radio. The latter give us a pretty good idea on an ongoing basis whether or not we are attracting and holding our audience.

We strive to be creative in all aspects of our business. In sales we have moved way beyond the old performance cost-per-point type selling. Our account executives must be marketing specialists as well as salespersons. Our approach now is designed to help the client's key decisionmakers cut advertising costs, improve their image, sell their values, and so on. In other words, we help them understand their needs and market to those needs.

Bonneville has done some creative things in its Finance Department. (I made that statement to a gentleman one day and he said, "Boy, I don't want anyone in my Finance Department being creative with figures. I want to know exactly what money has come in and what money has gone out.") Well, we do know what money comes and goes, but Bonneville has designed and adapted finance systems that take advantage of advanced concepts to make us most effective. We have internal audits, computerized accounts payable, accounts receivable, general ledger, and payroll, and we have operational reviews. We are currently working on a payroll dump into our personnel system to help us complete technical reports for management with greater ease and accuracy. We transmit accounting reports between our divisions and home office over the phone or via satellite.

Creativity Starts with Top Management. Okay, so we're creative, but how do we go about getting the creativity we need?

I feel it all starts at the top with the vision and philosophy of the company president. Since its inception back in 1964, Bonneville has been blessed with the kind of top leadership that was committed to outstanding community service, planned personnel development, quality programming, profitability, and leadership in the effective use of the mass media in dealing with significant issues of our day.

Arch L. Madsen was president of Bonneville from its inception in 1964 until 1985 when Rodney H. Brady became president. Both men have set extremely high standards for themselves and for the company. Their personal integrity and values permeate the company. Their management style is participative, not autocratic. They realize that any accomplishments Bonneville makes will be through its people, and to get the most from people you must have enlightened managers.

It has been a tradition for over 20 years to have annual week-long senior management retreats where managers are exposed to different concepts by rubbing shoulders with gurus like Charles Garfield, Tom Peters, Ken Blanchard, Steve Covey, Mike Vance, Denis Waitley, and many specialists in the broadcasting, communications, and advertising industries.

Our managers are not told how to implement new ideas or concepts in operating their own divisions. They have the autonomy and flexibility to take advantage of the opportunities that may occur in their particular marketplace and to implement changes that are harmonious with their management's state of evolution. Corporate policies and procedures and corporate staff consultants provide guidelines to help assure the manager that the standards he or she and his or her team set will be legally, morally, and psychologically acceptable. However, we share the creative approaches used by the different managers.

Sharing creative ideas between the divisions means the idea may be utilized in another market or can be piggy-backed or adapted to work in another market. This sharing is done both informally and formally. The formal sharing takes place at our senior managers seminar and at our other group management seminars — our sales managers seminar, our business managers seminar, our personnel directors seminar, and so on. We have a section in our house newsletter where new ideas or new community service projects are outlined. We have special teleconferences to discuss matters that we want to address more creatively so that we can have a broad view of the matter and build upon each other's ideas.

At our 1985 Senior Management Seminar, the managers jointly redesigned our company mission and commitment statement and decided to enunciate our core values. This year at our annual seminar, we will create our vision — the legacy we want to leave our markets in five or ten years. Because of the business we are in and because of the communities, we have a unique opportunity to focus our efforts to make a difference. We will determine the kind of people we need to accomplish this vision and the kind of culture needed to attract, retain, and nourish these people.

Sharing Creative Ideas. Of course, creativity in all our areas of involvement emanates from Bonneville's greatest asset — its people. We have a lot of super-talented, committed people throughout our company. This is not an accident. Bonneville feels it is vital to hire and retain the right kind of people. Bonneville takes the time to analyze the contribution a specific position needs to make. Then it seeks a person with the required qualifications. In addition to the technical skills necessary, Bonneville looks for an individual who can buy into its core values, is willing to continue growing, wants to project the desired company image, and understands the need for and is willing to make the necessary effort to communicate effectively with each person with whom he or she must interact. Employees must be willing to work in a smoke-free environment and evidence their interest in industry and community involvement.

To attract and retain talented, committed, values-oriented employees, Bonneville provides an attractive physical working environment containing the latest technical equipment. Our employees designed a wage and salary program that measures each position's contribution and assures external and internal pay equity. We have incentive programs that provide profit-sharing when goals are exceeded or operating costs reduced. We have a comprehensive benefit package that includes medical/dental/short-term disability/long-term disability/ life insurance/accidental death and dismemberment/401(K) Thrift Plan/pension plan/Flex-spending account, and so forth.

Our company's management style gives an employee the responsibility and accountability for his or her assigned area of contribution. Each position has an updated job description that tells each employee what his or her areas of responsibility are. Currently we are working to establish performance standards for most positions.

Providing Growth Opportunities. Bonneville provides growth opportunity. We realize that to be leaders in our industry and in the communities we serve, we have to "stand on higher ground." For this reason, the corporation provides the resources to make it possible for each staff member to expand his or her horizons. The company encourages all management to annually attend a seminar or convention to keep them current in their area of expertise. We provide various in-house workshops and educational assistance and cross-training. We have various recognition programs to reward excellence. We are constantly trying to do a better job at sharing information, goals, plans, results, to keep everyone in the company informed, and to help them realize that they are an integral and necessary part of our commitment to provide quality broadcast entertainment, information, news, and values-oriented programming. At Bonneville, we must be effective as individuals and as a team if we are to enhance our company potential to serve and improve individuals, community, and society.

PART III

Exploiting Information Technology

26

Networking Is the Organization

Ellen S. Quackenbush, Group Manager, DEC

I would like to give you a business perspective on why everyone is talking networking today. For example:

- Why a worldwide banking network that supports 24-hour a day trading is considered essential for today's bank.
- Why a dealer network that lets customers order the exact car they want right from the dealer showroom and, at the same time, schedules its production on the factory floor is key to Detroit.
- Why networks which allow cross-functional teams of people to speed new products to market or customize products for the needs of local markets are taking hold in even the most traditional industries.

In short, I will discuss how and why companies are using networking to create the lean, mean, and flexible organization that will win in the 1990s.

Networking Has Come of Age. The role of information technology and especially networking has changed dramatically over the last 20 years. In the 1960s and 1970s, information technology was used to automate stable, well-understood areas of the business. Vertical functions with predictable information flow — such as payroll or accounting — were good candidates for this type of automation. These "vertical" information systems were typically designed, installed, and managed by corporate MIS departments, with little or no involvement of the end user. They were tuned for high performance, and typically included a dedicated mainframe and network for each business application.

This style of networking worked well when the goal was to optimize a stand-alone business function and provide efficient, vertical information flow within the organization. As long as the business requirements remained stable, functions did not need to cooperate across organizational boundaries and applications did not need to talk to one another; everything was fine. However, that is not today's business reality. It is no longer good enough to be an efficient organization; the goal for today and tomorrow is organizational flexibility. The efficient organization defines what it wants to do, and then drives costs to the ground. But if you, for example, have become efficient at making buggy whips, you are in trouble. What is needed today is the flexibility to identify and act upon market trends quicker than the competition, and to muster all of the resources in your organization to meet new market opportunities.

The goal now is cross-functional information sharing across the organization, which requires horizontal as opposed to vertical information flow. Order Entry has to work with Manufacturing and Distribution. Sales has to work with Marketing and Engineering. A flexible, open networking system is essential for them to all work together.

Today, networks are providing the information technology to support this new kind of flexible corporate infrastructure. They are being used to break down the barriers that developed in the 1960s and 1970s between functions, between applications, and between organizations.

It is not surprising that line of business managers, not MIS or communications managers, are using networking as a strategic resource to help manage their business as an integrated whole and to create the kind of organizational flexibility that will win in the 1990s.

Today's Business Pressures. Business pressures companies face today are very different from the ones they faced in the past and help to explain the push for flexibility and cooperation. Let's examine these pressures.

Time pressures. Time has become a critical metric for business competitiveness — time to market is watched as closely as cost in getting a new product to market nowadays. The pace of business processes has accelerated through automation of routine tasks, real-time operational control, and direct links to suppliers and customers. Shortened windows of opportunity are requiring faster decision-making processes. It is becoming increasingly important to recognize the early warning signs of market shifts and muster all the resources of your organization to respond to these changes.

Global competition. All companies that are significant in size have to compete on a global scale today. That does not mean being sensitive to local markets and diverse cultures. A product that is successful in France may not be successful in Germany or Japan. Often, a new approach to marketing, dealing with customers, and meeting local regulations will also be required. John Naisbit, the author of *MegaTrends*, describes this as the "simultaneous globalization and individualizing" of business offerings. The challenge is to have economy of scale and economy of scope at the same time. That is a very hard thing for an organization to accomplish: the idea of trying to be big and small at the same time. You want to be big to achieve economies of scale, yet you want to look small to best meet local needs.

Shifting market boundaries. Market and industry boundaries today are also shifting. It is becoming harder and harder for companies to answer the questions, "What business are we in?" and "Who are our competitors?" In some cases, information technology (in particular networking) is helping to redraw these boundaries. For example, look at the financial services industry. American Express, Sears, and Citibank seem to be spilling over into each other's business in a scramble for control of credit cards. Sears has opened a savings bank in California and both American Express and Citibank put merchandise circulars in their credit card mailings. The real confusion may be over our definition of the market. Each of these competitors has a very strong corporate network. Maybe the real business is operating a value-added network for electronic merchandising. It's not surprising that a major money center bank has been quoted as saying, "We're not a bank, we're a communications company."

Galloping technology. Add to this confusion a technology that is changing at a frightening rate. MIS managers don't talk the same language as telecom managers and line of business managers don't understand either of them. No wonder some business managers have a hard time keeping up with new technology and recognizing how to apply this technology to solve their business problems. Yet neither the technical expert nor the business expert has the whole answer. Both must cooperate to get the job done and learn to work in a cross-functional task force to develop innovative, successful ways to meet customer needs. Given this business environment, one of the worst handicaps a company can have is an unresponsive, closed organization. The traditional hierarchy, optimized for command and control, is the wrong organizational tool for today. It is designed to execute a known, stable objective and once its target is in sight, like the oil tanker, it has a hard time changing direction. A hierarchical organization makes it hard to see your business as an integrated whole, the way your customer sees it. It slows down the business process because cross-functional cooperation often only happens at the vice presidential level. Today's challenge is to build an organization that is integrated and efficient in its internal operations yet open and responsive to the external market.

What Business Are You In? One of the most important questions a company has to ask itself today is, "What business am I in?" The answer is not always self-evident. Yet the correct answer is often the key to future competitiveness. For example, look at the digital watch market in the mid-1970s. Texas Instruments invented this market by applying their expertise in electronics to watches. TI also applied the same manufacturing strategy that has made them successful in the electronics component industry — "pricing down the learning curve."

TI standardized on one design to drive costs down, and ramped up volume as fast as possible. At the same time, they encouraged demand by pricing aggressively, driving the price of digital watches down from $80 to $20. They expected that people would go in droves to the local drugstore and grab up all the Texas Instruments watches. However, customer demand was low. The problem was that the design TI standardized on was somewhat less than fashionable. Nobody wanted to wear TI watches. TI never actually went out to talk to customers to see what they wanted in a digital watch.

At the same time, a small Japanese manufacturer called Casio decided to enter the digital watch marketplace. They began to experiment with small design changes, and developed a dozen or so prototypes. Some models looked like jewelry, others used rugged packaging enclosures and looked like scuba-diving watches. Some had different colored straps. Some used LCD displays, others used LED displays and so forth. Casio tried to figure out what kind of niches or segmentation could be applied to the marketplace, and after a couple of months they figured out which ones sold best in the marketplace. They designed standardized components to satisfy those designs, and then started driving down their price. Within 18 months, Casio watches had replaced TI watches on store shelves because they were providing watches that people wanted.

What was the difference? The difference was in how they defined the business they were in. TI's goal was to build watches. Casio's goal was to satisfy watch customers. They also had a different view of their organization. TI focused on one function, manufacturing, and on being the best manufacturer in the business. Casio focused on the entire value-added chain and, in fact, included customers in their product development process. Casio built an integrated organization that could learn from and respond to the external market. They both met their goals, but Casio won the business.

The Traditional Hierarchy. The traditional multi-level hierarchy no longer meets the needs of today's business environment. There are a lot of reasons why this is true. First, the traditional hierarchy provides an emphasis on control and functional efficiency rather than management and adaptation. There is a focus on "not failing" in their functional role rather than succeeding as a whole organization.

Second, workers at all levels become frustrated. At operational levels, workers lack the resources and authority to adapt to market shifts. Only the really revolutionary — Big Bang — ideas reach the top where they can be acted on. Small ideas and incremental changes get lost in the process. Upper management feels disconnected from "the real business." By the time they get information, all the real world context has been filtered out by layers of middle managers. Viewed in this context, MBWA (Management By Walking Around) is senior management's attempt to bypass the layers of hierarchy to get down where the real work is being done.

Third, the traditional organizational solution has been to use staff and planning processes to coordinate the functions. But staff is expensive, adds overhead, and is really the wrong answer to the right problem.

Focus on Goals: Yours and Theirs. A new organizational model is needed, one that extends beyond functional roles and organizational boundaries to view the industry as a whole, and that recognizes cooperation between industry partners as the new competitive edge. Your business is more than just manufacturing or engineering — it also includes your suppliers and customers. No company operates in isolation.

When a business begins to look outside its own organization, outside of its own brick walls, to its "extended value-added chain" to identify potential partners, the resulting cooperation can be very powerful. For example, look at the concept of "Just-In-Time Manufacturing." The business justification for Just-In-Time Manufacturing is usually pretty simple — it is seen as a way to reduce inventory. The benefits are often misrepresented as "externalizing" the risk and the cost of inventory onto the supplier.

In practice, however, the greater benefit to be gained by Just-In-Time Manufacturing is the flexibility obtained through the close cooperation between the supplier and the manufacturer. Each organization becomes able to learn from, and adapt to, the other. When your suppliers know what your plans are, they can make investments to make sure that the quality and delivery schedules of their components will link directly into your manufacturing needs. They know what your specs are, and you know what their capabilities are, so you do not have to ask your supplier to do something they are not capable of doing.

It is counterproductive to view a supplier as somebody to pin up against the wall and say, "I need faster delivery, and I need a lower price," because ultimately you are both going to win, or both going to lose. In the long run, the manufacturer can have a faster time to market, because the supplier knows what the manufacturer will require. The manufacturer is able to eliminate a whole step in the manufacturing process — incoming inspection — because they know the supplier's operation well enough that the inspection in essence happens before the product or the part hits the loading dock.

An example of such a win-win cooperative relationship can be seen at Monsanto Fibers, which sells fibers to carpet-weaving companies. Monsanto Fibers puts terminals in its customers' factories to be sure they are using Monsanto's fibers correctly and have chosen the right fiber for the job. According to Monsanto, it is like having a quality control inspector at your customer's site. Ultimately, the customer gets a higher quality product and buys more of Monsanto's fibers. Monsanto sells more fiber. A win-win situation.

A similar example is that Firestone has developed networked links to the Ford Motor Company in order to design tires that meet the need of models still on Ford's drawing boards.

The result is that today, firms are creating partnerships and strategic alliances with their suppliers and their customers based on win-win opportunities. The flexibility that such extended value-added chain partnerships provide wins over the functional hierarchy every time. In a phrase, "Simple efficiency is no longer enough. . . ." It is not doing things faster, it is working smarter. As Harold McGraw, the CEO of McGraw-Hill, has said:

> The major cause of the failure of large corporations to maintain a competitive advantage is the failure to maintain the flexibility, innovative thinking, and all-out dedication of a smaller, owner-managed company.

Key words here are "flexibility" and "innovation" — to learn faster, and incorporate "smallness" into your way of doing business.

Organizations Are Flattening Out. What are companies doing to try to recapture the advantage of smallness?

One thing they are doing is simply downsizing their organization, reducing the number of workers and layers of management. The story is told in company after company — the firm cuts headcount by 10 to 20 percent and costs drop while quality and time to market either remain unchanged or actually improve. Why? Because the middle managers and central staff whose principal function, as Peter Keene has said, is to be "information pools and message switches" are the ones first removed.

Peter Drucker has called the resulting business form "the information-based organization" and describes it as a "symphony" of cooperating experts working toward a shared goal. According to Drucker: "Traditional departments . . . won't be where the work gets done. That will happen in task-focused teams."

The center of gravity in organizations is moving down — from the top of the organization in older command and control hierarchies to the middle of the organization today. Decision-making and the core organizational knowledge is also moving down to the middle level of "knowledge workers." These workers are more specialized, independent, and responsible for coordinating and defining their own contribution to the group effort. Communication with other members of a cross-functional team is key.

Knowledge Worker Effectiveness Requires Information Sharing. In effect, the most important role now required of these knowledge workers is no longer to be functional middle managers, but to be members of cross-functional teams responsible for solving broad business problems. Effective organizational communication is required between *ad hoc* cross-functional groups — teams that are set up and broken down to solve particular business problems or to drive to market a particular new product for a particular customer group.

For example, Campbell Soup and Procter & Gamble are two packaged goods manufacturers that are moving new product development and delivery out of headquarters into the field. Campbell Soup is a leader in customizing base products for local markets. For example, the Nacho Cheese soup in Texas is spicier than the standard version sold in other parts of the country. Campbell Soup is going so far as to decentralize much of their marketing staff and advertising budgets out into the field in order to do away with the functional or product blinders that sometimes develop in companies that are focusing on a headquarters-driven approach. Procter & Gamble, who originated the concept of the all-powerful "brand manager," has similarly been taking steps to reorganize its middle management into cross-functional teams from R & D, marketing, manufacturing, and sales, in order to better meet the demands of more informed consumers and more powerful retailers. These cross-functional teams need a flexible communications technology that supports information sharing across functional boundaries.

New Form of Communication Required. The old style of organizational communications was based on a hierarchical structure, much like an organization chart. It focused on vertical flow and on economies of scale. The emphasis was on "not failing" in a certain function, as opposed to succeeding in cross-functional corporate goals.

The new form of organizational communication required by knowledge workers today focuses on the lateral, cross-functional flow of information — on information sharing, as opposed to information for management control. There is an emphasis on obtaining economies not of scale but of scope, enabling cooperating groups to work together more easily. The focus is on making an organization more adaptable, sensitive, and flexible to the market and marketplace needs. There is a goal of optimizing across functions, not within one function. Success is measured in terms of being responsive to customers, of sharing risk as opposed to allocating or avoiding risk.

Networking Is the Enabling Technology. But this does not mean scrapping your existing physical organization and rebuilding. Rather, the challenge and the opportunity is to use networking to create new patterns of information sharing within your existing organization. These "virtual organizations" overlay your current organization to support the cross-functional and inter-organizational groups that form to respond to changing market needs.

Take aerospace, for example. There aren't many firms in the industry and many government projects are too large for one company. Thus, to minimize risk and command the range of resources to complete a project, firms form inter-organizational teams to bid on large government contracts. These bidding teams don't follow any neat organizational boundaries. Engineering in Company A may be cooperating with engineers in Company B on one project and competing with them on another. Once the contract is awarded, the customer may wish to join this virtual organization to monitor progress on the project. Networking should be flexible enough, open enough, and standardized enough to support this interorganizational cooperation.

Corporate-wide "Enterprise Networks." A new style of networking is becoming a key asset in providing the flexible organizational communications that are now required. The old style of networking was hierarchical, emphasizing master/slave relationships between terminal and host. It was vertically optimized for efficiency, and typically would only function between a narrow ranger of systems developed by a single vendor.

A new style of networking is more appropriate for the organizational communications needs of the 1980s and 1990s. Today's new style of corporate-wide "Enterprise Networks" enable lateral and open information flow, and provide the flexibility to support global information sharing between functions, between applications, and in fact, between organizations. Today's networks need to accommodate a multi-vendor computing environment, based on international standards, to allow corporations to take advantage of the best technologies as they develop. They are optimized to connect islands of automations. They are designed from the beginning to openly support equipment from different vendors, and to integrate voice, data, video, and other communications technologies. They are designed to allow these multi-technology networks to be managed as a logical whole.

In fact, both the "old" and "new" styles of networking were developed in the early 1970s, albeit for different purposes. It is useful to examine why and how each evolved — in order to see the inherent strengths of each style, and their basic differences.

The first hierarchical computer networks began to emerge in the early 1970s. They were typified by IBM's System Networking Architecture (SNA). SNA was developed as a way of making the most efficient use of expensive mainframe resources. It allowed terminals in remote field sites to be connected to a centralized mainframe via a dedicated network link. The terminals could be used to enter and display data for a single mainframe application, without the need for local computers at the field sites. The SNA network architecture was optimized for efficiency and control, and provided the least-cost solution in an era when computers were very expensive — as long as the application, the business needs, and the communications flow requirements did not change.

At the same time, a completely different style of network began to emerge. It was first developed for the Department of Defense ARPANET network project as a means to directly connect all of the computers involved in the department's and related U.S. government research activities.

Unlike the commercial data processing mainframe applications for which SNA was optimized, ARPANET was designed to provide peer-to-peer connections between many diverse computing systems, both large and small, running a wide variety of applications.

The Department of Defense required a network that supported dynamic routing between many computer nodes, so that it could withstand node failures (for example, during combat conditions). NASA and other government agencies also required ARPANET to support cooperative research between universities and aerospace corporations. As a result, the ARPANET network was designed to accommodate multipurpose and diverse computing systems. It was designed to be rugged and capable of re-routing around failed nodes. It was designed to be very flexible in terms of ease of use and installation, and to be optimized for information sharing and unstructured work. It was the first large-scale peer-to-peer style network, and very successful.

Digital's networking products and capabilities are a direct descendant of the ARPANET style of networking. The Digital Network Architecture (DNA) was based on these same original ARPANET design considerations, and today provides the most powerful and successful implementation of peer-to-peer networking in use throughout the world.

Historically speaking, as SNA-style and ARPANET-style networks evolved into the 1980s, discussions concerning their relative merits bordered on the religious. It is important to realize that each architecture had its merits, and that each was designed to fulfill the needs of completely different customer bases. However, as we enter the 1990s, organizations are using peer-to-peer networking in areas of their business where flexibility and lateral information sharing is demanded. It is common to find a peer-to-peer logistics, distribution, and sales network "front-ending" a hierarchical order entry system. It is not surprising that peer-to-peer, ARPANET-style networks are in the spotlight today.

Requirements for the Network of the 1990s. What are the requirements for networking in the 1990s? Digital has identified four elements, which it calls its Strategic Network Vision.

The first requirement is "interconnectivity," that is, being able to plug two devices together and share the same wire. While this is certainly an important requirement, it is not useful by itself.

The second requirement is "interoperability." Interoperability is the ability for diverse devices to cooperate to perform useful work across the network. Interoperability requires that applications be able to cooperate in a transparent, flexible manner. Interoperability in a multi-vendor environment is certainly the largest challenge for business networking in the 1990s; it can best be achieved by adoption and conformance to the ISO/OSI international standards.

Third, "useability," is the ability to perform work that supports business objectives. A network must allow people to work together on problems to support the business needs. The network, in other words, must be a flexible enough system to adapt to changing business requirements as well as to support your current business strategy and business process.

Fourth, "manageability," is the ability to manage diverse systems and technologies across the network as a logical whole. The manageability of the network is necessary if it is to provide cost effective solutions to changing business requirements.

It is important to realize that all four of these requirements must be in place for a network to achieve its goal. You cannot eliminate any one of these without getting into trouble. If a network provides interconnectivity, but not interoperability, in a sense it provides just plumbing, without the intelligence to do useful, cooperative work. If a network provides useability without manageability, it can support business operations and strategy only if they are static. Without the ability to manage change, change can only be accommodated by *ad hoc* patches, and at a high cost. These are the four components of Digital's Strategic Network Vision. Digital has developed a strong networking product set to achieve each of these requirements.

"The Network Is Your Organization." In summary, let's take a look at what a well-designed network lets you do today and in the 1990s. From the business manager's perspective, the end result is a network that models the organization — a network flexible enough to adapt and support organizational goals and the current business process. This network does not limit what you do, but models what you decide to do. The network gives business managers the flexibility to do what they do best — run the business.

Looking from the bottom up, from a technical or MIS manager's perspective, the network is an architecture that allows technical experts to incorporate new technology as it matures, without disturbing the business applications that reside on top. It supports the business transparently, regardless of what the business requirements are. In essence the network becomes, and really is, your organization's system and way of doing business. The network gives the technical manager the ability to provide transparent access between systems, and transparently incorporate new systems and technologies to support the business.

Putting these two perspectives together, the network provides the partnership that companies are always elusively trying to create between technology experts and business experts. It lets the business person run the business, and it lets the technology expert run the network. It makes companies successful, and provides them with a winning strategy for remaining competitive in the 1990s and beyond.

27

Networking in the 1990s

Gil Piddington, Vice President of Networking, Unisys

I am responsible for program management of Unisys Communications and Networks Product and Marketing Programs. It's a great challenge and a lot of fun looking forward to networking in the 1990s and its impact on businesses and organizations of all types.

There are many forces at work driving change in our industry. I will mention a few and briefly relate their impact on businesses. First, deregulation in the U.S. telephone industry has opened the door partially to permit telephone companies to enter the computing business and computing companies to enter the telephone business. The competition that this has brought about has driven costs down while accelerating technological innovation. Second, technology for the integration of voice, data, and image today supports reliable digital transmission and very efficient use of bandwidth requiring fewer lines and much lower expenditure. Third, a combination of factors has fostered the rapid growth of private and hybrid networks. Organizations are becoming their own telephone companies. Thus the cost, throughput, and reliability of networking in the 1990s is changing the strategic business view of the network.

Open Architectures Help Solve Communications. I was thinking about the challenges we face in our industry, and it occurred to me that the way we develop managers in our universities and businesses has created a problem very analogous to that facing the computing and

301

networking industry today. We train people in very narrow, vertical, and incompatible shafts of development. Engineers, MBAs, sales and marketing people all have their own incompatible languages. They have each organized their worlds differently. Few are portable and few can communicate well outside their shaft, but the success of an organization is based on strong networking, eliminating the people-incompatibilities and focusing on common goals. Our success in world competition is dependent on our ability to cross over and break down cross-functional boundaries with open communications. In our industry, open architectures are helping to solve these problems, and they will play a major role in the 1990s in facilitating communications between people in the incompatible shafts.

Free market computing is upon us and growing at double-digit rates. These are computing systems based largely on industry standards. Clearly, open architectures will be at the vanguard of growth in the coming decade. Open operating systems, open system generation languages, and open networks are the cornerstones of this movement toward portable applications and heterogeneous, yet interoperable, networks. As you all know, "standards" can be interpreted and implemented differently. They are not a panacea. Conformance to a standard does not mean that different systems will communicate properly or that applications are completely portable. Interoperability testing of micros, mainframes, and departmental systems, as well as all other elements in the network, is mandatory for heterogeneous networking.

Current standards and those evolving for electronic data interchange, open document architecture, directory services, network management, and virtual terminal protocol will dramatically improve an enterprise's ability to communicate information within itself and to the outside world. The hopes, goals, and efforts are in place to permit a single terminal or workstation to access all computing systems in a network. The opportunity to employ a single electronic mail or store-and-forward messaging system across many incompatible computing systems is close at hand. It will be demonstrated at the COS-sponsored Enterprise Networking event in June 1988.

These open architectures will enormously increase the community of people who have access to information and thus drive up the bandwidth required for data networking. Today, voice occupies in excess of 80 percent of this bandwidth. In the coming decade, voice and data requirements are projected to achieve parity.

Private Networks and Hybrid Networks Flourish. This increasing demand, the technology which permits multiplexing of voice, data, and image, and significant cost savings are causing many organizations to install private networks and hybrid networks, which couple private and public voice and data networks. Large and medium-size organizations are installing T-1 backbone networks at a rapid rate. These are dedicated 1.544 MBS or 2.048 MBPS trunks which interconnect and route voice, data, and image traffic from telephones, terminals and workstations, computers, and facsimile transceivers. They service proprietary backbone data networks, such as Unisys BNA and DCA, DECNET, and SNA. Both public and private X.25 data networks can also be interconnected. And, of course, PBXs are connected to support voice traffic. Voice today can be compressed to provide up to ten calls across a 64 Kbps circuit that traditionally only carries one call.

The cost and control benefits of private networks can be enormous, but having your own network requires comprehensive management of that network. Today, this is a difficult task because each family of equipment from each of the many vendors represented in a network is managed by its own unique network management system. The growth in private networks demands a manager of network managers that will provide a single interface to and from the network for alarm handling, trouble ticket and configuration management, diagnostics, and so on.

Extending Networks for Competitive Advantage. Some organizations have already recognized the potential of networking for achieving strategic competitive advantage. I'm not just talking about voice, electronic mail, facsimile, data inquiry, and transaction processing within an enterprise. Rather, I am talking about shortening the business cycle by such moves as extending the network to the customer for order placement and to the supplier for acquisition of parts and raw materials, connecting common carriers for the on-line transmission of shipping instructions, and electronically delivering invoices to customers who in turn electronically transfer funds for payment. Though there are many examples today of these kinds of network applications, costs and incompatibilities represent severe limitations. In the 1990s, competition, open architectures, and private networks will justify these business interconnections. Competitive advantages will be realized from shortened order lead times, just-in-time manufacturing, and reduced working capital. Basically, networks will be employed to dramatically compress the "raw materials to revenue" business cycle.

Innovative organizations will also exploit the service opportunities of networks for both internal and external purposes. Training, advertising, documentation distribution, information retrieval, business applications, and financial transaction services will be available to more and more organizations and individuals because of open architectures and lower network costs.

Enterprises with excess capacity on their private networks will sell value-added services to their smaller customers and suppliers, offering them such things as lower cost telephone calls, electronic mail, and document distributions. These are but a few examples of how organizations will use networks to achieve strategic competitive advantage in the 1990s.

Whether you are in the business of supplying or using networks, more than ever before the race will be won by the swift. Those who can predict and react quickly to changes in technology and costs will be successful. Organizations must view their networks as strategic assets and deploy them as competitive tools in the 1990s.

28

Working Toward Open Systems Interconnection (OSI)

George Chang, Research Scientist, Bell Communications

I want to open by defining the meaning of Open Systems Inter-connection (OSI) and giving you some rationale for choosing it. I will present a conceptual-layer model often referred to as the Reference Model and briefly describe what each layer does and what protocols have been developed for OSI communications. Following this, I will discuss the process of developing the user-vendor "Implementation Agreements" for OSI products. I want to emphasize the importance of doing conformance tests to make sure that vendor implementation follows the implementation specifications. The interoperability test will insure that different vendor products can interwork.

Instead of using the traditional definition stated in OSI documents, I want to define OSI by using a simple triangular diagram. There are three distinct approaches to providing communications solutions.

At the lower right-hand corner of the triangle, there is the "Roll Your Own" (RYO) approach, which is perhaps the fastest way to get things rolling for a small community of users. This is, generally, very restricted with limited extension (or expansion) capability.

At the left-hand corner is the "Single Vendor Solution" (SVS) method. This approach is a viable one if most of your systems are from a single vendor. Again, this method has its own shortcomings when you want to interconnect with multi-vendor products.

The third method is the OSI method. OSI is designed to permit interconnection and interworking of multi-vendor systems in a fair and square way. What I mean by this is: "No individual or single vendor can change interface specifications without prior agreements from all concerned parties."

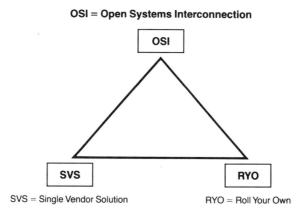

Figure 28.1 What is OSI?

Many criticize OSI as being a slow process. I agree with this observation and can even cite some facts. However, I would rather present a strikingly similar political analogy. If the SVS method is like a monarchy and the RYO approach equivalent to an anarchy, OSI is a democracy. The choice is yours.

Why OSI? Our definition of OSI means that an end system of one vendor can interwork with end systems from various vendors. Why do we need OSI?

As many of you may know, proprietary protocols and systems architecture from major computer manufacturers create problems of interconnecting different vendor products for distributed processing. Furthermore, when new applications and new communications technologies are introduced, the problem of interconnecting different end systems is compounded. Therefore, we need a conceptual master plan for interconnecting various vendor products within the international community. Given that rationale, the OSI Reference Model and the associated peer protocol standards will insure that application processes in different end systems will interwork in the OSI Environment.

OSI Model. The OSI model consists of seven layers, namely, the physical layer at the lowest level, the link layer, the network layer, the transport layer, the session layer, the presentation layer, and the application layer at the highest level.

The physical layer is concerned with the bit transmission between end systems. An example of this standard that many of you may be familiar with is the RS232 standard. The link layer is concerned with establishing, maintaining, and releasing data links. Additionally, it also handles the link-by-link error correction and flow control. The network layer is concerned with the proper routing and switching of data packets to the proper end destination. For an efficient and optimal throughput, segmentation and blocking of data may be done at this layer. Error recovery and flow control features may also be incorporated in this layer. The session layer makes sure that proper communications partners are established at the connection establishment time. This layer also deals with the organization and control of dialogue between communicating partners. More specifically, you want to know who you are communicating with, and whether you both talk simultaneously (two-way simultaneous) or take turns (two-way alternate). If you did not receive data (or message) completely and correctly from your communicating partner, you may request that your partner resend the data.

The presentation layer deals with the proper data representation (or language) that you and your communicating partners have agreed to. If there is a difference in terms of data representation, a "necessary translation" will be done in this layer. The application layer provides communications functions that interface directly with user application processes. Later, I will show you some application layer protocols developed by the international standards bodies.

Layer of OSI Reference Model. Alternatively, we can broadly divide the OSI Reference Model into two blocks. The upper layer block consists of the session, presentation, and application layers which can be considered as the user of the lower layer transport service. This latter service can be treated as a bit pipe or a network service depending on the layer boundary drawn.

Application Service Elements (ASE). Several application layer protocols have been developed by the international standards bodies. Namely, the international organization for standardization (ISO) and the International Telegraph and Telephone Consultative Committee (CCITT).

The File Transfer, Access, and Management (FTAM) and the 1984 Message Handling Systems (MHS) are the two most mature standards as of today. Many vendors are implementing products based on these standards.

Layer Protocol. Let's see how Application Data (AP Data) from an application process is put together in an OSI stack to accomplish data exchange between two application processes.

As an AP data enters the application layer, an application layer header (AH) is added to the AP data. The combined AH and AP data is termed a protocol data unit (PDU) for the application layer. The peer-to-peer communication is accomplished by PDU exchanges between peer entities. The application PDU becomes the (service) data unit as it enters the presentation layer. Again, a presentation header (PH) is added to the data unit to form a presentation PDU. This process is done for every layer as the data moves from the application layer down to the link layer. As the physical layer, the bits are moved across the "wire" from one end system to the other.

At the other end, the reverse process is done. That is, as the data moves up from lower layer to upper layer, the header of a given layer is removed. Finally, at the top of the application layer, the AP data is delivered from one end system to another.

File Transfer Application. Before going on, I want to show a real-world application where OSI is really needed. The example is a file transfer application between various end systems, ranging from mainframe processors to personal computers (PCs). What OSI provides you is the ability to move files between various end systems, whether they be IBM mainframes, a UNISYS mainframes, DEC's minicomputers, IBM PCs, or Apple's MACs. Users of one end system need not be concerned with the idiosyncrasies of other end systems.

OSI Implementation Agreements. The National Bureau of Standards (NBS) OSI Workshop has played an important role in moving OSI standards forward. The OSI Workshop was formed in February 1983 as a vendor/user forum for developing "Implementation Agreements" of OSI protocols. The workshops are held four or five times a year usually at NBS's facility in Gaithersburg, Maryland.

The first demonstration of OSI feasibility was done at the 1984 National Computer Conference (NCC). The following year, General Motors and Boeing Computing Service staged another OSI demonstration (the MAP/TOP demo) at the 1985 Autofact. The implementations were based on the Phase I Implementation Agreements made before the FTAM reached International Standards (IS) status.

The FTAM achieved its IS status in fall 1987. Subsequently, in December 1987, the NBS/OSI Workshop developed the stable Phase II Implementation Agreements. Many vendors now implement OSI products based on this stable document.

The Corporation for Open Systems (COS) was formed in 1986. I want to remind you that COS is developing the test capability to do conformance testing of vendor products. Similar activities are going on in Europe. The European effort includes the Standards Promotion and Application Group (SPAG) and European standardization organizations CEN/CENELEC.

Conformance and Interoperability Tests. The objective of the conformance test is to make sure that vendor products are implemented according to implementation specifications and conformance requirements. Two major areas in conformance testing are the capability test and the behavior test. The capability test will check all functional capabilities claimed by the implementors. The behavior tests will determine what observable behavior is permitted by the relevant protocol standards in instances of communications.

A well-planned and thoroughly conducted conformance test will increase the probability that different vendor implementations will interwork. Ultimately, we need to conduct multi-vendor interoperability tests to insure that OSI products from different vendors interwork as they should.

Conclusion. OSI Standards will provide a way to make interoperability between different vendor products possible. The Implementation Agreements developed jointly by users and vendors will be the base for developing interworking OSI products. To be sure vendors have implemented their products according to specifications, we need an unbiased third party to test for conformance and interoperability. Finally, I would add that future leaders in management information systems will play an important role in making OSI work.

29

Competing with Standards

Lincoln Faurer, President and CEO,
Corporation for Open Systems

I want to discuss how the ability to network multi-vendor products will encourage competition. Emerging computer technologies need open system interconnection (OSI) communications standards to meet the networking needs of the immediate future. Products and services based on OSI standards are going to accelerate the advent of easy linking of different brands of computers. This ease of coordinated use will foster increased competitiveness because vendors will concentrate more on superior features and less on interconnection.

Vendors/Users Benefit from Standards. Integrating computer systems is difficult and expensive, but standardized products will make the process easier. The competitive standing of computer and communications vendors will not be hindered by standardized products. Fortunately for them, and for users, they are willing to turn this opportunity to their advantage. And it is the users who are making this possible, by forcing the standards issues.

Integrating open systems into our information processing environments should definitely stimulate competition among communications and computer product vendors. As users find that they can resolve their information processing problems using products and services from multiple vendors in open systems environments, the competition for the attention of the user will intensify. Vendors are well aware of this, and that is why they are moving towards OSI.

Because OSI and ISDN are international standards, they will facilitate introduction of foreign products in the U.S. market. In addition, U.S. manufacturers who understand the potential are certainly moving to penetrate the overseas market.

The availability of OSI and ISDN products and services will exert a powerful stabilizing force on the industry. The market for open systems technology will expand, and product and interface longevity should increase. Under these conditions, users will be more willing to invest. Purchases will be viable for a reasonable length of time.

These are the thoughts I want to expand on for you today. First let's review OSI. I'll fill you in on how COS is working with OSI to bring about better opportunities for competitive computer and communications products by accelerating the introduction of multi-vendor interoperable OSI products and services into the marketplace.

OSI Provides Interoperability. The OSI model developed by the international organization for standardization (ISO) is a guideline for developing products that conform to open systems interconnection standards. The goal of OSI is to ultimately allow all conforming computer and communications products to link without expensive add-on equipment, black boxes, or programmers who do nothing but connectivity work.

OSI deals with communications standards. These can be compared to performance standards in that design features and production characteristics are left up to the vendor. Thus, users can compare equipment proposals on the basis of features and economic considerations, because suppliers address the standardized performance requirements specified in requests for quotations. Users will have a greater variety of need-specific products to choose from and will know that they will work together, while the vendor can still provide a unique product identity.

Vendor-independent standards, like OSI, will increase competition on the basis of quality rather than functionality, and quality will translate into reliability and service. More good news: Increased competition will result in price and performance battles.

Users will continue to choose whatever architecture meets their needs, just as they have in the past. The only expected difference for them will be the tremendous improvement in selection and features.

A common misconception is that OSI will create sameness in the computer industry and depress the market. That, my friends, is pure hogwash. Let's compare OSI to the stereo industry, and you'll see what I mean.

If you walk into a stereo store today, you can choose an amplifier, turntable, and speakers, all from different vendors, and they will operate together. This interoperability is the result of standards and their application across a broad market. Surely no one can claim that the stereo market has suffered as a result of this standardization. On the contrary, it has undergone tremendous growth. OSI will do likewise for the computer industry, as users can choose from myriad multi-vendor products to solve their processing problems.

One example of an obvious need for standardization is the field of connectors for fiber optic applications. Over 20 types of connectors have been designed for fiber optic applications, all by different manufacturers. But none are interchangeable.

If standards had been established prior to production, high quality interchangeable connectors would have been available earlier, and many economic and technical problems could have been avoided. The need for interoperability is definitely here.

COS Members Abandon Proprietary Approaches. Both IBM and DEC are COS members. Both are developing products based on OSI. But neither of them is ready to abandon their existing proprietary architectures and protocols. Naturally! Why give up something you've dedicated years of work to produce, and that has done well for you, when it can be used in conjunction with non-proprietary OSI products? These companies are working to strategically allow OSI product integration into their existing proprietary networks.

When the IBM PC was released, it grew into a de facto standard, proving that standards can increase competitiveness and reduce prices. The enormous benefit demonstrated by the standardized PC design has inspired computer buyers to push for standards throughout the industry. IBM PCs and ensuing clones became the closest thing to generic computers the industry has ever seen. The same basic PC software runs on products covering a wide price and performance range. Consumers compare and buy many different brands, depending on specific need and price. That puts unprecedented power in the hands of buyers.

For years, all that was available to users were stand-alone proprietary products, those that need private protocols to operate properly. They all inhibit interworking efficiency. OSI, on the other hand, opens the door to interoperability and increased networking opportunities.

Practical Networking Needs Multi-Vendor Environment. When you buy the same brand of system for all your information processing requirements, you are simulating interoperability by using only equipment from one manufacturer. But in so doing, you are accepting whatever solutions are offered by that single manufacturer. And that's not what practical networking is all about. Practical networking is a multi-vendor OSI environment, where each requirement is solved by the best possible product, and in which all the disparate products interwork in one efficient, networked information processing environment.

Anyone in the audience who works in procurement at Ogden ALC at Hill Air Force Base is well aware of the constant battle to break out sole source items. Once they are broken out and go competitive, you can expect a fair and reasonable price for the items you are procuring.

In the case of computer and communications products and services, many manufacturers are the sole source for (or appear to have a monopoly on) certain products. Worse yet, you are forced to rely on one vendor for the products you need if you decide to expand your system, even if that vendor's products don't afford the best possible solution to your requirements.

Facilitate Multi-Vendor Networking. If you are not familiar with Manufacturing Automation Protocol (MAP) and Technical Office Protocol (TOP), then you should know that they comprise a set of internationally recognized computer communication standards, based (with few exceptions) on the OSI reference model and protocols. MAP will facilitate multi-vendor networking on the manufacturing floor, while TOP deals with networking needs of technical office data. MAP is driven primarily by GM, TOP by Boeing — both are COS members. Both GM and Boeing, and indeed the many members of the MAP/TOP users group, recognize the need for their future systems to operate in an OSI-conformant, multi-vendor environment. Both GM and Boeing are therefore highly active participants in COS, and the 1500-plus member MAP/TOP user group is an alliance associate of COS.

World Governments Demanding Interoperation. The United States government's recent commitment to OSI signifies widespread use of OSI in the future. The desire to purchase OSI-based products will have an effect similar to GM's insistence on compliance to MAP. The government OSI users group, consisting of almost every major government agency, is completing the government OSI profile (GOSIP). GOSIP is slated to become a federal information processing standard (FIPS), providing an outline for government procurement of OSI-conformant systems. The Department of Defense (DOD) will adopt OSI protocols as a full co-standard with the DOD protocols when GOSIP achieves FIPS status, scheduled for early 1990.

The impact of the GOSIP requirement, given that the U.S. government is the largest single procurer of computer and communications products in the world, is massive. It will impact not only all government users, but vendors, systems integrators, and government contractors, as well.

Government plans for implementation of OSI call for interoperation with DOD protocols, for the expected life of those systems supporting the DOD protocols. TCP/IP is a widely used networking system. It is very similar in structure to OSI, and serves as a good starting point in using OSI protocols, since widespread OSI availability is still a few years away.

A new law went into effect in the United Kingdom government in February. The law requires conformance to international standards in government computer contracts valued at more than $115,000, forcing vendors to comply to OSI standards. The law was created by the European Commission of the Common Market, and while Great Britain is the first to enact it, the commission's goal is an open market by 1992 for all of Europe. Great Britain issued its own internal government GOSIP specification in 1986.

In Australia, the National Protocol Support Centre was established in 1987 to aid procurement offices in moving toward open systems, and to help specify commitment and development toward international standards.

With the availability of truly compatible multi-vendor products, I believe that competition will expand and that there will be fewer and fewer instances of sole source procurements. When products can be confidently linked, it won't matter who the manufacturer is, all products will interconnect. As long as there is an independent means of testing products to verify that they really conform to predetermined standards, then buyers can be sure that the competition is real and the product is sold for a fair and reasonable price.

The United States Defense Communications Agency (DCA), Army Information Systems Command, National Communications System, and the National Bureau of Standards (NBS) are all COS members. As COS members, they all have a say in the technical direction of COS, the methods used, and the products selected for the development of conformance tests.

Gateways Being Eliminated. Any business that needs systems integration, protocol converters (black boxes), or emulators to make products work together uses gateways. One gateway is required for each interconnection between different brands. Depending on the size of your business, this can require many gateways — and grow to be very expensive. In determining that multi-vendor networked information systems environments were desirable in the first place, the information technology world realized early on that the tremendous proliferation of gateways needed to make such networks possible would be unwieldy and expensive.

Many firms use equipment from multiple companies to avoid being stuck with a single product line. Many of them use gateways while awaiting the onset of truly compatible products. Products built to meet common standards depend on tests for conformance to base and functional standards, and they don't require gateways. This is the COS approach.

Standardization Requires Conformance Testing and Licensing. Ease of networking is the objective of developing products that conform to product specifications or implementation agreements, based on agreed-upon international standards. Conformance testing is therefore clearly required as a prerequisite to facilitated multi-vendor networking.

Many computer and communications vendors are working to develop the products that will make true compatibility a reality. COS was developed not only as a means of arriving at widely accepted, consensus product specifications, but also as a means of pooling resources to reduce the extremely expensive development costs that the development of conformance tests incurs. Most, if not all, manufacturers who are now COS members were previously working on their own version of OSI-standard systems. Unfortunately, many of the individual versions would have had difficulty achieving eventual compatibility because each would have been based on a slightly different set of options than the others — hence the need for consensus products specifications, a major benefit of COS.

This is also why, if we opt for using standards over gateways or proprietary systems, we need proof that products conform to given standards. Conformance testing and licensing will provide much greater probability of future interconnectivity in accordance with standards. It is also why a major part of the COS budget is devoted to our test development activity, and to developing an integrated test architecture that meets the foreseeable needs of COS members and the industry as a whole.

In 1987, our first OSI-conformance test products were introduced. They are transport, IP, lower layers (802.4), FTAM, and MHS. Following the MHS and FTAM applications, COS will focus further on the lower layers of the OSI reference model, and on network management.

COS's in-house testing and licensing center should be operational this year. It is functioning even now in a specialized way. Member and nonmember companies will be able to bring in or connect product test implementations to the COS testing system for evaluation. COS testing will impose minimal restriction on how vendors implement their OSI-compliant products, and will follow international standards for "conformance testing."

Electronic Mail and File Management. File transfer, access, and management (FTAM), and electronic mail (X.400 MHS) are level seven OSI protocols. FTAM is a method of storing and transmitting files that will allow users to remotely move large data files between different types of computers.

For many PC users, electronic mail is their most important interface with the mainframe. Many large companies have in-house electronic mail systems allowing employees with PCs or terminals to send E-mail to one another.

But what constitutes an electronic letter to one system may come across as just gibberish to another. Thus, the reason behind the X.400 standard: It will create a universal electronic mail interface, where mail will easily transfer from one system to another.

With OSI you can use the same communication protocol to interconnect between internal or external systems. X.400 MHS and FTAM are available only through OSI — and their features rely on OSI's connectivity. The functionality of X.400 MHS and FTAM, as well as future OSI-defined protocols, will only be available in OSI-conformant systems.

Demonstrating Interconnectivity. If you are not already aware of it, I'd like to tell you briefly about Enterprise Network Event '88 International, or "Enterprise," an exposition to be held in Baltimore in June of this year. Enterprise is one of the most unique expositions ever staged in the information technology arena, and I believe it's going to be an exciting experience for both the participants and attendees. COS is co-sponsoring "Enterprise" with the MAP/TOP users group, June 6-9 at the Baltimore exhibition center.

"Enterprise" will demonstrate the MAP/TOP and COS protocols that vendors will use to interconnect their products to simulate one operational business environment or enterprise. The MAP/TOP users group has adopted the COS platform as a subset of its MAP/TOP version 3.0 specification. COS will provide conformance tests for the COS-supported protocols, which are file transfer, access, and management (FTAM), and message handling services (MHS).

COS's conformance tests should expedite the development process for FTAM and MHS, as well as MAP/TOP-compatible products. These products should then be widely available during 1988 and 1989.

The demo will connect eight on-site areas and the remote U.K. site in a demonstration of a full manufacturing enterprise, all integrated on a MAP/TOP network. The staging areas being developed independently by their sponsors are:

- process control and facilities management
- engineering and production functions
- corporate operational functions
- subcontracting functions

- engineering and planning functions
- assembly and test functions
- an aerospace coalition for specialized aerospace production
- the corporation for open systems, the Enterprise's invoice capability
- the Communication Network for Manufacturing Automation (CNMA), a consortium of European vendors and users who will be linked by X.25 from England to simulate a remote parts manufacturer.

The overall goal of the COS booth is to demonstrate products based on international standards as a vehicle to the interoperation of information systems in multi-vendor environments. The exhibits in the COS booth will show how a communications network based on COS protocols may be used in tying together OSI-based proprietary systems, and will drive home the importance of conformance testing in achieving interoperability. These exhibits are in keeping with the theme of the COS booth, "COS promotes vendor harmonization through OSI."

To show how OSI is an effective solution to interconnection, the COS booth will demonstrate enterprise-wide and local applications involving remote file transfer using FTAM and electronic messaging using MHS. The COS booth local applications will be using both local area network (LAN) and wide area network (WAN) technology to demonstrate MHS and FTAM functionality.

Examples of the MHS local applications include urgent requests for parts, and a supplier connection scenario. COS will award certificates to those who correctly answer questions on OSI given in an FTAM-based quiz. To demonstrate interconnectivity in connection with the COS quiz, FTAM will be used to retrieve the quiz from a file server and to deliver a certificate giveaway to a certificate server.

Within the COS booth, vendors will also be participating in the global FTAM, MHS, and Enterprise applications. Each one of the sponsored booths will demonstrate either the COS or MAP/TOP 3.0 protocols.

Testing of five major network functions will be demonstrated. COS is sponsoring the development of tests for file transfer, access, and management (FTAM) and message handling services (MHS or electronic mail). The industrial technology institute (ITI) is coordinating the development of tests for manufacturing message services, network management, and network directory service protocols. This development will actually be done by a consortium in Europe (CCT).

I hope a number of you will be traveling east to experience "Enterprise" this June. It will give you a great opportunity to see first-hand what interoperability holds in store for all of us.

Conclusion. I hope it is obvious that interoperability is a need not just for the future, but for today. Standardization is necessary to implement coordinated use of multi-vendor products and services. It will stimulate, rather than stifle, competition. Networks of the future will employ standardized products; today's users and vendors are seeing to that. And, last but not least, standardization requires conformance testing.

The problems in determining the most effective and economical ways to develop open systems products and services are everyone's problems, and the solutions are for the benefit of all concerned. But the majority of vendors and users world-wide have narrowed the solution down to network linking via OSI.

OSI paves the way for the creation of new products that will integrate with existing proprietary networks, facilitate multi-vendor environments, and perhaps eventually replace today's proprietary systems. As I said before, existing suppliers see OSI as an opportunity to expand their markets. Most, if not all of them, have begun to develop new product offerings based on OSI.

The desired dimension of multi-vendor connectivity may be several years away, but COS is striving to bring it closer as quickly as possible. With the help of users and vendors alike, we can reach that goal.

30

Integrated Services Digital Networks (ISDN)

Edward Botwinick, Timeplex

I thought it would be helpful to cover two subjects: first, an introduction to ISDN, and second, ISDN from the perspective of Unisys networks and Timeplex, the world's leading supplier of private ISDN networks.

During the past several years most telephone networks in the industrialized world have been converting to digital technology at a prodigious rate. The rapidly improving economics of the fiber optic transmission plant have swung the balance so that the transmission plant of most telephone systems is rapidly migrating to a mostly digital environment. Similarly, the switching plant is also becoming digital, taking advantage of the low cost, high reliability, and flexibility of digital electronics. Once these major components of a telephone system are digital, it is a relatively simple extension to bring the digital interface directly to the customer premise, providing the users with broadband digital options for the transmission of any digital information — voice, data, and image — through the same network. ISDN is really a set of standards to insure maximum connectivity via the switched network, globally, with uniform control and switching software to establish connections across the network. We anticipate widespread deployment of ISDN over the next decade and have taken positive steps in our own product development to allow our customers to utilize this exciting new capacity.

There is a great tendency in the information systems world to seek out global truths and monolithic solutions. Those of us in the networking business have learned the hard way that there is no monolithic approach, and there is no unique solution to any networking application. Although some industry observers have characterized ISDN as a universal cure for everything including the common cold, we believe that ISDN simply represents an additional transport and switching alternative with a specific set of price/performance characteristics to be weighed and balanced against other alternatives in the user's overall environment.

Scenario for Using ISDN. Although there is a significant amount of confusion and skepticism in the market place regarding what ISDN will do for the user, ISDN is inevitable, and it is important to understand where it fits. Let me discuss some possible scenarios for using ISDN in a typical hybrid — that is a combined public/private T-1 network.

Using an integrated, digital access line, the user has access to a multiplicity of services, both switched and dedicated, together with a signalling network that can be used to provide enhanced services or transport user-to-user signalling information.

ISDN is a technology that has been thrust on the user by four communities of interest: local exchange companies, interexchange carriers, equipment vendors, and standards organizations. They — or we — have two fundamental motives:

1. To reduce operational costs in the network. Carriers view ISDN as a natural evolution of the network, and Bellcore has shown that ISDN will prove in for a telephone company with as little as six percent penetration over eight years, with no incremental revenues. This is significant when it comes time to justify ISDN expenditures to the regulators.

2. To increase revenue potential. Once this digital network is in place, the carriers expect to increase network usage, attract data traffic on the network, and offer enhanced services, accessible via ISDN. Likewise, the traditional telecommunications equipment providers see ISDN as an opportunity to churn the embedded base of equipment in an otherwise stagnant market.

The missing party so far in the ISDN story is the user. The interesting phenomenon about users is that, in general, they are confused about what ISDN will do for them, but they expect to implement ISDN anyway. What do they expect?

- They expect cost reductions for services and access charges and lower personnel expense for managing the networks.
- They anticipate an additional networking alternative that will fit into hybrid networks, delivering new functionality.
- They hope that they can obtain from the carrier improved control of ISDN based switched networks.
- They also expect access to new, and as yet undefined enhanced services that will assist them in operating their own business more profitably.

Timing in Implementing ISDN. Any large scale network upgrade such as ISDN will take an extended period of time due to the capital expenditures involved. Timing of deployment is a very important market factor. ISDN timing will be based on:

- Standards convergence — the standards are far from complete.
- Digitization of the network and availability of local digital access.
- User demand which will probably grow very slowly because of the lack of identified applications.
- Regulators may slow down deployment in the U.S. as they frequently do.

But have no doubts, ISDN is coming. Beta tests and trials have begun and will continue through next year. Our company is using these trials to gain experience in the technology and applications of the technology to business problems. Limited standard service will begin in 1989. However, the roll-out will be slow. Availability from most carriers will occur during the early 1990s and widespread deployment sometime in the mid-1990s.

Internationally, the situation is somewhat different. Government policy in many places is stimulating ISDN and retarding alternatives as a mechanism for retaining value-added services on the public network, and supporting local equipment makers to protect employment. Many countries already have pilots with paying customers, and full service roll-out should be available earlier in many other countries than in the United States.

ISDN Costs/Pricing. The most important open issues are: How much will ISDN cost the user, and what will the ISDN pricing strategy be?

In America, ISDN pricing must be cost-based to satisfy regulatory concerns. Within these cost constraints the carriers must execute a pricing strategy designed to both stimulate network usage and to increase profitability with value-added traffic and services. However, since users are confused about ISDN service benefits, deployment decisions will be principally based on demonstrable cost reductions.

We also believe that the traditional higher price for switched service relative to dedicated lines will continue under ISDN. Therefore, we expect a continuation of the current high growth market for versions of the Timeplex network resource managers that provide gateways to the ISDN environment.

Dedicated private networks will continue to be the principal backbone for larger users at least in the United States and Great Britain because of their low cost, special applications, and user control. ISDN will emerge as a principal option for connecting low usage facilities to the backbone network, for traffic overflow, and for access to the public services.

ISDN Program at Timeplex. We have a very active ISDN program at Timeplex. This program includes planning and participation in trials. A recent telecommunications manager's survey indicated that users were not getting important ISDN planning information from their vendors. Therefore, we are filling this void with ISDN training programs and seminar participation. Our focus is to describe how ISDN fits in with private and hybrid T-1 networking. We are also active participants in the ISDN standards organization.

ISDN prototype development is currently in progress, and we will begin live trials shortly. At this time our objectives are to get hands-on experience with the ISDN technology, obtain further customer input on ISDN requirements, and solicit user feedback on our ISDN applications.

At Unisys, we are ready for the introduction of ISDN. We are now planning the introduction of ISDN capability in the Timeplex product line, where we have identified four principal applications:

1. ISDN hybrid networking applications for handling peak loads, or for alternate routing, when primary facilities fail.
2. ISDN distributed access permits users who are not within a reasonable distance of an ISDN service node to gain access to ISDN based services.
3. ISDN service access permits the user to gain access to services offered by competing ISDN networks anywhere in the world.
4. ISDN branch office networking permits small locations to be connected to a backbone network via ISDN.

Timeplex and other existing users can continue to benefit from private networks, and can add ISDN access as needed, when it becomes available. Here, ISDN will be used to supplement private networking.

Conversely, in areas where ISDN is the principal transmission facility, virtual private networks will be constructed using ISDN-only network resource managers. Most importantly, all of the Timeplex ISDN capability will soon be available in conjunction with Unisys's traditional Datacom networking architectures, as well as with our emerging open network implementation.

31

Planning Operations Systems Networks*

Daniel Minoli, Scientist, Bell Communications

Many corporations need a network to interconnect their automated support systems with user terminals to permit corporate-wide access. The Bell Operating Companies (BOCs) are no exception. They need a flexible and efficient internal communications network, termed the Operations Systems Network (OSN), to assist them in carrying out their business.

A layered, standardized, vendor-independent architecture, which employs the BOC's own resources such as Integrated Services Digital Network (ISDN), the Intelligent Network (IN), and other plant facilities, is likely to be the optimal course of action for the BOCs. Such an architecture would allow technology independence and the ability to exploit the economic benefits of the latest engineering improvements.

Introduction. The Information Age has had a significant impact on the corporate environment by demanding instant accessibility to engineering, marketing, scheduling, work force, forecast, and financial data, among others. This is particularly true for industries that are characterized by real-time, geographically disseminated, and labor-intensive elements (banks, brokerage firms, airlines, telecommunications firms, etc.)

---

* This chapter was co-written by J.J. Amoss.

To meet business needs, in the 1960s and 1970s many companies developed operations systems (OSs), that is, management information systems, decision support systems, executive support systems. These systems generally encompass order processing, inventory control, budgeting, and so on. The next step, which came in the 1970s and 1980s, was the establishment of an Operations Systems Network (OSN) that interconnects these automated support systems with user terminals to permit corporate-wide access. Generally the goal has been to deliver all necessary data via a small or large number of desk terminals.

Existing and anticipated services to the community of business and residential customers cannot be provided in a cost- effective manner without adequate communication resources. This paper aims at sensitizing network planners to the importance of designing networks that can fully meet the strategic business requirements of the organizations they support in the 1900s. OSN networks provide a pivotal corporate resource which can impact positively their overall future posture and efficiency.

Clearly, a well designed OSN must be a cost-effective data communications network that meets all technical and business requirements. These requirements include, among others: security, acceptable response time for all types of required transactions, support for all pertinent interfaces, high availability and reliability, maintainability (network control and component management — hardware and software), modularity, integrity and simplicity, consistency, upgradability and expandability, and appropriate geographical and topological scope.

Current OSN planning activities at Bellcore are directed toward two goals. First is defining an "open" or vendor-independent communications architecture based on the Internal Organization for Standardization (ISO) Open Systems Interconnection (OSI) Reference Model and related protocol standards. The use of interface specifications based on these standards will provide the necessary flexibility and choice of vendor products. Second is use of BOC network architectures and services, where practical. This includes use of the existing public packet switching network (PPSN), and the evolving Integrated Services Digital and Intelligent Network/2 (IN/2).

What Is an OSN? The OSN includes the collection of terminals, the communications portions of operations systems (hardware and software to implement communications protocols), the communications portion of network elements (for operations-related traffic), and the communications facilities interconnecting these elements. It is concerned with internal BOC communications to support operations. Traditionally this has included data communications areas such as terminal-to-operations systems, operations system-to-operations systems, and operations systems-to-network elements.

Typical OSN topologies that require a communication architecture and a strategy are:

- cluster controller — OSN — same LATA CPU;
- luster controller — OSN — same LATA CPU1 — same LATA CPU2;
- CPU — same LATA CPU, bulk traffic;
- cluster controller — other LATA CPU;
- work center/wire center LAN;
- cluster controller — CPU with real time switching to other CPU;
- cluster controller — CPU with concurrent window to other CPU;
- printer sharing: CPU1 and CPU2 accessing same printer;
- co-located terminals and CPU;
- Network Element — OSN — same LATA CPU,
- Embedded Operations Channels;
- word processor vendor A — word processor vendor B;
- wireless/mobile data terminal — OS; and
- synthetic voice terminal — OS.

Each of these topologies must be addressed in detail to establish ISDN and IN implementations and transition strategies.

Possible areas for future OSN planning activities include voice communications, (real-time, conferencing, and store-and-forward); broadband communications (full motion video — slow-scan and high resolution, videoconferencing, freeze frame, and graphics); facsimile; and videotex.

Four groupings of data sources and terminations characterize OSN users: work centers, wire centers, data processing centers (DPCs), and minicomputer maintenance and operations centers (MMOCs).

OSN data traffic can be grouped into four classes: bulk, inquiry/response, store-and-forward, and wire center data. Bulk data accounts for about half of the OSN traffic volume and consists of large messages, typically greater than 100,000 characters, with large bandwidth requirements in one direction (for delivery) and small bandwidth requirements in the other (for confirmation). Bulk data usually has no critical response time requirements. Inquire/response data accounts for about 30 percent of the OSN traffic volume, averages several hundred characters (typically 100-character inquiries and 1500-character responses) and has an average response time requirement of 4-8 seconds (including host processing). User pressure will be to reduce this delay. Wire center data is between network elements and operations systems (OSs). Message size and response time requirements vary greatly for this class of traffic. Store-and-forward data is typically printer traffic generated by OS-to-terminal communications.

OSN Target Architecture. Most BOCs utilize several different technologies in implementing their OSN. These technologies include the Bell Administrative Network Communications Systems (BANCS), packet network, private lines, local area networks, and vendor proprietary networks. This existing OSN environment has a number of characteristics typical of many current large corporate networks. The environment is fragmented; it has a number of different communications protocols and interfaces, resulting in high costs for development, maintenance, and operations; and it suffers from a lack of global network management.

OSN planning is taking place in an environment where forecasted requirements, service definition, standards, product availability, and expected technology costs are in a state of flux. With this in mind, the following set of objectives is established for the OSN target architecture:

- Make optimal use of BOC services by taking advantage of synergies between BOC internal and commercial service offerings.
- Protect the investment represented by the installed base hosts, applications, terminals, cluster controllers, and so on.
- Allow user access to services using shared, rather than dedicated facilities.
- Provide the ability to tailor services to the needs of individual OSN network users.
- Provide a multi-media communications environment where the network need not be concerned with the type of information being transmitted or processed.

To meet these goals, the following elements are being considered as the building blocks of the OSN target architecture.

- *Integrated Services Digital Network.* The transport element of the proposed target architecture is ISDN. ISDN provides packet switching, circuit switching, and channel switching. When evolved to ISDN, OSN networks will provide dynamic capabilities and control to satisfy OSN requirements.
- *Intelligent Network.* The Intelligent Network will provide control needed for flexible service establishment. IN aims at introducing maximum flexibility by providing modular reusable functional components that can be combined to define new services These software-defined functional components will allow the OSN target architecture to cope with the evolution of technology, vendor products, user requirements, and more rapid introduction of new services. IN is also expected to allow the tailoring of services to individual OSN users.
- *Open Systems Interconnection (OSI) Protocols.* These are critical elements of the proposed architecture for the 1990s and will assist in providing vendor independence.
- *Local Switching Element (LANs).* Another component of the OSN architecture is local switching element with data switching capabilities, value-added functions such as protocol conversion, local user services, and local network management capabilities.
- *Gateways to Integrate Portions of Vendor Proprietary Architectures.* Gateways will allow integration of proprietary architectures into the OSN architecture.

With the proposed architecture, there will be opportunities to integrate transmission, switching, access, signalling, and operational and administrative functions to support multiple services.

ISDN will provide the transport functionality and IN will make the network more intelligent. Some of the intelligent characteristics exhibited by the proposed architecture are:

- *Protocol Independence.* This means that any host and any terminal can communicate directly.
- *Implementation of a Truly Distributed Environment.* For a number of economic, administrative, or pragmatic reasons, OSs have been deployed on physically separate (and often geographically dispersed) hosts. A user may need to access hosts that are in two locations serially or even in parallel.
- *Redundant Cost-Effective Networks.* As more businesses become dependent on the real-time availability of mechanized systems, a reliability is critical. This implies both availability implemented with redundant logical links, but not necessarily redundant physical links as

well as availability implemented with redundant logical machines, but not necessarily redundant physical machines.

- *Security.* As more businesses become dependent on computerized tools, the risk to vital data (customer records, corporate forecasts, plant records, etc.) increases. While host-based security is one approach to the problem, recent well-publicized events of networks in question cooperating in the infraction effort point to a need for network-based security. "Closed user group" is one possibility.
- *Network-Resident Services.* Many functions performed by hosts, front-end processors, cluster controllers, or other adjunct devices may be best handled by the network. In addition, there is an opportunity for network-based services. Some examples include messaging services, including message storage and medium conversion, and dynamic bandwidth allocation.

The proposed architecture will offer several benefits. Using existing BOC public networks increases the potential for sharing facilities and services, as well as operations, maintenance, and administrative functions. Use of these network-based services should increase user capabilities. The proposed architecture will minimize problems associated with incompatibility by using standards to the maximum extent. Standard interfaces between major components will allow the use of products (switches, computers, software, and so forth) independent of vendors and allow each component to evolve with minimal impact on other components. The proposed architecture will include software-defined capabilities to allow customization and evolution of services.

OSN Transition Issues. Some of the issues likely to affect transition to an ISDN/IN-based architecture include technical and protocol matters, available services and geographic coverage, and interworking and gatewaying with traditional data communication architectures (proprietary systems, LANS, and so on).

ISDN deployment depends on the cooperation of three parties: carriers, data and voice communication CPE manufacturers, and end users. Individual carriers will control the evolution timetables for their respective regions by assessing their own needs, market goals, capital investment opportunities, PUC support, and other factors. Detailed transition plans for the migration of the OSN to the target architecture should become formulated in the next couple of years as ISDN and IN deployment and planning proceeds.

In the meantime, four basic phases in the development of an ISDN plant are:

- *Phase 1.* Feasibility and engineering phase. Worldwide research by carriers and interested parties, including standards activities (circa 1976-1986).
- *Phase 2.* Various field trials of the technology and initial services (1984-1989) with ensuing technical refinements.
- *Phase 3.* Service maturation phase (1987 and beyond):
  Defining advanced services
  Developing standards
  Developing communications equipment that exploits the new technology
  Developing OSs that allow management of new service components such as service establishment, updating of customer records, billing, and maintenance
  Filing and FCC/PUCs acceptance of tariffs
  User's analysis of service (the user needs to conclude that the service is cost effective)
  InterLATA ISDN deployment (in cooperation with interLATA carriers)
  Geographical penetration
- *Phase 4.* Market acceptance phase (1989 and beyond).

All of these phases must happen although there may be some temporary overlap or parallel occurrence. The service definition and deployment and the market acceptance phases are the most crucial for the evolution and ubiquitous employment of ISDN in the plant.

The feasibility and engineering phase started several years ago and culminated with the 1984 CCITT basic recommendations. This phase will continue for a number of years to address certain areas still under investigation, such as rate adaption, broadband, and higher level signalling protocols. The U.S. trial phase started in mid-1986 and is continuing into 1988. The service maturation phase will start as an outgrowth of the trial evaluation effort. This phase will start in mid-1988 and will continue into the early 1990s. This phase will involve iterative, incremental types of effort. The market acceptance phase will overlap the service maturation phase. There are three participants in this phase: carriers who will provide the technology and services, equipment manufacturers who will build the necessary hardware and software, and the end users. This phase must follow the trial phase and preliminary aspects of the service maturation phase (tariffs, some geographic penetration, and some equipment availability). Dates are forecast for 1990, 1995, and beyond.

Many related plant modernization efforts are already underway and will assist the migration toward ISDN. These efforts include plant digitization, deployment of fiber, introduction of digital switches, and deployment of the Common Channel Signaling network based on Signaling System Number 7. ISDN is thus part of a broader evolution: the transition of the plant from analog to digital technology (carrier and fiber-based). ISDN provides a framework for the future evolution of the plant.

The progression of ISDN-based services considers three dimensions — ISDN functionality, its geographic scope, and time. For example, a BOC may decide to make a plant transition to ISDN which begins with a basic digital offering for metropolitan business customers and then grows in functionality and geographic scope over time. Another BOC may choose to cover a wider geographic area (business and residential, metropolitan and suburban) in a very short period of time and then add advanced functionality later only for metro business customers (BOC3). Another BOC may wait before offering basic 2B + D access, and then wait again before increasing functionality (BOC5). Another BOC may wait for the standards and technology to mature and only then offer service to metro business customers (BOC6).

At an early stage, ISDN services will most likely be at the transport layer for replacing traditional point-to-point links. Typical OSN applications would include: interFEP links (using basic or primary interfaces), cluster controller-to-FEP links (using basic interfaces), links to remote medium speed printers (using basic interfaces), T1-rate channel extenders (using primary interfaces or possibly broadband interfaces), and LANs.

Access to ISDN will be through terminal adapter (TA) equipment providing standard RS-232-C ports for traditional data communications equipment. Data subrates of 8 kbps, 16 kbps, 32kbps, and other traditional rates (2.4 kbps, 4.8 kbps, and 9.6 kbps) may be either rate-adapted or multiplexed with other subrate channels and transmitted on the B channel. This feature will be useful during a transition phase where DTEs may initially operate at transitional speeds, until upgrades from equipment vendors make full use of the new available bandwidth. User packet services and signalling functions to provide OSN services is envisioned. Geographic coverage will be small. This early phase is forecast for early 1988 until 1990.

At an intermediate stage of the transition, OSN elements, such as CRTs, cluster controllers and hosts, will interconnect directly through ISDN using native ISDN interfaces such as 2B + D, 23B + D and, possibly, broadband. The equipment will start to become generally available from major vendors in this time frame. In addition, the widespread use of ISDN packet-switching services will materialize. Some broadband services at greater that DS-1 rate will be available for use and some IN/2 data services will be used by the OSN. This phase is believed to encompass the 1991-1994 period.

At an advanced stage of the transition, additional OSN applications will emerge. Geographic coverage of ISDN and IN/2 will increase. This stage will make full use of the ISDN signalling channel and IN/2 control capabilities. This phase is anticipated to start in 1994.

Advanced data networks architectures are possible in the 1990s by employing ISDN, IN, and other BOC facilities. These architectures will be able to support the BOC's internal data requirements, as well as those of commercial users.

32

The Information Explosion

Susan Hitchcock, Operations Manager, Southern Bell

The Information Age explosion is here. Information users have witnessed significant growth in all three information sources — voice, data, and video. And although voice communications continue to occupy a major share of telecommunications activity, techniques such as bit-rate compression and ever-increasing bandwidth promise to rapidly expand both the demand for, and the transport capability of, data and video.

Acceptance of ISDN. How will telecommunications networks and the local operating companies accommodate this heavy demand for integrated information services? The answer is a resounding one — through the Integrated Services Digital Network, or ISDN.

ISDN is the network architecture of the future, and will provide a pipeline for *simultaneous* transport of voice, data, and video signals throughout the public switching network. This architecture will take advantage of rapidly developing communications technologies to provide users with cost-effective, end-to-end digital connectivity to support a wide range of both narrowband and broadband services. Users will have a single, integrated, user-friendly point of access to these services, with some control and flexibility over how they use the available bandwidth. Basic narrowband ISDN access is through a 2B + D basic rate or a 23B + D primary rate interface (a B-channel is 64 kilobits-per-second and a D-channel is 16 kilobits-per-second).

The telecommunications industry supports ISDN for four primary reasons. First, ISDN will allow telecommunications providers to offer users new services with corresponding new revenue streams. Secondly, the ISDN architecture provides a less costly means of offering service. Thirdly, ISDN is a major step toward an intelligent public switched network, with customer control over the use of the available bandwidth. Finally, the industry is actively participating in the development of international standards.

ISDN architecture will support all varieties of customers, from the residential to small and large businesses to corporate common carrier accounts. The common factor among this diverse customer range is the personal computer and the expanded communications capabilities that it has generated. ISDN service offerings will include both items that are available today, such as basic dial tone and Centrex service, plus expanded features such as simultaneous voice, data, and video; home security and energy management; and videotex services.

There are several key customer acceptance tests for ISDN. The first is feature transparency: Will the new ISDN architecture be able to communicate with the embedded existing network without losing services currently available to customers? A second test is portability: Can one user terminal work with all manufacturers' ISDN equipments at designated transmission speeds? A final test is cost: Will ISDN offerings be less expensive than those over the existing network? Several cost studies, including one from Bell Communications Research, indicate that mature ISDN will provide significant savings for telecommunications users. These savings are fundamentally the result of comparing the cost of one ISDN line that can handle voice, data, and video, with the cost of three or more individual lines for non-integrated services.

Strategic Plans/Development of ISDN. As rapidly as technology is changing, Southern Bell believes that the deployment of broadband ISDN (BISDN) will begin before narrowband is pervasive in the network. BISDN will offer all of the services of narrowband ISDN, plus new features such as video telephony, video teleconferencing, video retrieval on an interactive, demand basis, and high-speed data transmission. The industry began trial deployment of narrowband ISDN in 1987, and expects to begin BISDN deployment in 1989. By the late 1990s, telecommunications networks should include a pervasive BISDN overlay, with some self-adjusting capability. By the year 2000, we should see widespread deployment of self-adjusting BISDN networks.

Southern Bell's strategic plans have called for aggressive positioning of the network to provide for digital transmission with the bandwidth and speed capabilities to serve any customer on demand, where feasible. Specific strategies include:

- Converting 100 percent of network switches to stored program control by the end of 1989
- Deploying the next generation switch as the primary replacement for the 1A ESS, providing features such as internal load balancing, full digital connectivity, fast packet/circuit hybrid capabilities, and both broadband and narrowband access
- Aggressively deploying fiber, including fiber to the living unit as soon as economically feasible
- Deploying Common Channel Signaling System Seven (CCS7) as an integral building block for ISDN
- Enhancing Operations Systems to support software service provisioning
- Constructing a nodal architecture that allows for "self- healing" on a non-service affecting basis

Southern Bell has made significant progress in implementing these strategies. By the end of 1988, 99 percent of all switches will be stored program control. Fiber shipments continue to increase, while copper shipments are projected to decrease dramatically over the next five years. Fiber is currently present in over 54 percent of Southern Bell's feeder routes. By the end of 1988, 87 percent of available local loop facilities will be provided through pair gain equipment, with almost half of those served by fiber. Southern Bell cost studies show that fiber to the living unit will become cost effective in 1990 for basic telephone service, and sooner with additional revenue services such as a second line to the residence. By 1990, Southern Bell expects to accommodate 100 percent of interoffice facility growth requirements, 80 to 90 percent of feeder route growth requirements, and up to 50 percent of distribution loop growth requirements on fiber.

Early in 1988 in Atlanta, Georgia, Southern Bell began the first commercial roll-out of ISDN service. The customers for this first application include Prime Computer, Inc., Trust Company of Georgia, Hayes Microcomputer Products, AT&T, and CONTEL. Each of these customers are "leading edge" companies who are interested in higher efficiency and lower cost voice and data services. Over the next two years, Southern Bell plans to expand ISDN installations in several locations throughout its four-state region, serving high-growth customers interested in advanced services, on a willingness-to-pay basis. Southern Bell is also pursuing an ISDN terminal, which will provide user-friendly access to the ISDN network. Southern Bell has communicated its ISDN plans to terminal vendors, and has identified several strong terminal candidates which may ultimately be recommended to ISDN customers. Currently, Southern Bell has just under 400 ISDN lines in service, with plans to increase this to 315,000 ISDN lines and 9,822,000 CCS7 lines within the next five years.

Southern Bell is testing ISDN services over a fiber network at a Florida subdivision called Heathrow. Heathrow is an upscale residential and business "city of the future." As EPCOT is Disney's Experimental Prototype Community of Tomorrow, so Heathrow is Southern Bell's Fiber City of the Future. Through a joint venture with Northern Telecom and Heathrow Development, Southern Bell will implement advanced telecommunications services in phases. Over the next two years, these will include the first residential ISDN offering, the first ISDN offering over fiber, and the first application of two-way voice, data, and video over the same single mode fiber.

ISDN Pitfalls. There are still a number of issues associated with ISDN/BISDN deployment. One of the most significant is the establishment of international standards. After a series of meetings and compromises, a February 1988 agreement in Seoul, South Korea shows promise in resolving this issue. This agreement essentially endorsed one of the specifications from the Hamburg Agreements in 1987, and calls for a 155 megabit-per-second interface capable of supporting coexisting circuit and packet based services and providing bandwidth on demand.

The demand for efficient information services is clear. Both the business and the residential information services markets continue to grow at dramatic rates. With the software-provisioned, self-healing network of the future, customers will enjoy user-friendly integrated access to features not even dreamed about a few short years ago. Despite some of the pitfalls that ISDN has experienced over its short history, it continues to be the strongest, most promising network architecture to lead us into the Information Age and into the realm of global telecommunications in our lifetime.

33

Administrative Productivity Through Information Technology

Ronald Whittier, Vice President of Direct Marketing, Intel

Intel is an information technology company in two ways. First, we're a manufacturer of information technology products. Over the past 20 years, we've built a reputation as being a supplier of micro-computer solutions. We sell about $2 billion worth of information technology products a year.

Second, Intel is a user of information technology products. We use a variety of such products in all facets of our business — in manufacturing, in development, and in the administrative areas.

Usually I talk about Intel as an information technology company in the first way. In this chapter, I will address us as a user of information technology.

Enhancing Productivity in the Plant and Office. Productivity programs are common for manufacturing companies. And Intel certainly has a major focus on getting factory worker productivity up — and we take a lot of pride in showing 30 percent productivity improvement in our plants over the last two years. Much of the productivity increase is due to computer-aided manufacturing or automation.

Likewise, with the shortage of skilled design engineers, high-tech companies like Intel make significant investments in improving the productivity of engineers as measured by the improvements in time-to-design complex microcomputer chips. Again, part of the solution involves massive increases in the computing power supporting each design engineer. The CAD workstation market growth is strong evidence of this trend.

What's good for the factory and the design lab is also good for the office. Demands for streamlining operations to increase margins have led to productivity enhancement programs in the office aimed at the administrative side of the business. Productivity here is measured by the revenue-per-administrative-person. And, once again, the significant increase in productivity can be ascribed to the implementation of "Info Technology" in the work place. This increase will be the basis of my remarks on administrative productivity.

Let me describe two elements of this productivity enhancement program.

Administrative Productivity in 1975. Information technology is being implemented in parallel at a variety of levels within the administrative function. One area that has been dramatically affected is the individual worker. As recent as 13 years ago, standard office equipment consisted of a typewriter and a telephone. These two pieces of equipment had a number of problems.

The typewriter was better than the pen, but by today's standards it was equally primitive. The problem was one of keystrokes — there were just too many involved: the original draft, edited versions, the final draft, "original" copies, retyping at remote locations. From a productivity standpoint, it's axiomatic that you should only keystroke a given piece of information one time (or less). The typewriter left a lot to be desired.

Looking at the telephone, the major problem in the office was trying to reach the person you needed — it was common to play phone tag.

Administrative Productivity in 1985. The era of the typewriter has changed in a revolutionary way. By 1985, the PC had arrived and in most modern offices, the typewriter had been eliminated. For the administrative support staff, the word processing function on the PC made the typewriter inefficient in comparison. The spreadsheet capability and application software allowed the office staff to perform project management tasks in a much more efficient manner. By 1985-

86, the professional and support staff had converted to PCs, and the increased productivity actually allowed the necessary staff reductions of the 1986-1987 time period.

Also by 1985, electronic data communication arrived to the desk top. It was no longer necessary to find co-workers with whom you could leave a mail message. But the capability goes well beyond this — it is possible to transfer data files (text, graphics) over these communication links.

This form of information technology enhancement continues uninterrupted. Additional functions continue to be added to the desk top information system. The capability has gone beyond increasing the productivity of the individual, or even the small work group that provides the basic administrative support. The revolution that grew to replace the phone, typewriter, calculator, drawing table, etc., has now reached the point of providing enhanced enterprise productivity.

Order Processing, 1975. Beyond the "simple" problems of the desk top, there are problems that involve complex transaction processing in the major administrative functions of the company. In the sales and marketing function, the most complex system is that which controls the order processing function. For example, in the order processing system at Intel in the 1975 period, the customer sends an order to Intel, and if the order finds its way through the system, the customer ultimately receives the product ordered and an invoice.

Computers were used as a department tool to store, report, and retrieve information. Communications between customers and vendors and between departments were handled with telex machines, typewriters, and mail.

Order Entry Throughput-Time, defined as the time elapsed between a customer submitting a P.O. and a vendor responding with a delivery date, was measured (manually) in terms of number of days. Seven to ten working days was not uncommon.

Customer inquiry TPT (from receipt of customer question regarding backlog or shipment to response to customer) was also measured in terms of days. Seven to 14 working days was not uncommon. All warehouse activity was manual, with TPT running as much as three to four days.

One way to characterize the complexity was by the 12-step process and the lack of electronic communications. It took approximately 300 workers to run this system for $300 million in revenue, around $1 million revenue per employee working in the sales administration area.

Order Processing, 1987. A dozen years later, in 1987, the system has been greatly simplified. Computers are now used as a company-wide system. They still store, report, and retrieve data, but in addition, they automatically and instantaneously communicate between different departments. Typewriters, mail, and telex machines have been totally eliminated as communication vehicles. In addition, computers process tasks which were previously handled by human intervention, such as scheduling delivery, generating acknowledgements, generating shipping instructions in remote locations, printing shipping papers, and generating invoices. Mail is now used only for customer-to-vendor information flow.

Order entry TPT is measured in terms of hours — generally running 24 to 72 hours with 75 percent of that TPT being "mail" time between customer and vendor. In the warehouse, robotics has replaced the manual pick activity. Warehouse TPT generally runs 24 to 48 hours. It took approximately 115 workers to run this system at $1.93 billion in revenue, around $17 million revenue per employee working in this area.

Order Processing, 1990s. Where does this system go next? On to something called EDI, Electronic Data Interchange: the "Paperless Office." This is the computer-to-computer exchange of intercompany business documents and information. This means that Intel and its customers can exchange all information necessary to run their supplier-vendor business relationships electronically. Information on all aspects of order processing between customer and vendor is handled "on-line" and "instantly" by electronic data interchange. Standards for computer formats and third-party networks allow for customers and vendors to communicate using their system designs.

Once EDI is implemented in the 1990 time frame, the order processing system will be simplified even further so that all communications are electronic; the interface with purchasing is eliminated. The customer's MRP system "talks" directly to the vendor's Order

Processing system. Invoices are also sent computer-to-computer. Computers now function as complete, closed loop business processing systems. Order entry TPT will be measured in terms of minutes. The customer has the capability to look at his backlog "on-line" on the vendor's system. The number of people required to implement this kind of a system: 135 workers for $3 billion in revenue, around $22 million per employee in sales administration.

Conclusion. In summary, we see that computers have had a profound effect on the most complex corporate information systems supporting the enterprise. This has happened in parallel with the automation of the desk top. There's more to come. Ultimately, the systems will be integrated.

Let me conclude with a few remarks on the obvious implication of this to the administrative worker, whether that be clerical worker, project leader, or department manager.

First, we all need to learn to type or, more correctly today, how "to move the mouse so that we point at the little house." Further, you should sign yourself up for a lifelong training/investment program in the area of information technology. Each year there is more hardware, more software to learn to keep up with information technology.

Why should you do this? The most productive and successful companies, the most productive and successful individuals, are those effectively using information technology — it's fundamental to being competitive. But you have to use and implement this technology in an intelligent, informed way. Think of this as an investment; there is "good" information technology and "bad" information technology. If you invest in the bad stuff, your productivity, over the long haul, will go down.

To be able to implement this technology both personally and in a commercial enterprise, you need to be trained in it and understand it; you need to be a sophisticated user.

This means that you either become knowledgeable about information technology so that you can use information technology, specify information technology, pay for information technology, and effectively implement the technology, or you become a very non-productive, non-competitive employee.

34

Du Pont Exploits Emerging Technologies

John Taylor, Manager, Du Pont

I have had the good fortune to be both a participant and an observer in a company that has done very well at dealing with advanced technology. What company is this? This company has the first supercomputer to be acquired in the chemical industry, has a global electronic mail network with over 46,000 users interconnected, is a recognized leader in the use of electronic data and interchange, and is a recognized leader in the commercial exploitation of expert systems. This is Du Pont.

Du Pont is roughly a 140,000 employee, $30 billion per year diversified manufacturing company. It has "industrial departments" in it which make and sell various products. I call Du Pont a diversified manufacturing company because we produce chemicals, automotive finishes such as car paints, pharmaceuticals, medical diagnostics and medical equipment, textile fibers for all sorts of uses, electronic products, engineering plastics, oil, and coal, and many other products.

In addition to the industrial departments, we have "staff departments" like many companies do — Finance, Legal, External Affairs, and others. Among the staff departments are the "technology departments" in Du Pont. There are three of these — the Central Research & Development Department, of which I am a part, the Information Systems Department, which is the corporate MIS function, and the Engineering Department. These three departments report to a Senior Vice President of Technology. These three departments alone will spend about $13 million in 1988 for advanced technology in computers and systems. This is independent of the activities of the industrial departments who are also doing things for their own agendas.

The objective of these expenditures is not to anticipate emerging technologies; rather it is to exploit emerging technologies for the purpose of competitive advantage. And in that light, I have changed the title of my essay to indicate that we are really interested in "Exploiting Emerging Technologies."

I have three key messages for you today. First, competitive advantage is simply lead time on a maturity curve. Second, technology is not the problem. Third, resource deployment is.

Maturity Curve and Competitive Advantage. Let us explore each of these points. At the risk of insulting your intelligence, let me review what a maturity curve or a life cycle curve is. The ordinate is utility or usefulness; the abscissa is time. Technology is born in invention and during its youth it is experimented with. The experiments reveal the true benefits which the technology offers and then there is a rapid period of growth as suppliers and users alike race to deploy it and reap the benefit before others do. During maturity, the technology is a commodity reasonably accessible to anyone. After maturity comes aging, when the technology declines in the face of other, newer, technologies. Incidentally, actual death is usually slow to take place, but there's an erosion and a displacement as new technologies overshadow the old.

The second line in front of the maturity curve represents taking advantage of technology before most others; competitive advantage is the difference in time between your ability to rise up that first line and the time when everybody else can get it. One characteristic of competitive advantage based on technology is that it will go away in time. It is getting there first that counts.

Opportunities Limited by Resources, Not Technology. My second observation is that technology really is not the problem — usually. There is a cornucopia of emerging technology to which we could devote resources. We simply do not have enough resources to meet all of the opportunities. If we are going to achieve competitive advantage we want to act early enough to obtain lead time. This means that there is risk associated with it; in fact, the earlier you try to exploit a technology the greater the risk. The amount that the three technology departments have budgeted to expend in this area this year is $14 million — that is a limited resource; and so this brings me to the last point.

Resource deployment is the problem. Fundamentally, what we are trying to do is optimize the resource deployment to obtain a business benefit before others can achieve it. We need to recognize the business opportunity which means we must be in close contact with the business. They, not the technologists, are the people who will receive the benefit; they, not the technologists, are the people who are close to the customer and recognize the bottom line objectives of the company. The technologists must communicate the availability of new technology and help the businesses recognize the opportunity; a true partnership is necessary between the information science specialists and the people running the business. Once the opportunity and the technology have been identified and the opportunity has been judged to warrant the expenditure and the risk, then the resources, the people and the money, must be committed and they must be committed in sufficient measure to realize the benefit.

Let me show you five examples from Du Pont where we have done this at different stages. I can only share the benefits with you in a qualitative sense, but I think you will get a sense of the business opportunity we were going after, what technology was used, what we did, what resources were expended and how, and what the results were.

Exploiting Global Electronic Mail. First, let's talk about global electronic mail. We have three mainstream technologies in our company: IBM (370 architecture only), Digital Equipment Corporation VAX technology, and HP 3000s. We have mail systems operating on all of those. The driving force here was Du Pont's evolving with foreign subsidiaries. Around 1980 we began to shift our emphasis and we became what is commonly referred to as a multinational company, but it was a U.S.-based multinational company. We are now going through "globalization." We are becoming global corporate citizens because we believe that to compete effectively in the global marketplace we must run our businesses as if they were global enterprises. As an example of this, the Lycra business in our Textile Fibers Department is operated by a European who lives in Geneva. For us to fully realize the global competitive opportunity, we must overcome the barriers of time and distance to communications. This led us to conclude that global electronic mail across the three technologies was a strategic imperative. The technology used was a combination of "interconnects" and "global directory services." Interconnects are the ability to pass messages from one technology or from one vendor to another. It is important to realize that a global electronic mail system is useless to you if you have no way of finding the address of the person on the other end, so the global directory services were an important part of this effort. This was a non-trivial task — $2 million spent over two years. The result is that we have 46,000 users on three architectures interconnected in a very graceful way.

Exploiting Artificial Intelligence. The next example I would like to use relates to the commercial exploitation of artificial intelligence. We realized that if we had an aggressive program to exploit artificial intelligence, we could get substantial leverage out of the human experts that exist in Du Pont today. We are generally considered a technology company, so we have a fair number of these experts. Some of them are aging and facing retirement so we had a strong business reason to capture their knowledge. The vehicle that was used was a pretty simple set of tools; it was expert systems shells running on both PCs and mainframes. We formed an AI task force; we spent roughly $4 million over the last two years doing this. This was about 12-15 people whose job it was to plant seeds of expert systems, to go about the company training people, helping people find opportunities and train them and leave them self-sufficient for the continuation of these expert systems. There are 100 systems in commercial use today; there are 300 presently under development and the target is to have 2000 of them commercially operational within the company by 1990. We are highly confident that we will achieve this. I cannot reveal the actual payback to you, I can only tell you that we have repaid the $4 million several times over — a winning proposition.

Exploiting Electronic Data Interchange (EDI). We are recognized as one of the first non-financial services companies to have a major thrust with regard to electronic data interchange (EDI). This is the exchange of business transactions between ourselves and our customers and vendors. Fundamentally, our goal is to make it easier to do business with us so our primary target is our customer. We are trying to create what is referred to as switching costs. We want our customers to love doing business with us, and rely on information that they can get from us in a graceful and speedy way, so much that it becomes a barrier to their stopping doing business with us and going to do business with somebody else. These are called switching costs. We used fairly standard techniques — batch transaction exchange and interactive access. Obviously standards were important in this activity, standards for the format of various business documents. We created an Electronic Data Interchange Task Force at the corporate level to build a conduit to the customer base and to handle the standards negotiations and the various other things necessary for success. Basically, they have become an assistant to the business to make EDI come about and to enhance their relationship with their individual customers. It cost about $2 million over a couple of years; we have over 100 companies with EDI batch transactions exchanging with us routinely and about 500 users with interactive access to our systems today.

Exploiting Supercomputers. Du Pont was the first and is still the only company in the chemical industry with its own supercomputer. We saw an opportunity to provide a unique computing resource in support of our research activity. The decision was precipitated by an unsolicited offer from Cray Research, Inc. They had a used CRAY 1A taken in trade, and they approached us with a very attractive lease on this used machine. I manage the Scientific Computing Division which provides computing services to the scientific community. I went to my customers and said, "You have a number of people within your organizations who believe that in-house access to a supercomputer would be a valuable asset. Here is an opportunity to do it inexpensively; you will probably never see a similar opportunity again. Are you willing to put $2.5 million on the table?"

We had taken the lease costs; we added to that the utilities, the space, the staff, the maintenance, the various other expenses that go with it. We determined that we could run it for $200,000 per month; the commitment was for a year. The research community said "yes," we will subscribe to this "experiment." The CRAY 1A was started up in January 1986. This past November we replaced it with an $11.39 million CRAY XMP; this attests to the success of the experiment. The value of an in-house supercomputer to an organization like ours is that the rates for the use of our supercomputer are anywhere from one-third to one-tenth of what we would pay if we went to a service bureau. So we have a substantial competitive advantage to the extent that supercomputers are useful to our scientific research.

Exploiting Compound Document Architecture. Finally the compound document architecture: Du Pont is a highly technical company. I have already mentioned our need to move communications about the world in a fast and facile fashion. It would be very beneficial to be able to communicate compound documents, such as documents that contain text, tables, data, and graphics, in revisable form on a global basis because technical information is so much a part of what we do.

Let me provide a simple example to describe the value of "revisable form." I have a document containing a spread sheet and I send it to you in revisable form. You can display it on your work station, click on the spread sheet, and you are in the spreadsheet package (with the data that came out of the document) enabling you to manipulate the data. This is a true compound document. Later on, we expect to further integrate faster and vector graphics, image, audio, and full motion video. The technology involved here is work stations; you really cannot accomplish this with terminals. Clearly, standards as well as software are an important part of it. To date, we have spent about $250,000 on the "Compound Document Architecture Study." We spent that money over two years and concluded that it is too early for us to get into full commercial exploitation. Nevertheless, we are piloting a number of approaches so that we can position ourselves to run up that maturity curve earlier than any other large corporation in America or in the world.

Summary. Well, this really brings me to the close but I would like you to remember three things:

1. Competitive advantage is lead time on a maturity curve.
2. We have more technology than we know what to do with.
3. Resource deployment to meet business needs is really the problem that we have to deal with.

I have positioned each of my five examples approximately where I think they lie on the maturity curve. EDI is nearing maturity; it would be relatively easy for others to do what we have done. In fact some of what they could do would be built on standards that we pioneered. Supercomputers — if you have $11.39 million, Cray would be glad to sell you one, so there is not a big barrier there. The barrier is having the guts to do it. Global electronic mail — if you have multiple technologies to span (and we have fewer than most), there is a significant technical and time barrier for you to do it. It is clearly achievable — we did it — but that is a little farther out for others to catch up with. AI — I think somewhat the same; recognizing the opportunities and deploying them. We will have 2000 AI systems by the year 1990; how many will you have? Compound documents — it is really very early and our confidence in our ability to climb this curve is really based on pilots right now.

These are my observations from watching a company that is trying to deal with the emerging technology challenge. I hope that they are useful to you.

35

Computer Simulation in Manufacturing

W. David Kelton, Professor, University of Minnesota

Simulation is a way of transforming one kind of information into a different form. The kind of information we want to receive is the useful kind, and the kind of information we input is not particularly useful by itself.

I will start by introducing and talking about modeling and how simulation is used, and then justify my existence by quoting some surveys about what gets used and what might be the perceived value of some of these techniques. Then, in order to try to make you understand my concerns about the use and misuse of simulation, we will look at an example and go inside a simulation to see what goes on there. I will discuss the information that emerges from the simulation and what you need to put into it. Both are substantial. Lastly, I will present my guesses of where this might be going.

Modeling and Simulation. Computer simulation is a method for studying systems that are too complicated for what we might call a "paper-and-pencil" analysis. Traditionally, we would look at a system and model it, for example, as a bunch of interconnected waiting line models or queues. Since the 1920s, people have been thinking about queuing theory and ways to get interesting answers out of queuing models. The problem is that only very simple models with assumptions that are far off the mark with respect to reality can be used this way.

For example, a manufacturing facility I worked on had groupings by machine type. There was one type of machine where the flow was more or less from left to right (although not completely; there is feedback, and so forth). In this group, there were five machines, a conveyor belt, systems of automatic guided vehicles, and an automatic storage and retrieval system. I don't know if it was simulated beforehand or not, but it was built that way.

There are a lot of questions a person might ask about a system like this. The primary one is what will be the production volume: How many parts per day, or per shift, will be produced? However, a long-term operational question would be: "What if we added a machine?" We might expect an improvement in production, but it is difficult to quantify. And if we have an opportunity to, say, add one more of this or that (if the cost is relatively the same), where should it go? In which group should the machine be put? And should there be a strategy if breakdowns occur?

These kinds of questions are very important in high volume production. There is a tremendous amount of money to be saved by thinking about how to operate systems this way. Now, I have said that this particular system does exist. It is operating. But it would have been better to simulate it beforehand, asking if this is the best physical layout for the equipment. Should they be clustered by machine type, or should they be put into cells under a different manufacturing style where certain part types would use certain machines?

The difficulty is that this is a complicated system and just one part of a large factory. Traditional methods such as queuing theory are not applicable here unless you make a lot of incorrect assumptions.

Let's talk about the general idea of modeling and simulation, starting with the assumption that there is a system of some sort to study, typically a manufacturing system. There are a number of methods we can use to study systems but I want to talk about where simulation fits into the picture.

The first thing we need to decide is whether or not we are actually going to fool around with the system itself. In a sense, that is the best idea because there is no question about whether we are looking at the right thing. So the best way to study a production line and see if we want to add a machine here or there would be to go in and do it. Add a machine here and run it for awhile. Then add it over there and run it for a while. Now that begins to stretch the corporation's fiscal

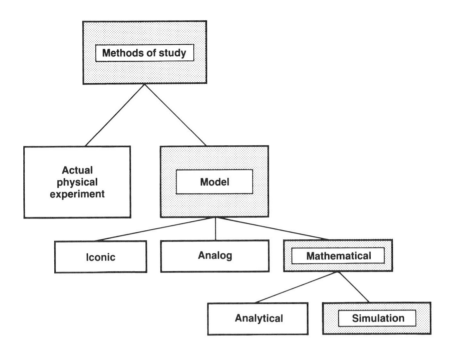

Figure 35.1 Methods of Studying Systems

side because it is a little difficult to say, "I'd like to experiment with each of these machines, which cost $180,000 apiece. I'll need two of them before I decide which one I really want."

A more extreme example would be in the health care area. Simulation is used frequently to size hospitals and emergency rooms. We would like to know how many nurses and doctors are needed in the emergency room and so we put some number in there and, well, that seems like enough. Let's try it with fewer, and if that does not work, we will increase the number.

There are systems that we simply cannot look at. An example of why we can't do this is that it simply does not exist yet. And there is no alternative to seeing a model of the system.

Now, in the minds of most people, the word "model" conjures up that oil company ad that showed guys learning how to drive supertankers, driving these things that were about 8 feet long around in a swimming pool to learn how to maneuver and dock them. Models like these are called *iconic models*. In manufacturing, there are things called *table-top operations models* that for all the world are like an electric train set. It is an actual model of parts staying here for a while and then being moved over there. It is nice to do but difficult because it is not easy to change things and watch the results. But lots of people are doing research by looking at iconic table-top models of manufacturing systems.

Analog models — like a thermometer representing air temperature or a speedometer — are probably not very useful in manufacturing. They bear no physical resemblance to what is being studied, but only measure something about it. It is difficult to think of analog models in manufacturing.

The kind of models I want to focus on are called, for lack of a better word, *mathematical models*. When I was going through school, I wondered what a model really was, but nobody ever told me. I finally figured out that a mathematical model is just a bunch of assumptions about the way something works. It is composed of logical assumptions as well as quantitative and numerical assumptions. In a sense, models are always wrong. A model is always an abstraction of reality, and so looking at a model is not as good as looking at the actual system. But in many cases, it is all we can do. We cannot look at the actual system. So suppose we make some kind of assumption about the way something works. We then have to think about how to study the mathematical model of the system.

Mathematical models may be amenable to what is called an analytical solution, and this is the traditional kind of textbook paper-and-pencil method (which often needs a computer anyway because the calculations are so involved). But an analytical solution gets you the answer to the question you are asking. What is the expected number of parts produced per day in the system? There are a number of things you can do with that. You can play with the parameters and see what would happen if this parameter changed. And it is easy to do with this little formula (or this little computer program). Analytical solutions to mathematical models are always preferable.

However, systems are often so complicated that it is impossible to build a realistic model simple enough to admit an analytical solution, and that is where simulation comes in. There are some pros and cons of analytical versus simulation models. In analytics we get exact results. Now it might sound silly; we are always looking for the answer and this is something that students find very difficult to grasp at first. When you write a computer program to do something, it prints something out and that is the answer. Simulation is not like that, unfortunately. The drawback of analytics is that we can only use them for relatively simple models. Simulation, on the other hand, gets us only approximate results, at least the type of simulation I am going to talk about.

Simulation is a poor word in a way because it can mean very different things. To an economist it means one thing; to somebody making flight simulators, it means something entirely different. In simulating things like manufacturing systems we are not going to get exact answers just as by building a simulation model, we are not going to get the same answer. And that can be upsetting. It is not that you or I are wrong; we are both right but just different.

With simulation we don't have to "look where the light is." A lady was walking along and saw a guy groping around the ground beneath a street lamp. She asked, "What are you doing?"

He replied, "Well, I lost my keys and I'm trying to find them."

"Oh, you lost them around here."

"No, I didn't lose them here; I lost them over there."

"Well, why don't you look over there?"

He replied, "This is where the light is."

One thing that happens with an analytical model is that there is a lot of "light" there. You get a lot of nice results. The trouble is that it may not be where the problem is; that is not where the keys are lost. With a simulation we have the luxury of dealing with more complex models and therefore more valid representations of reality. Analytical models often make a tremendous number of possibly offensive assumptions which do considerable violence to the extent to which the model represents the real system.

Usage and Value of Simulation. There have been surveys done about the usage and value of computer simulation. One was done in the journal *Interfaces*, which is the primary applications journal of the operations research and management science community, done nearly ten years ago. The survey asked 137 firms, "Which one of these techniques do you use?" *Statistical analysis* (These were their words; imagine getting a questionnaire like this and having to answer yes or no to words like this...) is used by something like 87 percent of the firms.

Simulation was close behind at 84 percent. *Linear programming*, a technique that most of us probably learned in a course somewhere, is not as widely used. Usage of *project management*, such as CPM, starts to fall off.

Thus, in 1979, four out of five large firms said that simulation was used in their company. If you asked about the operations research and management science techniques, I really do not think statistical analysis counts and so in this survey simulation comes out to be the most frequently used operations research technique. This was ten years ago when computers were more expensive, a lot slower, and simulation software was harder to use. I am sure that if this survey were repeated today, the numbers would be even more favorable toward simulation.

In a related survey, a questionnaire was sent to the cumulative graduates of the Department of Operations Research at Case Western Reserve University in Cleveland. This was the first such department in the world, so they have a lot of graduates. The ranking of the results indicated that the most successful subject they had learned there was statistics. Something called "systems forecasting" came in second; I am not exactly sure what a word like "systems" is supposed to mean. Simulation came in third.

Statistics is not really an operations research technique and "systems" is too general to mean much, and so once again simulation is apt to be the best thing that can be done. So I think, with the word properly defined, simulation comes out on top every time.

Basic Workings of Simulations. Let's look at a fictional example of what a simulation actually does. (See Figure 35.2.) In this situation, parts arrive in a kind of a two-stage process with interarrival times having an exponential distribution with mean one minute, join a FIFO queue, and then enter some kind of process. The processing takes between 0.7 and 0.8 minutes, assuming the uniform distribution here. They enter another queue for inspection, which takes between 0.8 and 0.9 minutes.

Ninety percent of the parts pass inspection and just leave the world as far as we are concerned. Ten percent of them fail and have to return for further processing. It would be possible for a particular part to fail inspection several times. I have tried to include something about breakdowns, assuming that the processor can go down. It stays up for an average of six hours, and when it goes down it takes between eight and 12 minutes to repair. The system starts out empty and we run it for two shifts.

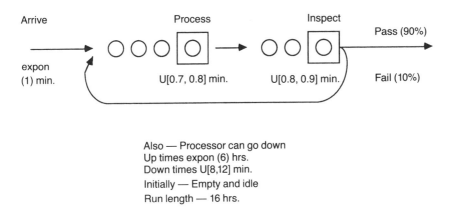

Figure 35.2 **Manufacturing Simulation Model**

Now, how would someone go about doing a simulation of this type? There are two world views of simulation modeling. Originally, the method used was called *event scheduling*. In event scheduling, we identify the character events. What happens that causes the system to change? In this particular system we have a part arrival, end-processing, and inspection, at which time it goes either here or there, and we also have this machine-up and machine-down business. Finally, the simulation ends.

So there are six different events happening in this system to cause it to change. We could then go to the computer and write a code to represent those events. This can be done in a general-purpose language like FORTRAN. These events are hooked together by means of a clock, representing time, and an event list, or sequence in which the events are going to occur. The clock and the event list interact to move through time from one event to the next and cause the events to happen in the order in which they actually occur.

In a simulation's engine room is a random number generator that determines specifically how often things arrive and how long it takes to serve them. Now, random number generators certainly do not interest very many applications people, but they do matter. I got up this morning and walked over to the local bookstore, picked up the management science text being used these days, and there it was printed in the chapter on simulation — one of the world's worst random number generators. You cannot just do something weird and come up with a good random number generator. It has been shown over and over that this particular one gives you wrong answers in a simulation. I am not saying inefficient or inaccurate — I am saying wrong. The methodological issue right at the bottom is the random number generator. It is incredible that these things perpetuate themselves.

Another way of looking at this is that, instead of identifying characteristic events, we identify characteristic players in the model, sometimes called entities. Other languages call them processes or transactions. Here we have "parts" entities (two servers) and we have to model this breakdown some way. Breakdowns are usually thought of as "demons" seated off to the side who go in, kick the processor, and then sit on it for the time period representing repair time. Then these demons let go and wait until they decide to go in and kick it again.

Simulation works by telling a little story about what happens to a "typical" entity as it "flows through the system." This usually requires a specialized simulation language — a specialized piece of software. It took a while but I coded this in FORTRAN (with event-scheduling logic) and it took about 600 lines of code. Process-interaction logic lets you do things a lot quicker and a lot easier, but it does require the software and may limit your flexibility.

I will show you a process interaction program in a simulation language called SIMAN, just one of the simulation languages I could have used. I create a part, it gets in a queue, it seizes a processor, it stays there for a while, it releases the processor, it gets in another queue, it seizes the inspector, it stays there for a while, it releases the inspector, and then it branches into "Done" where it leaves (meaning it passes inspection) or it fails inspection and gets back into the queue again.

This is a natural way to describe systems like this. We need a separate part for the breakdown demon: Create one, wait around for an up time, go kick the machine by preempting it, and then return. But there are details. What happens when the demon kicks the machine down? There is a modeling assumption here that requires attention because it matters. It can tell you whether or not to buy this machine. The disposition of the preempted item must be dealt with in a particular way.

This is only one of the several simulation languages widely used in the United States. This particular one requires that details be placed in a different file altogether, like a super data file specifying things about distributions and what I want to watch and how long to run it, and so forth.

When noting output, it is important to look at the time in system and at the quantity produced, in this model, for instance, 955 good items on one day. Although some of these were recycled several times, this was the production figure for that day. Time in the system averaged about ten or 11 minutes. If I look at equipment utilization, the processor was busy 84 percent of the time and the inspector over 90 percent of the time. These utilization statistics are of interest, for example, if instead of a manufacturing system, this were a computer system where a server is any sort of expensive CPU. The processor queue averaged three or four parts and the inspection queue averaged five or six parts. The worst they ever got was 26 and 22.

One limitation is that this was one run. I did this once driven by a random number generator, a good one in this case. Had I used a different random number generator, or a different stream, I would not get these numbers out. A simulation is an experiment, and doing it once is like growing a tomato and making conclusions about the effect of the fertilizer. Or it is like throwing a die once, watching it come up three, and concluding that every side of the die is three.

This is the big problem in using simulations. You run it once and so the analysis is woefully inadequate. Unfortunately, in many cases simulation is misused exactly this way. It is difficult to build large simulation models and, once the thing is operating, you may feel that it is over and you just run it. Well, you are not done. If you don't do something beyond this, you have wasted a lot of time.

Information Out. I would like to get these kinds of results and I could add a second inspector to see how it would increase my production. Those are the kinds of things typically done in a simulation.

Let's continue this example. Say I have a space problem and would like to put a capacity on the buffers. (See Figure 35.3.) Maybe I will put 12 on the one in front of the processor and ten on the one in front of the inspector. This is only a guess right now. (I am just doing a simulation. These are numbers inside a computer, nobody is getting hurt, no production is lost, and therein lies modeling's value.)

So I would change these buffer capacities by trying several different values. This is the first result, when I had no buffer capacities. Now if I reduce the buffer capacities to 12 and ten, my production drops off a little bit, from 955 to 948. The time in system drops off also because I am forcing my queues to be shorter. If somebody wants to leave and they can't, they stay there. If somebody wants to come in and they can't, they are lost to the system. That was the assumption made. It does not seem like a great production loss, so let's see if I can squeeze the buffer capacities down further. Production drops off, but what happens there? I get smaller buffers, but more production. Does that make sense? Maybe — but maybe not. There are some anomalies here and maybe they were trying to tell me something. Maybe there is some synchronization going on.

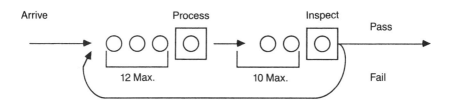

Figure 35.3 Putting Capacities on the Buffers

Looking at the statistical properties of the output can be a reliable tool. The output information we get from simulation is statistical information and a statistical analysis of the simulation is required. In this case, by running each scenario five times, I got 979 — which is really an extraordinarily large number for that system. It was just the luck (or unluck) of the draw.

I did not cook this up to illustrate a point. This actually happened with this model. And with a sample size of five or so, I can move on to some traditional statistical analysis — like making a confidence interval. These confidence intervals tell me, in a sense, how much uncertainty I have in the simulation output information. In this case, with infinite buffers, my production will be someplace between 924 and 951. This may seem like unacceptably wide parameters to you. We could improve it by increasing the sample sizes the way normally done in statistical inference. From this we can conclude that the buffers could be decreased without appearing to hurt production materially. Again, I think these intervals are too wide. I prefer pinning down the result better.

I am afraid many people doing simulation ignore this step. It is not enough in running a simulation to start it and stop it arbitrarily and look at the resulting numbers with the assumption that is it. We saw that this number would be pretty misleading. My earlier result is really very strange and just the luck (or unluck) of the draw. Simulation information is, I think, misleading information. This is a little better but we can still see degrees of inaccuracy. Something can be done about it.

Unfortunately, while fine for this model, the idea of replication is unacceptable for other kinds of simulation goals because traditional statistical methods do not work. A group of people who refer to themselves as simulation methodologists worry about how to design and interpret simulation output.

Information In. We need to build some sort of model early on in a simulation study. In the modeling activity, you can distinguish two distinct sorts of goals. One, for lack of a better word, I call a *qualitative model*. This is just a physical picture without getting down to analyzing the numbers. Considering this the first step, you have to understand what the system is, or what it will be, when it is built.

The other side is a *quantitative model* involving the actual specification of numerical values and parameters. How did I know in this little model that inspection times lasted between 0.8 and 0.9 minutes and they were uniformly distributed? In this case I made it up — because this is a made- up example. How would I reach these results in reality?

Here we have nine machine groups with nine different machine types. So we have to specify nine cycle time distributions. If these machines go up and down, I have to specify nine down time distributions and nine up time distributions, resulting in 27 distributions. With five different parts going through here, each one may require different machine times. Suddenly I have many different distributions to specify — a daunting task, to say the least. I cannot just stay at home and make them up because the assumptions of numbers and distribution forms matter in terms of output, and I can get completely different solutions depending on my choices for these input distributions.

Normally, this would be done by sending my industrial engineer out to the plant with a stopwatch and clipboard to record the time it takes to process this kind of part in the machine. When and for how long does this machine goes down? And how often do parts show up? I would come back and do some sort of statistical analysis to determine the probability distribution forms — is it exponential, uniform, normal, Weibull, or what?

In the automotive industry it has been said that data collection and specification of this input information is the most difficult and costly part of the project. It is harder than building the model, coding it in the simulation, and interpreting the results. Herein lies the difficult and unglamorous part. Another industrial person told me that the inability to convince management that reasonable distribution assumptions had been made caused the entire project to fail.

Although most of my own work has been done on output, I have begun to worry about the input analysis side. First of all, I have convinced myself that it matters. The choice of input distributions can make a tremendous difference in terms of output. I have developed what I think is a routine and easy-to-use method of dealing with the input distribution specification problem. It is 60 lines of FORTRAN that fits on one page.

What do you do without data? This often happens. You have no data, or you have data on the wrong phenomenon and you are not comfortable with imputing it over to what you really want. I have some suggestions for dealing with this: Routinize the data collection procedure. Take advantage of automatic sensoring. This capability is now becoming much more widespread. Involve simulationists in data collection design because that gets us to the point of being able to collect data on things we will need to make the simulation go.

Prospects. Simulation's main advantage is in allowing us to use the technique on realistic models without having to make a lot of assumptions. To be sure, we have to make some assumptions. But we do not have to start assuming away the world. Typically, in queuing theory, you have to assume things have exponential distributions because this is a convenient mathematical form. We do not have to do that in simulations; we can use whatever we think is appropriate. This gives us more valid models of reality and therefore more confidence in the relevance of the results.

I think it is better to get an approximate answer to the right question than the exact answer to the wrong question. I would rather take my dim little flashlight to where the street light isn't and have a look. I will have to grope around a little, and I might need some help, but at least I am not making the mistake of getting really nice answers to some irrelevant questions.

An interesting idea is to do an analytical study as a precursor to a simulation study just to get an idea of order-of-magnitude, qualitative kinds of results. For heaven's sake, don't believe the numbers. A pre-simulation analysis is an exciting possibility, just to get a rough idea.

The information flow in a simulation could look like Figure 35.4. We have some model structure, we have data from which we hopefully will get distributions, and that composes the simulation's input information. We can think of the simulation as some kind of a processor — as a black box or a program like any other computer program that takes input numbers, does something to them, and produces output numbers. The output numbers are really a transformation of the input distributions into the output distributions, which is what we are interested in.

I already know about the time it takes to process something on this machine. I really need to know how many I am going to make, exactly where the process time impacts on how many you can make — and simulation is the way to do that transformation. The output information is then used to assess system performance, to assess something about uncertainty in terms of these confidence intervals or a variance estimate, and ultimately, of course, to make decisions about what to do.

I think it is essential to manage the input and the output information appropriately, which means different things. Output information must be interpreted statistically. The proper statistical analysis of simulation output data is a complex issue. You cannot just take something out of traditional statistical analysis and carry it over to simulation the way I did in this example.

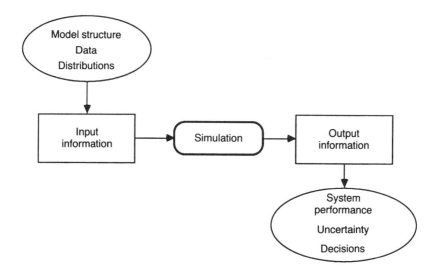

Figure 35.4 Information Flow and Transformation in Simulation

Input information must be managed properly. We have to worry about specific inputs to the simulation. We, of course, have to document the input and output data framework. This documentation, especially in a complex arena like simulation, is essential.

I think the use of simulation in manufacturing is going to increase. It is already widespread. Many vendors require that simulation studies be performed. Traditionally, simulation is used in systems design and perhaps in operation when it is already there. Off-line simulation is something that has been done for a while and now the idea of real-time control is available. It is now possible to do simulations on the factory floor to see what should happen.

There is a dark side to this whole issue. If you look at some of the trade magazines in the industrial engineering area, you will see some very attractive ads for simulation software. I worry that these ads are misleading and dishonest. There are things on the market now that some people call simulators. I call them ninth-generation simulation languages, and they are touted as being something anyone can use, and it is true. Anyone can use them.

I am concerned, however, because there are too many assumptions being made. You can have flexibility or friendliness — but you cannot have both. Things have gone completely on the friendly side and people are making assumptions that cause the results to be what they are. I am concerned about people who are unaware of some of the issues I have mentioned here using simulations. I apologize for the negative side to this discussion, but I worry about people throwing the die once without really knowing what they are throwing. Getting an incorrect answer is often worse than getting no answer at all.

Properly used, simulations give us tremendous insights into the design and operation of manufacturing systems. I see no real alternative.

36

Hidden Costs of Computing

Charlotte Cook Hofmann, President, Information Ideas

In business, there is a big push to improve, extend, and enhance — to make us better business people and our businesses more successful. We have a remarkable tool, the computer, to assist in this effort. Problems arise, however, when we are so busy using computers we don't have time to transact business. What follows is a discussion of those problems and suggested solutions.

Our management consulting firm investigates computing at a person-to-person, organization-by-organization level. In 1987, we were invited into a division of a large company with 3,000 people and a variety of computing resource problems. To learn about this organization, we interviewed 40 first- and middle-level department managers about their business. We asked whether their staff members were using their computing understanding and skills to fulfill the business goals of their organization.

During my eighth or ninth interview, the manager closed the door, sat in his chair, and placed his head in his hands, as if to catch a great weight. After a moment of silence, he said, "This isn't working for me."

I asked, "What isn't working?"

The manager said he had hired a promising young man to replace him upon his own promotion. The new man had excellent credentials, experience, and ability — but he was not computer literate.

Because the manager himself didn't understand computer technology and realized that his replacement should, he sent the new man to classes, about two days a week. After several months, the manager realized that he could not promote the new man.

He explained, "The new man is not attentive to the needs of the business anymore. He's fascinated with technology. He's teaching everyone how to work on their computers. That's wonderful — except I need a businessman, and he's become a technologist."

That was a startling story, but I thought it was only a fluke. Two days and four interviews later, however, I had another door closed and heard a similar story. This one was a sales story. The manager said, "He was one of my best salesmen, and I would do anything for him. He asked for a personal computer, and he got it."

At first, the salesman was automating this and checking that on his computer. Then he was showing his peers how to use their computers, too. The manager noticed that the salesman's sales began tapering off. The manager confronted the salesman, who responded with a series of excuses. When sales continued to fall, the manager fired the salesman.

When I asked about current sales figures, the manager said they were up 2 percent. The fired salesman, who had lost interest in making sales, had improved the ability of the others to make sales. The organization had lost one out of a sales force of five. Sales had not dropped 20 percent, but increased 2 percent. The point, however, is that the salesman had been hired to make sales, not support technology — so he lost his job.

The Issue: "Rapture of the Deep." In this company, two managers were faced with people they couldn't deal with. The two staff members lost touch with the business goals in favor of computing goals. At our company, we call this "rapture of the deep," a term borrowed from scuba diving. Overcome by ecstasy ("It's beautiful down here! I'm one with the ocean!"), some scuba divers throw off their life preserving equipment and drown. That's what computing technology does to some people.

In contrast, technology should extend and enhance the individual and that person's contribution to the productivity and success of the business, the ability to thrive and profit. All organizations need assistance with technology to reach their goals. But if a company is not in the computing or computer business, the keystroke or keyboard business, the data saving or archiving business, computing should only be used to improve the productivity and success of that company.

Language: Another Hidden Computing Cost. Consider how the computer has changed our language. Early in my career, I joined an information center, the crisis intervention and marketing side of the management of information services (MIS). Hired for my business, communication, and education experience, I had no computing skills, but my boss said, "I'm going to give you a guru who will answer all your questions."

One day I asked my guru about an operating system. He answered, "It's transparent."

I said, "No, it's not."

"It is transparent."

"It's not transparent to me."

"It was designed to be transparent, so it is."

"Even so, it isn't."

Increasingly frustrated, we realized our problem was communication, centering on the word "transparent."

My guru was a computer professional who uses language literally: "Transparent" means "clear as glass." I use language figuratively: "Transparent" means "clear," as in "I understand." Although most computer professionals have large vocabularies, these people (like the computers they work with) often have only one definition per word. Because computers don't use body language or intonation, computer professionals frequently are not astute in their understanding and appreciation of these language-enhancing matters.

A trade-off occurs. The more time spent mastering computers, the greater the loss of flexible "people skills." Whether we work on distributed or stand-alone information systems, our relationship with the computer is one-on-one and command-oriented. Therefore, one hidden cost of computing can be a need to re-acquaint staff with language and style once used and now abandoned in favor of "techno-speak".

Consider the Obedient Dog. The obedient dog has a one-to-one association between a word and an action. Some dogs only understand commands within the context of other commands. My dog will "stay" only when that command is preceded by "sit" and "down." Out of sequence, "stay" is a word the dog recognizes but cannot obey. Basically, computers are very obedient dogs. You tell them to do something, and they either understand what you said and proceed or they don't understand and, therefore, do nothing.

The problem is that people who spend four to eight hours daily in front of a computer start using language literally and in a command-oriented manner. As people grow confident and successful in their relationship with the computer, the style and quality of that relationship unintentionally carries over to their interactions with other people.

Consider how computer professionals often teach business professionals to use computers:

"Press this key to do that."

Frequently, there is no "please" or "thank you," no explanation as to what the key does. Just, "You want this to happen — press that key."

Instead of this kind of communication, we need to find a relationship with computers and computing that extends and enhances our skills as business people. Let's examine some ways to do this by exploring "rapture of the deep." Here is a suggested approach:

---

1. Recognize the problem and assess the situation.
2. Don't assign blame.
3. Recognize this problem as a management issue.
4. Decide between centralized and decentralized support of the business (knowledge) worker.
5. Commit the resources to fulfill the support decision.
6. Develop career paths for computing-literate business professionals.
7. Teach more business and less technology.

Table 36.1 One Approach to "Rapture of the Deep"

Recognizing the Problem. The simplest approach is to acknowledge "rapture" and its cost, primarily one of time and creativity.

Example: In some companies, "recreational reading" of vendor manuals is quite popular. Instead, the staff should read the *Wall Street Journal* or the business section of the local newspaper.

Example: Talented business people with rolled-up sleeves spend their time with tiny screwdrivers at the back of a micro computer. Should business staff know everything about technology? Should they be fixing hardware or hacking software? Or should they be determining how to do more and better business with their customers?

Succumbing to rapture of the deep sometimes costs business people in ways they did not anticipate. Although their job descriptions didn't include taking apart computers or serving as local technical experts, these raptured workers receive instant gratification from tasks associated with technology — and, because they are not doing what they were hired to do, their new-found skills frequently cost them their jobs.

These people are also passed over for promotions. One manager told of an employee who hadn't received a promotion in three years because "I can't afford to lose him." Whether this was true — or the boss didn't understand the employee's contribution — this undervalued employee was probably out looking for another job. One way or another, a loss to the organization resulted.

A tremendous antagonism can exist between MIS and local use of personal computers, a conflict between business users of PCs and the supposedly enemy camp of MIS and the mainframe. In one case, an organization (MIS) is being thrown out or an organization (other than MIS) is attempting to secede from the corporation. What a waste of time and energy.

When rapture is tolerated, an organization can go its own way technologically and implement its favorite solution at tremendous cost in dollars and technological momentum. This could even turn the company in a direction that is not in its best long-term interest.

Typically, a company spends between one percent and five percent of gross sales on MIS — a lot of money, but consider this: One study reported that, with all hidden aspects included, an individual PC costs about $20,000 per workstation per year. How many workstations can a company afford to sustain in an environment that disregards an integrated strategic approach? In fact, isn't MIS chartered to manage computing resources to the good of the company? Corporations spend millions of dollars for MIS and additional millions for PCs, perhaps without enough coordination and with business techies running their own empires. The cost of this tolerated technical anarchy can be equivalent to or greater than the cost of using MIS — and, without loyalty to the corporation, the techies may see only local needs and short-term goals.

"Personal computer" is a remarkable term. There's really nothing personal about a computer. PCs are not "personal" computers, but corporate assets. The staff should deal not with personal information, but with corporate information. Larger companies can multiply the numbers and see a lot of money being spent for so-called personal computers. Who benefits from this? Only the hardware and software vendors. They are benefitting, and their customers are losing money.

A major question is what to automate. With a bad case of rapture, business techies will automate anything and everything, just for the sake of automating. This should be viewed as an illness, one that presents a difficult situation for a company. This leads us to the second step.

Don't Assign Blame. If you have people who are crazy about technology, the answer is not to discharge or ignore them, but to reintegrate these valuable business technologists back into the company as high-tech business people. These people are telling you of their interest in technology and their need for support in this area. Also, they are succumbing to rapture because no one is reinforcing the investment of their energy in the business.

Think of these challenges as the unanticipated consequences of good intentions. Had you known this was going to happen, you would have planned for it. There is no reason to hold yourself responsible for this because this is a new and unique situation in the business environment.

Problem as Management Issue. Computing is a business strategy. Its success should be measured by future profits and movement closer to the bottom line. Also, rapture of the deep is a management/leadership issue. Some business people say they are installing computers to save money, but this is not the case. Computing is not a cost-saving strategy. For some time, computing will increase costs substantially, with implementation of technology and development of staff competency required to maximize the investment in technology.

We talk about productivity, but what does this mean? In most cases, nothing is created or manufactured, so this is not machine productivity. And it's more than individual performance.

When a secretary who could write 20 memos a week now has the ability to do five times that many, that's not productivity — it's overkill. We should look at the charter of the organization, use the computing facility to automate or innovate, and reach the goals of the organization sooner, more efficiently, or for the first time. Computing is the resourceful use of information, not technology. Computing power can extend and enhance business people beyond existing capabilities. Therefore, computing management cannot be delegated to professional or administrative staff. The costs are too significant and the implications too strategic to view the computing equation as anything other than a management issue.

Centralized or Decentralized Support. The issue is not centralized or decentralized support by internal service organizations. The only issue is provision of organized and timely support. Resources should be directed so time and energy are not spent spinning expensive high-technology wheels or frustrating creative business professionals. Companies that do not choose a support path open the door to internal anarchy. Those who are motivated to create their own support arena with no direction beyond their own short-term orientation will do so.

The number of amateur business techies who get into this arena can be as high as 10 to 20 percent of the total computing population. The professional computing organization can be outnumbered two to one, severely jeopardizing the corporation's investment in an integrated and evolving computing strategy. The answer is to encourage management to decide between centralized and decentralized support. Which approach is chosen is not as important as the fact that a choice is made and a commitment fulfilled.

Commit Resources. Management must follow up and follow through: Determine how to support the staff and then do it. Make the decision, commit the resources, and follow an appropriate course of action. To avoid rapture of the deep and combat the business techie threat, the company needs to give business professionals the appropriate support. For instance, although in some cases there should be a computer on every desk, the fallacy is that this must be done, with the expectation that everyone will use computers the same way.

As president of a small business, I am also chief salesperson. Should I be running the spreadsheets? Should I design databases? Should I be fixing my printer? Why would I want to? The more time I spend at the computer, the less I spend building the business. It's better for me to delegate many computing tasks and concentrate on developing business.

Career Paths for Computer-literate Professionals. Of course, our company still needs computing support, someone to handle maintenance, security, and so forth. That person in our company might spend 15 percent of her time in support activities. This is why larger companies have MIS groups or fully dedicated support personnel. The presence of this support is vital regardless of the budget that pays for it. Develop career paths for computing-literate business professionals.

Wherever career paths are inadequate and missing, unrest thrives. More time and resources are spent jockeying for positions (and nonexistent promotions) when people aren't provided opportunities to excel and be rewarded. Professionals and administrative people with strong technical ability are likely to leave, taking their expertise and their need for advancement to the competition.

Even the best possible techie should be given career path options. Without such options, the business techie will eventually move on and a certain replacement cost will accrue to the organization.

Teach More Business and Less Technology. This means solving computing literacy issues, analyzing current business challenges, and providing required business training. In developing your staff, develop them as business people. Today, more time is spent giving employees computing skills than business concepts and industry information. Approximately four hours are spent in computing skills training for every one hour spent in business training. Business is producing techies at the expense of nurturing creative and resourceful business people. This is not to suggest that technical training doesn't have its place. Management should make decisions about who should be trained and how much. Should a manager learn advanced programming? Who should attend courses on how to fix a PC?

Although spreadsheets are probably the world's simplest software, some software firms say it's a difficult subject. Therefore, many people approach them rather cautiously. When I taught spreadsheets, I found that the main problem was people in the class who had never done anything of a financial nature.

(After I asked one person, "What's a balance sheet?" and was told, "I don't know. My boss told me to take this class," I determined that spreadsheet classes were frequently substitutes for financial analysis classes.)

Learning a computer product is not a replacement for adequate and basis financial logic. How often have staff members enrolled in a software class, when they should have been in a business class?

In another case, project management software was distributed to six managers. Two weeks later, one manager was pleased with this software, and the other five panned it. The first manager questioned the others — and learned that they were struggling because they didn't know project management. How could they appreciate automation of a function they didn't even understand?

In the mailroom of one company, three-quarters of the incoming mail was magazines on technology. I saw this after I'd heard that there had been a decline in business magazine subscriptions and an increase in PC-related magazines. This should be a matter of concern. I would rather have my staff reading *Business Week* than *PC Week* — and not because the latter isn't a good publication. As management consultants working in a variety of industries, we need familiarity with the business of our clients. Therefore, understanding an industry provides us with reasons to pursue computing options and advances, not the other way around.

Conclusion. Staff members are the creative force and future of any business. If their attention is focused on activities that drain energy and resourcefulness from product and customer issues, the company is in trouble. To the extent that management avoids — or inappropriately delegates — responsibility for computing strategies and support, that is the extent to which the corporation is financing rapture of the deep.

PART IV

Company Practices for Enhancing Productivity and Quality

37

SMED: The Heart of JIT Production

Shigeo Shingo, President,
Institute of Management Improvement (Japan)

Do all of you know what these are? (Bananas) I wonder how much they cost. Let's suppose you can buy one for 15 cents. Do you eat the skin? No. And yet they sell these bananas to you by weight. The weight includes the skin and the fruit. The skin amounts to about 40 percent of the banana. I actually measured this once in my hotel room. So if you are paying 15 cents a pound, each of you is paying six cents, or 40 percent of that, just for the peel. In American production systems, I think we will also find a great deal of inedible skin. My goal is to build production systems that consist only of fruit.

Reducing/Eliminating Inventories. Improvements in American production systems are extremely superficial. I visited a certain company here that had an inventory control system. It was a three-dimensional stock warehousing system, and by inserting a card you could get any part out within three minutes, and they invited me to try it. I tried it and the part actually emerged in two minutes and 40 seconds.

"Isn't this wonderful," they asked me.

I said, "Yes, it's a wonderful thing, it's really magnificent."

They said, "I'll bet you don't have these in Japan, do you?"

I said, "No, we don't have these in Japan."

They said, "We thought you didn't have them in Japan."

I replied, "Well, you see, in Japan we don't need them because we send our parts directly from parts manufacturing to the assembly line eliminating any need for this stock in the first place."

In the plants associated with the Toyota group, for example, there is no stock like this. At the very end of final assembly, there is a small stock of finished goods. The parts are brought to the assembly line 15 times a day. U.S. plants often seem to have magnificent warehousing facilities. Do you make money on those? No. They are simply facilities permitting you to pay a lot of taxes. We don't have them.

Relationship between Setup Time and Lot Size. The concept of the economic lot size says that as you produce in larger and larger lots, costs will go down but inventories will increase. At the place where these two lines meet, you have what we refer to as an economic lot.

In the Toyota plant, I took a setup which took four hours and reduced it to three minutes. When you start doing something like that, suddenly there is no reason to worry about economic lots or anything of the sort. Another recent example is from a Japanese company called Saian Metals. They have 13 70-ton presses and, simply by pressing a button, are able to complete a changeover on all of them by using pneumatic cylinders and other devices. The changeover can be affected in 28 to 30 seconds and there is absolutely no stock or inventory of finished products. Also, stock does not pile up between processes. There is a continuous, smooth flow with no stock anywhere along the line. One worker may oversee ten presses. In something like this you see the real cause of the trade friction between Japan and the United States.

When my friends heard that I was to receive an honorary doctorate from Utah State University, they said, "Oh, that's terrible." I said, "Why is it terrible?" They said, "That means in America, people are beginning to understand and disseminate your ideas. Now Americans will start producing things cheaper and better than us and we will start suffering from reverse trade friction." So, I may actually be run out of Japan on a rail. I am letting you know this in advance so that if it comes to that, I will be able to live in America. Please treat me kindly when I show up.

Improving American Production Methods. This is what I mean when I say that in the United States (1) improvements have tended to be

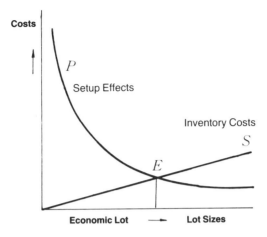

Figure 37.1 The Economic Lot Size

superficial and (2) you have failed to deal with more fundamental improvements. This, I think, is the first great mistake being made here. The ideas I have come up with, including the SMED (single-minute exchange of die) system, the ability to change dies in a few minutes or even a few seconds, and the complete elimination of defects, really have a genesis in the ideas of Frederick Winslow Taylor and Frank B. Gilbreth. I have always had a tremendous respect for Taylor and Gilbreth. (And I have never forgotten that they were Americans...). In America you have to return to Taylor and Gilbreth and change the direction you took from their studies. I point this out in my book, *The Sayings of Shigeo Shingo: Key Strategies for Plant Improvement* (Cambridge, MA: Productivity Press, 1987).

For 200 years, America has lead the world in production management. Looking toward the future, even in Japan, we will all run into trouble if the United States fails to continue to lead in some way or other. Everyone has to participate in continuous improvement.

History of Production Revolutions. Looking at world manufacturing history, we find a number of production revolutions. The first great innovation occurred in the 1770s with the division of labor. This revolution changed our perception of production. Whereas before, a single worker producing at maximum capacity could make 200 pins a day, with division of labor productivity could be increased.

For instance, by using ten people and dividing the various tasks involved, productivity could be increased 200-fold. Another effect was that various kinds of complex tasks were broken down into simple components, so that rather than having only skilled workers performing production tasks, ordinary workers could achieve the same results. Productivity therefore rose dramatically. Workers became better paid and more money started flowing in society. There were more goods in the marketplace and more people able to buy them. The economy expanded. In a crude sense, that is what happened in the Industrial Revolution. The key point being that the simplification of the work process resulted in increased productivity.

The next production step forward was extending the power of the human hand by adding the powers of steam and coal. This was followed by the next step — equipment improvement. Whereas, for example, a machine that had only performed cutting now had the ability to insert or remove the piece on the machine. This brought us toward the concept of machining centers. To give machines the measurement precision we needed, we developed numerical control (NC) machines.

We were moving in the direction of programmed manufacturing. We spent a lot of time transferring the functions of the human hand to machines but managed to forget about functions of the human brain. We forgot to add a judgment capacity to these machines. Today, however, by attaching sensors and so forth to machines to detect abnormal situations, we are moving in the direction of true automation.

It has been said that there are 23 identifiable steps in moving from human hands, or human fingers, to complete automation. But it has also been said that 20 of those steps are really no more than mechanization — not automation.

Pre-Automation Reduces Labor Costs. I have already said that in the course of these improvements we have neglected the transfer of human judgment to machines. While touring the plant of U.S. aircraft manufacturer, McDonnell Douglas, I saw workers sitting and watching machines — just sitting with their arms folded watching the machines. I asked, "Why are you sitting there? What are you doing?" The answer was that they were waiting for abnormal situations to arise.

Sensors do this function in Japan, freeing workers from their machines. At Toyota, for example, we have 50 machines that cut cylinders and only two workers monitor them. In every case, sensors are attached to the machines. When anything abnormal occurs, a warning is given and the human monitor corrects the problem.

The two functions we are discussing here are (1) checking for abnormal circumstances and (2) correcting whatever is wrong. In Japan, we often divide these two functions into having the machine do the checking while the humans do the fixing. We call this *preautomation*, and this approach has allowed us to reduce most labor costs considerably.

Another important point is that in Japan, even if our machines sit idle for a certain period of time, we make every effort to have human beings work at their full capacity. This is because, while machine costs depreciate over time, you always have to pay your workers.

To maintain a flow system, there are times when it is necessary to buy a new machine and put it on the line. But when possible, we construct our own machine, usually for one-tenth of a new machine's market price.

America Concentrates on Keeping Machines Busy. While American managers seem concerned about running their machines at full capacity, it is okay for workers to sit idly and watch the machines run. We Japanese have exactly the opposite approach. We want to keep our workers working full time and it is alright if the machine stands idle for a while.

Matsushita Electric, for example, has a flow system that requires about ten changeovers a day. To keep the system going, they installed a machine that on the market would have cost ¥3 million. They built it themselves, however, for ¥600,000. This way they were able to put together a system that could accommodate ten changeovers each day and still produce in extremely small lots. As a result, they have no inventory. In any case, our idea is that, under certain circumstances, it is alright to keep the machines idle. This is difficult for Americans to understand. I have a feeling that in the United States there are many instances in which you have neglected to provide machines with this judgment function. Isn't it true that American managers start complaining when machines are idle? And yet we can make very inexpensive machines.

Taylor's Scientific Management. The next great revolution in production occurred in the 1880s with Frederick Taylor and his indepth study of machine cutting. He invented high-speed tool steel and analyzed human labor and fatigue. Frank Gilbreth conducted human motion studies. These two people made great strides in applying scientific methods to work operations.

My method of asking "Why?" five times comes from Frank Gilbreth. The point here is that you must continue to think about the purpose of the work being done. In America, you spend all your time watching and worrying about the actual work being done. But you do not give much thought to why setup times are so long.

At Ford, they reduced a setup that had taken five hours to two minutes. Why was that possible? When I first went to the Granville-Phillips plant three years ago, I noticed a chart on the wall and asked Daniel Bills, their president, what it was.

He said, "It charts our defect rate."

"Why do you chart defects?" I asked.

"Because," he said, "our people can look at it, realize they have to pay more attention, and thereby improve it."

And I said, "That's ridiculous. You don't need a chart that is like a death certificate."

A small chart for the company president is fine. But you do not need great big charts for the world to see.

When I asked Mr. Bills what his biggest problem was in terms of defects, he took me over to an operation where they had two vessels they were welding together with solder and a burner flame. The trouble was that inside the vessel, a printed circuit board and the solder on it were melting from the heat of the operation. He told me that the defect rate on this particular operation was 10.7 percent.

I asked Mr. Bills to tell me what was actually being done here. His answer was: soldering.

I then asked, "How do you melt the solder?"

"With a burner," he replied.

I said, "No, no, no, no!"

"Well, we're actually soldering with the burner's flame."

I again said, "No, that's not it either. You're soldering with the *heat* of the burner's flame. Instead of aiming the burner here, why not move it around like this so you only melt the solder around the edges."

Suddenly, the defect rate dropped from 10.7 percent to zero. Cases like this are rampant in American as well as in Japanese factories. So to return to fundamental improvements, I refer back to the ideas of Taylor and Gilbreth.

Human Feelings Are Important. I think all of you are familiar with the so-called Hawthorne experiment. At Hawthorne, they conducted an experiment in which workers performing an operation gradually had the level of light increased. The results showed that as it got brighter, productivity improved. Then, reversing the experiment, they lowered the light level and found that productivity still improved. These results showed that apart from the physical circumstances of operations, human feelings were also very important to productivity. Being the center of attention inspired the workers more than the level of light. The Japanese took these principles and developed such things as "management by objectives" and JIT.

Around 1965, MIT Professor McGregor developed a theory of human types, X-type and Y-type. His idea was that X-type people did everything possible to avoid work, whereas Y-type people carried out work independently and autonomously.

In the 1800s, American factories were being organized and new labor was being brought in from other countries, from places where such structured physical work did not exist. In any case, managers of that time looked on workers as basically lazy and unwilling to work. Their attitude was, "If you don't do the work, you won't get paid."

At the time, of course, nothing like labor power existed. If work decreased, people would simply be laid off. In Japan, our approach differs. We have lifetime employment. When General Motors and Toyota, in a joint venture, set up the NUMMI plant to produce automobiles near San Francisco, they found that even Ford workers wanted to join up.

When asked why American workers would want to come and work at a Japanese plant, they said they liked the security of knowing that their jobs were there until retirement. Even if their salaries were not the greatest, these people liked the idea of doing a number of different jobs in the factory. Other benefits included a company cafeteria where workers and managers ate side by side.

Japan is a small country with about 120 million people and few natural resources. All we have is human labor. Without hard work, we cannot survive. This has created a situation in which maybe 90 percent of our people are Y-type. What they want is job security, an opportunity to work at a variety of tasks, and high wages. This has been accomplished at some U.S. companies, too, such as Omark Industries and Mr. Bills' company, Granville-Phillips. These are non-union companies where they refer to the workers as "our people."

I think the number one failing of American companies is treating workers as X-type. And I think we would see tremendous changes if workers were treated as members of a company's family. These manufacturing revolutions have taken place because the United States has provided the opportunities. In the future, American factories should take the leadership in production improvements.

Misunderstanding the Relations between Process and Operations. There is another great defect in the thinking used by American companies. It is a defect in the way Americans think about production. Production activities consist of two phenomena: processes and operations.

Actually, in 1921 Frank Gilbreth realized the importance of the process phenomenon. He announced this in a paper to the American Society of Mechanical Engineers (ASME). This extremely important phenomenon was discovered in the United States — but then a great error was made. The mistake was that a *process* was seen to be a large-scale unit of production analysis, whereas an *operation* was seen to be a small- scale unit of production analysis. The delusion here is that if you improve a small operation, if you improve one small part of all the production, then the whole production system will improve. That is the mistake. I think production is a network of processes and operations.

There has been no understanding in the United States of the two-axis structure. On the Y-axis, you have a product starting with raw materials moving through certain steps in a single flow to become a finished product. On the X-axis, at each stage, you have various kinds of workers — transport, inspection, or machining workers — working on the processes in specific operations. Americans have concentrated on the horizontal axis, looking at how to improve the productivity of individual machines or workers. They have neglected to look at the vertical axis, or the process.

Gilbreth identified four phenomena within the scope of a process. He said a process consisted of (1) processing or machining, (2) inspection, (3) transport, and (4) storage. I have adopted this view of production. Even though in America you know this, you still tend to look at processes and operations as lying on the same axis. In 1945, I realized that they, in fact, were on different intersecting axes and I announced this to the Japan Management Association.

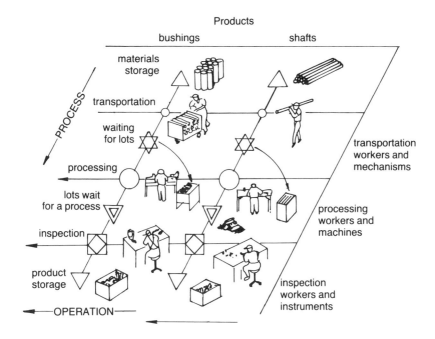

Figure 37.2 Structure of Production

I can give you a lot of examples. In this country, you have been paying a lot of attention to centering a die on a machine. You have used various kinds of electric and mechanical devices to make the adjustments just right. These are what I call *operational improvements*.

I would approach it differently by simply supplying some blocks, shims, and guides to center the dies when they enter the machine. This requires no operational improvements. This very simple change improves the whole process, which is why I feel *process improvements* have much greater importance than operational improvements.

Source Inspection and Defect Prevention. Originally we had what I call judgment, or discriminative, inspections, where goods produced were inspected for defects. The idea was to eliminate the defectives and only send approved goods on to the customer. This, of course, did not reduce defects, so Americans came along with the very clever idea of what I call informative inspections. When a defect was located you would return it to the place where the defect occurred. Action would be taken to correct the defect and thereby reduce the defect rate.

We studied this system in Japan and benefited tremendously from improvements in quality. Indeed, American-style quality control, in this sense, has been very significant. Yet, this approach will not reduce defects to zero. I want to keep reducing the defect rate. Because there is no number less than zero, I am working at present to bring things down to zero.

Let me explain this. The American approach to inspection has you checking for defects, performing feedback, and then taking action to correct the problem. The way I see it, a defect results from something else. It comes from a careless mistake or an error. I want to perform this feedback and action loop at the level of that careless mistake so the product is caught before it becomes defective.

For example, if you have to weld six points to the periphery of a disk, you can attach a counter to the welder so that every time it reaches six, it releases the workpiece and allows you to move on to the next process. If six welds have not been performed, the workpiece will lock informing you that something must be done. Also, there is a timer on it, and if a weld has not been made after 15 seconds, the workpiece will lock, and once more you will have to go and check. This system, which is very simple, creates a zero-defect operation, even though careless mistakes still occur.

With spot-welding, you might also have a secondary current available to send through the weld as soon as it is made and the workpiece is still on the machine. This way you will know that a current will flow through the weld. You can have meters underneath to measure this. If the current is insufficient or incorrect, you know to go back and remove whatever is obstructing it. Again, in this way, you can assure yourself that defective items will not be produced.

In an SQC approach, you might use snap checks for this. Various statistical methods can be used for insuring quality in such cases. Snap readings reduce the time and trouble required to check for defects. The way we do it, however, is to check every item. We call it 100-percent inspection.

With human beings, there are two kinds of forgetting: (1) We can forget things and (2) we can also forget we have forgotten. Because we all forget things, we can use mechanisms such as counters or a secondary current to catch that careless forgetfulness before it creates a defect. In Japanese, the word for "careless mistake" is *poka* and "to avoid" or "proof" is called *yoke*. So I refer to these devices as *poka-yoke*.

You have to remember that these very simple devices provide 100-percent inspections. They inspect every single item that goes through. The simple counter and locking device for the workpiece performs inspections without increasing trouble for the human workers. The devices are inexpensive, too. In Japan, this would cost something like ¥ 30,000 ($300) or less. Surely for U.S. companies it is no big deal to pay $300 in return for zero defects on this weld.

Koga Metals in Japan has 18 spot welding machines performing this kind of work. Out of 250 million pieces, they had no defects. I understand that American plants cannot reduce their defect rates to zero or eliminate defects entirely. Maybe this is because by eliminating all defects, American quality control engineers would lose their jobs...

Minimizing Transportation with One-Piece Flow. Let's talk about transportation. Transportation is a negative factor. It increases nothing but costs. Two years ago in Paris I visited the plant of perhaps the world's number-three machine tool manufacturer. I noticed that the machines were laid out with similar machines grouped together. I said this was one way to insure having a lot of transport. They said it was not a problem because they had a chain conveyor to carry parts from one machine to another, thus eliminating the need for arranging machines according to work flow. I said to them, "Look, this is does not improve transport — it improves transport operations." To improve transport you must eliminate as much of it as possible. Therefore, arrange machines according to the process flow, and in those cases where it is absolutely necessary to transport, it might be more efficient to have a machine do the transporting rather than human workers. You may need forklifts to bring raw materials from the warehouse to the line, but between machines, you shouldn't need transport devices.

I should point out that in Japan, too, there are lots of forklifts being used between machines, but I think a lot of these are companies where the managers get rebates from the forklift companies. I should also say that at the companies where I consult, there are no forklifts moving things between machines. Perhaps U.S. managers also receive rebates from forklift manufacturers.

Minimizing Storage with One-Piece Flows and SMED. Next, we will discuss storage. Why do Americans think it is good to produce a lot of items at once? Why do you even have the idea of an economic lot? It is because your setup times are long. If you could make the change-overs in 30 seconds, small lots would be more desirable, presumably.

If the customer places an order a week in advance, and you can produce a product in half a day, then you don't need stocks of finished products. Also, if between processes, you have a one-piece flow (lots of one item), and you have a single flow throughout the entire process, you can reduce production time from three weeks to perhaps three hours. Are U.S. companies specifically producing to accumulate inventories of finished products, or to accumulate inventory between processes?

Granville-Phillips, for example, is faithfully following the ideas that I am talking about. They have reduced their production cycle to a matter of hours so that when an order comes in, they start producing that order then. Therefore, they have no stocks of finished products. Also, because their machines are arranged by process flow, there are no stocks between machines.

These changes have allowed them to save about half their amount of plant space. I also gather from Mr. Bills that labor costs have been reduced 60 percent. Granville-Phillips can then use the extra space and workers to make new products. And from what I gather, they are making so much money, they don't know what to do with it.

I returned after a year to Granville-Phillips and asked Mr. Bills if he was following my suggestion of having people ask, "Why?" three times. He said, "Yes, and our profits have risen three times." The following year I went back and said, are you asking, "Why?" three times. He said, "No. Actually we are asking "Why?" six times." I said, "Does that mean your profits have risen six times?" And he said, "Actually, they've only gone up five times." Recently I have learned that they have increased their spending on research and development three times.

From his point of view, presumably, company presidents whose plants fail to achieve such results must look pretty silly. The reason is that the money he saves, both in space and worker time, is being plowed back into more and more production, and this, in turn, brings in more money. Maybe this has allowed him to repay his bank loans, I don't know. Maybe banks are going to him and saying, "Here, borrow more money." The trouble with bank money is the interest you have to pay, so you want to use as little as possible. What you want to do is make more money.

Non-Stock Production. I am very unhappy about the common perception of the Toyota production system as a JIT system. In America, you have JIT institutes and JIT study groups and so forth, and that's fine. It is a fine thing to do, but more fundamentally you want to reduce setup times to 30 seconds. You want to be able to reduce your lead times to three hours. You want to be able to produce those ten items when an order for ten items is received.

At one company where I consulted, the Asahi National Illumination Company, a maker of fluorescent lamps, they may get an order for ten items one day requesting delivery by the next day. So they put their production system into action and produce the ten lamps by 2pm the same day and send it by overnight express. The product is at the customer's door the next day.

At Matsushita Electric's washing machine division, they start with raw materials such as the body of the washing machine, which they stamp. They do the bending of the body, they paint it, and they attach the various parts. They assemble the whole machine, and from the very beginning of this process until the time it is ready to be delivered to the customer, it only takes two and a half hours. This particular plant used to produce one type of washing machine in fairly large lots, and usually only one type a day. They have long since abandoned this approach and now produce, say, 100 type-A washing machines, 50 type-B washing machines, and so forth in a single day. This has allowed them to eliminate the tremendous warehouse facilities they previously had to maintain.

The point here is that until now we have looked at stock as a necessary evil. We haven't liked it, but have thought of it as necessary. Suddenly, when you realize you can make changeovers in 30 seconds, when you realize you can reduce production cycles to half an hour, is it really necessary?

I understand that Utah is Mormon territory. Regarding human nature and so forth, I am sure you receive good guidance from the

Church. But in terms of production, you should be listening to the teachings of Dr. Shingo. By doing that, you will be able to produce better and make more money. In the Bible, it says that those who believe will be saved. If you believe in what I tell you, you will be saved. I ask you at Utah State University to understand my ideas and spread them throughout the country, throughout the world, even to Japan, and help contribute to world prosperity.

I am told that Japanese cars are very popular in the United States, especially as second cars. When I ask why, I am told that it is because, first of all, they don't break down. Secondly, they are of high quality and, although this has changed somewhat, relatively inexpensive. I assure you that if U.S. manufacturers produce high quality, inexpensive cars that don't break down and are bigger, the way American cars are now, they will make tremendous inroads into the Japanese market. Maybe within three years, U.S. legislators will say no to Japanese imports. If it comes to this, and American cars are flooding Japan, I would like to ask you all, please, to buy a Japanese car.

Building New Production Systems in America. The ideas just discussed I refer to as a non-stock production system (NSP). You can read about it in my most recent book entitled *Non-Stock Production: The Shingo System for Continuous Improvement* (Cambridge, MA: Productivity Press, 1988). I encourage you to read my books: *A Revolution in Manufacturing: The SMED System, Zero Quality Control: Source Inspections and the Poka-yoke System,* and *Study of the Toyota Production System from an IE Viewpoint.*

I want you to think of today as commemorating the start of an effort to build a new production system. Unfortunately, some people at the top in Japan, people at universities in Japan, don't listen to what I have to say very much, but I think perhaps that if they find out that American academics and managers are interested in it, they'll learn right away.

The system that I'm espousing today is something that will reap great rewards for you. Some of you may say that it's not possible in this country, because basically in Japan, we have Y-type workers, and here we have X-type workers, with a mix of X- and Y-type workers. But from what I've seen in individual plants, there are cases in which individual plants have in fact succeeded with these methods.

All of you are familiar, I think, with the so-called Volvo production system. Volvo production system assumes that workers are X-type workers, and they treat them that way. I've been to Volvo and I asked them, "Why are you doing this?" While it is true that the Volvo approach may make things a little bit more comfortable for the workers, the fact is that the country's budget deficit will go further and further into the red.

In building this new system, you have to start to change from a view of workers in which you see them as lazy, into a view of workers where you see them as interested in participating and in working.

You may keep inventory around to protect you from various fluctuations and conditions, but if you follow what I'm saying, by reducing or eliminating defects, if you cut setup times down to the 30 second level or so, and if you set up one-piece flows so that your production periods become dramatically shortened, all of a sudden there's no need for these stocks.

On the plane flying over here, I was reading a book about the Soviet Union. It said that in the Soviet Union, money makes love to goods, but in the United States, goods make love to money. Apparently in the Soviet Union, you have to have money on you all the time, because if you see a line where people are waiting for some desirable product, you immediately want to be able to get in line to buy it.

When a Japanese artistic group went to the Soviet Union they told the story of a visit to a farmer who brought out a trunk full of money and said, "Do you have any idea how hard it is to have all this money and yet be unable to buy anything with it?" Russians visiting Japan encounter an entirely different situation. There are no lines and department stores are full of products. People don't have the money to walk around with and buy the products. Russians visiting Japan apparently take home a lot of transistor radios and other electronic goods.

In America, goods are produced in order to make money. This is what I mean by goods making love to money. To survive in the United States you have to keep producing goods and keep making money. To do that, you must continuously be improving your manufacturing efficiency. If you don't, you will not survive in today's world.

Can U.S. Improve Its Production System? Make those banana skins as thin as possible. Eliminate them as much as possible. In your own factories, then, the challenge of the future is to set up production systems that, as much as possible, eliminate that 40-percent inedible banana skin. At a press conference I gave last year in New York, a reporter asked me if I thought the system I have described can be achieved in the United States. I replied, "The question isn't whether you think it can be improved or not. The question is whether or not you're going to do it. If you can understand the new system I'm describing," I said, "then the only thing left is for you to do it."

I cannot believe it possible that America's pioneer spirit has been lost. When I arrived in Salt Lake City, I found a land surrounded by gold mines and copper mines and so forth. You had to have people here who worked those mines very hard. I am sure there are some hard workers with that pioneering spirit still left around here. To put together this new production system, we have to develop a new frontier spirit. Go forth!

38

Putting Shingo Methods to Work in U.S. Business

Daniel Bills, President, Granville-Phillips

When we asked what action we could take to produce the greatest improvement in our productivity, the answer surprised us in both its power and generality. Because the overall productivity of a company depends on so many variables, it seems improbable that a single type of action can make much difference. Also, because each business is unique with different markets, customers, products, and methods, one would not expect to find a single type of action that has general applicability.

Looking for Opportunities to Increase Output. The productivity of a company can be expressed as:

$$\text{Productivity} = \frac{\text{Output}}{\text{Input}} = \frac{\text{Ideal Output} - \text{Wasted Output Opportunities}}{\text{Ideal Input} + \text{Wasted Resources}}$$

Many in manufacturing tend to regard waste as merely scrap and rework — a paltry 2 percent of the sales dollar at most. Our recent work has convinced us that a large portion of the resources of a typical business are wasted on non-productive activities. It appears we waste so much of our available resources on useless activities that we miss many valuable opportunities to increase output. Thus, waste of resources affects both the denominator and the numerator, causing productivity to be much lower than it could be. When viewed this way, waste is not just a few percentage points of sales but is much larger and causes a huge drag on business results. Improving productivity by eliminating all forms of waste appears to be the largest opportunity any company has. The search for how to eliminate this waste deserves management's full attention and resources.

Proper selection of output opportunities can produce large improvements in productivity. However, in this presentation I will only examine how to reduce waste of resources in achieving a pre-selected output result.

Managing Cause and Effect. Along with many other companies, we have been using Japanese engineer Shigeo Shingo's methods at Granville-Phillips to achieve large increases in productivity. When I asked why these methods are so successful, I gradually came to the realization that the Japanese are managing cause and effect. They do not leave their desired business results or effects to chance as we tend to do. The Japanese patiently study the causes of the results they want and then take action to produce these causes in the correct order. Few have been as patient or as effective as Mr. Shingo, a developer of the Toyota Production System.

Some believe that the Japanese are, by nature, much more patient than we are and that we can never hope to achieve their type of results. This belief misses the point. Managers must be very patient in achieving the causes of business goals but at the same time very impatient with the waste of resources on useless activities. We must be patient at managing cause and effect and impatient with everything else. Many managers tend to get it the other way around.

The management of cause and effect was masterfully and humorously illustrated by Rube Goldberg during his lifetime in cartoons at which I marveled as a child. Goldberg drew contraptions where, for example, a rabbit leaping for a carrot sets off a chain of events that causes the gates of opportunity to open. We can learn much about the subtle characteristics of managing cause and effect by studying these cartoons.

When the rabbit jumps for the carrot, a string attached to the rabbit's leg causes a gun to fire at a pail of water. The water drips into a container gradually raising the water level. The rising water floats a candle up under a teakettle. The steam from the kettle causes a turbine to turn, reeling in a rope attached to the gates, thus causing the gates to swing open.

In this example the rabbit leaping on the carrot is the root cause of the gates' opening. The root cause is that certain result that must occur next to produce the desired end result. As each sequence of action is completed, it becomes the cause of the next sequence leading ultimately to the desired end result. Root action is that type of action that, when completed, produces a root cause.

As we follow the action through the process we note that the root action changes with time from one type of root action to another. After the rabbit has caused the gun to fire, the dripping water is the root action that will cause the gates to open. After the teakettle boils, the steam exiting is the root action that will cause the gates to open. If the candle is out, there will be no steam. If the candle is not burning, then the completed action of lighting the candle is the root cause of the gates opening. Obviously the desired end result of the gates opening only occurs if all of the appropriate actions are completed in the proper sequence given existing conditions.

Now that we understand some of the characteristics of root action and root cause, we can explore what can cause waste of resources in business. In business we usually seek to produce the same type of result over and over again whether it be to produce one widget after another or to achieve sales goals year after year. Imagine an ideal process that repeatedly produces a desired business result with zero waste. This ideal process would consist of an appropriate sequence of results carefully selected to cause the end result with minimum use of resources. What type of changes will introduce waste into this waste-free process? Obviously the addition of unneeded actions will cause waste. Each time we operate the process, resources will be consumed on unneeded activities. Another change that will cause waste is any omission of required actions. Each time we operate the process, we will need to improvise when we come to the omitted action in order to achieve the end result. If we execute any actions out of sequence we will introduce waste over and over again. The greatest amount of waste will occur if there is no well-defined sequence of actions for achieving the end result. Each time we try to achieve the end result we must devise a new sequence of causes and results.

Note that each of these changes to our ideal waste-free process causes waste and each change involves taking non-root action. Can it be that taking non-root action is the root cause of waste in business? I believe taking non-root action is the root cause of all waste.

It is important to realize that cause and effect is operating in business, as in any endeavor, at all times according to the natural laws of physics, chemistry, biology, and so on. Cause and effect cannot be avoided. Chains of cause and effect are present in any business at all times. These chains are usually far more complex and difficult to understand and follow than in the previous cartoon example. Typically there are an incredibly large number of possible actions a manager can take at any time. Returning to the cartoon analogy, there are often rabbits, dogs, cats, tigers, lions, canaries, and so forth, scattered all over in business. Each can jump this way and that way. Each may be tied to a gun, a cannon, a grenade or a pea shooter aimed here and there. Certain of these possible actions can become root causes of a desired business result, but most are only distractions leading to huge waste.

Methods of Identifying Root Action. How is a manager or employee to know what is the specific root action that must be taken at any given time? Obviously, if it is required to achieve the end result over and over, it is highly wasteful to have to search around for what is the root action to take at any given time. What is required is a set of directions specifying exactly those results that must be produced in a certain sequence to achieve the desired business result with minimum use of resources. As each result is completed, the next result becomes the root cause of the end result. Discovering how to design such a process involving minimum use of resources is a challenging task requiring more time than is available here.

We can obtain some clues about how to design appropriate processes by carefully studying what has worked well for the Japanese. For example, Just-In-Time (JIT) manufacturing is a technique that helps reduce the amount of resources required. The resulting small lot production helps to insure that if there is any deviation from the prescribed series of results leading to the end result, the minimum number of products will be affected. Single-minute exchange of die (SMED) methods help make small lot production possible. A JIT process requires far fewer resources than a conventional process.

Even when all parts of the business process are apparently in place, a manager often finds out too late that conditions have changed. The rabbit is sick, the gun misfires, or someone has forgotten to fill the teakettle. These unanticipated situations continually change the expected course of cause and effect and the desired end result is not achieved. Mr. Shingo teaches a very effective method of repeatedly asking "Why?" until the root cause of a changed condition or a defect can be identified and eliminated.

The root cause of not achieving an X-percent increase in profits next year may be that the manager has not requested our set-up people be trained in Mr. Shingo's methods of fast set-up. Because our set-ups take so long, our lot size must necessarily be large. Thus, defects are identified too late in the manufacturing cycle. Hence, waste is high, productivity is low, and we will not achieve an X-percent increase in profits next year, given today's conditions.

It is easy for this manager to grasp that he should set a goal of having his set-up people trained at once in Mr. Shingo's methods of fast set-up. If he takes this root action — a simple request — then a whole chain of cause and effect can be set in motion. His set-up people can be trained, set-up times can be decreased, lot sizes can be reduced, defects can be decreased, productivity will rise, and net profits will eventually increase. Of course, he can anticipate that all this will not occur so smoothly. The rabbit will get loose, the teakettle will develop a leak, and so on. These defects in the chain of cause and effect that form the process can and must be removed as they occur by identifying the root cause of each defect and taking appropriate action.

Acting on Root Causes. What type of root causes have we implemented at Granville-Phillips? We used to keep our production lines going at all cost. Defective components or assemblies were simply put aside where they would conveniently be out of sight. Then we decided to have our employees stop the line and remove the root cause of a defect before resuming production. The occurrence of a defect is now the root cause of an immediate improvement in our processes. Think what a powerful improvement tool this is! This one simple decision to stop the line when a defect occurs and remove the root cause permanently forces each defect we find — and we found many at first — to be a root cause for improvement.

Our set-up times used to be so long that our lot sizes necessarily had to be large. After seeing actual die set-ups being made in a few minutes in Japan, I made the decision to have our people trained in Mr. Shingo's methods of fast set-up. This decision enabled us to produce all products in small lots and was a root cause of greatly increased productivity.

We used to produce products in large lots with resulting large work in process inventory and many defects. I took action on a root cause several years ago and decided to produce products in lots of five or less. This one decision caused defects to be greatly reduced.

Prescription for Improving Productivity. Here then is my prescription for greatly improving productivity:

1. Understand thoroughly the concept of root action and root cause.
2. Devise a process that requires the minimum amount of resources for achieving the desired end result.
3. Operate the process, stopping to permanently remove the root cause whenever a defect occurs.

Developing an effective process for each type of business result is one type of action that will produce the greatest improvement in productivity. Using Shingo methods helps to produce a more effective process.

39

Employee-Driven Productivity at Omark Industries

Lawrence White, Plant Manager, Omark Industries

I want to explore the methodology and philosophy of what we've accomplished over the last five years. I want to talk about employee-driven productivity.

Many people are not familiar with Omark Industries. It is not a byword recognized in most households. We manufacture cutting systems for chain saws. We do not manufacture chain saws or power heads. We manufacture cutting chain, guide bars, and the drive sprocket that transmits power from the motor to the chain. We sell our product in over 120 countries in the world and have three factories and distribution warehouses around the world.

Three-Pronged Approach to Productivity. We have a three-pronged approach that we have used since 1982 in implementing our systems. You can think of three converging circles that overlap and compliment each other. First is *employee involvement* as follows: "Our philosophy on employee involvement is to have an environment and culture wherein all employees freely express their opinions, ideas, and solutions to situations or problems. They accept responsibility and exercise judgment and authority wisely. They are proud of our people, products, and customers. They work together and are committed to improvement and they know that this is their company."

Our philosophy on Total Quality Control (TQC) is "to have an environment and culture wherein all employees believe that the people who receive their product or service are their personal customers. They understand their customers' requirement and needs, control their product or service through statistical analysis and process control and do it right the first time, constantly improve customer service, and measure results.

Our philosophy on Zero Inventory Production (ZIP) system is "to have an environment and culture wherein all employees are dedicated to supply goods and services based on customer requirements — what they want, how they want it, when they want it are involved with the cycle of lowering inventory to reveal hidden wastes and eliminating the causes.

Richard Schonberger wrote in his book *World Class Manufacturing*, "In my judgment, Hewlett Packard is further along in implementing Just-In-Time than any other non-Japanese-owned company except perhaps Omark Industries."

Ask Employees to Be Involved. There are a lot of different types of productivity that you can work on inside a company. I want to talk about the employee driven portion as compared to other productivity sources. What we do is ask our employees to be directly involved in managing things within the organization. We want them to be involved in designing their own work stations, improving the process, and be personally a part of the things that relate to improving productivity on the job. As Robert Hall says in his book *Zero Inventories*, "Any system at the bottom base is a human system."

From our perspective, people are the most important resource we have in the company. Employee involvement is one of the key strategies we use to improve productivity. We are trying to improve the way we manage. At the same time, we are continuing to share more and more of these techniques with our people to enable them to participate. We are a manufacturing company and the base of America is manufacturing.

Eighty percent of the people and the brain power in industry is on the shop floor in manufacturing and for years and years, unfortunately, those people were told, "You are paid to work, not to think." There is a terrible waste of creativity in that sort of environment. We try to fully tap and utilize that creative capacity, implement it into our system, and take advantage of all those ideas and that mental power.

Create a Comfortable Environment for Employee Involvement. We want to create an environment where people are comfortable being involved in Omark's success, where they can be recognized and feel that they are directly involved and part of the business. We are training our people in the same techniques and skills that management people have benefitted from in the past to effectively address and solve problems. We train our people in the seven basic problem-solving skills that are really the bottom line of industrial engineering techniques that are taught to most engineers. They include things like brainstorming, histograms, data collection, force field analysis, and so forth. These are very straightforward, simple techniques that all our people can handle. We also found out that they can handle statistics as well. A lot of people haven't been to school for 20 or 25 years. So, we provided them with a two-day algebra refresher course immediately before they attended statistics classes. It is now standard for employees to receive 80 hours of statistical training during their first year of employment.

Once these tools are learned, they are immediately applied on the job. We call our methodology "training" as compared to "education." Typically, education is where you go to class and learn a subject; then you go on to another subject. With training as we define it, we want our people to go to class, be trained, go back to the job, and immediately apply it so that it becomes institutionalized knowledge.

Empowering Workers to Improve Systems. Using statistics, workers control the quality of the process rather than the quality of the content. Content quality typically is called conformance quality. In manufacturing, that relates to making sure that all of the specifications on the engineering blueprint are met. Traditionally, workers only have a 10- or 15-percent influence on this conformance quality. Most of it is dependent on the equipment and tools they are given. What we are doing is empowering them to work on the other 85 to 90 percent of the quality opportunity. The productivity reward is in improving the system or process. By controlling the quality of the process, you control the quality of the content.

This leads us to two conclusions: First, to narrow variations in the way we manage, we have to apply quality improvement techniques to the management processes, just as in manufacturing processes. As a matter of fact, if you study the entire movement in Japan, Total Quality Control (TQC) is not directly related to statistical quality control or any of the other traditional quality kinds of issues that are thought about in the United States. TQC, in Ishikawa's book *What Is Total Quality Control?*, is described as quality in the process of management. It is proper planning, execution, follow-up, and corrective action.

Second, we want to make sure that all of our employees are part of management so that they understand what the bottom line is all about, who the customers are, and where the opportunities lie. In other words, we need to share the responsibilities of management with every employee.

Traditional Supervisory Model

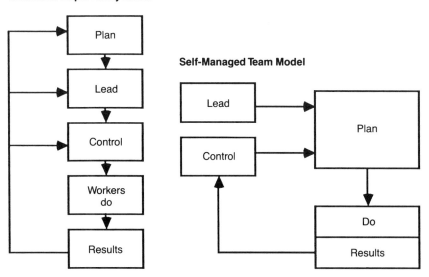

Figure 39.1 Model for Meaningful Work (Myers, 1970)

Self-Management Model. Here is a model from a book by Meyers published in 1970. This is the traditional top-down supervisory role. The supervisor is responsible for planning, leading, and controlling. The workers execute. The supervisor audits the results, revises the plan, tells people what needs to be changed and what needs to be controlled. The input essentially is from one person.

At Omark we believe the more appropriate model is the self-managed team model where the leader or supervisor provides leadership about what needs to be accomplished. He doesn't necessarily dictate how it is to be done. He lets the team members participate in the plan and execution, evaluate the results, and come back to make adjustments for additional improvements in what was accomplished the first time around.

As we continue to improve the way we manage our business, we want to continue expanding this concept of self-managed teams. These teams address the following issues:

- Building meaningful work models for a whole task
- Developing workplace values and norms
- Identifying outputs and standards
- Accessing information
- Designing organization/task structures
- Communicating
- Training
- Interpersonal skills
- Technical skills
- Scheduling people/machines/materials/improvement effort
- Staffing
- Leadership
- Performance feedback
- Improvement
- Discipline

This is a very revolutionary idea in the United States and a lot of people who have been trained in traditional management methods feel like they're losing control. Control, however, is in leadership — not management. The issues are to build meaningful work models for the whole team, develop values and norms that differ from traditional methodology, identify outputs and standards, and so on.

Stages in Self-Management. We find that our teams go through three stages in the general process of change or revolutionary advancement. First, they change their present frame of reference by developing a mutual picture of what the goals are all about. Everyone has to understand what we want. Second, they define the implications of where we are going. And last, they commit themselves to action so that everybody is working both for the organization and for themselves.

We believe that employee-driven productivity is the source of productivity for the future. It is the only way that business is going to survive in North America. We plan to continue in this direction. Our corporate mission is to be the best managed company in North America. We know that if we can engage the power and the minds of our people, our mission will be accomplished.

Organizational Values. We have two basic organizational values. First, we are very confident about our people. We know that they are committed to themselves and will deliver the efforts needed to make the organization prosper. The key words here are that *our people are committed to themselves*. Second, they have to understand who they are working for. If they work for the company, the way they approach their work on a daily basis is a lot different than if they understand that they are actually working for themselves. Everyone must trust that all these efforts are going to be supported and equitably rewarded.

Investment in Training. Listed below are the efforts we have undertaken to prepare the background for allowing this transition to happen. These hours, broken into three categories, are the typical amount of training an employee will go through. All employees participate anywhere you see the term "Users." We find this gives people a base of material and knowledge to use in solving everyday problems on the job.

ZIPS	Team visits to Japan	
	ZIPS study teams — Shingo books	20 Hours
	Leaders — Zero inventory class	35 Hours
	Users	6 Hours
TQC	Users (SPC I)	32 Hours
	Leaders (SPC II)	32 Hours
	Engineers/Facilitators (ED I-IV)	164 Hours
	Marketing Staff	32 Hours
	Users (GDT I)	22 Hours
	Designers/Interpreters (GDT II)	20 Hours
EI	Members (Basic EI)	8 Hours
	Leaders	24 Hours
	Facilitators	Ongoing

Table 39.2 Investment in Training

Productivity Results. The following table shows some of the results achieved during the last five years:

(FY '83 – '87)	
Raw Material Inventory/Unit	Down 31%
Work-In-Process Inventory/Unit	Down 65%
Production Through-Put Time	Down 64%
Floor Space Required/Unit	Down 27%
Cost of Poor Quality/Unit	Down 32%
Cost of Scrap/Unit	Down 65%
Labor Productivity (Units/Hour)	Up 40%
Actual Cost/Unit	Down 15%
Actual Units Produced	Up 54%

The first item shows that we measure our raw material

Table 39.3 Productivity Results

The first item shows that we measure our raw material inventory in dollars per unit produced. What we are measuring is the number of dollars of inventory we have for each unit that we produce. We have decreased that by 31 percent in this five-year period. Moving down the list, our work-in-process inventory has been reduced 65 percent. Production through-put time was reduced 64 percent. The floor space, the square footage for each unit we produce, has been reduced by 27 percent. Cost of poor quality, which we define as scrap, sort, rework, warranty, and disposition of deviating material, is down 32 percent. Scrap per unit is down 65 percent. Labor productivity, that is actual units per hour, is up 40 percent. The actual cost of the product has declined 15 percent and this includes inflation. We haven't increased our prices for five years. The bottom line is that all of this was going on while we were increasing our output by 54 percent.

I think these are testimonials to the kind of results most manufacturing companies can expect if they get into these programs and make the investment. These figures include the training investment. It's all on-the-job training where people are off in a classroom during their own work time. They are being paid for their classroom hours while someone else is doing production. This is what we mean by employee-driven productivity. And it is working successfully at Omark.

40

Ford's Use of Shingo's Methods*

James Torvinen, Ford Motor Company

I am excited about this opportunity to share with you some of the experiences we have had at the Ford Motor Company's Van Dyke Plant in the field of single-minute exchange of die (SMED). Our exposure to the concept began with a productivity conference, such as this one, conducted by Dr. Shigeo Shingo. The conference was conducted in Washington, D.C. several years ago. Since then, Dr. Shingo has visited our facility to assist in implementing the SMED program.

First, I will acquaint you with our plant and the history of our press shops. Next, I will cover the application of SMED at Van Dyke. Finally, we will look at the impact SMED has had on our manufacturing operations.

Van Dyke's Press Shops. The Van Dyke Plant is one of seven plants in Ford Motor Company's Transmission and Chassis Division. Our facility is located 30 miles northeast of Detroit on a 180-acre site in Sterling Heights. By Ford standards, Van Dyke is a mid-size plant with approximately 2 million square feet of floor space. The press shop occupies 200,000 square feet or 10 percent of the plant. Our products include rear axle assemblies for light trucks, front suspension, upper arms, lower arms, rear suspension, front arms, rear

---

* See Appendix: "Ford's Experience with Shingo Methods"

arms, struts, transmission components, and steering column brackets. Our manufacturing equipment in the press shop includes presses from 100 tons to 1,000 tons. Our transfer presses vary from 600 tons to 3,000 tons. The tonnage describes manufacturing pressures required to produce the parts. Our production materials vary from 0.070 inches to 0.200 inches in thickness depending on the product.

Need for Frequent Changeovers. In 1986, the Van Dyke press shop bid on Taurus, Sable, and Aerostar business. Winning the contracts, the press shop now found its tradition of dedicated presses would create major problems. The new business would load existing presses with up to six different dies. In fact, the 3,000-ton transfer presses would have to go from one die to five. During 1986, these changeovers and our inexperience in this area led to four major emergency outsourcing buys. Outsourcing buys result from the inability of the supplier to meet customer demand. Each of these buys cost our operation $200,000.

The pressure for change is obvious. Our labor and overhead cost were also high as we ran overtime and weekends to meet production schedules. To protect changeovers, large inventories of raw materials, in-process parts, and finished parts were maintained. The need to improve changeover procedures was immediate and pressing.

Introducing SMED. Into this critical situation plant manager Gifford M. Brown introduced the concept of SMED. To learn about SMED, the plant's productivity manager and I attended the Washington conference. The major areas of SMED are preparation, outside work, and inside work. Wherever possible, you delete inside work, transferring necessary activities to outside work.

Returning to the plant, we selected the five-station progressive die press. On this press we run six parts, none of which are common. Frequent changeovers on this press were of major concern to us. These changeovers took between three and seven hours to complete.

Our first effort in SMED was training. We trained diesetters, operators, and we trained ourselves to listen and act upon changes. We then practiced, but this was only the beginning.

Next we installed a display board. On it we wrote which press, which day, and which parts were involved in changeovers. We also listed how long each changeover took.

Our first action on the dies involved the subplates. This action commonized the dies. The subplates on the bottom and the top adjust the height. The die can be distinguished by the color contrasting with the subplates on the top and bottom. Each die was outfitted with the commonized subplates. We then commonized the bolt length for the four bolts in the top subplate. This enabled us to limit bolt adjustment to one-half a turn for die changeovers. The bottom subplate was modified with a "V" block on one side and flat stop on the other side. The intent of this modification was to insure positive location of the die, left to right and front to back. This resulted in the same location for each die everytime. The bed of the press was then dowelled on the bolster itself. The pin was the size of the slot in the subplate, again designed to commonize die locating.

We next eliminated the pins and the cushions designed to raise the dies when the parts are being formed. We installed nitrodyne cylinders instead. Each die now has a self-contained nitrodyne gas cylinder.

Changeover on Komatsu: Largest Press in U.S. Our success with these actions was then transferred to the 3,000-ton Komatsu which is 56 feet long, 30 feet high, and 13 feet deep. At the time we made our modifications it was one of the largest presses in the United States. It has 14 transfer stations, each die being equal in size to the die we addressed previously. Under each ram, there are seven dies. It is a double-ram press. The Aerostar lower arm, left and right hand (the arm being 0.189 inches), the Mustang or Fox arm, right and left hand lower, and the Taurus station wagon common, right and left hand, required five separate sets of tools.

In addition to the previously discussed changes we purchased eight rolling bolsters for the presses. The rolling bolsters were designed to increase the setup work which could be done as outside work. Tracks were installed to roll the bolsters to the press, away from the press, and into the press. Since our process changes were made to existing equipment, electric motors had to be fitted to the bolsters to allow for direction changes. Blank destackers were added to accommodate the various part configurations. We were required to move the blanks from the blankers press to a stack system located on the front of the press which would be common to all parts or at least easy to changeover using a bar or pin assembly, which is in fact what we did. To commonize the sets of 14 dies, we added sham packs. Presently, we are able to interchange the dies in any of our presses. Digital ram readouts were added to each column of the ram, capable of reading the ram location. This enables us to make accurate first-time settings with proper location for the bolsters, eliminating the need for time-consuming adjustments. Quick disconnects on the rails, electrical in nature, as well as quick disconnects for air and lubrication were installed, allowing operators to make the changes in place of skilled workers such as electricians and pipefitters.

Results of SMED: Changeover Reduced from Six Days to Six Hours. The results of this effort were astronomical. The 3- to 7-hour changeover has been reduced to 2.3 minutes. Our intent is to continue to drive this number down. One action underway is the purchase of a Unico feed to allow speed settings to be made with the push of a single button. Our experience had shown that the die could be installed quicker than the feed adjustment could be made. The 3,000-ton Komatsu press took up to six days to changeover. This time has been progressively reduced to 14 hours and now is averaging between 6 and 9 hours. Effectively this changeover is "outside" work as it is accomplished during our third, non-production shift. Our present goal is to reduce the time to 4 hours by the end of 1988. We are confident this goal will be met.

Performance in terms of labor and overhead operating costs improved by 24 percent during the 1986-87 period. This translates to $1.2 million. To put this in perspective, remember, this is a one-year improvement in an operation that is only one-tenth of the plant's activity. The scrap level in 1986 was 130 percent over budget. The 56-percent improvement we realized through the SMED application equates to $250,000. The just-in-time impact on our floats resulted in a reduction from 50,000 to 100,000 pieces down to the present 10,000 to 12,000 pieces. This figure is still being reduced.

We at Van Dyke are enthusiastic practitioners of these SMED techniques. I would like to express by appreciation to Dr. Shingo for his assistance in launching our program. Productivity seminars, like this one, should also be recognized for the valuable contributions you make in bringing the latest manufacturing concepts into the field. Finally, I would thank our plant manager, Gifford Brown, for his support and encouragement in this endeavor.

Appendix

Ford's Experience with Shingo Methods*

Part I: SMED. In a hit play or movie all the public sees is the final, polished product, unaware of the behind-the-scenes problems that had to be overcome. When American car buyers made hits of the Ford Motor Company's Taurus and Sable models, they were seeing the final, polished products. They were unaware of the behind-the-scenes efforts at improving quality and cutting costs. Those efforts occurred in offices and on shop floors in factories like the one described below, Ford's Van Dyke plant in Sterling Heights, Michigan, one of seven in Ford's Transmission and Chassis Division.

Big Changes. When Gifford Brown took over as plant manager of Van Dyke in December 1985, he quickly became aware of the big changes that were going on in the press shop. Prior to 1985 all of the forming or transfer presses were dedicated to a single part. Changeovers were infrequent or nonexistent. There was little or no demand for quick, efficient die changes. But with the advent of the Taurus, Sable, and Aerostar vehicles, the situation changed dramatically — formerly dedicated presses had to handle several parts.

Located on 180 acres, the Van Dyke plant makes a variety of chassis parts for front- and rear-wheel drive passenger cars and light trucks, such as rear axles, suspension arm assemblies, and high-precision components for automatic transmissions. The total of "things to build" every day, according to Brown, is about 75,000 units. To do it, Van Dyke employs roughly 1,600 hourly and 250 salaried workers. The plant has an annual payroll of $64 million and annual sales of $630 million.

With 2 million square feet, the plant is a medium-sized facility by Ford standards. But its press ship, taking up 200,000 square feet,

* From the *Productivity* Newsletter, (Norwalk CT: Productivity Inc., March/April 1988).

houses the largest presses in Ford's manufacturing system, two 3,000-ton Komatsu presses stretching 30 feet high, 56 feet wide, and 13 feet deep. Changeovers used to take five to seven days.

Starting small. In the beginning of 1986, the plant's ability to handle frequent changeovers was being "severely tested," Brown recalls. During that time, the plant had to resort to emergency outsourcing of work four times. "Unfortunately," says Brown, "the actions took place when the subject of outsourcing had become a very sensitive issue with the workforce."

Besides upsetting the workforce, sending work out of the plant created logistical problems. Operating costs were higher than planned, and inventories of raw materials, work-in-process, and finished stampings were reaching unmanageable levels. "We needed a rapid improvement in our ability to manage regularly scheduled die changeovers," says Brown.

The plant's productivity manager and press shop superintendent became familiar with Shigeo Shingo's Single-Minute Exchange of Die (SMED) system during the spring. They had some skepticism about SMED initially, but, more importantly, they accepted the principle that significant improvements were necessary.

Shingo developed the SMED system while consulting at Toyota Motor Corp. when the Japanese automaker was implementing its landmark just-in-time (JIT) production system. In order to accommodate the many rapid die changes that JIT demanded, Shingo developed an approach for reducing changeover to less than ten minutes.

"To accelerate the learning curve and move the plant in the SMED direction quickly, we decided to start with one of the smaller presses, a 400-ton Danly," Brown explained. "It uses several progressive dies to produce six different parts that are cycled over the same press. Given the frequency of changeover needed to maintain efficient inventory levels on the six parts, we had ample opportunity to find out in a short time what worked and what did not." Here is what worked:

- Changeover teams were organized and provided the opportunity to practice their procedures.
- A display board was set up on the exterior of the press shop office to record the changeover times achieved by the teams.
- Subplates were added to progressive dies to standardize mounting thicknesses, locations, and die shut heights to eliminate making ram adjustments.
- Locator pins were installed in bolsters to standardize stops for sliding dies into the press.
- All new dies were designed with self-contained nitrodyne gas systems to eliminate press cushions and bolster air pins.

As these features proved effective on the 400-ton press, they were applied to other progressive die presses, as well as to the more complicated and larger transfer presses. But Brown notes that "the greatest challenge in all of this, and the opportunity for the most significant improvement" was represented by the two giant, 3,000-ton presses.

The first step was to install rolling bolsters and imbed tracks in the shop floor. These measures facilitated the movement of the bolsters in and out of the presses and to the die staging and set-up area. "We currently use a complement of eight rolling bolsters to service these presses," Brown says. Self-contained electrical motors drive the bolsters back and forth, while a heavy-duty lift provides up and down movement.

In addition to the features developed for the smaller presses, the following were developed for the Komatsus and other transfer presses.

• Blank destackers were redesigned to facilitate quick change from part to part.
• Shut heights were standardized with shim packs.
• Digital ram position indicators were installed on the Komatsus.

"In terms of reduced changeover times, they have in fact achieved SMED on the 400-ton Danly that they used for experimenting and learning," Brown says. Changeover times that once averaged two to three hours now average less than five minutes. On the Komatsu presses, average changeover time was cut from five to seven days to eight to twelve hours. "They are confident of further reductions in the near future," says Brown.

Other benefits flowed from the changeover improvements. In 1986, performance to average budget for labor and overhead was exceeding plan up to 43.5 percent in the third quarter. Average performance for the first seven months of 1987 was reduced to a low of 0.3 percent over plan in July, or an improvement of 43.2 percent in the ten-month time frame. I do not mind telling you that a turn-around of this magnitude caused those serious thoughts of outsourcing the entire operation that were forming in late 1986 to evaporate quite rapidly.

Quality made a dramatic turnaround, too. Average 1986 scrap performance peaked in the neighborhood of 130 percent over budget, while the average for the first seven months of 1987 went as low as 93.8 percent below budget and on an average was 35 percent under budget for the full time frame.

"Needless to say this also was a most welcomed development, given the intensity of our competition in the race to determine who really is number one in quality," Brown says.

"We are delighted with the tremendous progress we have made in this area in a relatively short time frame. Despite these gains, we are still a long way from home in many respects, but we are encouraged with results so far."

To any managers thinking about adopting the SMED philosophy, Brown advises to "jump-in and charge ahead full speed."

Part II: Poka-yoke. Van Dyke currently is testing and experimenting with a variety of poka-yoke applications. Shigeo Shingo, inventor of poka-yoke, describes it as a system that carries out 100 percent inspections and gives immediate feedback when errors or defects occur. Combined with source inspections, a poka-yoke system can lead to a zero quality control system which can virtually eliminate the need for statistical quality control.

"As typically happens, we implemented our first device in response to a problem," Brown says. Van Dyke machines and assembles daily 1,600 front spindles, a composite knuckle and stem part for Ford's Aerostar model.

Early in the program spindles occasionally arrived at the St. Louis assembly plant having missed an operation. "These parts raised havoc with the assembly operation because they simply would not assemble to vehicles," Brown explains.

An investigation showed that a part occasionally could miss an operation and proceed through the rest of the process undetected.

After some experimenting, the problem was solved with poka-yoke. Special details were designed into the fixture at the operation following the one that was occasionally missed. This way, the part could not be positioned unless the troublesome preceding operation had been performed. Says Brown, "This seemingly simple mechanical solution, which was relatively inexpensive to incorporate, has proved effective." The operation has not been missed since the fixture modifications were made.

Lend an ear. Another problem affected a front knuckle machining operation for the Taurus in which four holes were drilled at once. "We had experienced improperly drilled holes and broken taps on the drill station," Brown recalls. Again, faulty parts were getting through the rest of the process and winding up at the assembly plant. To eliminate the problem, a sound detection system was installed to monitor the vibration frequency and triggered a shut off of the machine before the drill broke.

"The effectiveness of this has been verified by the reduction in the incident rate of the defect to zero," Brown says. This success has made him optimistic about the final results of several other experiments to eliminate defects.

Seeing is believing. In a critical automatic assembly operation, needle bearings, a roller bearing, and a retainer ring are assembled on each of three journals on a tripod joint.

During launch of this operation, some needle bearings periodically would not be assembled. The mistake was very difficult to detect after the assembly had exited the machine. Even worse, incomplete needle bearings would result in premature failure of the total assembly. "It was imperative that a system by devised to prevent the process from continuing unless the full complement of needle bearings was present," Brown says. After looking at several approaches, a poka-yoke vision detection system was installed.

The system uses a video camera process to determine if the assembly has the right number of needle bearings. The machine is shut down automatically if the full complement of needle bearings is not present.

"Our experience since the incorporation six months ago has been 100 percent successful with respect to preventing incomplete assemblies from getting through," Brown says. "During that time, we did go through a learning curve, due to the sensitivity of the equipment, to develop the proper program to minimize the rejection of acceptable parts. We now feel the bugs have been fully worked out and we are actively pursuing similar applications on other machining lines."

These three examples of mechanical, audio, and visual devices represent the diverse approaches to mistake proofing. Brown says that the experience with these and other applications has made employees more aware about how integrated the processes are. They recognize more readily the interdependence of one operation to another.

"In addition, the benefits derived from supplementing our SPC process control efforts with strategic applications of poka-yoke are significant. In our continuing pursuit of ever-improving levels of quality, cost, and customer satisfaction, the recognition of all of these programs as essential elements in a total manufacturing system is paramount to achieving the goals necessary to our continuing success.

"I encourage any who are contemplating SMED or poka-yoke techniques to forge ahead and experience the abundant opportunities these techniques will reveal."

41

Computer Integrated Manufacturing: The Continuous Journey

Jodie Ray, Senior Vice President Industrial Automation
Texas Instruments

I would like to share with you the strategies and tactics that Texas Instruments (TI) is using to successfully implement computer integrated manufacturing (CIM) and meet today's worldwide competitive challenges. The combination of our efforts in each of these three areas determines our progress. Similar commitments, skills, and corporate conditioning are required for progress along a continuing journey.

All of you recognize the real-world competitive challenges of getting superior products into the hands of our customers. These challenges demand special product features, but also higher quality, faster response time, greater flexibility, reduced costs, and continuing improvement as yesterday's excellence becomes today's norm. To deliver advanced products to our customers has required advanced manufacturing concepts, processes and technologies as well. I'd like to address those and their impact as we go along.

TI Growth and Background. Semiconductor cycles have impacted TI's growth. Several major innovations have fueled our long-term success. I call your attention to the industrial automation emphasis in 1987 which I will address later.

We are an international company with approximately 50 plants in 17 countries supplying our products in close proximity to the markets they serve. In addition to our plants in the United States and Europe, we have four plants in Japan and several others in the Pacific Basin. All of these sites are linked by our wide area information network including over 40,000 on-line terminals (more than one for every two employees).

Our semiconductor business has faced severe competitive pressures, particularly in the past two years. International teamwork has met significant success in improving quality, productivity, and implementing high technology automation.

We have been driven to develop manufacturing processes and technologies parallel with our product developments. We use material-handling robotics, guided vehicles, and standard control systems in our semiconductor manufacturing. Where possible, we use available equipment, but often we develop new technology ourselves to maintain our product and manufacturing leadership.

We believe we are one of the most automated of all semiconductor and defense electronics systems manufacturers. In addition, we supply small business computers, calculators, and artificial intelligence products. We share the lessons learned and the technologies developed across all the businesses within our company. These technologies cover processes such as machining and assembly, philosophies such as flexible and just-in-time manufacturing, equipment such as vision and guided vehicles, and the enabling control and communications systems.

I'd like to focus on what we are doing in three key areas to extend our CIM thrust: the continuing emphasis on the nurturing of our total quality culture; the implementation and evolution of intelligent approaches to automation — with particular emphasis on the role of artificial intelligence for industrial applications; and, finally, the integration of our factories.

Total Quality Culture. It is easy for industry to look immediately to the technology of CIM to provide the answer to competitiveness. But much can be accomplished and, in fact, must be accomplished before the first capital request is signed. For a company to be successful, it must be willing to develop or redevelop a total quality culture. That culture must include a management commitment to a change in the way of doing business, people training at all levels (from our suppliers through all our operations to our customers), and a comprehensive set of visible measurements that can show progress to all those involved.

At TI, quality has been a major thrust for the past decade. It must be sought in every step of every job that we do — no matter who our customer is (external or internal): the next workstation, the downstream process, the secretary in the next office, the accounting department, the shipping dock, and so on. We feel this dedication to quality is an important foundation for successful automation and, in fact, has been the driving force for most of our automation programs.

In addition, it can serve to lead the way on broad involvement, education, and training initiatives. Our approach has been top-down education and training: First, with our officers and managers attending the Crosby Quality College; then, pyramid instruction down through our professional staff in Dr. Juran's methods; and later, selected instruction in statistical quality control, Taguchi methods, and so forth. It is based on multi-discipline quality improvement and effectiveness teams at all levels of the organization which nurture a culture of continuous problem solving and improvement.

We have also established a quality management system and database against which our business management is measured. Beyond this, quality is now an important dimension of individual performance reviews.

Quarterly reviews of each major TI division help drive a vibrant program with customer-valued results indicated by 137 quality awards in the past three years. We are most proud of the Deming Prize. In 1985 our Higi plant was the first U.S.-owned Japanese plant to be awarded the coveted Japanese National Prize (which requires years of preparation, training, and data collection).

Automation/Artificial Intelligence. When the foundation effected by a total quality culture is in place, automation and CIM can succeed. The next step in the journey is the incremental implementation of intelligent approaches to automation.

We have 700 integrated circuit assembly machines, where vision is used to align, route, and attach the finite connections between chips and mounting frames. Fifteen years ago, TI began using internally developed cameras and processing coupled with TI-built, vision-equipped manufacturing machines. Higher resolution vision is now even more important as semiconductor geometries continue to shrink to submicron dimensions and bar sizes increase dramatically as we integrate more functions on each device. Today, throughout our business, we have over 3,000 TI-developed vision systems in daily manufacturing use.

Since the early 1970s, we have seen a hundred-fold increase in integrated circuit assembly productivity through the use of these intelligent machines. Moreover, the increase in quality yield and reduced capacity needs has also been dramatic.

Another example of TI-developed intelligent machines is our automated guided vehicle (AGV) that moves along any path — under vision-aided, flexible computer control — unencumbered by guide wires or floor stripes and capable of operating in our strict clean room environments. Along with robots, many of them also computer vision-aided, these systems were developed by TI because of unavailability in the open market.

Another example is our mobile robot. It is a TI AGV equipped with an on-board robot used for machine tool replenishment in one of our defense business fabrication plants.

Artificial Intelligence. In recent years, we have been investing heavily in artificial intelligence (AI), and I would like to illustrate how we are applying this technology to solve real world problems. We have found that industrial use of AI is becoming one of the first beneficiaries of this technology. The evolutionary path that TI has taken in the industrial applications of AI has involved progression from initial simple applications to interactive training, closed-loop process control, scheduling, and code generation. For example, four years ago, our original manufacturing AI efforts dealt with simply embedding the troubleshooting instructions in a machine diagnostic as an off-line expert advisor.

Another expansion in scope took place through a knowledge engineering project with Corning Glass. Previous attempts to mathematically model one of their 160-foot-long TV picture tube annealing ovens were unsuccessful. The oven has dozens of heaters, baffles, and ports used to manually profile the temperature through the oven for different TV tube models. The 12-hour thermal time constant of the oven prevented effective control feedback. TI and Corning engineers developed an AI-based simulator that allows the process engineer to see the effect of control settings in faster than real time. A planning system was then built to determine the control settings required to give a desired annealing profile. The underlying breakthrough was the ability to model and control the oven process through a heuristic, or rule-of-thumb, approach without any mathematical equations.

We have also expanded the use of AI to include coupling video graphics and artificial intelligence diagnostics into an interactive maintenance and training system. This results in a "just-when-needed" maintenance system that can adapt to an operator's capability or can train an individual at the point of need, avoiding the costs of initial training and low retention of information not routinely used.

Eventually, we project AI delivery to the factory floor using a portable AI maintenance terminal. Such a unit may have more than 600 MB of built-in optical memory — that's more than several complete sets of encyclopedias — and yet, no keyboard, to reduce intimidation for blue-collar users.

In parallel with the expansion of the process complexity and capabilities, we are developing delivery vehicles that embed artificial intelligence within our control systems, even including knowledge in the control loop. For example, Calgon uses a system for on-line monitoring and diagnosis of water treatment applications. It uses over 1,000 rules to cover hundreds of diagnostic situations.

In a related example, a terminal screen displays a new industrial programming capability. This is the first step toward intelligent software. The process engineer graphically creates a manufacturing process flow diagram and the intelligent software system then automatically documents the design and generates the machine/control code necessary to run the control system. This will significantly lower control system design, development, and maintenance costs.

Integrated Factories. Although intelligent machines and technologies are important, the real business impact is achieved by coupling these technologies, controls, and methodologies into integrated factories. Computer, controllers, and software are the technologies that tie the factory together.

TI's concept of computer integrated manufacturing is broader than traditional definitions. I'd like to concentrate on the area and cell levels of factory control that tie our machines and material flows into integrated manufacturing operations.

We have been evolving computer-based cell controllers for the past eight years — from initial functionality in 1979 to a fan out of more comprehensive versions in the past two years. This year we are completing development of our third generation of cell (or block) control capability. We intend to make it modular, flexible, and portable so we can fan it out generically across internal applications. In addition, we are considering it for external introduction later. While our emphasis is on incremental connectivity, our system architecture supports full plant or factory "total solutions," as well.

I want to describe three of the many examples of fully integrating the manufacturing technologies into functioning factories.

Our facility in Sherman, Texas, is used to build defense systems on a fully integrated, flexible, just-in-time basis with paperless capability. It consists of an automated warehouse, six machining cells, final assembly, and so forth, tied together with automated material delivery and fully integrated computer control. In one of these machinery cells a tracked robot moves material between 14 machines for various machining, finishing, and inspection steps. That 14-machine cell is manned by two operators. This facility has achieved a 61-percent productivity increase, a 45-percent reduction in cycle time, and an inventory reduction of 47 percent — all through automation and integration.

We are very pleased that this factory has received the 1987 Lead Award from the Society of Manufacturing Engineers. This award is given once annually for demonstrated leadership and excellence in the application and development of computer-integrated manufacturing.

I'd like to move now to another defense systems facility, our Trinity Mills metal fabrication shop in North Dallas. Here we are completing a more recent flexible manufacturing project. It has four machining centers, wash station, inspection machine, deburr robots, and a wire-guided material AGV. The wireless intelligent tool delivery mobile robot I described earlier is now being added to this system. This system is achieving spindle turn times in excess of 80 percent in production.

Lessons Learned. In our drive for manufacturing excellence, we have learned valuable lessons. One is that the trouble with CIM is also its strongest attribute: It exposes inherent problems whether in design, operations, or management systems. These problems must be understood and corrected before further automation. Horror stories can occur when projects just blindly automate their problems before jointly solving them. In all cases, the total process and flow should be questioned, simplified, and smoothed before automation. Much can be gained at this stage before automation is invoked.

The goals we have set are: total quality control, improved design quality, resolution of the MRP and JIT conflict, lower absolute costs, timeliness, flexibility, and the ability to manage continuous change. The competitive need to achieve these goals must be (1) automation and (2) to facilitate the cultural change. These goals can only be achieved through a broad concept of resource sharing, information sharing, and analysis sharing, cutting across all traditional disciplines. This is what transforms CIM from a "big watcher" role to a "big helper," called in by the operator or the maintenance technician, and so on, who feels he is participating in and, in fact is the owner of, the process.

In production, the objectives we are striving for are our two highest cost elements: (1) material at 50 percent and (2) indirect labor at 40 percent. CIM can extend electronic data interchange and our quality systems to our vendors. At TI today we execute over 33 percent of our material orders by computer. In the indirect areas, CIM can download, upload, communicate in all directions, control configuration, enforce specifications, document trends, and so on, instantaneously all the way out to our customers. It offers the potential of reducing or eliminating the NC programming and process planning layers of our current approach. In summary, it can insure the right information at the right place at the right time to allow the process to be managed (with less resources) by the right actions at the right time.

Further enhancements can occur in the direct cost area as well. First, the ability to acquire real time statistical information may change our appreciation for quality and how we can use it strategically. The operator now has graphical process and machine trends plotted against thresholds and limits. Training at this operator interface level can be continuous with real time interactive text and graphics. And everyone up the line can be more effective with a real time "information window" versus weekly or monthly printouts. This window should be an information summary at each level with a "zoom" capability for problem solving.

Summary. Let me summarize what we at TI have learned in our journey so far. First, simplify the design of the product and the process using a multi-discipline team. Second, involve, educate, and train at all levels. Next, use statistical process and quality controls in every area possible. Only automate where justified, using CIM incrementally as it is needed. Always strive for continuous improvement.

We have found the journey from the quality foundation through intelligent automation and factory integration can yield remarkable real results. For example, the actual negotiated contract pricing for the HARM (high speed anti-radiation missile) from TI's first contract in 1982 through FY86 improved each year in spite of inflation. We have reduced cost on an 81-percent learning curve and have been cited by the U.S. Navy as the best cost reduction performance of any of their missile programs.

In general, absolute numbers for improvements will vary with the specific applications; but many other examples across TI in the past few years fall right in line with the high end of the benefits reported in a study by the National Academy Press. I point out significant improvements in lead time, quality, and design in addition to those advantages more traditionally associated with automation.

In conclusion, we believe quality, productivity, and CIM in its broader definition are becoming essential strategic elements of our business. At TI the strength of our industrial automation thrust derives from combining excellent technology with our unique application experience to deliver required solutions. We intend to continue our own progress in our own plants and to build a major external business on those strengths.

42

Kodak's Copy Products Quality Program

Dale Esse, Manager of Product Quality, Eastman Kodak

An integral part of any successful quality improvement project is the active, continuous support of upper management. Their positive attitude and active involvement fosters a dynamic, team-oriented environment which transcends all working levels. To maximize achievements in this type of atmosphere, new philosophies must take root and continuous improvement must be encouraged.

This paper describes the Quality Improvement Program implemented at the Copy Products Division of Eastman Kodak Company, a program which utilized the above philosophy to effect significant cost savings and quality improvements. Characteristics of this improvement program that will be detailed include: (1) a strong emphasis on teamwork and communication, (2) assembly's ownership of quality, (3) the replacement of in-process quality control (QC) inspection with a final product quality assurance (QA) audit, and (4) a redirected focus on customer-perceived quality.

Background. Since the start of Kodak's Copy Products Division in 1975, traditional 100-percent inspection had been used throughout the assembly process. In recent years, however, copier competition, both foreign and domestic, threatened to replace Kodak's share of the marketplace with similar high quality products at lower costs. In 1983, a newly appointed Copy Products QC management recognized many drawbacks of the 100-percent inspection system such as:

- 100-percent inspection is not 100-percent effective.
- 100-percent inspection is essentially a sorting process of good products from bad.
- 100-percent inspection is not cost-effective.

In addition, assembly had little responsibility for quality and no apparent incentive for building it right the first time. QC inspection acted as a "police force," enforcing corrective action after the product was assembled (defect *detection*, not defect *prevention*). The accepted philosophy to improve quality was to increase the frequency of inspection. Acknowledging the "proof of the need," a management team of recognized leaders from assembly, quality control, and manufacturing engineering started discussions to develop a plan that would reduce QC inspection from 100 percent to sampling. A strong resistance to change the traditional 100-percent inspection system was quite obvious and due, primarily, to the fear of changing the long accepted social positions of QC and assembly. That is, the QC "empire" would be significantly reduced and assembly would be forced to accept the responsibility for building a quality product. These concerns and many others were addressed by the management team and a three-phase quality improvement plan was formulated that would change phases as quality improved and stabilized.

The Phase I, II, III Quality Improvement Plan was implemented late in 1983 on all KODAK EKTAPRINT Copier/ Duplicator products. The use of statistical sampling principles was required for each phase of the plan to maintain an *acceptable outgoing quality limit* (AOQL). However, applying these principles to a highly complex, low-volume product, such as the EKTAPRINT Copier/Duplicator, proved to be a formidable challenge. The AOQL number derived for each assembly area had to be *estimated* based on histogram data of the actual average nonconformities per unit for that area. This histogram data would determine where each assembly area would start:

- Phase I (100-percent inspection with controls) — where product quality was poorest and required all phases of the step-down process.
- Phase II (Lot Sampling) — where product quality was better and Phase I was not required.
- Phase III (Continuous Sampling) — where product quality was best and Phases I and II were not required.

Major characteristics of the Phase I, II, III Quality Improvement Plan included:

- Management presenting the plan to the copy products community in an attempt to educate a majority of the people prior to implementation.
- Management demonstrating their commitment to the plan by holding weekly roundtable discussions with assembly, QC and manufacturing engineering to address problems and concerns.
- Establishing acceptable control limits that were realistic.
- Distinguishing between a major and minor defect with a major defect having priority for corrective action over a minor defect.
- Shifting phases or lowering control limits only on the consensus of QC, assembly, and manufacturing engineering.
- Implementing a formal failure analysis system to insure management-controllable problems would get resolved.
- Using the Pareto Principle in failure analysis to enable QC and manufacturing engineering to utilize their time on the critical few problems.

Phase I. Phase I was the continuance of 100-percent inspection, but control limits were added that defined the maximum number of nonconformities on an inspected unit which assembly should not exceed. To establish the control limits, a team comprised of assembly, manufacturing, and QC engineering evaluated those inspection criteria that were important to the product's function and then categorized each inspection check as major or minor. A major is defined as a check that, if nonconforming, would cause the Equipment Service Representative (ESR) to correct it during installation, cause noncompliance to regulatory agency or safety requirements, or result in a service call at a future date. This could be due to a numerical value which significantly exceeds its specification or a condition that would decrease reliability.

The team then reviewed histograms of the past nonconformity data for the specific assembly area in order to establish control limits. A minimum of one month's data was reviewed with only major nonconformities being considered. If an inspected unit did not exceed the established control limit, the unit was accepted, repairs were made by assembly and re-inspected for subject repairs only by QC. But if an inspected unit exceeded the control limit, assembly was required to repair, re-evaluate, and re-submit that unit to QC for 100-percent re-inspection. The detainment of product due to assembly's re-evaluation and QC's re-inspection provided assembly with an incentive to build it right the first time. During operation of the plan, results were continually reviewed by assembly and QC and the control limits were systematically tightened (lowered).

Once assembly minimized the number of operator-controllable errors, a need was recognized to formalize a system that would address the management-controllable errors. The system developed, called the Failure Analysis (FA) Plan, generated a Failure Analysis Form for each major nonconformity found during inspection. This form served a dual purpose. First, it acted as a tool to initiate specific corrective action. An FA Team comprised of a representative from manufacturing engineering, assembly, QC supervision, and QC engineering was contacted to collectively analyze the specific nonconformity and, where possible, establish a corrective action sequence. Where immediate corrective action was not possible, the FA Form was held "open" until corrective action was complete. In areas where a high number of FA Forms were generated, it was necessary to apply the Pareto principle. In this manner, analysis was done on the significant few versus the "trivial" many. Secondly, the FA Form served as a data reporting tool to be entered into a computerized central data bank. Reports could then be extracted on a routine or special basis to assist in determining those problems that should be addressed. Examples included yield reports, high runner reports, and overall nonconformity reports.

When a particular assembly area achieved and maintained a previously agreed upon control limit goal, Phase II was implemented.

Phase II. This phase utilizes the lot concept wherein assembly formed lots of a predetermined size and inspection evaluated a random sample from the lot.

Phase II used the same major nonconformity criteria as Phase I. The same team that set the control limits under Phase I established a control limit which was the basis for the acceptable sampling criteria for Phase II. As the assembly area progressed through Phase II, the limit was continually reviewed and tightened.

In most assembly areas, a lot size of five units was used which maintained both good product flow and minimal statistical validity. When assembly informed inspection that a lot was ready for audit, inspection verified lot integrity and selected the sample unit(s) forming the lot utilizing a random sample selector (common die). Inspection completed the entire inspection procedure and noted all major non-conformities found on the sampled units. When a noncomformity prevented checklist completion, on-the-spot repairs were made, with those nonconformities still counting towards the total. Upon completion of the checklist, all conformities were verified by both assembly and inspection supervision. If the number of major nonconformities exceeded the establishment control limit, the entire lot failed and was returned to assembly for correction (that is, all uninspected units were checked for the nonconforming conditions found on the inspected unit(s). After repairs were made, all units were subjected to a screening operation by assembly. This previously established screening checklist insured that all units could pass inspection on the second submittal. The screening procedure was modified and updated by assembly, as necessary, to serve this purpose. The entire original lot was then resubmitted to QC for re-inspection. A random sample was taken which may or may not have contained the previously inspected unit(s). The same procedure applied as on initial submittals except tightened (lowered) control limits were established on re-inspection.

Several unique reports were used under the lot plan. One was a yield chart that showed in percentage the daily progress of initial sampling and re-submittals. This chart also acted as an indicator: High consistent yields indicated that the control limit could be tightened. In addition, a weekly lot sampling report was issued which included both the above data and a running list of nonconformities. These reports were used at weekly roundtable discussions that covered the positive as well as the negative results encountered.

During Phase II, when assembly firstline supervision recognized the benefits of improved (faster) product flow, they became very proactive for quality improvement and this resulted in significant quality gains. This enabled assembly to reach the goals required to implement Phase III sooner than anticipated.

Phase III. In Phase III, we continued using the same major nonconformity criteria and Failure Analysis System as used in Phases I and II. The initial step was to establish the control limit, average outgoing quality limit (AOQL), and the inspection sampling rate. This step determined the type of plan used and was accomplished by reviewing the nonconformity data for the specific assembly area for at least the past four weeks.

The plan began by inspecting a specified number of units in a row at 100 percent. This value was dependent on the particular average outgoing quality limit and inspection rate chosen. Once the value was achieved, a unit was randomly selected for inspection upon the completion of the assembly process. This random selection process was accomplished through the use of a random sample selector. Once selected, the unit was subjected to a complete inspection. If the number of major nonconformities found during inspection did not exceed the established control limit, the unit was accepted; repairs, if necessary, were made and inspected by QC; and continuous sampling continued per the specified sampling rate.

If the number of major nonconformities exceeded the established control limit, the unit was returned to assembly, repairs were made and re-inspected by QC. The next four units that completed the assembly process were then subjected to 100-percent inspection. The concept of inspecting four units in a row was necessary to maintain the AOQL that was chosen. If the four units met the control limit, sampling resumed according to the specified rate. If any of the four units exceeded the control unit, 100-percent inspection continued until the specified number of units in a row successfully passed inspection.

In addition to the timely and accurate nonconformity reports used throughout all three phases, a status sheet and yield chart were also utilized. The status sheet was used by inspection to keep track of the number of units inspected and not inspected so that they could accurately monitor the specific stage of the plan they were in. The yield chart was similar to that of Phase II except that sampled units were plotted instead of lots.

Overview of Success of Phases I, II, III. The Copy Products Phase I, II, III Quality Improvement Plan was very effective in reducing nonconformity rates and significant cost savings resulted. The plan also proved that product schedule did not have to be sacrificed for good quality (See Figure 43.1). Also, there were large assembly savings in rework, scrap, and overall product costs such as reduced work-in-process and reduced floor inventory, resulting in faster throughput.

The increased awareness towards the Phase I, II, III Quality Plan also brought about many changes in attitude and philosophy. The antagonistic feelings that once existed between assembly and QC

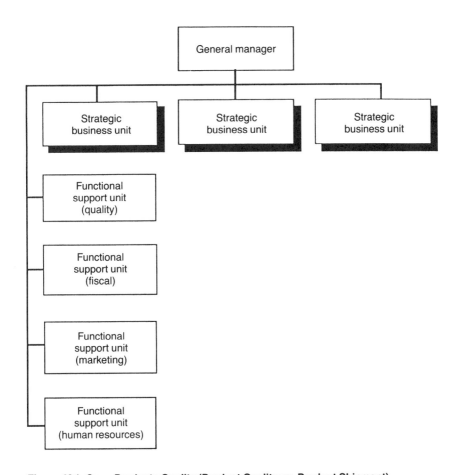

Figure 42.1 Copy Products Quality (Product Quality vs. Product Shipment)

evolved into a productive, team-oriented relationship between the two groups. Assembly acquired a strong incentive to build it right the first time and recognized the need to assume responsibility for quality. Overall, the copy products community saw the need to be cost effective to remain competitive and to take a closer look at the customers' needs and how the customer perceived the quality of our machines.

To meet these needs and our mutual goal of zero defects, a plan had to be devised that went beyond the Phase I, II, III Plan and would give total responsibility of in-process quality to assembly and enable inspection to make the transition from controlling in-process quality to controlling final product quality.

QA of the Future. By 1985, quality had substantially improved (primarily due to assembly's ownership of quality) and QC inspection became a redundant process. Once again, the management team devised a step-down plan not only to reduce QC inspection but to eliminate it entirely from the building process. In Phase I, II, III, QC inspection audited products based on design specifications (that is, assembly set-up specifications) but the QA of the Future Program focused on realistic standards (that is, quality as the customer perceived it). Inspection transitioned from in-process quality control (QC) to final product quality assurance (QA). As an area met a control limit of zero major noncomformities 90 percent of the time, QC inspection was withdrawn from that area and assembly assumed full responsibility. The QA auditing of the final product was based on input from our customers (marketing and the customer equipment service personnel).

The QA of the Future Program received total management commitment and, because of this continued support, quality gains were significant with all in-process QC inspection systematically eliminated in less than one year. In addition, feedback from within the factory and from the field indicated the quality levels continued to improve.

The QC inspection group has been reduced significantly since 1983. With this elimination of QC inspection, assembly has had to implement plans to hold the quality gains. One of these plans (detailed later) evaluates and compares actual assembler performance. Other plans implemented in the QA of the Future Program include a final product acceptance audit and a ten-level conformance audit of packed units. These audits focus on one main theme: Audit the product based on functional performance, not on assembly set-up specifications.

FPAA (Final Product Acceptance Audit). Final Product Acceptance Audit (FPAA), implemented in early 1986, is a random sampling QA audit of the final product and is based on customer-perceived quality. Various major definitions include:

- Control limit (C) is the number of major nonconformities allowed per unit and is based on previous data.
- Modified control limit (Cm) is a tighter control limit than "C". Initially, Cm is 75 percent of control limit but as quality improves and stabilizes, Cm is reduced to 50 percent of control limit.
- Major nonconformities have been split into two categories, A and A'. An A' is a nonconformity that would be adjusted by an Equipment

Service Representative (ESR) as part of the normal machine installation, therefore not added into the total nonconformities that are charged against the control limit, (provided that assembly can demonstrate that the condition can be adjusted within acceptable limits). A nonconformity would not be adjusted by an ESR as part of the normal machine installation and would require additional time to adjust it to acceptable limits.

- A product engineering organization was formed at this time which combined in-process QC engineering functions with the manufacturing and design engineering functions to more effectively support the production process.
- All nonconformities are verified by a team representing product engineering, assembly, QA supervision, and QA engineering and classified as A, A', or minor (low priority) nonconformity. The purpose of this is to provide immediate feedback to the assembly line and prompt product engineering for any necessary corrective action.

Initially, a specified number of completed units is audited per the FPAA checklist and the data compiled. The control limit is determined from the data and sampling begins by randomly selecting a completed unit for audit prior to shipment. For example, if the sample rate is one-third, an average of 33 percent of all units is chosen for auditing over a period of time.

Several improvements have been incorporated into the FPAA plan to make it a "user-friendly" plan and increase its chance of success. One feature is the modified control limit to control limit. This is an early warning indicator that the quality of machines has worsened and that there is a high potential for exceeding control limit if the problem is not addressed. Screening of units by assembly is one option that has been used to improve and stabilize process quality. Other modifications have been incorporated which easily identify the quality of the assembly process at any given time.

Another improvement of the FPAA plan is the use of the rolling average. In Phase III (continuous sampling), each unit inspected was plotted against the control limit. This resulted in many large "spikes" on the chart for nonconformities per unit. A rolling average of nonconformities per unit tempers the "spikes" and allows assembly time to stabilize the process before it goes out of control and exceeds the control limit. For most Copy Products applications, a five-unit rolling average has been used successfully (that is, each point plotted represents one audited unit with its number of nonconformities averaged with its number of nonconformities found on the previous four units audited).

Other key programs have been implemented to aid assembly in the transition from assembler to assembler/inspector. Two of these plans are summarized in the following sections.

Critical Parameter Monitoring. Critical Parameter Monitoring (CPM) is a variable screening process audit performed by assembly as inspection is removed. The purpose of CPM is twofold: (1) to provide the assembly supervisor with a tool to guarantee acceptance quality levels in his or her area and (2) to allow the supervisor to take a closer look at individual assemblers on a frequent basis.

The assembly supervisors for each assembly area are responsible for monitoring critical parameters on their assemblies before they shift to the next assembly area (their customer). The critical parameters are defined by each assembly supervisor with input from product engineering. The basic guideline for defining critical parameters is: A critical parameter is one that, when not set-up properly, could directly affect machine performance, customer satisfaction, and/or final product acceptance audit.

The length of the CPM checklist, the percentage of units monitored (a minimum of 10 percent of the production schedule is required) and the frequency at which each assembler is monitored (a minimum of two audits per assembler per week is required) are determined by the assembly supervisor and reviewed, where appropriate, with product engineering to maintain consistency. The data generated from CPM Aadits (distributed once a month) helps to determine possible assembly processes that drift with time, prioritizes problems for corrective action, reduces risk of floor line purges, clarifies assembly procedures and identifies potential problems with specific assemblers.

Assembly Discrepant Report. The Assembly Discrepant Report (ADR) is a reporting system of all problems found during the assembly build process or CPM audits that need further engineering analysis. A failure class is assigned to each nonconforming condition such as: parts — mechanical, assembly area responsible or under investigation. The name of the person designated for implementing corrective action and target dates for completion are also recorded on the ADR. Meetings are held bi-weekly (chaired by the assembly general supervisor) to update the status of each ADR to insure proper follow-through to completion. All ADR's are recorded into a central database for retrieval at any time.

Conforming Audits. Copy Products has enhanced the product audit testing by implementing a 10-level conformance audit that confirms the unit is fit for customer usage by auditing all possible customer environments. The operating procedure states that every four weeks, a specified number of units (2 percent of the shipping schedule) must be removed from the packaging area prior to shipment. They are unpacked and set up in the factory per installation procedure used by our field service personnel. These units are then audited at certain "levels" such as high altitude, environmental, regulatory, or customer usage. By the end of a four-week period, these units will have been audited on at least one of the ten "levels." The results of the conformance audit testing provide management with timely information on product early life performance, reliability, and conformance to specifications.

Conclusion. Until 1983, Copy Products Division operated on principles that proved to be not only costly but essentially ineffective in achieving and holding any real quality gains. Our products cycled their way through an elaborate maze of queues; waiting to be inspected, repaired, reinspected, and moved to the next queue. This operating philosophy failed to keep pace with modern aspects and advantages of active Quality Improvement programs. Today, the Phase I, II, III and QA of the Future Quality Improvement plans have shifted full responsibility for in-process quality from quality assurance to assembly. This transfer of responsibility has been accomplished without any significant amount of added cost to assembly.

In addition, inspection has changed from its former role of in-process sorting to its new role of auditing final product based on the customer's needs. The gains in quality and cost reductions include:

- An overall average major nonconformity per unit reduction of 90 percent on all EKTAPRINT products since the implementation of the quality improvement program.
- A 70-percent reduction of QA personnel with a direct labor savings of nearly $3 million since 1985.
- A 50-percent reduction in QA unit cost.
- Significant reductions in rework costs (that is, from 12.5 percent to 8 percent on one product alone).

The social consequences of assuming new responsibilities has been overcome and a more productive environment has evolved. As continuous improvement is encouraged and rewarded by management, the gains to date will not only be held but exceeded. Continuous improvement must become a part of a company's culture, taught and practiced at every level. The Copy Products Division of Eastman Kodak is well on its way to achieving such a culture.

43

Total Quality Control: A Breakthrough Approach to Teamwork at Hewlett-Packard

Julie Holtry, Marketing Manager, Hewlett-Packard

Dr. Juran has certainly impacted Hewlett-Packard's approach to quality improvement. He has taught us many things. But he has particularly helped us to focus on driving cultural, attitudinal changes in our environment: changes which facilitate quality improvement.

Attitudinal and Cultural Changes. Juran says, "Before anything will be done, there needs to be a 'breakthrough in attitude' — a belief that improvement is possible. And even after someone has figured out how the improvements can be achieved there is still the task of convincing everyone involved that the new method is worth a try — 'a breakthrough in cultural patterns.'" He is making an important statement to corporate management today and has reaffirmed a conclusion that we have reached at Hewlett-Packard.

Managers have a new job today: creating attitudinal and cultural changes in the workplace. Perhaps this job is the most important job of the coming decade.

Why do I say this? What is happening in business today that warrants such a conclusion? It is becoming quite clear that the world has become one very interdependent marketplace, and global competition has become increasingly fierce. Companies are being forced to change the way they do business with their customers.

This competition has even changed the way nations govern themselves. For example, you can't open a newspaper today without reading about legislation that's intended to address our import-export imbalance.

And many of you are aware of a U.S. law recently enacted to emphasize quality. This is the National Quality Award established for the purpose of encouraging American businesses to practice effective quality control. The first awards will be presented in November of 1988.

The fact is that competition is demanding much more from us — and quality is becoming a key differentiator, and a strategic issue which must be used as a competitive advantage. In order to do this, quality needs to be managed differently today. Managers need to make breakthroughs in cultural patterns in our current workplace. They must create a revitalized environment where a shared vision becomes the driving force for quality improvement and teamwork is used to effectively execute these strategic visions.

We have found an approach that is helping us create this kind of environment and achieve results in quality improvements — results that can give us the kind of competitive edge we need to compete in global markets. The approach is called "Total Quality Control."

But before I get into this topic, let me put my remarks in some kind of context as to our company. I am not certain how familiar many of you are with Hewlett-Packard; who we are, what we do, what we look like. Hewlett-Packard is headquartered in Palo Alto, California. HP is an international manufacturer of measurement and computation products and systems used in industry, business, science, health care, and education. HP equipment is used in many different ways. An HP financial calculator can help you figure out the financing for a new home. An HP electronic test instrument helps car makers check for vibrations so the car you drive will have a smooth ride. An HP analytical instrument can measure the chemicals in suntan lotion to make sure it protects you from sunburn. An HP desktop computer helped design the fuel system for an airplane that you might have flown in. And if someone you know ever has a heart attack, an HP medical electronic product can help revive that person quickly.

HP sales in 1987 were $8.1 billion. From 1977 to 1987, the company's net revenue grew at an average annual rate of more than 20 percent. HP has 82,000 employees worldwide, a network of 410 sales and support offices and distributorships in 78 countries. Besides U.S. plants, we have research and manufacturing facilities in Europe, Japan, Canada, Latin America, and Southeast Asia.

First, I think it's important to review a little of our quality history. What we know of quality management today certainly reflects our experiences from the past. Then I want to show you how we've adopted the philosophy and methodology of TQC to a key management process — the process of strategic planning and implementation. It's through this process that we have attained the greatest breakthroughs in creating the "Juran" environment of shared visions, teamwork, and continuous quality improvement.

HP's Experience with Quality. Looking at our early history, I can honestly say that focusing on quality isn't really new to HP. We've focused on providing product quality excellence since the company was founded in 1939. But our perception and understanding of quality today is certainly much different than it was then. In fact, it's much different than it was just a few years ago.

Quality began moving to the forefront of company concerns at HP in the late 1970s because, like many other companies, we were feeling the increased demands of competition in the marketplace. Technology was becoming more of a commodity. It wasn't enough to be making a superior product anymore. One calculator can only be so much better than another; we had to lower our prices. In order to do that we had to lower our own internal costs of doing business.

So in 1979 we conducted some cost of quality studies. In every case, we found that our costs of not doing things right the first time were from 30 percent to even 50 percent of our revenues.

It was in response to this finding that our president and CEO, John Young, set what he calls a "stretch objective," or what we call "10 percent." He challenged us to improve the reliability of our hardware by a factor of ten in ten years — by 1990.

Why a factor of ten? To force us to change our basic approach, our "same old way" of doing things, and to change our expectations about what is possible. Had he asked for just a 30 percent improvement, we probably wouldn't have been motivated to try fresh approaches to our tasks.

To respond to this challenge we sent study groups to our joint venture in Japan, Yokogawa Hewlett-Packard, or what we call YHP. YHP had made astounding gains in quality improvement through their adoption of Total Quality Control (TQC). They began their efforts in 1977 and in only five years these were their results:

- Manufacturing cost down 42 percent
- R&D cycle time down 52 percent
- Failure rates down 79 percent
- Productivity up 120 percent
- Market share up 193 percent
- Profit up 244 percent

Redefining Quality. So all these experiences, the forces of competition and cost of quality, YHP successes and the 10-percent goal, helped to shape our current understanding of quality and actually led to our redefinition of quality.

At HP, we have found that our customers are actually redefining the quality of our products today. Quality no longer just means hardware or software reliability or durability. It now means customer satisfaction for the "total business relationship" with the customer — the quality of our documentation, the quality of our sales interactions, the way we ship the product, bill our customer, and so forth.

And we found that not only was quality the route to customer satisfaction but it was also the path to improved productivity. Where we found areas of high quality, we found high productivity. Where we identified areas of low quality, we identified unproductive areas. And so, pursuing quality became critical in the way we managed our business. In 1980, HP launched a company-wide TQC effort.

Total Quality Control. Before I give you some concrete examples of our results, let me take a moment and tell you how we are defining TQC at HP. It is probably not much different from how many of you have studied it or how other companies are defining it.

TQC is a management philosophy and a way of operating totally committed to quality that focuses on continuous process improvement. TQC views every aspect of the business relationship with the customer as a process that can be continually measured and improved through the use of scientific methods. Perfection is the goal. The methodology requires universal participation and a teamwork approach to problem solving. The results are "customer satisfaction."

The "customer" concept applies to both external and internal customers, and requires every person and every unit in the organization to regard itself as both a producer and a customer, and insist on receiving and delivering products and services of perfect quality at each stage of the process until they reach the end user. Thinking of colleagues as customers produces a subtle, but powerful change in people's attitudes. It helps foster the cooperation among departments and divisions that is so essential to a decentralized company like HP.

The bottom line to TQC is that it makes you ask seven very basic questions. Who are my customers? What do they need? What are their measures and expectations? What is my product or service? Does my product or service meet their needs and expectations? What is my process for providing their need? What corrective action is required to improve my process?

Searching for the answers to these questions fosters a shared vision. Mapping out the direction of a group's activity helps everyone agree on what they are actually doing or should be doing and how to measure their performance. And when a group reaches consensus on how to measure the success of their efforts, you've gone a long way toward building a unified team.

TQC Results in Manufacturing. That is enough theory. Let me briefly describe some of our recent results and give you some examples of the way TQC forges teamwork.

In the early 1980s our manufacturing facilities were the first to follow YHP's lead. For example, within two years our business computer manufacturing operations were able to reduce manufacturing cycle time from three weeks to four days. Inventory went from four months to one month. And they were able to accomplish this with 20 percent fewer people.

After we gained experience in manufacturing, we turned our focus to other production environments. The use of TQC in the product repair centers has enabled our U.S. support organization to reduce their repair turnaround time by 25 percent without increasing the size of the work force.

TQC Results in Credit Control. Let's look at how TQC helped our accounts receivables performance. We have an operation that, in essence, serves as our catalog sales division. They book about 25 percent of all our orders each year, most over the telephone. Most of the sales are small.

In 1984 our overdue collections in this division were $652,000. Management was unhappy, as were the customers whose shipments were put on "hold" because they weren't paying their bills. As the HP credit people dug into the problem via TQC methodology, they turned up some surprising and embarrassing facts. In many cases, customers weren't paying their bills due to our errors — specifically, delivery to the wrong address, wrong product, wrong price, and so on. HP improved their internal processes, dropping overdue receivables to $218,000 within two years. That is $434,000 less invested in the business in the form of uncollected funds.

The aggregate results of these kinds of efforts throughout the Company are large. Overall company-wide inventory savings have been $542 million and a natural spin-off of this has been floor space savings of $200 million. Company-wide accounts receivable savings have been $150M.

TQC Engenders Teamwork. These accomplishments hinge on the kind of teamwork that TQC engenders at HP. Let me tell you another story that illustrates TQC teamwork in action. This is a case where it would have been easy for the situation to deteriorate into a finger-pointing session between divisions of HP, but it didn't.

We have an operation in Roseville, California, called Computer Support. It's responsible for supplying repair parts and exchange assemblies for all our computers worldwide. Until recently, they had a less-than enviable reputation with their customers, who are HP's field sales representatives. Their delivery time just wasn't fast enough. So they used TQC methods to analyze thoroughly their own repair process and identify what slowed things down.

Their information showed them that 80 percent of their delivery delays were caused by waiting for just 20 percent of the parts they needed (Juran calls this "the vital few") and that those parts, in turn, came from other HP divisions. They didn't point an accusing finger at the guilty divisions. Instead they put on an educational roadshow that they took around the company. It mapped the entire process of repairing customer orders (or end user orders) — from the customer, to HP customer engineer in our field organization, to SMO (the Roseville computer support operation), to the supplying HP division, back to computer support, and then back to customer engineers when repaired.

This broad, informative picture — and its focus on internal and external customers — convinced the other divisions that they were an integral part of a very broad and important process. They are now much faster in sending parts to Computer Support, because they understand better how their own actions affect customer satisfaction. They see themselves as part of the same team.

Use of TQC in Strategic Planning. I want to spend my last few minutes talking about an application to TQC that has perhaps the greatest single potential for achieving breakthrough results at HP — TQC applied to strategic planning and implementation, or what the Japanese call *hoshin kanri*.

The word *hoshin kanri* is actually derived from two chinese characters — *ho*, meaning direction and *shin* meaning needle as in a compass. *Kanri* means policy. So the literal translation of *hoshin kanri* is "direction of policy" or what we call strategic planning.

There's a little story behind how we adopted *hoshin*. One day, a renowned Japanese quality consultant was visiting one of our divisions. He asked the general manager if he could see his annual plan. The general manager responded, "Sure, I have it right here in my desk." He reached into his desk, brought his only copy out, dusted it off, and presented it to the consultant. The consultant lifted it up to his nose, took a little sniff, and said to our general manager, "This annual plan smells a little musty. Smells like it doesn't get out of the drawer very often." On another occasion, in another division, after receiving the general manager's annual plan, this same consultant very nicely turned to him and said, "This is a very nice 100-year plan, extolling perpetual virtue."

Well, it wasn't too hard to see his point. Some changes needed to be made in our planning and implementation process. As you may know, Juran places a great deal of importance on planning. We needed to make our annual plans living documents. We needed objectives that were clear, realistic and could be completed within an annual time frame, and that could be measured. In addition, we needed implementation plans that were truly capable of driving a change throughout the organization.

So we began to implement a structured objective-setting process where objectives, strategies, and measures are all hierarchically linked together, spanning all functions of the business. This is the *hoshin* process. It is not my intent to walk you through this process in detail, but our planning is a process — a continuous cycle with no beginning or end. It really starts with an annual review — an analytical review of the previous year's objectives and accomplishments. Key issues are identified and analyzed from the bottom up to determine how much improvement or change is required in the next planning cycle, say one year. Extensive detailed and structured planning follows with a plan deployed at each level linked with all other plans being developed.

Here's how the plan's deployment works. A strategy and measure at one level of management will become an objective and goal to the next level down: "How" a manager wants to accomplish an objective (or his strategy) becomes the "what" that has to be done by the next level down (their new objective).

Finally, the strategies come to life through detailed implementation plans. Essential to the implementation process is periodic review. Built-in progress checks and reviews verify that the strategies were correct, the implementation is progressing, and the goals will be met. And if not, course changes are required. Of course, getting through this process is not the ultimate goal: The ultimate goal of *hoshin* is improved performance. And we are getting results!

Hoshin kanri fosters a shared vision and creates changes in people's attitudes — employees are motivated because they belong to a general movement in which they are directly participating and contributing to the achievement of the strategic issue. Managers are motivated because they can be assured that the objectives they are working on are directly tied to key customer concerns and are aligned with their boss's priorities. Juran, as you may know, calls this kind of participation one of his "rules of the road" for implementing change.

We are obviously sold on the effectiveness of TQC. We feel it is a very important tool for our managers as they face difficult challenges today. Assuredly, the adoption of TQC underscores the value of achieving breakthroughs in teamwork to enable us a strategic foothold in world markets. Thank you, Dr. Juran, for helping us see the light!

44

Managing Quality/Productivity Improvement at McDonnell Douglas

Henry "Hank" Todd, Vice President, McDonnell Douglas

I want to share my views with you on managing quality/ productivity improvement for maximum effectiveness. To do this, I will be discussing what we feel are key management actions, how they have been implemented at McDonnell Douglas Astronautics Company facilities in Huntington Beach, Monrovia, California, what the result has been, and how we go about maintaining the focus on quality and productivity.

Key Management Actions. Although quality is the responsibility of everyone in the organization, there are some key actions that management must take up front to set the example and get the process started. They are strategic thinking, communication, managing by natural work groups, training for the new culture, ethics, and operating in the new environment. I will discuss each in detail.

Strategic Thinking. First is strategic thinking. So you don't confuse it with strategic management, strategic thinking, at any level, is simply understanding where you are going before you address how you are going to get there. Sandy McDonnell, our CEO, verbalized his vision of the McDonnell Douglas Corporation through what he called the five keys to self renewal. When fully implemented, strategic management, quality/productivity and ethical decision-making will provide us the desired cultural environment to be a self-renewing corporation. Our most important productivity assets are our human resources.

Communication. The next step is total communication. If we expect our personnel to think strategically and support our efforts, we must provide them with all the necessary information. McDonnell Douglas has documented the five keys in corporate policy No. 2 and we continue to emphasize our goal through the corporate newsletter, videos and division/component communiques. In addition, it is a standing agenda topic for all major meetings as well as regular staff meetings and is the focus of our annual "all hands" meeting with all employees in the division.

Management by Natural Work Groups (NWG). Management by natural work groups (NWG) is another key management action. The more you involve your people in the decisionmaking process, the easier it is to make rapid change. This system of management overcomes the natural incompatibility between an organization designed hierarchically and today's participative approach. We feel there are three types of NWGs — vertical, horizontal, and combination as defined here. By utilizing this type of management system, the people can more easily identify their responsibility for quality/productivity improvement in their daily activities. This moves them towards greater self-management.

Training for the New Culture. This concept drastically changes the degree of responsibility each individual has in managing our business, so we are obligated to provide the proper training. In the past two years alone, our people have participated in 276,600 hours of multifaceted training. We focus on the development of the individual as well as the various processes used in quality/productivity improvement. Voluntary participation in Lou Tice's "Investment in Excellence" combined with consultants like Peters, Drucker, Covey, and Blanchard and the proven processes of Deming, Juran, Conway, and the Productivity Center provided them the tools to operate successfully in the new environment.

Ethics. Intrinsic to each of these ethics. Much has been written and said about ethics, but by comparison, little has been understood. It is the understanding that makes the difference and, I might add, the common understanding that creates a climate of trust and re-spect. We have summarized understanding ethics as an awareness of, and sensitivity to, the ethical content of daily decisions, choosing the best solution among the alternatives, addressing the fairness of the action or decision about to be implemented, considering all affected parties — employees, customers, shareholders, stakeholders, the community, our nation, even our competitors.

Operating in the New Environment. Operating in the new environment places a new responsibility on management to connect the purpose and financial performance of the organization to the individual and the job performance of the NWG. Two years ago, Huntington Beach reorganized into strategic business units with a concentrated customer focus and functional support units (FSU) that streamlined our support actions. This change facilitated implementing the system of management by natural work groups which strives to use teamwork to achieve common objectives and institutionalizes greater self-management.

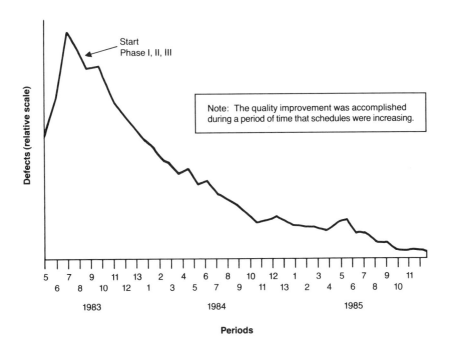

Figure 44.1 A Sample Organization Chart

This sample organization chart may help you to better visualize the difference between a matrix-type organization and one which utilizes the SBU/FSU (Strategic Business Units/Functional Support Units) concept.

Implementing Natural Work Groups. At McDonnell Douglas we have implemented both internal and external natural work groups. Internally, they are within and across SBUs and FSUs. We have productivity center NWGs that are program focused and action team NWGs that focus on an individual part or parts within a given program. Externally, we have PANH — partners advancing to new horizons — which involves our suppliers in quality/productivity improvement. Our inter-division/intercomponent NWGs are formed to take advantage of shared capabilities.

Establishing a Common Objective. Managing change of this magnitude can be extremely difficult unless you establish a common objective that everyone within the organization can identify with and contribute to. By identifying one overriding significant business issue you remove the roadblocks. The SBI at Huntington Beach is to catch and beat our competition and improve customer satisfaction. We and our suppliers must increase quality and reduce costs through productivity improvements in our systems and increasing performance. Our measurement of success is a doubling of sales and return on investment in the time frame of 1985 to 1990.

Tangible Results. Does it work? You bet! We have tangible results. Since 1984 our business base has doubled, our expected growth in 1988 is to a total of $890 million, and our 1987 backlog was the highest ever for our division. We feel comfortable in projecting that by 1990 we will not only meet our ROI goal, but we'll exceed our goal of doubling sales. Management hasn't done it and cannot do it alone — it takes everyone in the organization managing quality/ productivity improvement on an individual and continuous basis.

Maintaining the Focus. Based on these facts, it would be very natural to feel we can now sit back and relax, but nothing could be further from the truth. Now, more than ever, it is critical to maintain the focus and build on that success. When I talked about communication, I mentioned an annual "all hands" meeting. From the sessions just concluded, we identified our five most important issues for 1988 as demonstrating quality performance on existing contracts, winning one major program and keeping all programs sold, enhancing employee productivity, improving the competitive posture and accountability of SBUs and continuing progress toward the SBI goals.

We went on to identify how we can resolve these issues:

- Reduce cycle (flow) time
- Focus on product quality and delivery
- Achieve promised objectives — doing things better
- Improve the quality of engineering drawings
- Complete the implementation of productivity center NWGs
- Continue to implement the path program
- Achieve 100-percent launch success on all programs
- Continue to embed cultural change and the five keys
- Achieve a better understanding of the various degrees of participative management and expand its use
- Allocate our asset base and working capital base to provide accurate feedback to the SBUs and FSUs.

Of course, these aren't the only things we can do and we recognize that. They are, however, the seeds that start the process — the "what if we..." and the "we could..." ideas that bring us right back to involving the individual in managing quality/productivity improvement.

Summary. In summary, the keys to managing quality/productivity improvement for maximum effectiveness are: (1) strategic thinking — understanding where you are going before you address how you are going to get there; (2) communication — providing personnel with all the necessary information as well as continuous feedback on progress; (3) managing by natural work groups — implementing a working environment that involves all personnel in day-to-day problem solving and decision making; (4) training — providing the wherewithal to do it; (5) ethics — creating a climate of trust and respect; (6) eliminating fear; and (7) operating in the new environment — do it — and enjoy the results! Everyone wins — the customer, the company, the stockholders, and the employee.

45

The Quest for Sustaining Quality Improvement

James Talley, Vice President of Quality, General Dynamics

General Dynamics has been the leading defense contractor for six of the last nine years. We are number 36 on the *Fortune* 500 list of the largest U.S. industrial corporations. With over $9 billion in annual sales, we operate in all 50 U.S. states and 50 foreign countries. Our 100,000 plus employees are highly motivated to *turn out the best products that meet and exceed contract performance requirements at or below the agreed-to cost, and at or ahead of the required schedules*. That is our definition of quality.

We are proud to have our General Dynamics F-16 aircraft be declared one of the 100 products that America makes best. *Fortune* magazine, March 28, 1988, determined the finest of their kind. The criteria was it had (1) to be state-of-the-art and the height of innovation and technological advancement, (2) to be the most durable of its kind and provide good to great value for the price, and (3) to have or hold market share.

So I want to share what we at the Fort Worth Division of 28,000 Texans started in 1981 and, at the support and push of President Ollie Boileau and Executive Vice President of Aerospace Dick Adams, implemented in General Dynamics. We call this quest for quality — Quality Improvement Program (QIP).

Chronology of Quality Improvement. Where do we start? We assessed our facilities against the business base and determined that we must upgrade our capabilities. So in 1976 we started our factory modernization process, going from batch manufacturing to process flow manufacturing. Then in 1977, with the assistance of the U.S. Air Force we started the Technology Modernization concept. The USAF put up $25 million to do manufacturing conceptual studies and General Dynamics invested $100 million in implementation equipment. This concept and Industrial Technology modernization with the supplier base is the subject for a future presentation. So in 1980 we linked productivity and quality together and started QIP. The Quality Improvement Program was laid out and we ventured into the cultural change.

General Dynamics started with the strategy that "what management cannot measure...it cannot control." So, we agreed:

- The company must have a specific productivity and quality improvement program.
- A company policy must be published.
- The program must be staffed.
- Practical measures must be identified and defined.

The concept of QIP was to:

- Promote quality awareness among all employees
- Involve all personnel in the improvement process, from top management to staff and line employees
- Provide intensive training to each department, at every level, teaching the values of quality disciplines and how to profit from them
- Establish measurable goals in each department that align with the corporate common goals, making department management fully accountable in their performance and merit reviews for goal achievement

The program was established to make an immediate cultural impact. This was done to:

- Gain immediate benefits from near-term improvements in scrap, rework, yield, engineering changes, product support and material
- Obtain far-term rewards by steadily improving user requirements, proposal schedules, design considerations, communication, and release to production
- Continually update measurements and targets to ensure a dynamic, on-going program with self-sustaining properties

The Quest for Sustaining QIP. How have we done? The corporate and division policies were released February 4, 1981, as shown. Of particular note is paragraph two which states that quality is every department's job; the Quality Assurance Department's job is final acceptance of the products.

General Dynamics
Executive Memorandum
No. 81-2
4 February 1981

      TO: *Division General Managers, Subsidiary Presidents, and Corporate Directors of Quality Assurance*

SUBJECT: *Quality Assurance Responsibility*

1. It is General Dynamics' policy to provide quality products and services commensurate with the standards demanded by our customers. It is the Division Manager's responsibility to establish and maintain sound, cost-effective quality practices in his division.

2. Each General Manager will be held accountable for obtaining the requisite quality and for insuring that proper actions are taken in engineering, manufacturing, materials, and quality assurance. All other functions also shared in the responsibility to deliver quality products and services.

3. General Dynamics recognizes the vital importance of its product and services in our national economy and defense and that of our foreign customers. This policy will not be compromised.

                             O.C. BOILEAU
                             President

Table 45.1 General Dynamics Corporate Quality Policy

1. General Manager
   Divisional overtime

2. Contracts

3. Production Operations
   * First time yield
   * Scrap labor
   * Scrap material
   * Rework/repair

4. Logistics
   * Service report response

5. Finance

6. F-16 Program Office
   * Deviation/waivers

7. Research and engineering
   * Avoidable engineering drawing changes

8. Electronic Manufacturing Center

9. Quality Assurance
   * Material review frequency
   * Inspection escapes

10. Human Resources

11. Data Systems Central Center

12. Materials
    * On-time deliveries to production
    * Accepted purchased items

* Corporate Common

Table 45.2 Quality Improvement Parameters

Next was the extensive QIP training! We selected Dr. Joseph Juran as the quality guru to lead our march into being among the best. We selected our top corporate and division management and locked them up for two days of quality immersion. Dr. Juran and the three gurus from the Navy, Army, and Air Force lectured the 118 executives on the intricacies of quality improvement in San Diego, California. We then took Dr. Juran and Frank Gryna to the four aerospace divisions and trained 2,010 additional management personnel.

Many more were trained and are still being trained through a wide variety of media.

The corporate common measures that were selected were done by a panel of 13 experts. These corporate common measures, along with some other selected Fort Worth measures, are shown below. These measures have definitions for collecting and measuring and are briefed as part of each division's performance at the corporate quarterly and annual performance reviews.

Corporate Common Parameters Cost Savings vs. 1982 Baseline Data				
Function	**Element**	1983 $ Savings	1984 $ Savings	Total $ Savings
General Manager	Overtime Reduction	13,965,255	3,165,721	17,130,976
Engineering	Avoidable Engineering Changes	3,601,360	17,462,396	21,063,756
Program Office	Deviations Waivers per Aircraft	798,560	823,200	1,621,760
Production	First Time Yield	172,415	180,155	352,570
Production	Direct Labor Hours for Scrap	202,051	*1,859*	200,192
Production	Value of Raw Material Scrap	294,340	176,237	470,577
Production	Direct Labor Hours for Rework/Repair	1,339,881	583,201	1,923,082
Material	Production Material On-Time Delivery	*57,016*	*1,360,708*	*1,417,724*
Material	Purchase Item Acceptability	70,401	204,223	274,624
Logistics	Service Report Response Time	52,752	68,283	121,035
Quality Assurance	Rejection Reports for Material Review Action	464,821	1,349,770	1,814,591
Quality Assurance	Nonconforming Items Which Escape Planned Inspections	*55,451*	275,943	220,492
QIP Grand Total Savings		**20,849,369**	**22,926,562**	**43,775,931**

Table 45.3 Corporate Common Parameters

The Payoff. So we have implemented a program, a process of quality improvement. Is it paying off? We think so, and the record backs up that statement. Our corporation will do nearly $10 billion in sales for 1988 with backlogs of greater than $21 billion. The F-16, the M-1 tank, the Stinger missile, the Trident submarine, and so on, are top of their line products for the USAF, Army and Navy. The F-16 is being sold to 17 nations, with more countries interested.

But, those are gross indicators, so let's get more specific — back to the QIP that has been described. We did not have really good hard data in all measured functions until 1982, so that's the baseline. As you can see, we had savings of $43,775,931 for 1983 and 1984; it is even more for the ensuing years. Overtime is a good indicator of each division's performance. A division should plan on about 5 percent overtime, 7 percent according to government studies in an alarm system. Plus, much more than 5 percent dramatically impacts the quality of work due to tired people, out-of-station work, shortages, and so forth. Engineering change rates indicate it wasn't done right the first time and this really impacts the procurement/material and production departments. The studies we have done across the corporation show that avoidable engineering changes or make-it-work changes are $4,000 to $6,000 each, so you can see that doing the design right can create significant savings.

Summary. We have implemented a formal quality improvement program. We defined a process; it is run by top management; it involves all the employees — not just the production floor; and we are continuously training. We have started our quest, we have seen significant improvements, but we still have mountains to climb and boulders to overcome.

We believe that meetings and seminars like Utah State University's Partners Program are part of that continuous climb for excellence and the survival of this great country.

46

Improving Service Sector Productivity

William McCormick, President, Fireman's Fund

Let me begin with one observation: Productivity in the service sector is the same as productivity in the manufacturing sector. If that surprises you, consider the fact that both sectors define productivity in the same way; that is (to borrow a page from Webster), "Yielding or furnishing results, benefits, or profits; or yielding or devoted to satisfaction of needs." In other words, doing something useful and doing it in a way that is, in some sense, profitable.

Both the service and manufacturing sectors have the same tools at their disposal. At American Express, perhaps the nation's best known service company, automation has long been the key to greater productivity. Previously, when cardmembers called with a complaint or a question concerning a bill, employees had to pore through files to see what the records showed. All of that took a lot of time. Now a computer does all of that on a screen. Whenever a cardmember calls, all the information required — name, address, recent transactions, billing status — is instantly available and the problem is resolved with a few keystrokes. Corrections are made and the information in the central computers changes. That's clearly an improvement in productivity. It's much the same at a company like R.J. Reynolds. Five years ago, RJR had machines that made 4,000 cigarettes an hour. Now the company has machines that make 9,000 cigarettes an hour and manpower needs have decreased substantially. Once again, we have a clear improvement in productivity. Both sectors have the same objective and utilize the same means to achieve that end; only the size and nature of the machine vary.

The Du Pont Formula. Both sectors have other tools, as well. The problem is that they don't always make the best use of them. To understand this, let's examine another definition of productivity, namely the classic Du Pont formula:

$$\text{ROE} = \frac{\text{Net Income}}{\text{Sales}} \times \frac{\text{Sales}}{\text{Assets}} \times \frac{\text{Assets}}{\text{Equity}}$$

Return on equity is probably the best known and most widely accepted method of measuring productivity (profitability) among different industries and businesses. It also provides the foundation for and explanation of much of what is happening in the business world today. It tells us a lot about the basis of our competitive stance with Japan and the rest of the world.

Let's take the first item, net income divided by sales or return on sales. What drives that number? First and foremost — prices. The higher the prices, the higher the return on sales. However, in today's competitive world there is little room to raise prices. In the past, whenever General Motors raised prices, the other domestic auto makers would go along and that's how costs were covered. They can't do that anymore. The Japanese competition, as well as GM's domestic competitors, won't let them. The same is true in chemicals, insurance, banking — almost any industry you can name. The ability to raise prices is greatly constrained because world competition has put a real limit on how much you can get for your product.

So what's left? Expenses. The lower the expenses, the higher the return on sales. How do you lower expenses? You have three tools to work with: manpower, materials, and interest, the cost of capital. Those are the three top components of expense. That's why companies like RJR automate. It lowers their personnel cost per cigarette made. That's why other companies try to use substitute materials — such as plastics instead of steel — to lower unit material costs.

That's also why still other companies work very hard to lower their cost of borrowing: The lower the cost in interest rates the higher return on sales.

But there are limits here as well. In the United States, we have the highest cost labor market in the world. In some countries, people work for bare sustenance. Our standards of living are different; we believe workers should have a house, two cars, a television set, and so forth.

Then there's the cost of material. For better or worse, material costs are fairly universal across the globe, if you exclude the cost of tariffs and transportation. Thus, most companies pay pretty close to the same amount of money for materials.

Lastly, there's the cost of money. Here the playing field is also uneven. In Japan, interest rates are 5 percent because they have a stable currency and they have fiscal discipline in their government. In the United States, interest rates are hovering around 10 percent. Why? Because people are afraid of inflation. For the better part of this century, the real cost of borrowing money has been 3 percent. Anything higher than that is based on expectation, either real or imagined, of inflation. Thus, because the Japanese are better fiscal managers than we are, they have a stable currency and a lower cost of money.

Let's consider the second item, sales over assets. That's asset turnover. It's important because it tells you how much revenue you are getting per dollar of total assets tied up in business. It's a measure of yield on total investment. That number varies greatly by industry. An industry like advertising is labor-intensive. There is very little capital, so asset turnover ratios are very high. On the other hand, a capital-intensive industry such as petrochemicals will have a very low sales-to-assets number. But the important thing to remember is that, while the ratio may vary greatly from industry to industry, variations within an industry are based on brainpower.

Japanese Attain High Asset Turnover. Let me just give you an example involving the auto industry. In the past, managers worked hard to get 2:1 asset turnover. That translates to a revenue of $2 billion total on assets of $1 billion. Why? The big number there is inventory. In American factories and mills, goods were piled up floor to ceiling. Then, the Japanese came along and invented just-in-time inventory. Instead of moving goods from factory to warehouse, and from station to station within a warehouse, goods arrive the minute they are needed. The reason the Japanese can do that is because their people never miss a delivery date and never deliver poor quality parts.

The Japanese do something else as well. In the United States, we used to make only one kind of car at a time, all black ones for a while, then all yellow ones. The reason was that it was too difficult for a manufacturer to make different models. If you go to a Honda factory, down the assembly line will come, one after the other, all kinds of different cars: two-door, four-door, a red one, a green one, a blue one, one behind the other. Why? Because Honda's sophisticated manufacturing techniques allow it to make products in sequence to fill a container that goes to the United States or somewhere else in the world. The cars go right into a container and onto a ship and they're on their way. They don't sit in a warehouse. Hence, there is less finished goods inventory. That's where brains come in.

What about American brainpower? Can we duplicate the Japanese talent for innovation? Yes. What will it take? Better quality and better service standards and higher standards of execution among all of our suppliers. It is possible. And it is imperative. In Japan, the asset turnover is in the range of three or four to one. In the United States, it is in the range of two or three to one. If you have the same return on sales, and the same labor cost, and if your asset turnover is 50 percent greater, your return on equity will be 50 percent greater as well — say 15 percent, rather than 10 percent. That's quite a difference! There's huge leverage in that number. It allows our competitors to charge less and still make the same return we make. That's where the competition gets fierce.

So far, I've considered the first two terms of the Du Pont equation. The last term is assets over equity, or financial leverage. The players here are investment bankers, and the game involves the capital structure of the business. The main issue here is how much funding comes from where. In the best of all possible worlds, most of it comes from payables and other free money that people owe you. However, more frequently, much of it comes from debt on which you pay interest. There is also equity that comes from people who are investing capital. Depending on how much risk you want to take, this second term — debt — can become very big. You can then have very little equity for a given amount of assets. The good news is that it allows you to make a lot of money, as long as nothing goes wrong. The bad news is that, if you make a mistake, you are out of business.

All of American business is leveraging up in order to make a good return. They are adding much leverage and risk instead of working on the second, brainpower-dependent factor. Now the Japanese, among others, are leveraging up as well. Where it all will lead is anyone's guess.

Productivity: The Human Factor. So much for the economic side of productivity. What about the people factor? In the Du Pont formula, the only place where people expense occurs is in the first term, net income over sales. And there, they are considered only as a cost factor — something to be controlled or reduced.

If that's the case, the question becomes, how do we control the cost of the human factor? In my experience, there are only three ways to improve manpower productivity and reduce the relative costs of people. Guess what the first one is? Make them go away. Automate your operations. Why? Well, I don't know about you, but I've always found that people are ornery beasts. They don't always do what you ask them to do. They sometimes look out the window when they should be welding a part or they don't show up because their child is sick or has a problem in school. So the first secret of success in increasing productivity is to automate. Frankly, I find that a little disturbing because, like you, I'm a member of the human species. But automation is a fact of life. It's happening in the auto companies with robots; it's happening in the insurance business with computers. It's simply something we have to accept to remain economically viable.

But the good news for us homo sapiens is that we can't eliminate people altogether. And if we have people, there are only two ways to manage them. The first choice is to manage conflict. We are all familiar with that. It all begins with children, doesn't it, when they say "Mommy, I want a cookie." "No." Children want to do one thing, parents want another, and there's conflict.

We see the same type of conflict on another level in business. Take the assembly line of 40 years ago. People were expected to put the bolts in and the nuts on as cars moved down the line. The work wasn't very interesting. Management saw its main task as enforcing discipline and monitoring attendance.

Motivating People by Integrating Work/Play. There are still a lot of jobs in this world like that. Generally speaking, they get done by managing conflict by using what one writer calls the KITA school of management.

KITA is short for "kick in the ass." There are two ways to apply it. One is negative feedback: the "do it or else" school of management. You threaten to kick your employees or to withhold pay or privileges if they don't show up, or you install a time clock. The other way to do it is positive kicks in the backside — so-called incentives, such as more attractive surroundings, privileges, wages, and so on.

The underlying assumption in both cases is that the worker doesn't want to do the work and, therefore, you either have to kick him or give him an incentive. Either way, it's an enforcement system. Using positive incentives is far more subtle and a great deal nicer, but it's the same basic mechanism. And it is used, and it will be used, as a way to get work done here in the United States and abroad.

The trouble with the KITA method is that it only works well when you can measure output in quantifiable terms, such as keystrokes per minute, or tons of coal per hour, or number of cars per day. However, in our increasingly technological world, where more and more of the work product is intellectual, measurement becomes much more difficult. The old methods simply don't work as well. How do you measure intellectual productivity? How do you measure whether somebody is thinking or not, or whether their ideas are good? And once you come up with a way to measure this type of productivity, how do you encourage it?

Let me give you a simple example. I have twins, age 11. My daughter loves to read. My job as a manager is simple. We hop in the car and go to the bookstore, and she picks out five or six books and off she goes to read. She's excited by reading.

My son, on the other hand, doesn't like to read. So I try to override his objections with a little KITA. Needless to say, it doesn't work very well. He has nowhere near my daughter's enthusiasm to read. And none of the "forcing" techniques — the incentives and the threats — have been effective. In the end, it all comes down to self-motivation.

It's the same in business. We need to get people to manage themselves. And the way to do this — the way to motivate and make people productive — is to make them excited about what they're doing. We've got to get better at creating jobs in which people are turned on by the work itself, not because someone is standing over them.

To do this, we must begin by understanding and honoring the importance of work in our lives. Nietzsche once said, *"Leben ist arbeit und lieben"* (life is work and love). That is a pretty sobering thought. It asks us to put aside all of the distractions and diversions life offers or imposes, to think of our lives in terms of just two things, and then to ask ourselves how we're doing. The results can be disconcerting! Fortunately, the Lord made us pretty durable, and I, for one, can tell you that you can run a long time on empty. The question is, should you? Or should you ask others to? I think not. The effect on the human spirit is too devastating. I'd like to think that we were intended to use that durability and strength for better things.

I also think that my old friend Nietzsche would agree. After all, he also observed, *"Arbeit muss Liebe nicht Mühsal sein"* (work should be love not labor). It is a worthy ideal. The question is how to achieve it?

I think that the key is to integrate work and play. You have to love what you are doing. Robert Frost, one of my favorite poets, offers an interesting insight in his poem, "Two Tramps in Mud Time." Stating that his goal in life is to unite his vocation and avocation, he uses the analogy of his two eyes creating a single image.

The story behind the poem is interesting. Frost's hero is out chopping wood for his house in the woods when two tramps appear. They stop to watch, and the man chopping wood thinks, "They want me to hire them to chop the wood, so that they can earn their meal." Frost concedes that the tramps have a point, but the fact is our friend loves to chop wood. It isn't work for him; he does it because he loves it. The thought is somewhat similar to Thoreau's observation, "When you chop your own wood it warms you twice: once when you chop it and once when you burn it."

Both stories tell us that the difference between work and play is not physical exertion. Consider Frost's woodcutter, or the amateur athlete who runs ten miles a day.

Nor is it a matter of mental exertion: how many of us spend hours playing chess, or computer games, or studying esoteric subjects? Certainly, money represents one dividing line, but for people for whom work is play, there is something more — a fulfillment of a higher need.

Maslow, one of our great behavioral scientists, recognized that there is a hierarchy of needs which he expressed as a pyramid. At the base of the pyramid are the physiological needs: food and shelter. At the next level is safety or security; above that are social needs, such as a sense of belonging. Above that are ego and self-fulfillment.

The two values at the top — ego and self-fulfillment — are where the magic is. It's kind of scary when you think that the top of the pyramid — those things which we hold most dear — are built on a base of McDonald's french fries, but that's the way it works. It's hard to conquer the world — or change it — on an empty stomach. But once we have met those basic needs, we can move onto the realm of the spiritual and the intellectual. And in that realm, motivation depends on ego and self-fulfillment.

Oliver Wendell Holmes observed, in the spirit of the Greek ideal, "The only happy person is a person whose work allows him to function to the full extent of his ability." It is only when we honor the values at the top of the pyramid that we really turn people on — that we turn work into play. The precise motivating factors may vary; it may emerge as a chance for achievement, or an opportunity for growth; it may be the challenge of an external task or an inner goal. Whatever they are, if we allow people to pursue them, in an environment where there is recognition and fairness and a sense of caring about the quality of the work that is done, we will never have a problem with productivity, whatever business we choose for our life's work.

Honoring Your Own Needs. So far, I have talked about business productivity. Now I'd like to talk about personal productivity.

In this life, we are blessed with a surfeit of diversions. There are pastimes and obligations, telephone calls and business activities, and so on. Unfortunately, sometimes there is so much going on that we don't have the time to really think about what it is, after all, that we were sent here to do on this earth. It's difficult to focus on what really motivates us and what we want to do with our lives. We have little time to spend on our own values and on our own goals. We are frequently so preoccupied with reacting to people and events that we forget to think about what we want to achieve. We rarely have time to ask, much less resolve, important questions such as, "What do I really love to do?"

And it is a question that deserves a lot of thought. It's funny: When you do what you really like and you're good at it, it's amazing how God kind of puts wind at your back and carries you along. Let me give you an example. I happen to like variety and change. I'm intrigued by intellectually challenging problems. That's one reason that I've enjoyed working at a lot of different jobs and places. I've worked for Admiral Rickover building nuclear submarines. I've worked for McKinsey and Company, where I was able to tackle many different kinds of problems. I spent a wonderful year in East Africa, where I worked for Julius Nyerere, reorganizing the government of Tanzania. I've worked at American Express, where I served as president of four divisions in six years. And I've enjoyed Fireman's Fund. We were very pleased in 1986, when *Forbes* magazine named us the most improved insurance company in the country. In short, I've done what was right for me, and I've loved my work. But mine is not the only path, nor should it be.

I had a friend in high school who loved something different. He didn't like variety or intellectual challenge. He liked skiing. So when I was studying physics and stretching my mind with other intellectual puzzles, he was skiing. When it came time to choose a college, he enrolled at a college in Vermont. Why? So he could ski. Unfortunately, he couldn't major in skiing, so he studied marketing. It was four years of Calvinist effort on his part. When it came time to take a job guess who he worked for? Head Ski Company. Guess why? He loved skiing, and he spent his twenties going around ski areas trying out all the new skis and skiing.

Then, AMF bought Head. The culture of the company changed, and he didn't like it as much. So, he took some money and bought a little ski shop in Sun Valley. He now owns a ten-store chain. He's making a lot of money and he loves his life and guess what he does everyday? He skis.

The point is that you can make a pretty good life by following your star. Take Steve Jobs of Apple or Bill Gates of Microsoft, or an engineer who loves engineering. Or a secretary who loves her work and the company of her co-workers. Or a housewife who loves raising her children. As long as each of us is doing what we want to do, we do it well. And, not coincidentally, the productivity benefits are enormous.

The reverse is true as well. A woman who wants to be in an office or a laboratory instead of at home with her children shortchanges herself and her children by remaining home. And the one who wants to be at home with her children has a hard time giving 100 percent at the office.

The same principle applies to all of us. We see that at Fireman's Fund all the time with people who are in the wrong line of work. There are people who should have been in sales but were placed in underwriting, and vice versa. Once they recognize the problem and get to the right spot, their creativity takes off. We never have to supervise them again. And, in an era in which knowledge rather than physical output is more and more the product, that human factor becomes increasingly important.

Conclusion. The productivity gap has widened in recent years. Average U.S. business productivity grew at 3 percent a year from 1950 to 1965. From 1965 to 1973, the rate was 2 percent; and since 1973, it has barely crept along at 1 percent.

We've tried a lot of things in recent years to remedy the situation. We've reorganized and we've restructured. We've merged and acquired. We've changed our names and launched flashy advertising campaigns. We've dislocated 30 million jobs in the manufacturing sector in the last ten years. And yet, we have failed to close the productivity gap. The United States still lags behind countries such as Italy and Great Britain in business productivity and per capita GNP.

Perhaps the time has come to try something new — or, more precisely, something old. More than 200 years ago, Adam Smith observed that economic growth depends on the free exercise of talent and creativity.

It is a sentiment echoed by Peter Drucker, who wrote more than 40 years ago that an institution must be organized to bring out the talents and capacities of its people; to encourage people to take the initiative, give them a chance to show what they can do and a scope within which to grow.

The power of the individual has always been the foundation of American success. Perhaps, in this time when corporations are being encouraged to get back to their roots — to stick to what they do best — that we as managers re-vitalize that most American of American of traditions: to honor the individual; to give him — or her — the tools needed to get the job done — and then to get out of the way.

47

ConAgra's Approach to Quality and Productivity

John Phillips, Assistant to the Chairman, ConAgra

I would like to discuss what we at ConAgra have found over the years to be a proven productivity plus and probably the backbone of our company. ConAgra — I think you will agree as you hear about our management philosophy and our culture — is very unique among large companies today, which is one of the reasons we try to keep it that way. ConAgra jumped 18 places on the 1988 *Fortune* "500" list — we are now number 41. Fourteen years ago when all this started we were, I believe, about number 400. So something that we're doing is working.

Utah State and the world of education overall have changed in the 30 years since I graduated from this campus. The world of business has also changed in that time. Words that might have characterized business in 1958 when I graduated could have been bureaucratic, autocratic, conformity, keep your nose clean, policy manual, dress code, and so on. Today, you might more often hear words like involvement, participation, open management, think tank, team effort. Unfortunately in practice, there are too many companies today operating as they operated in the 1950s.

At ConAgra we believe the single most important key factor to our success is our ability to unleash the power of the individual. That's the backbone and the thrust that weaves itself through our total culture. I'll expand on this as we go forward.

Company Turnaround. First I think that in order to understand the ConAgra of today and what we hold important, one really has to understand where we come form. A scant 14 years ago, in 1974, ConAgra would best be characterized as being a medium-size midwestern company operating in flour milling and poultry production — and in big trouble. In 1974, our company had $34 million worth of equity and $160 million worth of debt — we lost $12 million that year. If you lived in or around Nebraska and read the newspaper, it was like watching a soap opera. It wasn't a question of whether ConAgra was going to fail or not; the question was when. Interestingly enough, on the open market, you could have purchased the whole company in 1974 for $10 million. Today, that price would be over $2 billion.

By 1988, things had changed dramatically. Sales have moved from $600 million in 1974 to invoiced and managed sales of almost $18 billion today. I say invoiced because if you read our annual report, you wouldn't see a number quite that large. Unlike some of our competitors, in our commodity trading businesses we don't report invoiced sales. We report as sales the margins that we get on those sales. But if we reported all of our invoiced and managed sales, we'd be about $18 billion.

ConAgra's profit has gone from that $12 million loss to $272 million pre-tax profit today. Our return on common shareholders' equity has gone from a negative to one of the highest in the food industry. We've averaged over 22 percent in the last five years. Employment has moved from 5,000 people to about 50,000 today.

In ConAgra in 1974 we held no significant market shares. Today we enjoy market leadership in agricultural chemicals, flour milling, fertilizer merchandising, red meat, poultry, seafood, and frozen foods. We also have a strong presence in processed meats, grain merchandising, and worldwide trading.

We made a conscious decision about 48 months ago that if we were going to continue our growth in earning power, we had to become a multi-international company. From that beginning, today we have about 50 international offices in about 25 different countries.

ConAgra's Culture: Power of the Individual. I've often been asked, What's the one thing most responsible for ConAgra's dramatic turnaround?" The answer is simple: the power of an individual. That individual happened to be Mike Harper, who is currently our chairman and CEO, but as we went forward it became the power of a number of individuals.

We often hear the term "team effort" used. Well, I'd like to talk about that a little bit. I'd like to give you some examples of why we think using team effort as a rallying point is sometimes not getting at the real crux of the motivation or the productivity that might be available.

When Mike Harper came to ConAgra in 1974 to try and help save the company from bankruptcy, one of the first things he concentrated on was the balance sheet. And one of the first things he saw when he looked at the balance sheet was that the flour milling inventories represented a tremendously large pile of money. He didn't know at the time whether they were too large or too small to do the proper job that a good flour milling company would do. But there were 15 flour mills and each one of them was managed by an individual manager, and that manager individually was responsible for delivering the quality and the quantity of products to his customers in his region.

Well, each one of them was asked and challenged to reduce their inventories 10 percent and not sacrifice quality or service. Now, did Mike know that 10 percent was the right number? No. But each said, "I can do it." Now when you asked 15 different managers, they didn't say "We can do it." They said "I can do it. I commit to do it." This was not their usual way of operating. Full grain bins in the flour milling world is a comfortable way to be. You know you're not going to run out, and you know what you've got in quality. We all know that change from the normal is pretty scary. But they committed to it *individually*, and they did it *individually*. Then they committed to another 10 percent, and they did that. It was *not* a team effort. These were 15 individuals committed to doing what they could to save their company. And they played a big part in reducing our debt at that time by over $70 million in about four months.

Company Philosophy. By 1976, it became obvious that ConAgra was going to stay afloat. So, Mike and half a dozen of his key people and a couple of folks that he called on from the outside literally went up on a mountaintop in Colorado and tried to decide "what do we want to be, now that we're going to stay afloat." They asked, "Where do we want to take this company?"

Well, they came away committed to a philosophy which remains the foundation of our company today. It takes on several characters.

One is that we decided to be a basic food company, and, broadly defined, that means to operate between the farm and the table. You probably won't see us in jet engines in the near future.

They set four basic financial objectives, which I'll talk about a little later. But the belief was and is today that committed individuals are the most productive when the target is clearly defined.

Family of Independent Operating Companies. One of the most important things to come out of the 1976 era was getting articulation of what has become our ConAgra culture. The desired organizational climate was first described as independent operating companies. We believe that independent operating companies attract the best people in the industry because good people like to be held responsible and they like to run their own show. Independent operating companies keep from creating bureaucracy. Layers of bureaucracy in many large companies and governments tend to take all the energy level and all the actionability out of growing a business. In the food business we work on large volumes and razor-thin margins. So if you're not actionable to take advantage of something as soon as it happens, it will probably go on by you.

We also characterized ourselves as a family of businesses — independent operating companies, but within a family. Those family members can draw on the overall strengths of the family. I characterize independent operating company presidents as timber wolves. Timber wolves, as most of you know, hunt independently nine months out of the year and do very well. But three months out of the year they choose to run in a pack and pull down bigger game than any one of them individually could get on their own. And that's what we try and encourage among our independent operating companies: to run their own show but understand that they have the ability to operate as a family, or hunt as a pack.

Committed People Who Are Free To Act. We also characterize our culture as surrounding ourselves with committed people. We don't want involved people — we want committed people. And if there are a few of you out there who don't understand the difference between involvement and commitment, I'll ask you if you had scrambled eggs and bacon for breakfast this morning? The hen was involved; the pig was committed.

We also try and create an atmosphere where people feel free to act without fear. One thing that happens in bureaucracies is that people start creating their own little piece of turf, and their biggest job and their biggest concentration becomes protecting and building that turf. The fear of doing something new, because I might lose some of that turf, or I might put it in jeopardy, really stifles the growth of a lot of organizations. We try and create an atmosphere where people feel free to disagree and challenge; it's okay to argue, it's okay to fight — as long as you're fighting for the same causes. In short, we try to create a culture that releases the power of the individual.

There are a lot of implications when you emphasize individuals. For example, what do individuals do, and what do committees do? Well, we in our company don't feel that committees get much of anything done. We have, for instance, a management executive committee composed of the top seven or eight people in our company. The idea there is that every one of our employees across the world is represented by one person on that committee. We have only one rule in our executive committee: We never vote. When somebody throws a problem or an opportunity on the table for our executive committee, that individual is the responsible executive who's going to finally make the choice one way or another of what he does, if he does anything, and which direction. But he's got a lot of friends in the same family and a lot of them are pretty high-powered people who have gotten a lot done over their lives, and he has that resource available to him.

We have a pretty fair football team in Nebraska. The Aggies realize that; unfortunately, Oklahoma hasn't got the message. We've all heard the saying, "A chain is only as strong as its weakest link." Let me talk about how we look at a football team. We don't look at it as a team effort. A football team doesn't win, in our estimation, unless most of its 11 players win individually. And when you think that way you can never say at the end of a skirmish, "The team let me down." And when you get to that point in your individual assessment of your efforts, you really know that within yourself you have the power to win.

People Want To Be Led, Not Managed. I want to make it clear that I am not talking about structural power, the power that you have because you own the company or because you're the boss. Someone once described the power of hierarchy as a set of gears. When that gear up at the top turns about a quarter of an inch, somewhere down the line there's some poor little gear that's running like mad. You need to hope and be sure he's running in the right direction and he's running on something worthwhile. So people who have hierarchical power have to be very careful about the way they exercise it.

United Technologies ran a great series of thoughtful ads in the *Wall Street Journal* a while back. One was called "Let's get rid of management." It said, "People don't want to be managed, they want to be led. Who ever heard of a world manager? You can lead your horse to water, but you can't manage him to drink." And finally the ad says, "If you want to manage somebody, manage yourself; you do that well and you're ready to stop managing and start leading." I believe there's a lot of truth in that ad. And we at ConAgra are committed to trying very hard to lead and not to manage.

There are a number of different styles of leadership. Soupy Sales once said, "There's no limit to where a person can get with a kind word and a gun." Well, that is not real leadership. It is a form of management.

You have all heard of the mushroom style of leadership. Perhaps you've experienced it; hopefully you haven't practiced it too much. That's when you keep your people in the dark, you cover them with manure, and eventually you can them.

Leadership is an individual act and it has great power to bring about action and change in any organization. When I was interviewing college graduates and people for jobs, the one main thing I looked for was the trait of leadership. Was the person a leader in his church? Was he a leader on his athletic team? Did he evolve as a leader in his fraternity or in his community? If he went into the service, did he just mark time there, or when he came out, was he several ranks up and had much more responsibility than when he went in?

And the one trait I really look for other than the fact he or she has assumed those leadership positions along the way is whether the person is dissatisfied. Is he or she a dissatisfied person? Not grumbly, but do they say to themselves, there's got to be a better way. If I could get every one of our employees in ConAgra one pill, it would be a pill that when they came to work in the morning, they'd say, "There's got to be a better way of doing my job." I don't care whether it's a secretary or somebody on a production line or an executive. If every one of them said that and strived to go home that night having made a contribution, having found a better way to do it, you couldn't keep a harness on where this company would go.

Individual Freedom and Commitment To Make Right Decisions. One way leaders of an organization can increase the power of individuals is to change the culture of the organization. That's really what happened at ConAgra. We changed the culture of the organization, what the organization holds sacred, and what it concentrates on. I mentioned our corporate philosophy that emphasizes notions of freedom to act, encourages risk-taking, acceptance, and assumption of responsibility, and an environmental climate that stresses openness, support, trust, and competence. Leaders can have a great impact on an organization — I don't care what organization it is — by impacting on the culture and the environment.

Let me give you a little food for thought. We have today about 50,000 employees in ConAgra. I would say very conservatively that every one of those 50,000 employees probably makes 100 decisions a day. That's 5 million decisions a day in ConAgra. Now I'm sure that if I was personally making all those decisions, they'd all be right. But what we have to do is influence those 50,000 people to make good decisions based on their power as individuals.

Let me give you an example. If you take a quality assurance inspector on one of our bacon lines in the Armour Food Company, whether it be in Louisville, Kentucky; Mason City, Iowa; or San Antonio, Texas; that individual has the power to gain us a customer or lose us a customer for life. And that person doesn't make 100 decisions a day. He or she makes many thousands of decisions a day about the quality of the product that goes out with our brand name on it. Somebody's going to buy that bacon and say that's indicative of what Armour bacon is all about. Well, if we threaten that individual inspector so he won't let any bad bacon out, what's going to happen? No bacon is going to get out. On the other hand, if we don't care, he's going to let all the bacon pass, and that's even more disastrous. Management's task is to create an environment where the individual feels the freedom and commitment to make the right decision most of the time.

Shared Visions Shape Individual Behavior. Another way to increase the power of individuals is to create a sense of shared commitment. I mentioned earlier that we set our company's fundamental strategies and our four basic financial objectives at that 1976 meeting in Vail. And we decided early on to go public in declaring our goals and values and measuring ourselves against those goals and values.

We were probably one of the first major companies in the country that put in writing and published to our stockholders and to the public what our financial objectives were and then measured ourselves against them each year. Now it's gotten fairly popular. But they're not just external objectives. They are the way we manage internally.

Shared visions shape individual behavior, and sharing a common goal does not restrict the power of the individual. It focuses it. We believe that's extremely important. We want every ConAgra employee to commit individually to those objectives that we annually publish on pages four and five of our annual report. Those are a 20-percent return on common shareholders' equity, a 14-percent earnings per share trend line growth, a commitment to a conservative balance sheet — 35 percent maximum long-term debt-to-equity ratio. And in our business we also attempt to zero out our short-term debt at the end of every year. Now there's a lot of dancing that goes around to do that because at any given time we'll have substantial short-term debt. But what zeroing out that debt does in a cyclical commodity business is demonstrate the liquidity of our balance sheet. That's very important, particularly to our creditors.

We've met our financial objectives now for 12 straight years, although we don't promise to do that. We're not a stairstep earnings company. If you want to invest in a company that's going to commit to give you an earnings increase every quarter in every year, then I suggest you don't buy ConAgra, because some of our businesses are cyclical commodity businesses.

Now the return in those cyclical commodity businesses over time is very good, but you can't expect an increase each year and each quarter. I was associated with a company one time that had a lot of good points to it, but one of the unfortunate points is that if we got down to the end of the quarter and we weren't going to show an increase in earnings, we'd rip the guts out of all of our marketing programs and all of our advertising programs, and we were making long-term decisions based on short-term facts. Too much of that goes on today.

Our most important objective is that 20 percent ROE. When we acquired Armour Food Company, Greyhound chairman John Teets came on our board. After one of the board meetings, he said, "You know, I think that all the ConAgra managers and employees have got 20 percent ROE tattooed on their shorts." We of course went out and had shorts made with "20% ROE" on them. Well, Mike Harper shared that story with a *Fortune* reporter. It resulted in a *Fortune* photo of Mike holding up his shorts with "20% ROE" on them — and nationwide coverage, thanks to the wire services. We got a lot of dignified headlines out of that like "Undercover Story Breaks at ConAgra" and "ConAgra Executives Keep Deep-seated Goals in their Underwear." I guess that's one way of publicizing our objectives. It did get around a lot.

Praising Improves Worker Productivity. The fundamental difference in leaders is the way they use their own power. I'm sure you can think about certain people when you hear this. Some people lead by trying to be the best personally. This is a leader who emphasizes the difference between him and his associates, clearly placing himself at a significantly higher level and value. This leader often, in fact, is a superior performer, and he or she emphasizes their power over others.

Some leaders adopt the Borden's milk theory of power. That is that power comes in quarts, and if I give you a quart, that's a quart less that I have.

We would suggest that an alternative approach is to exercise power by trying to increase the power of your associates. This can be done by conveying a positive regard for them. One thing we do at ConAgra, and I credit Mike with starting this, and now it's very much a part of our being — we don't spend a lot of time trying to correct the shortcomings of our employees. We choose to spend a lot of time building on their powers, building on their strengths.

We have found that if we've got somebody who's really good at something, if we'll just praise that, and really say that they're the best there is in that, it gets even better and so does everything else along with it. And that person goes home at night walking about six feet high instead of going home at night thinking "Boy, all I heard all afternoon was how bad I am." We have found that to be very, very productive. If you openly expect top performance, top striving, innovation, and commitment to excellence, you're going to get it.

Creating Community of Individuals with Power. We have spoken of a culture stressing individual responsibility and independence. We've touched on the importance of pride and the power of the individual. Does it really make a difference? Well, I personally believe it does. One example: If you had $30,000 in 1974 and if you were crazy enough to invest it in ConAgra stock and you put it in the bottom drawer, today, even after October 19, it's worth about $2.5 million.

That increase in stockholder wealth is due entirely, in our opinion, to a large number of individually committed people at ConAgra. There's no limit to what the power of the individual can cause to happen.

Our job as leaders is to create a situation where we have a community of individuals who feel they have power to get things done and change their world. Commitment to a shared vision will move the organization toward that vision, but commitment is a voluntary act — and commitment can only be made by individuals who feel their own personal sense of power. You can't commit to something unless you really feel you've got the power within yourself to get it done.

Effective leadership and power as individuals build a culture of pride. Individuals who recognize and use their own personal power will be the best of the best.

A friend of mine, General Jack Chain, heads up the Strategic Air Command. I've been privileged to be involved and know something about their bombing competition. When you see four or five people in an aircraft, each one committed to being the best at what he does in that aircraft — and you see the pride in how tall they stand when they're recognized as the best among their peers — anybody who doesn't have something well up inside is not paying attention.

In short, we believe there is a direct correlation between the success of ConAgra over the last 14 years and going forward and our ability to help unleash the power of the individuals who help to manage and to run our company.

PART V

Guidelines for Managerial Action

48

Managerial Guidelines for Productivity and Quality Improvement

Y.K. Shetty and Vernon M. Buehler, the Editors

Management has traditionally viewed productivity and quality as two aspects of production, not as key strategic elements for company viability and profitability. In today's global market, however, such a perspective is a prelude to business failure.

Challenged by intense international competition, heightened customer expectations, and declining profitability, U.S. firms are finding that they must improve productivity and quality, as demonstrated by the well-publicized actions of many companies. However, with few exceptions, many companies are unable to match the productivity and quality levels of their overseas competitors. Recent studies conducted by the American Society for Quality Control and American Productivity Center showed that even though corporate executives strongly believe productivity and quality, together with speed of delivery and timely creation of new products, are the most critical competitive issues facing American business, many do not know how to achieve these goals. This is mainly because productivity and quality improvements require company-wide commitment and an appropriate investment in time, resources, and managerial action. It also requires major changes in corporate philosophies and operating systems.

Despite these challenges, some companies are successfully using proven methods for enhancing productivity and quality. Based on the experiences discussed in this book and elsewhere, the following clear guidelines have emerged:

1. *Productivity and quality must have the firm commitment of top management.* This commitment should be reflected in a company's philosophy, goals, policies, and priorities. Top management must lead, inspire, and involve itself in creating a culture for consistent productivity and quality throughout the organization.
2. *Productivity and quality must be recognized as competitive issues and must be part of a company's performance goals and strategy.* The concern for productivity and quality must be integrated into how the company conducts its business. Productivity and quality, like any other strategic aspects of business such as profitability, growth, market share, and innovation, should be strategically managed.
3. *The human side of an organization is the key to consistent productivity and quality improvement.* Research and company experiences clearly show when proper attention is paid to people, productivity and quality naturally follow. Managers can take these several steps to enhance productivity and quality more specifically through people:
   - Recognize that company employees are the key to productivity, quality, and customer service. Employees and managers at all levels should be convinced that productivity and quality are part of every job and critical for their company's success.
   - Develop and implement employee policies and practices on selection, socialization, training and education, performance appraisal, reward system, employee involvement, and communication to promote consistent productivity, quality, and customer service.
   - Pay special attention to employee recruitment, selection, and socialization. Spend a considerable amount of time in selecting the right employees best suited for company success. Instill company values on product quality and customer service. Once selected, employees should be intensely socialized on company culture — norms, systems, and procedures relevant to productivity, quality, and customer service.
   - Reinforce this socialization process through continuous training and education for consistent productivity and quality performance. Training is especially crucial due to changing technology and labor shortages. Training programs should be designed to provide extensive awareness of productivity and quality, each employee's role in the productivity and quality process and the importance of quality to company, quality technique, and the job skills to support the quality and productivity improvement.
   - Incorporate productivity and quality into performance appraisal and reward systems. Make sure that quality achievement — doing it right all the time — is an important element of every employee-manager's and non-manager's performance measurement and reward system.

- Encourage employee participation and involvement, despite the difficulties of implementation. Employees are a natural source of input for productivity and quality improvement. Every person from the CEO to the hourly employee needs to be involved in exploiting the limitless creativity of all people. Employee involvement can be achieved through informal directions, suggestion systems, quality circles, joint/labor-management committees, and other such devices.
- Utilize effective communication systems throughout the organization. Company goals, plans, and strategies can no longer be tightly held by top management since it is essential that all levels of the organization be well informed. The overall content of the message should reinforce the deep commitment of management. The message should create an awareness and understanding of the role of productivity and quality to employees and their companies. It should instill a deep desire to consistently apply these concerns to on-the-job matters.

4. *Productivity and quality are closely linked and are essential for gaining competitive advantage.* Though there are many ways to improve productivity, product quality is a significant means for improving productivity. Product and service quality reduces costs and improves productivity. Twenty-five to 30 percent of manufacturing cost — a substantial cost savings — accrue from reduced rework, scrap, and lower inspection, warranty, and product liability costs. Focus must be placed on value-added activities and elimination of wastes, such as unnecessary inventories, inspections, storage, handling, and so forth. Quality also affects a firm's sales and market share. Customers who prefer quality products are willing to pay more. Customer loyalty and the uniqueness associated with quality are difficult barriers for competing firms to surmount.

5. *Vendor quality programs are increasingly important to improving productivity and quality.* Material costs represent an increasing percentage of total costs relative to direct labor and overhead. This plus the growing use of outsourcing makes it important that companies pursue vendor quality programs such as joint statistical process control, communicating the importance of quality to vendors, joint product development, and tightening specifications.

6. *Productivity and quality standards and measures are preconditions for success.* Explicit productivity and quality standards should be established on the basis of reliable information. Productivity and quality information must be appraised in determining whether the company is doing well according to a historic and/or competitive comparison. Also, the source of the problems as well as opportunities for improvement must be determined through comprehensive appraisals. Establish customer-driven quality standards. These will enable a company to develop realistic productivity and quality goals and improvement programs. Once standards are set,

the next step is to maintain performance through proper measurement, appraisal, reporting, and corrective action.

7. *A variety of innovative technological and management programs have the potential for enhancing productivity and quality.* Programs for improving productivity and quality are apparent from measurement of current performance. New improvement programs may be necessary to meet company goals on productivity and quality.

Among the technological programs are Computer-Aided Design (CAD), robots, Material Requirement Planning (MRP) systems, electronic data interchange (EDI), process controls, Computer-Aided Inspection Testing and Process Design (CAI, CAT, and CAID), automated materials handling, computer controlled machinery (CCM), and automated data collection methods. Innovative management methods being used include JIT, and many ideas for increasing worker participation, improving quality, developing manufacturing strategies, integrating systems, restructuring supply networks, and training. Noteworthy among the manufacturing innovations for improving manufacturing processes are those developed by Shigeo Shingo on the single-minute exchange of die (SMED) concept, the Poka-yoke defect-prevention system, and the non-stock production techniques for eliminating inventories and other wastes.

These programs have been developed by quality experts such as W. Edwards Deming, Philip B. Crosby, Joseph Juran and others. The American Productivity Center, a privately funded non-profit organization dedicated to increasing productivity, assists companies in developing productivity improvement programs. Programs and techniques must be tailored to the problem and business situation. No single technique or program is best for all companies. Productivity and quality problems must be precisely defined and the attributes and limitations and different approaches must be recognized.

8. *Information and manufacturing technologies play a key role in enhancing productivity and quality.* These technologies include factory automation, computer integrated manufacturing, office information systems, flexible manufacturing, and artificial intelligence. Information technology and manufacturing must be given strategic considerations if they are to reach their full potential.

Excellence in manufacturing can be facilitated by using new technologies, positioning manufacturing strategically, and developing a long-range plan in which manufacturing plays a key role. Traditionally, investment in these manufacturing improvements has been made using conventional accounting methods. This fails to account for intangibles such as better quality, greater flexibility, faster time to market, quicker order processing, and higher customer satisfaction. For example, the use of flexible manufacturing enables factories to rapidly shift from one product to another, cuts lead time, and speeds their response time to customer needs. This drives down economies of scale and minimizes inventories.

9. *Recognize that all company activities have potential for improving productivity, product, and service quality.* Improvements in productivity and quality are realized through close cooperation between managers and employees, between departments, and between the company and its vendors. Remove barriers between functional specialists and create a climate for teamwork. Teamwork not only improves productivity and quality but increases the competitive position by shortening the time for product development and commercializing new innovations. Close cooperation and teamwork can be greatly facilitated by the integration of systems including manufacturing and functional systems.

10. *Initiatives aimed at continuously improving productivity and quality must* be managed for optimum results. Improvement must be planned, organized, monitored, controlled, and continuously revitalized. Continual incremental steps that improve quality and productivity offer better results than infrequent large efforts. For enduring results, productivity and quality improvements must be fully integrated into the total management of a company.

Taken together, these guidelines provide a framework for making productivity and quality improvement efforts successful. They are guidelines, not rigid rules. These guidelines have to be adapted to meet the unique situation of each company. Improvements require planning, effort, and resources, and will occur over time. Sustained and long-term success requires diligent action by all employees — managers and non-managers. Managers must recognize that quality and productivity improvement often require major changes in organizational philosophy, culture, and operating systems, changes which are difficult and which require patience, hard work, commitment, and discipline. However, consistent improvement in productivity and quality can provide powerful leverage to achieve both competitive advantage and profitability. This means providing products and services with a quality level that not only meets but exceeds customer expectations.

Bibliography

Abernathy, William J. *The Productivity Dilemma: Road Block to Innovation in the Automotive Industry.* Baltimore: Johns Hopkins University Press, 1978.

Abernathy, William J., B. Clark, and A.M. Kantrow. *Industrial Renaissance: Producing a Competitive Future for America.* New York: Basic Books, 1983.

Abernathy, William J., and Robert H. Hayes. "Managing Our Way to Economic Decline." *Harvard Business Review* (July/August 1980): 68-81.

Adam, E.E., Jr., J.C. Hershauer, and W.A. Ruch. *Productivity and Quality — Measurement as a Basis for Improvement.* Englewood Cliffs, N.J.: Prentice-Hall, 1981.

Adams, Harold W. "Solutions as Problems: The Case of Productivity." *Public Productivity Review* (September 1975): 36-43.

Adler, Paul S. "A Plant Productivity Measure for 'High-Tech' Manufacturing." *Interfaces* (November/December 1987): 75-85.

Allen, David, and Victor Levine. *Nurturing Advanced Technology Enterprises: Emerging Issues in State and Local Economic Development Policy.* Westport, Conn.: Praeger, 1986.

Alston, Jon P. "Three Principles of Japanese Management." *Personnel Journal* (September 1983): 758-63.

Alvesson, Mats. *Consensus, Control, Critique: Paradigms in Research on the Relationship Between Technology, Organization and Work.* London: Gower, 1987.

Anderson, John C., and Robert G. Schroeder. "Getting Results from Your MRP System." *Business Horizons* (May/June 1984): 57-64.

Anderson, John C., Roger G. Schroeder, and Gary D. Scudder. "White Collar Productivity Measurement." *Management Decision* (Winter 1986): 3-8.

Andrew, Charles G., and George A. Johnson. "The Crucial Importance of Production and Operations Management." *Academy of Management Review* (January 1962): 143-47.

Ardolini, C., and J. Hohenstein. "Measuring Productivity in the Federal Government." *Monthly Labor Review* (November 1974): 13-20.

Argote, Linda, Paul S. Goodman, and David Schkade. "The Human Side of Robotics: How Workers React to a Robot." *Sloan Management Review* (Spring 1983): 31-41.

Baig, Edward C. "America's Most Admired Corporations." *Fortune* (January 19, 1987): 18-31.

Baillie, Allan S. "The Deming Approach: Being Better Than the Best." *Advanced Management Journal* (Autumn 1986): 15-24.

Baily, Martin N., and Alok K. Chakrabarti. *Innovation and the Productivity Crisis.* Washington, D.C.: Brookings Institute, 1987.

Bain, David. *The Productivity Prescription: The Manager's Guide to Improving Productivity and Profits.* New York: McGraw-Hill, 1986.

Bakewell, K.G.B. *How to Find Out: Management and Productivity.* New York: Pergamon Press, 1970.

Bastone, Eric, and Stephen Gourlay. *Unions, Unemployment, & Innovation.* New York: Basil Blackwell, 1986.

Basu, A.P. *Reliability and Quality Control.* New York: Elsevier, 1986.

Baumgardner, Mary. "Productivity Improvement for Office Systems." *Journal of Systems Management* (August 1981): 12-15.

Bewley, W.W. "America's Productivity Decline: Fact or Fiction?" *Financial Executive* (April 1982): 31-35.

Bittinger, Raymond E. "Organization Value Analysis and Opportunity Review for Productivity Enhancement." *National Productivity Review* (Summer 1987): 250-56.

Blair, John D., and Carlton J. Whitehead. "Can Quality Circles Survive in the United States?" *Business Horizons* (September/October 1984): 17-23.

Blau, G., and M. Rosow. *Trends in Product Quality and Worker Attitude: Highlights of the Literature.* Studies in Productivity No. 3, Scarsdale, N.Y.: Work in America Institute, 1978.

Bloom, G.F. "Productivity: Weak Link in Our Economy." *Harvard Business Review* (January/February 1971): 4-14.

Bobbe, Richard A., and Robert H. Schaffer. "Productivity Improvement: Manage It or Bust It?" *Business Horizons* (March/April 1983): 62-69.

Bohlarder, G.W. "Implementing Quality-of-Work Programs." *MSU Business Topics* (Spring 1979): 33-40.

Botkin, James, et al. "The Innovators: Rediscovering America's Creative Energy." *Library Journal.* (January 1985): 83.

Bradford, David, and Allan Cohen. *Managing for Excellence.* New York: John Wiley, 1984.

Brief, Authur P., ed. *Research on Productivity: Multi-disciplinary Approach.* New York: Praeger, 1984.

Briskin, Lawrence E. "Productivity and Competitivity: Measures of Industrial Efficiency." *National Productivity Review* (Spring 1987): 177-79.

Britney, Robert R., et al. "A Comparison of International Productivity Centers." *National Productivity Review* (Winter 1986/1987): 71-76.

Brockner, Joel, and Ted Hess. "Self-Esteem and Task Performance in Quality Circles." *Academy of Management Journal* (September 1986): 617-23.

Buehler, V.M., and Y.K. Shetty, eds. *Proceedings: Managing Productivity Enhancement: Company Experiences.* Logan: College of Business, Utah State University, 1979.

_____ . *Productivity Improvement: Case Studies of Proven Practice.* New York: AMACOM, American Management Associations, 1981.

Buffa, Elwood S. "Making American Manufacturing Competitive." *California Management Review* (Spring 1984): 29-46.

_____ . *Meeting the Competitive Challenge: Manufacturing Strategy of U.S. Companies.* New York: Dow Jones-Irwin, 1984.

Buijs, J. "Strategic Planning and Product Innovation — Some Systematic Approaches." *Long Range Planning* (October 1979): 23-24.

Burch, E.E. "Productivity: Its Meaning and Measurement." *Atlanta Economic Review* (May/June 1974): 43-47.

Burck, C.G. "Working Smarter." *Fortune* (July 15, 1981): 68-73.

_____ . "What Happens When Workers Manage Themselves." *Fortune* (July 27, 1981): 62-65.

Burgelman, Robert, and Leonard R. Sayles. *Inside Corporate Innovation.* New York: The Free Press, 1985.

Burnham, D.C. *Productivity Improvement.* New York: Columbia University Press, 1973.

Bylinsky, Gene. "America's Best-Managed Factories." *Fortune* (May 28, 1984): 16-24.

Callon, Michel, et al. *Mapping the Dynamics of Science and Technology.* Dobb's Ferry, N.Y.: Sheridan House, 1986.

Capannella, J., and F.J. Corcoran. "Principles of Quality Costs." *Quality Progress* (April 1983): 17-21.

Caron, Paul F., and Stanley J. Haddock. "Developing a Quality Assurance Program." *Internal Auditor* (December 1986): 37-42.

Case, Kenneth E., and Lynn L. Jones. *Profit Through Quality and Quality Assurance Programs for Manufacturers.* Norcross, Ga.: American Institute of Industrial Engineers, 1978.

Chew, Bruce W. "No-Nonsense Guide to Measuring Productivity." *Harvard Business Review* (January/February 1988): 110-16.

Chinloy, Peter. *Labor Productivity.* Cambridge, Mass.: Ballinger, 1981.

Christopher, William F. *Productivity Measurement Handbook.* Cambridge, Mass.: Productivity Inc., 1983.

Clark, K.B. "Impact of Unionization on Productivity: A Case Study." *Industrial & Labor Relation Review* (July 1980): 451-69.

Cole, Robert E. *Work, Mobility, and Participation: A Comparative Study of American and Japanese Industry.* Berkeley: University of California, 1979.

———. "Will Quality Control Circles Work in the U.S.?" *Quality Progress* (July 1980): 30-33.

———. "Learning from the Japanese: Prospects and Pitfalls." *Management Review* (September 1980): 22-28.

———. "The Japanese Lesson in Quality." *Technology Review* (July 1981): 29-34.

Cole, Robert E., and D.S. Tachiki. "Forging Institutional Links: Making Quality Circles Work in the U.S." *National Productivity Review* (Autumn 1984): 417-29.

Collier, D.A. "The Service Sector Revolution: The Automation of Services." *Long Range Planning* (December 1983): 10-20.

Committee for Economic Development. *Productivity Policy: Key to the Nation's Economic Future.* New York: Committee for Economic Development, 1983.

Connell, G.W. "Quality at the Source: The First Step in Just-in-Time Production." *Quality Progress* (November 1984): 44-45.

Cook, M.H. "Quality Circles — They Really Work, But." *Training and Development Journal* (January 1982): 4-6.

Corn, Joseph J. *Imagining Tomorrow: History, Technology, and the American Future.* Cambridge, Mass.: MIT Press, 1986.

Cosgrove, Charles V. "How to Report Productivity: Linking Measurements to Bottom-Line Financial Results." *National Productivity Review* (Winter 1986/1987): 63-70.

Craig, C.E., and R. Clark Harris. "Total Productivity Measurement at the Firm Level." *Sloan Management Review* (Spring 1973): 13-29.

Crandall, N.F., and L.M. Wooton. "Developmental Strategies of Organizational Productivity." *California Management Review* (Winter 1978): 37-46.

Crosby, Philip B. *Quality Is Free: The Art of Making Quality Certain.* New York: New American Library, 1980.

———. *Quality Without Tears: The Art of Hassle-Free Management.* New York: McGraw-Hill, 1984.

Crystal, G.S. "Motivating for the Future: The Long-Term Incentive Plan." *Financial Executive* (October 1971): 48-50.

Cummings, L.L. "Strategies for Improving Human Productivity." *The Personnel Administrator* (June 1975): 40-44.

Cummings, Thomas G., and Edmond S. Molloy. *Improving Productivity and the Quality of Work Life.* New York: Praeger, 1977.

Dale, B.G., and J. Lees. "Quality Circles: From Introduction To Integration." *Long Range Planning* (February 1987): 78-84.

Davis, L., and A. Chern, eds. *The Quality of Working Life*. New York: The Free Press, 1975.

Davis, L.E., and James C. Taylor, eds. *Design of Jobs*. Santa Monica, Calif.: Goodyear Publishing, 1979.

Deal, Terrence E., and Allan A. Kennedy. *Corporate Cultures: The Rites and Rituals of Corporate Life*. Reading, Mass.: Addison-Wesley, 1982.

_____. "Culture: A New Look Through Old Lenses." *Journal of Applied Behavioral Science* 19 (1983): 498-505.

Dearden, J. "How To Make Incentive Plans Work" *Harvard Business Review* (July/August 1972): 117-24.

Delbecq, Andre L., and Peter K. Mills. "Managerial Practices that Enhance Innovation." *Organizational Dynamics* (Summer 1985): 24-34.

Deming, W. Edwards. "Improvement of Quality and Productivity Through Action Management." *National Productivity Review* (Winter 1981-1982): 12-22.

_____. *Quality, Productivity, and Competitive Position*. Cambridge: MIT Press, 1982.

_____. *Out of the Crisis* Cambridge: Massachusetts Institute of Technology Center for Advanced Engineering Study, 1986.

Dermer, Jerry. *Competitiveness Through Technology: What Business Needs From Government*. Lexington, Mass.: Lexington Books, 1986.

Devanna, M.A., C. Fombrun, and N. Tichy. "Human Resource Management: A Strategic Approach." *Organizational Dynamics* (Winter 1981): 51-67.

Dewar, C. *The Quality Circle Handbook*. Red Bluff, Calif.: Quality Circle Institute, 1980.

Drucker, Peter F. "Entrepreneurial Strategies." *California Management Review* (Winter 1985): 9-25.

_____. "The Discipline of Innovation." *Harvard Business Review* (May/June 1985): 67-72.

_____. *Innovation and Entrepreneurship: Practice and Principles*. New York: Harper and Row, 1985.

Edwards, S.A., and M.W. McCarrey. "Measuring Performance of Researchers." *Research Management* (January 1973): 34-41.

Eilon, S., B. Gold, and J. Soesan. *Applied Productivity Analysis for Industry*. New York: Pergamon Press, 1976.

Eldrige, Lawrence A., and Charles A. Aubrey, II. "Stressing Quality — The Path to Productivity." *Magazine of Bank Administration* (June 1983): 20-24.

Fabricant, Solomon. *A Primer on Productivity*. New York: Random House, 1971.

Feigenbaum, A.V. *Quality Control*. New York: McGraw-Hill, 1951.

_____. *Total Quality Control: Engineering and Management*. New York: McGraw-Hill, 1961.

Fein, Mitchell. *Rational Approaches to Raising Productivity.* Norcross, Ga.: American Institute of Industrial Engineers, 1974.

———— . "Improving Productivity by Improving Productivity Sharing." *The Conference Board Record* (July 1976): 44-49.

Ferris, G.R., and J.A. Wagner, III. "Quality Circles in the United States: A Conceptual Reevaluation." *Journal of Applied Behavioral Science* 21 (1985): 155-67.

Fitch, Thomas P. "Putting the Emphasis on Quality." *United States Banker* (May 1984): 28-32.

Fitzgerald, L., and J. Murphy. *Installing Quality Circles: A Strategy Approach.* San Diego: University Associates, 1982.

Flynn, Patricia M. *Technological Change: Production Life Cycles & Human Resource Planning.* Cambridge, Mass.: Ballinger, 1987.

Follini, J.R. "Production Certifies the Quality of Its Work." *Industrial Engineering* (November 1971): 10-17.

Fombrun, C.J., Noel M. Tichy, and Mary Anne Devanne. *Strategic Human Resource Management.* New York: John Wiley, 1984.

Foote, George H. "Performance Shares Revitalize Executive Stock Plans." *Harvard Business Review* (November/December 1973): 121-30.

Ford, Robert N. "Job Enrichment Lessons from AT&T." *Harvard Business Review* (January/February 1973): 96-106.

Forrester, J.W. "Innovation and the Economic Long Wave." *Management Review* (June 1979): 16-24.

Foulkes, Fred K., and Jeffrey L. Hirsch. "People Make Robots Work." *Harvard Business Review* (January/February 1984): 94-102.

Freeman, Christopher. *Design, Innovation & Long Cycles in Economic Development.* New York: St. Martin's Press, 1986.

Frost, Carl F., John H. Wakely, and Robert A. Ruh. *The Scanlon Plan for Organization Development: Identity, Participation, and Equity.* East Lansing: Michigan State University Press, 1974.

Fuchs, Victor R., ed. *Production and Productivity in the Service Industries.* New York: Columbia University Press, 1969.

Gadon, Herman. "Making Sense of Quality of Work Life Programs." *Business Horizons* (January/February 1984): 42-44.

Gainsburgh, Martin R. "Productivity, Inflation, and Economic Growth." *Michigan Business Review* (January 1971): 15-21.

Gale, Bradley T. "Can More Capital Buy Higher Productivity?" *Harvard Business Review* (July/August 1980): 78-86.

Garvin, David A. "Quality on the Line." *Harvard Business Review* September/October 1983): 65-75.

———— . "What Does 'Product Quality' Really Mean?" *Sloan Management Review* (Fall 1984): 25-43.

———— . "Quality Problems, Policies, and Attitudes in the United States and Japan: An Exploratory Study." *Academy of Management Journal* (December 1986): 653-73.

_____ . *Managing Quality*. New York: The Free Press, 1987.

_____ . "Competing on the Eight Dimensions of Quality." *Harvard Business Review* (November/December 1987): 101-9.

_____ . *Managing Quality: The Strategic and Competitive Edge* New York: Collier Macmillan, 1988.

Geare, A.J. "Productivity from Scanlon-Type Plans." *Academy of Management Review* (July 1976): 99-107.

Gerstein, Mark S. *The Technology Connection*. Reading, Mass.: Addison-Wesley, 1987.

Gilder, George. *The Spirit of Enterprise*. New York: Simon & Schuster, 1984.

Gitlow, Howard S., and Shelly J. Gitlow. *The Deming Guide to Quality and Competitive Position*. Englewood Cliffs, N.J.: Prentice-Hall, 1987.

Gitlow, Howard S., and Paul T. Herts. "Product Defects and Productivity." *Harvard Business Review* (September/October 1983): 131-41.

Glaser, Edward M. *Productivity Gains Through Worklife Improvement*. New York: Harcourt Brace Jovanovich, 1976.

_____ . "Productivity Gains Through Worklife Improvement." *Personnel* (January 1980): 71-77.

Gold, Bela. "CAM Sets New Rules for Production." *Harvard Business Review* (November/December 1982): 88-94.

Goldberg, Joel A. *A Manager's Guide to Productivity Improvement*. New York: Praeger, 1986.

_____ . "New Technology and Human-Resource Productivity: An Uneasy Alliance." *National Productivity Review* (Winter 1987/1988): 54-60.

Gray, D.O., and T. Solomon. *Technological Innovation: Strategies for a New Partnership*. New York: Elsevier, 1986.

Grayson, C. Jackson, Jr. "Productivity's Impact on Our Economic Future." *The Personnel Administrator* (June 1975): 20-24.

Greenberg, Leon. *A Practical Guide to Productivity Measurement*. Rockville, Md.: BNA Book, 1973.

Griffith, Gary. *Quality Technician's Handbook*. New York: Wiley, 1986.

Gritzmacher, Karen J. "Visual Control Tools: A Hidden Productivity Factor?" *National Productivity Review* (Autumn 1987): 314-23.

Grootings, Peter. *Technology and Work: East West Comparisons*. Wolfeboro, N.H.: Longwood, 1986.

Grove, Andrew S. *High Output Management*. New York: Random House, 1983.

Gryna, Frank M., Jr. *Quality Circles: A Team Approach to Problem Solving*. New York: AMACOM, American Management Association, 1981.

Guaspari, John. *Theory Why: In Which the Boss Solves the Riddle of Quality*. New York: AMACOM, 1986.

_____ . "The Role of Human Resources in 'Selling' Quality Improvement to Employees." *Management Review* (March 1987): 20-25.

Hall, Peter. *Technology, Innovation and Economic Policy.* New York: St. Martin's, 1986.

Hallett, J.J. "Productivity and Quality: The Never Ending Quest." *Personnel Administrator* (October 1986): 22-27.

Hanley, J. "Our Experience with Quality Circles." *Quality Progress* (February 1980): 22-24.

Harrington, James H. *The Improvement Process: How America's Leading Companies Improve Quality.* New York: McGraw-Hill, 1987.

Harrison, Jared F. "Why Won't They Do What I Want Them to Do?" *Improving Performance and Productivity.* Reading, Mass.: Addison-Wesley, 1978.

Hayes, Glenn E. "Quality and Productivity — The Education Gap." *Quality* (October 1982): 50-51.

Hayes, Robert H. "Why Japanese Factories Work." *Harvard Business Review* (July/August 1981): 57-66.

Hayes, Robert H., and Kim B. Clark. "Why Some Factories Are More Productive than Others." *Harvard Business Review* (September/October 1986): 66-74.

Hayes, Robert H., and R.W. Schmenner. "How Should You Organize for Manufacturing?" *Harvard Business Review* (January/February 1978): 105-18.

Hayes, Robert H., and Steven C. Wheelwright. "Link Manufacturing Process and Product Life Cycles." *Harvard Business Review* (January/February 1979): 133-40.

_____ . *Restoring Our Competitive Edge: Competing Through Manufacturing.* New York: John Wiley, 1984.

Heaton, Herbert. *Productivity in Service Organization.* New York: McGraw-Hill, 1977.

Hershauer, J.C., and W.A. Ruch. "A Worker Productivity Model and Its Use at Lincoln Electric." *Interfaces* (May 1978): 80-89.

Hershfield, David C. "Barriers to Increased Labor Productivity." *The Conference Board Record* (July 1976): 38-41.

Hickey, James J. *Employee Productivity: How to Improve and Measure Your Company's Performance.* Stratford, Conn.: Institute for the Advancement of Scientific Management and Control, 1974.

Highlander, Cyrus C. "Six Steps to Unit Productivity Improvement: A Corporatewide Effort at Upjohn." *National Productivity Review* (Winter 1986/1987): 20-27.

Hill, Chris T., and James Utterback, eds. *Technological Innovation for a Dynamic Economy.* New York: Pergamon Press, 1979.

Hinrichs, John R. *Practical Management for Productivity.* New York: Van Nostrand Reinhold, 1978.

_____ . "Avoid the 'Quick Fix' Approach to Productivity Problems." *Personnel Administrator* (July 1983): 39-43.

Hise, Richard T., and Stanley H. Kratchman. "Developing and Managing a 20-80 Program." *Business Horizons* (September/October 1987): 66-73.

Holzer, Marc, ed. *Productivity in Public Organizations.* New York: Kennikat, 1976.

Hornbruch, F.W., Jr. *Raising Productivity.* New York: McGraw-Hill, 1977.

Horwitch, M. *Technology in the Modern Corporation: A Strategic Perspective.* New York: Pergamon, 1986.

Hostage, G.M. "Quality Control in a Service Business." *Harvard Business Review* (September/October 1975) 98-118.

Hutchins, Dave. "Quality Is Everybody's Business." *Management Decision* (Winter 1986): 3-7.

Hyer, N.L., and V. Wennerlov. "Group Technology and Productivity." *Harvard Business Review* (July/August 1984): 140-49.

Hykes, Dennis, and Colin Herskey. "Cultivating Entrepreneurism in Smokestack Industries." *Management Review* (March 1985): 38.

Iacocca, Lee, and William Novak. *Iacocca: An Autobiography.* New York: Bantam Books, 1984.

Ingle, Sud. *Quality Circles Master Guide: Increasing Productivity with People Power.* Englewood Cliffs, N.J.: Prentice-Hall, 1982.

Ishikawa, Kaoru. *Guide to Quality Control.* Tokyo: Asian Productivity Organization, 1972.

Jacobs, Herman S., with Katherine Jillson. *Executive Productivity.* New York: American Management Associations, 1974.

Jacobson, Robert, and David A. Aaker. "The Strategic Role of Product Quality." *Journal of Marketing* (October 1987): 31-44.

Jehing, J.J. "Profit Sharing, Motivation, and Productivity." *Personnel Administration* (March/April 1970): 17-21.

Judson, A.S. "New Strategies to Improve Productivity." *Technology Review* (July/August 1976): 61-67.

_____ . "The Awkward Truth About Productivity." *Harvard Business Review* (September/October 1982): 93-97.

Juran, Joseph M. *Quality Control Handbook.* New York: McGraw-Hill, 1974.

_____ . "Japanese and Western Quality: A Contrast in Methods and Results." *Management Review* (November 1978): 20-28, 39-45.

_____ . "Japanese and Western Quality — A Contrast." *Quality Progress* (December 1978): 10-17.

_____ . "Product Quality — A Prescription for the West." *Management Review* (June 1981): 8-14.

Kanter, Rosabeth Moss. *The Change Master: How People and Companies Succeed Through Innovation in the New Corporate Era.* New York: Simon & Schuster, 1983.

_____ . "Frontiers for Strategic Human Resource Planning and Management." *Human Resource Management* (Spring/Summer 1983): 9-21.

Katzell, M.E. *Productivity: The Measure and the Myth.* New York: AMACOM, American Management Association, 1975.

Kelly, Charles M., and James M. Norman. "The Fusion Process for Productivity Improvement." *National Productivity Review* (Spring 1983): 164-72.

Kendrick, John W. *Understanding Productivity: An Introduction to the Dynamics of Productivity Change.* Baltimore: Johns Hopkins University Press, 1978.

_____ . *International Comparisons of Productivity and Causes of the Slowdown.* Cambridge, Mass.: Ballinger, 1984.

_____ . *Improving Company Productivity: Handbook with Case Studies.* Baltimore: Johns Hopkins University Press, 1986.

Kendrick, John W., and Daniel Creamer. *Measuring Company Productivity* rev. ed. New York: Conference Board, 1975.

Kendrick, John W., and E.S. Grossman. *Productivity in the United States: Trends and Cycles.* Baltimore: Johns Hopkins University Press, 1980.

King, Robert. "Listening to the Voice of the Customer: Using the Quality Function Deployment System." *National Productivity Review* (Summer 1987): 277-81.

Kohl, R., et al. "Can America Meet Foreign Competition? A Treatise on Productivity." *Journal of Small Business Management* (January 1982): 56-58.

Kolmin, F.W. "Measuring Productivity and Efficiency." *Management Accounting* (November 1973): 22-24.

Konz, S. "Quality Circles: Japanese Success Story." *Industrial Engineering* (October 1979): 24-37.

Kreitner, R. "Identifying and Managing the Basics of Individual Productivity." *Arizona Business* (May 1976): 3-8.

Krigline, Alan G., and Jonathan S. Rakich. "Productivity Improvement Through Better Problem Solving by Supervisors." *National Productivity Review* (Winter 1987/1988): 61-70.

Kwan, Ik-Whan, and John W. Hamilton. "Measuring Technology: A Case Study of Office Automation." *Journal of Systems Management* (November 1987): 19-23.

Landau, Ralph, and Dale Jorgenson. *Technology and Economic Policy.* Cambridge, Mass.: Ballinger, 1986.

Langdon, Richard, and Roy Rothwell. *Design and Innovation: Policy and Management.* New York: St. Martin's, 1986.

Langevin, Roger G. *Quality Control in the Service Industries.* New York: AMACOM, American Management Association, 1977.

Lawler, Edward E., III. "Human Resource Productivity in the 80s." *New Management* (Spring 1983): 46-49.

Lawler, Edward E., III, and John A. Drexler, Jr. *The Corporate Entrepreneur.* Los Angeles: Center for Effective Organizations, University of Southern California, Graduate School of Business, 1980.

Lawler, Edward E., III, and Gerald E. Ledford, Jr. "Productivity and Quality of Work Life." *National Productivity Review* (Winter 1981/ 1982): 23-36.

Lawler, Edward E., III, and S.A. Mohrman. "Quality Circles After the Fad." *Harvard Business Review* (January/ February 1985): 65-71.

Lawrence, Colin, and Robert Shay. *Technological Innovation, Regulation, and the Monetary Economy.* Cambridge, Mass.: Ballinger, 1986.

Lefton, Robert E., V.R. Bussotta, and Manuel Sherberg. *Improving Productivity Through People Skills.* Cambridge, Mass.: Ballinger, 1981.

Lele, Milind M., and Uday S. Karmarker. "Good Product Support Is Smart Marketing." *Harvard Business Review* (November/December 1983): 124-31.

Leonard, Frank S., and W. Earl Sasser. "The Incline of Quality." *Harvard Business Review* (September/October 1982): 163-71.

Lesko, Matthew. *Lesko's New Tech Sourcebook.* New York: Harper and Row, 1986.

Levering, Robert, Milton Moskowitz, and Michail Katz. *The 100 Best Companies to Work for in America.* Reading, Mass.: Addison-Wesley, 1984.

Limpercht, Joseph A., and Robert H. Hayes. "Germany's World-Class Manufacturers." *Harvard Business Review* (November/December 1982): 137-45.

Link, Albert N, and Gregory Tassey. *Strategies for Technology-Based Competition: Meeting the New Global Challenge.* Lexington, Mass.: Lexington Books, 1987.

Lokiec, Mitchell. *Productivity and Incentives.* Columbia, S.C.: Bobbins Publications, 1977.

Lubar, Robert. "Rediscovering the Factory." *Fortune* (July 13, 1981): 52-64.

Lubben, Richard T. *Just-In-Time Manufacturing: An Aggressive Manufacturing Strategy.* New York: McGraw-Hill, 1988.

Luke, High D. *Automation for Productivity.* Huntington, N.Y.: Krieger, 1972.

MacKinnon, Neil. "Launching a Drive for Quality Excellence." *Quality Progress* (May 1985): 46-50.

Maidique, M.A. "Entrepreneurs, Champions, and Technological Innovation." *Sloan Management Review* (Winter 1980): 59-76.

Main, Jeremy. "Ford's Drive for Quality." *Fortune* (April 18, 1983): 62-70.

Maital, Shlomo, and Noah M. Meltz. *Lagging Productivity Growth.* Cambridge, Mass.: Ballinger, 1980.

Mali, Paul. *Improving Total Productivity.* New York: John Wiley, 1978.

Mammone, J.L. "Productivity Measurement: A Conceptual Overview." *Management Accounting* (May 1980): 36-42.

Martin, James. *Technology's Crucible: An Exploration of the Explosive Impact of Technology on Society during the Next Four Decades.* New York: Prentice-Hall, 1986.

McBryde, Vernon E. "In Today's Market, Quality is Best Focal Point for Upper Management." *Industrial Engineering* (July 1986): 51-56.

McConnell, C. "Why Is U.S. Productivity Slowing Down?" *Harvard Business Review* (March/April 1984): 102-11.

Mehl, Wayne. "Strategic Management of Operations: A Top Management Perspective." *Operations Management Review* (Fall 1983): 29-36.

Mensch, Gerhard O. *Stalemate in Technology.* Cambridge, Mass.: Ballinger, 1979.

Metzger, Bert L. *Increasing Productivity Through Sharing.* Evanston, Ill.: Profit Sharing Research Foundation, 1980.

Miles, Raymond E., and Charles C. Snow. "Designing Strategic Human Resources Systems." *Organizational Dynamics* (Summer 1984): 36-52.

Miller, Donald B. "How to Improve the Performance and Productivity of the Knowledge Workers." *Organizational Dynamics* (Winter 1977): 62-80.

Mills, Stephen, and Roger William. *Public Acceptance of New Technologies.* New York: The Free Press, 1986.

Mitroff, Ian I. *Business Not As Usual: Rethinking Our Individual Strategies for Global Competition.* San Francisco: Jossey-Bass Publishers, 1987.

Monden, Y. "Adaptable Kanban System Helps Toyota Maintain Production." *Industrial Engineering* (May 1981): 29-46.

Mooney, M. *Productivity Management.* Research Bulletin No. 127. New York: Conference Board, 1982.

Mudel, M.E., ed. *Productivity: A Series for Industrial Engineers.* Norcross, Ga.: American Institute for Industrial Engineers, 1977.

Munchus, G., III. "Employer-Employee Based Quality Circles in Japan: Human Resource Policy Implications for American Firms." *Academy of Management Review* 2 (April 1983): 255-61.

Murphy, John W., and John T. Pardeck. *Technology and Human Productivity: Challenges for the Future.* Westport, Conn.: Greenwood, 1986.

Naisbitt, John. *Megatrends: Ten New Directions Transforming Our Lives.* New York: Warner, 1982.

———. *Reinventing the Corporation* New York: Warner, 1985.

Nassr, M.A. "Productivity Growth Through Work Measurement." *Defense Management Journal* (April 1977): 16-20.

National Center for Productivity and Quality of Working Life. *A Plant-Wide Productivity Plan in Action: Three Years of Experience with the Scalon Plan.* Washington, D.C.: 1975.

———. *Improving Productivity: A Description of Select Company Programs, Series 1.* Washington, D.C.: December 1975.

———. *Improving Productivity Through Industry and Company Measurement.* Washington, D.C.: October 1976.

National Commission on Productivity and Work Quality. *A National Policy for Productivity Improvement.* Washington, D.C.: 1975.

National Research Council Staff. *Scientific Interfaces and Technological Applications.* Washington, D.C.: National Academy Press, 1986.

Naumann, A. "The Importance of Productivity." *Quality Progress* (June 1980): 18-26.

Ouchi, William. *Theory Z: How American Business Can Meet the Japanese Challenge.* Reading, Mass.: Addison-Wesley, 1981.

_____ . *The M-Form Society.* Reading, Mass.: Addison-Wesley, 1984.

Packer, Michael B. "Measuring the Intangible in Productivity." *Technology Review* (February/March 1983): 48-57.

Padgett, T.C. "Getting Supervisory Help in Improving Productivity." *Training and Development Journal* (January 1987): 48-50.

Papacosta, Pangratios. *The Splendid Voyage: An Introduction to New Sciences and Technologies.* Englewood Cliffs, N.J.: Prentice-Hall, 1986.

Pascale, Richard Tanner, and Anthony G. Athos. *The Art of Japanese Management: Applications for American Executives.* New York: Simon & Schuster, 1981.

Peeples, Donald E. "Measuring for Productivity." *Datamation* (May 1978): 222-28.

Peloquin, J.J. "Training: The Key to Productivity." *Training and Development Journal* (February 1980): 49-52.

Peters, Thomas J., and Nancy Austin. *A Passion for Excellence.* New York: Random House, 1985.

Peters, Thomas J., and Robert H. Waterman, Jr. *In Search of Excellence: Lessons from America's Best-Run Companies.* New York: Harper and Row, 1982.

Pierre, Andrew J. *The Technology Gap.* New York: New York University Press, 1986.

Pinchot, Gifford, III. *Intrapreneuring.* New York: Harper and Row, 1985.

_____ . "Innovation Through Intrapreneuring." *Research Management* (March/April 1987): 14-19.

Pipp, Frank J. "Management Commitment to Quality: Xerox Corp." *Quality Progress* (August 1983): 12-17.

Pitt, Hy. "A Modern Strategy for Process Improvement." *Quality Progress* (May 1985): 22-28.

Porter, Michael E. *Competitive Strategy.* New York: The Free Press, 1980.

Quinn, James Brian. "Technological Innovation, Entrepreneurship, and Strategy." *Sloan Management Review* (Spring 1979): 19-30.

Ramquist, Judith. "Labor-Management Cooperation: The Scanlon Plan at Work." *Sloan Management Review* (Spring 1982): 49-55.

Randall, R. "Job Enrichment Savings at Travelers." *Management Accounting* (January 1973): 68-72.

Ray, G.F. "Innovation as the Source of Long Term Economic Growth." *Long Range Planning* (April 1980): 9-19.

Reddy, Jack, and Abe Berger. "Three Essentials of Product Quality." *Harvard Business Review* (July/August 1983): 153-59.

Rees, A. "Improving the Concepts and Techniques of Productivity Measurement." *Monthly Labor Review* (September 1979): 23-27.

Regan, John F. *Even More Productivity: Expanding Effectiveness & Efficiency in Plant.* Philadelphia: Swansea Press, 1987.

Reich, Robert B. *The New American Frontier.* New York: Times Books, 1983.

_____ . "The Next American Frontier." *The Atlantic Monthly* (March 1983) 43-58.

_____ . "Entrepreneurship Reconsidered: The Team as a Hero." *Harvard Business Review* (May/June 1987): 77-83.

Richardson, John H. "Manpower and Material — Overlooked Elements of Productivity." *Production Engineering* (August 1983): 30-31.

Roberts, Edward B., "Generating Effective Corporate Innovation." *Technology Review* (October/November): 1977.

_____ . *Generating Technological Innovation.* New York: Oxford University Press, 1987.

Rockart, John F. "An Approach to Productivity in Two Knowledge-Based Industries." *Sloan Management Review* (Fall 1973): 23-33.

Rogers, F.G. "Buck." *The IBM Way.* New York: Harper and Row, 1986.

Rolland, I., and R. Janson. "Total Involvement as a Productivity Strategy." *California Management Review* (Winter 1981): 40-48.

Ross, Joel E. *Productivity, People and Profits.* Reston, Va.: Reston Publishing, 1981.

Ross, Joel E., and Lawrence A. Klatt. "Quality: The Competitive Edge." *Management Decision* (Winter 1986): 12-17.

Ross, Joel E., and William C. Ross. *Japanese Quality Circles and Productivity.* Reston, Va.: Reston Publishing, 1982.

Ross, Joel E., and Y.K. Shetty. "Making Quality a Fundamental Part of Strategy." *Long Range Planning* (February 1985): 53-58.

Ross, R.L., and G.M. Jones. "Approach to Increased Productivity: The Scanlon Plan." *Financial Executive* (February 1972): 23-29.

Ross, Timothy L., and Denis Collins. "Employee Involvement and the Perils of Democracy: Are Management's Fears Warranted?" *National Productivity Review* (Autumn 1987): 348-59.

Roy, Robin, and David Wield. *Product Design and Technological Innovation.* Philadelphia: Taylor and Francis, 1986.

Ruch, William A., E.E. Adam, Jr., and J.C. Herschauer. "Developing Quality Measures for Bank Operations." *Bank Administration* (July 1979): 47-52.

Rumberger, Russell, and Gerald Burke. *The Impact of Technology on Work and Education.* Philadelphia: Taylor and Francis, 1986.

Rutigliano, Anthony J. "An Interview with Peter Drucker: Managing the New." *Management Review* (January 1986): 38-42.

Ryan, John. "The Productivity/Quality Connection — Plugging in at Westinghouse Electric." *Quality Progress* (December 1983): 26-29.

Schaffer, R.H. "Productivity Improvement Strategy: Make Success the Building Block." *Management Review* (August 1981): 46-52.

Schainblatt, Alfred H. "How Companies Measure the Productivity of Engineers and Scientists." *Research Management* (May 1982): 10-18.

Schlesinger, Leonard A., and Barry Oshry. "Quality of Work Life and the Manager: Muddle in the Middle." *Organizational Dynamics* (Summer 1984): 4-19.

Schmenner, Roger W. "Every Factory Has a Life Cycle." *Harvard Business Review* (March/April 1984): 121-27.

Schonberger, Richard J. *Japanese Manufacturing Techniques: Nine Hidden Lessons in Simplicity.* New York: The Free Press, 1982.

_____. "Just-in-Time Production: The Quality Dividend." *Quality Progress* (October 1984): 22-24.

_____. *World Class Manufacturing.* New York: The Free Press, 1986.

Schonberger, Richard J., and James P. Gilbert. "Just-in-Time Purchasing: A Challenge for U.S. Industry." *California Management Review* (Fall 1983): 54-68.

Scott, Bruce R. "Competitiveness: 23 Leaders Speak Out." *Harvard Business Review* (July/August 1987): 106-123.

Sepehri, Mehran, ed. *Quest for Quality: Managing the Total System.* Technology Park, Atlanta: Industrial Engineering and Management Press, 1987.

Shaw, Eric, and Joel E. Ross. "Improving the Productivity of Service Organizations." *Industrial Management* (September/October 1987): 21-24.

Shaw, John C. *The Quality-Productivity Connection in Service Sector Management.* New York: Van Nostrand Reinhold, 1978.

Shaw, John C., and Ram Capoor. "Quality and Productivity: Mutually Exclusive or Interdependent in Service Organizations?" *Management Review* (March 1979): 25-28, 37-39.

Sherman, George. "The Scanlon Concept: Its Capabilities for Productivity Improvement." *The Personnel Administrator* (July 1976): 17-20.

Sherman, H.D. "Improving the Productivity of Service Businesses." *Sloan Management Review* (Spring 1984): 11-23.

Sherman, Stratford P. "Eight Big Masters of Innovation." *Fortune* (October 15, 1984): 66-84.

Shetty, Y.K. "Key Elements of Productivity Improvement Programs." *Business Horizons* (March/April 1982): 15-22.

_____. "Management's Role in Declining Productivity." *California Management Review* (Fall 1982): 33-47.

_____. "Managerial Strategies for Improving Productivity." *Industrial Management* (November/December 1984): 24-28.

_____ . "Corporate Responses to the Productivity Challenge." *National Productivity Review* (Winter 1984-1985): 7-14.

_____ . "Quality, Productivity, and Profit Performance: Learning from Research and Practice." *National Productivity Review* (Spring 1986): 166-73.

_____ . "Product Quality and Competitive Strategy." *Business Horizons* (May/June 1987): 46-52.

Shetty, Y.K., and Joe Barrett. *Productivity: A Resource Guide*. Roy, Utah: Barrett Management Services, 1981.

Shetty, Y.K., and Vernon M. Buehler, eds. *Quality and Productivity Improvements: U.S. and Foreign Companies' Experiences*. Chicago: Manufacturing Productivity Center, 1983.

_____ . eds. *Productivity and Quality Through People: Practices of Well-Managed Companies*. Westport, Conn.: Quorum Books, 1985.

_____ . *Quality, Productivity and Innovation*. New York: Elsevier, 1987.

_____ . *Productivity and Quality Through Science and Technology* New York: Quorum Books, 1988.

Shetty, Y.K., and Joel E. Ross. "Quality and Its Management in Service Businesses." *Industrial Management* (November/December 1985): 7-12.

Shingo, Shigeo. *Non-Stock Production: The Shingo System for Continuous Improvement*. Cambridge, MA: Productivity Press, 1988.

_____ . *A Revolution in Manufacturing: The SMED System*. Cambridge, MA: Productivity Press, 1985.

_____ . *Zero Quality Control: Inspection and the Poka-Yoke System*. Cambridge, MA: Productivity Press, 1986.

_____ . *The Sayings of Shigeo Shingo: Key Strategies for Plant Improvement*. Cambridge, MA: Productivity Press, 1987.

_____ . *Study of the Toyota Production System from an IE Viewpoint (Revised)*. Cambridge, MA: Productivity Press, 1989.

Sibson, Robert E. *Increasing Employee Productivity*. New York: American Management Association, 1976.

Siegel, Irving H. *Company Productivity: Measurement for Improvement*. Kalamazoo, Mich.: W.E. Upjohn Institute for Employment Research, 1980.

Sinha, Madhav H., and W.O. Willborn. *Essentials of Quality Assurance Management*. New York: John Wiley, 1986.

Skinner, W. "The Productivity Paradox." *McKinsey Quarterly* (Winter 1987): 36-45.

Smith, Martin R. "Improving Product Quality in American Industry." *Academy of Management Executive* (August 1987): 243-45.

Spenser, Lyle. *Calculating Human Resource Costs Benefits: Cutting Cost and Improving Productivity*. New York: Wiley, 1986.

Statistical Quality Control Handbook, 2d ed. Indianapolis: AT&T Technologies, 1956.

Stebbing, Lionel. *Quality Assurance: The Route to Efficiency & Competitiveness.* New York: Halsted Press, 1986.

Stenkerd, Martin F. *Productivity by Choice: The 20-1 Principle.* New York: John Wiley, 1986.

Stevenson, H.H., and D.E. Gumpert. "The Heart of Entrepreneurship." *Harvard Business Review* (March/April 1985): 85-94.

Stewart, William T. "A Yardstick for Measuring Productivity." *Industrial Engineering* (February 1978): 34-37.

Strebel, P. "Organizing for Innovation Over an Industry Cycle." *Strategic Management Journal* (March/April 1987): 117-24.

Strong, E.P. *Increasing Office Productivity: A Seven-Step Program.* New York: McGraw-Hill, 1962.

Struthers, J.E. "Why Can't We Do What Japan Does?" *Canadian Business Review* (Summer 1981): 24-26.

Swartz, G., and V. Constock. "One Firm's Experience with Quality Circles." *Quality Progress* (September 1979): 14-16.

Sylwester, David L. "Statistical Techniques to Improve Quality and Production in Non-Manufacturing Operations." *Survey of Business* (Spring 1984): 11-17.

Takeuchi, Hirotaka. "Productivity: Learning from the Japanese." *California Management Review* (Summer 1981): 5-19.

Takeuchi, Hirotaka, and John A. Quelch. "Quality Is More Than Making a Product." *Harvard Business Review* (July/August 1983): 139-45.

Tatum, Toby, and Rick Page. "Labor Productivity's Relationship to the Cost of Labor and Profitability in the Restaurant Business." *National Productivity Review* (Winter 1987/1988): 28-33.

Taylor, B.W., and K.R. Davis. "Corporate Productivity: Getting It All Together." *Industrial Engineering* (March 1977): 30-36.

Teece, David J. *Strategy and Organization for Industrial Innovation and Renewal.* Cambridge, Mass.: Ballinger, 1987.

Thompson, Harry, and Michael Paris. "The Changing Face of Manufacturing Technology." *The Journal of Business Strategy* (Summer 1982): 45-52.

Thompson, Phillip C. *Quality Circles: How To Make Them Work in America.* New York: AMACOM, American Management Association, 1982.

Thornton, H. Patrick. "Designing for Global Competition." *Management Review* (January 1988): 60-62.

Tichy, Noel M. *Managing Strategic Change: Technical, Political and Cultural Dynamics.* New York: Wiley-Interscience, 1983.

Tichy, Noel M., Charles J. Fombrun, and Mary Anne Devanna. "Strategic Human Resource Management." *Sloan Management Review* (Winter 1982): 47-61.

Townsend, Patrick L. *Commit to Quality.* New York: John Wiley, 1986.

Twiss, Brian. *Managing Technological Innovation.* White Plains, N.Y.: Longman, 1986.

U.S. Congress, House Committee on Science and Technology. *The Future of Science: Hearing Before the Task Committee on Science Policy of the Committee on Science and Technology.* Washington, D.C.: U.S. GPO, 1986.

U.S. Department of Labor, Bureau of Labor Statistics. *The Meaning and Measurement of Productivity.* Washington, D.C.: U.S. GPO, September 1971.

Vicere, Albert A. "Managing Internal Entrepreneurs." *Management Review* (January 1985): 31-33.

Vough, Clair F., and Bernard Asbell. *Tapping the Human Resource: A Strategy for Productivity.* New York: AMACOM, 1975.

Wadsworth, Harrison M., et al. *Modern Methods for Quality Control and Improvement.* New York: Wiley, 1986.

Wait, D.J. "Productivity Measurement: A Management Accounting Challenge." *Management Accounting* (May 1979): 24-30.

Walsh, D.S. "Analyzing and Solving Productivity Problems." *Training and Development Journal* (July 1980): 70-74.

Walter, Craig. "Management Commitment to Quality: Hewlett-Packard Company." *Vital Speeches* (August 1983): 22-24.

Walters, Roy W., and Associates, Inc. *Job Enrichment for Results: Strategies for Successful Implementation.* Reading, Mass.: Addison-Wesley, 1975.

Walton, R.E. "Quality of Working Life: What Is It?" *Sloan Management Review* (April 1976): 13-22.

Welch, J.L., and D. Gordon. "Assessing the Impact of Flextime on Productivity." *Business Horizons* (December 1980): 61-62.

Werther, William B., Jr., et al. *Productivity Through People.* New York: West Publishing, 1986.

Wheelwright, S.C. "Manufacturing Strategy: Defining the Missing Link." *Strategic Management Journal* (January/March 1984): 77-91.

_____ . "Restoring the Competitive Edge in U.S. Manufacturing." *California Management Review* (Spring 1985): 26-42.

Wheelwright, S.C., and R.H. Hayes. "Competing Through Manufacturing." *Harvard Business Review* (January/February 1985): 99-109.

White, B. Joseph. "The Internalization of Business: One Company's Response." *Academy of Management Executive* (February 1988): 11-19.

Wiley, Jack W., and Bruce H. Campbell. "Assessing the Organization to Identify Productivity-Improvement Opportunities." *National Productivity Review* (Winter 1986/1987): 7-19.

Williams, Kathy. "Enhancing Productivity Through Automation." *Management Accounting* (July 1981): 54-55.

Wilson, A.H. "Engineering and Productivity." *Engineering Journal* (March 1977): 22-26.

Wise, J. "Setting Up a Company Productivity Program." *Management Review* (June 1980): 15-18.

Wood, Robert, Frank Hull, and Koya Azumi. "Evaluating Quality Circles: The American Application." *California Management Review* (Fall 1983): 37-53.

Wooten, Leland M., and Jin L. Tarter. "The Productivity Audit: A Key Tool for Executives." *MSU Business Topics* (Spring 1976): 31-41.

Wunnenberg, C.A., Jr. "Productivity in the Warehouse: Who Needs to Automate?" *Management Review* (October 1977): 55-58.

Yager, Edward. "Japanese Managers Tell How Their System Works." *Fortune* (November 1977): 126-40.

Zeldman, M. "Moving Ideas from R & D to the Shop Floor." *Management Review* (December 1986): 24-27.

Biographical Notes

Mylle Bell is Director of Corporate Planning at BellSouth Corporation in Atlanta. A Georgia native, she graduated from Emory University. Prior to joining BellSouth in 1985, she spent 12 years with General Electric in management positions that included General Manager-Systems Operations with responsibility for GE's factory automation products. Previously at BellSouth she served as President of Bell-South International, the division responsible for all international activities. Among her varied memberships, she serves on the Boards of Directors for the Atlanta Red Cross and the U.S./People's Republic of China Joint Executive Committee.

Richard H. Bierly was elected Senior VP Human Resources of Unisys in 1986. He joined Burroughs in 1983 as VP HR after leaving IBM where he was director of personnel for Americas/Far East Corporation. He was elected Senior VP of Burroughs in 1984. During his 27 years at IBM, he worked in all aspects of HR management. He graduated in sociology from St. Lawrence in 1956.

Daniel B. Bills is co-founder, Chairman of the Board and President of Granville-Phillips Company, Boulder, Colorado. He holds a number of patents in the field of ultra-high vacuum and has been responsible for numerous innovations in vacuum technology. He has taught undergraduate and graduate courses in physics at Washington State University and has authored and co-authored a number of papers in surface physics, gaseous electronics, and vacuum technology. Dr. Bills is a past president of the American Vacuum Society and in 1983 was elected an Honorary Member. He holds a B.S.E.E. and an M.S. in Physics from Washington State University and a Ph.D. in Physics from Harvard University.

Jean M. Bishop is Vice President of Employee Relations at Bonneville International Corporation. She has also served as Assistant Vice President of Personnel and Personnel Director. She has been Personnel Coordinator and Personnel Assistant at Associated Food Store.

She has studied at the University of Utah, Brigham Young University, University of Michigan, and American Management Association.

Patricia J. Blair is Director of Corporate Personnel for Transamerica Corporation. She also acts as an internal consultant on personnel issues to Transamerica affiliate companies. She earned a B.S. in Business Administration from the University of San Francisco and an M.B.A. in Human Resource Management from Golden Gate University. She has professional experience with Ampex Corporation as well as with several Transamerica affiliate companies. She is active in civic, professional, and cultural organizations.

Norman Bodek is President of Productivity, Inc., dealing in productivity and quality improvement. He publishes the *Productivity* and *TEI* newsletters; conducts "Productivity the American Way" conferences; operates Productivity Press; conducts study missions in Japan, Europe, and United States; and consults on participation, automation, and efficiency.

Edward Botwinick is a Senior Vice President and member of the Management Board of Unisys Corporation and is President of Unisys Networks. He was Chairman of the Board of Directors and CEO of Timeplex, Inc., from 1977 until its acquisition by Unisys in January 1988. He was employed in various engineering, marketing, and management positions in the semiconductor industry. He received a B.A. in Physics from Columbia College and a B.S. in Electrical Engineering from Columbia University's School of Engineering. He is Vice Chairman of the Columbia University Engineering Council, on the Advisory Board of the Center for Telecommunications Research, and the Advisory Board of Wolfensohn Associates, L.P., a leading venture capital investment partnership.

James M. Buchanan has devoted himself to developing the contractual and constitutional bases for the theory of economic and political decision-making. In so doing, he has become the leading researcher in the field now called "public choice theory." He studied at Middle Tennessee State College and the University of Tennessee before receiving his doctorate from the University of Chicago in 1948. From 1957 to 1967, he taught at the University of Virginia in Charlottesville, where he directed the Thomas Jefferson Center for Studies in Political Economy and Social Philosophy. After a short interlude at the University of California in Los Angeles, he became professor at the Virginia Polytechnic Institute in Blacksburg in 1969, where he, with Gordon Tullock, founded and led the Center for Study of Public Choice. In 1982 the Center was moved to George Mason University. He received the Nobel Memorial Prize in Economics in 1986.

Vernon M. Buehler is a professor of business administration, assistant dean for business relations, and director of the Partner's Program at Utah State University's College of Business. He holds an M.B.A. from the Harvard Graduate School of Business Administration and a

Ph.D. in economics from George Washington University. He has been active in the field of government and business relationships and his articles have been widely published. He has taught public policy and business environment courses since 1972. He co-edited, with Y.K. Shetty, *Productivity Improvement: Case Studies of Proven Practice* (AMACOM, June 1981); *Quality and Productivity Improvements: U.S. and Foreign Companies Experiences* (Manufacturing Productivity Center, Illinois Institute of Technology, Chicago, March 1983); *Productivity and Quality Through People: Practices of Well-Managed Companies* (Quorum Books, 1985); *Quality, Productivity, and Innovation: Strategies for Gaining Competitive Advantage* (Elsevier Science Publishing Co., 1987); and *Productivity and Quality Through Science and Technology* (Quorum Books, 1988).

Rosa M. Bunn is Manager of Community & Economic Affairs at the Adolph Coors Company. She manages one of the most innovative and exciting examples of a corporate volunteer program in America known as the VICE squad (Coors Volunteer In Community Enrichment) and the ADVICE squad (Additional Duties Volunteers In Community Enrichment). She is involved with a variety of boards and non-profit organizations. She finds time to work with Coors philanthropy program which handles contributions for these same non-profit groups.

George K. Chang worked for the IBM Research Center for two years and the Ford Scientific Laboratory for two and a half years. He joined Bellcomm (a Bell Company) in 1967. He is a Distinguished Member of Technical Staff in the Protocol Analysis and Standards Organization in Bell Communications Research. He has been actively involved in the standardization of the File Transfer, Access, and Management (FTAM) protocols. He was the chairman of the "Workshop on Analytic and Simulation Modeling of IEEE 802.4 Token Bus Local Area Networks", sponsored by the U.S. National Bureau of Standards. He received his B.A. and M.A. in Physics from UCLA and Ph.D. from Rutgers University.

Kathleen Dole has had 15 years experience in designing, implementing, and administering pay, incentive, and benefit programs for the John Hancock Financial Services network of companies. Currently, she is Executive Consultant with primary responsibility for finding ways to compensate and motivate key executives through major strategic changes, corporate reorganization, and downsizing. Kathie is certified as a compensation professional by the American Compensation Association, is currently participating in the certification program of the International Foundation of Employee Benefits, and recently completed the Management Development Program at the University of California-Berkeley School of Business.

Kent Druyvesteyn has been director of the Corporate Ethics Program for General Dynamics since 1985. From 1981 to 1985 he was Dean of Students and Director of the MBA Program for the Graduate School of Business at the University of Chicago. He was Executive Director of the Richmond VA Independence Bicentennial Commission. He was editor of *Virginia Cavalcade* and has served in various editorial capacities for several other periodicals. He has been Chairman of the Board of Trustees of the Graduate Management Admission Council and served on the Board of Directors of International House, University of Chicago.

Dale P. Esse is Manager of Production Quality Assurance for the Copy Products Division of Eastman Kodak Assurance Programs for production of all Kodak Ektaprint Copier Equipment. In the course of his 18 years as an engineer and manager, he has traveled extensively in the development and implementation of quality programs. He received his B.S. in Mechanical Engineering from the University of Wisconsin. He has completed several courses in both quality and management, including the Juran course on Management of Quality and Management of Managers Seminar at the University of Michigan Graduate School of Business Administration.

Lincoln D. Faurer joined the Corporation for Open Systems (COS) in 1986 after retiring from a 35-year Air Force career with the rank of Lieutenant General. As Chairman of the COS Strategy Forum, he coordinates and recommends task priorities for the corporation. The Strategy Forum is an assembly of delegates from COS member companies that recommends the overall technical direction for COS.

Armand V. Feigenbaum is President of General Systems and the originator of Total Quality Control (TQC), which is the approach to quality and productivity that has profoundly influenced management strategy in competing for world markets in the U.S., Japan, and elsewhere. General Systems designs and installs integrated operational systems for corporations worldwide, with emphasis on improvements in quality and productivity. He is the author of *Total Quality Control*, now in its 3rd edition and in several languages. His honors include the Edwards Medal of the American Society of Quality Control, the National Security Industrial Associations Award of Merit, and the Union College Founders medal. He holds Ph.D. and M.S. degrees from the Massachusetts Institute of Technology.

Charles Garfield formed Peak Performance Center in California and for over 18 years has interviewed and examined more than 15,000 high achievers. Peak performers are results-oriented and motivated by a sense of mission, have the ability to assess strengths and limitations and to act accordingly, and do not wander too far from their goal. They are team builders and players, having the capacity for innovation and change.

C. Jackson Grayson is Chairman of American Productivity Center in Houston. He has an M.B.A. from the Wharton School and a Ph.D. from Harvard Business School. He served as Chairman of the U.S. Price Commission, where he received national recognition. He is a CPA and member of the Board of Directors of Lever Brothers, Sun

Company, IC Industry, and Potlack, Tyler, Harris, and Browning corporations. He has also been a newspaper reporter, a special agent of the FBI, and a manager of a cotton farm.

David Halberstam is one of the best known authors in America. He first came to national prominence in the early 1960s for his reporting on Vietnam. At the age of 30, he was awarded the Pulitzer Prize. Two of his books are considered landmarks: *The Best and the Brightest*, and *The Powers That Be*. His latest book, *The Reckoning*, seeks to explain why Japan has replaced the US as the dominating world giant. *Harpers's* magazine called him "a legend in American journalism".

Susan B. Hitchcock is an operations manager in Southern Bell's Headquarters Network organization in Atlanta. In this position, she is responsible for lending support to the company's Network Strategic Plan. She has been with Southern Bell since 1967 serving in the traffic department, switched services operations, and implementing major account centers. A native of Kentucky and a graduate of Agnes Scott College in Decatur, Georgia, she is active in education programs such as the Governor's Committee for Post-Secondary Education and the Adult Literacy Program.

Charlotte Cook Hofmann is President and founder of Information Ideas, Inc., an Oakland, California, consulting company that specializes in helping corporations implement computing as a business strategy. She received national attention for her findings and recommendations on "Rapture of the Deep," the condition that results from business staff becoming infatuated with technology. Her interviews have appeared in *Newsweek*, *The Wall Street Journal*, *Business Week*, *Computer-World*, *InfoSystems*, *InformationWeek*, *Data Training*, and *InfoWorld*. She is co-founder and Director of Product Development for The Knowledge Transfer. She developed a class on effective selling to MIS managers. She is a graduate of the University of California, Berkeley. She has served as Chairperson of the Bay Area Society of Information Centers and is currently the Vendor Coordinator of BASIC.

Julie Holtry is Corporate Quality Marketing and Communications Manager for Hewlett-Packard Company, in Palo Alto, California. She is responsible for promoting company-wide quality control (CWQC or known as Total Quality Control) to HP employees and customers worldwide. She has held management positions in the Personal Computer Marketing organization. She was National Merchandising Manager for Atari Corporation and Senior Director of Customer Service for a Major U.S. airline. She received her B.S. in Business Administration from the University of Arizona in 1969 and an M.B.A. in 1983 from Pepperdine University.

Bobby Inman is Chairman, President, and CEO of Westmark Systems, Inc. a Texas-based defense industry holding company. He graduated from the University of Texas in 1950 and entered the Naval

Reserve as an Ensign. He was the first Naval Intelligence Specialist to attain four-star rank. Between 1974 and 1982 he served as director of Naval Intelligence, director of NSA, and department director CIA. From 1983 to 1986, he served as chairman and CEO of the Microelectronics and Computer Technology Corporation (MCC) in Austin, Texas. He is chairman of the Federal Reserve Bank of Dallas and a member of the Boards of Directors of Flour, Oracle, Science Applications International, Xerox, Southwestern Bell, Texas Eastern, and Tracor. He is a volunteer director of the Atlantic Council and Council on Foreign Relations. He is a member of the National Academy of Public Administrators and the Trilateral Commission, and a trustee of Brookings Institute, Southwestern University, and Saint James School.

Raymond H. Johnson is an industrial-organizational psychologist who joined the Employee Relations Staff at Ford Motor Company after receiving his doctorate from Michigan State University in 1973. His current position is Consulting Associate of Employee Development Strategy and Planning Department. At Ford, he has been involved in a variety of human resource management programs. He initiated the development of career planning systems, and helped develop the Employee Involvement process credited with much of Ford's worldwide employee attitude survey program, and he has chaired the Mayflower Group (a national survey consortium of *Fortune* 100 companies). For the past two years, he was chief consultant to an executive task force concerned with culture change at Ford.

W. David Kelton is Associate Professor of Management Sciences in the Carlson School of Management at the University of Minnesota. He received a B.A. in Mathematics and M.S. and Ph.D. in Industrial Engineering from the University of Wisconsin-Madison, as well as an M.S. in Mathematics from Ohio University. He has published papers in several journals and been a frequent presenter at conferences. He is on the editorial boards of *Operations Research* and *IIE Transactions*, has been a reviewer for several journals, and was the Program Chair for the 1987 Winter Simulation Conference. His current research interests are in computer simulation methodology, statistical inference on stochastic processes, queuing, and quality control. He is a member of ORSA, TIMS, ASA, and SCS and is currently the Secretary-Treasurer for the TIMS College on Simulation.

Harold A. Loeb is Senior Vice President and Manager of the Los Angeles office of Hay/Huggins Company. He has over 20 years experience as an actuarial consultant specializing in the design, financing, and administration of all types of benefit plans. He is an Associate of the Society of Actuaries, a Member of the American Academy of Actuaries, and an Enrolled Actuary. He received his B.S. in Mathematics from Brooklyn College and continued his studies at New York University's Graduate school of Business Administration.

Ray Marshall is Audre and Bernard Rapoport Centennial Professor of Economics and Public Affairs at the University of Texas. From 1977 to 1981 he served as Secretary of Labor under President Carter. Other positions include: member of Board of Trustees, Carnegie Corporation; chairman, Board of Trustees, Institute for the Future; member, Board of Directors, National Policy Center; member, Executive Committee, Southern Regional Council; member, Board of Directors, U.N. Association; member, Advisory Committee, Office of Technology Assessment; senior advisor, Shearson Lehman Management, Inc.; trustee, Population Reference Bureau, Inc.; member, National Council, American Association for Advancement of Science; Member, National Research Council; and member, American Competitiveness Council. He holds a Ph.D. from UC Berkeley and has authored or coauthored 25 books and approximately 100 articles.

William McCormick is Chairman and CEO of Firemans's Fund Insurance. He is a member and/or Director of the Bay Area Council, National Center on Financial Services, Commonwealth Club, CA Roundtable, and SRI Advisory Council. He holds an M.S. from George Washington University and is a Yale graduate. He was a commissioned Lieutenant U.S. Navy, where he served on the Atomic Energy Commission staff of Admiral Rickover.

Dan Minoli has approximately 15 years experience in the telecommunications field. He has worked for Bell Telephone Laboratories, ITT World Communications, Prudential-Bache Securities, and is currently working for Bell Communications Research (Bellcore) as a strategic planner. He has published over 130 technical and trade articles; some of his work has been translated into German, French, and Spanish. He is an Advisor for DataPro Research Corporation. He is also an Adjunct Assistant Professor at New York University's Information Technology Institute, in addition to being on the Board of Advisers. He has been a columnist for *ComputerWorld* magazine and a reviewer for the *IEEE*.

Neal Orkin is an Assistant Professor of Legal Studies at Drexel University's College of Business and Administration in Philadelphia. He holds a B.S. in Electrical Engineering from Drexel and a J.D. from Temple University. He worked as an engineer prior to his teaching and legal experience. He is now a labor arbitrator for the American Arbitration Association. His articles have appeared in *The Harvard Business Review, The European Intellectual, Patent World,* and *Copyright World.*

John B. Phillips was named assistant to the chairman of ConAgra in September 1986. He joined ConAgra in January 1981 as President of Banquet Foods and a Corporate Vice President. In November 1981, he was named President and CEO, ConAgra Prepared Food Companies, and President and CEO, ConAgra Refrigerated Prepared Food Companies. He was with Campbell Soup for 22 years. He joined Campbell

Soup after graduation from Utah State University with a B.S. in Economics in 1958. Later, he served as advertising manager and general manager for Swanson Frozen Foods; vice-president of frozen foods for Campbell's Pepperidge Farm; director of personnel administration for Campbell; and president, vice president, and general manager of Swanson Frozen Foods.

Gilbert W. Piddington has worked in the information systems industry 20 years in a variety of sales, marketing, programming, computer operations, and program management assignments. Currently he is responsible for all Unisys communications and networking product programs including market requirements, competitive analysis, development engineering budgets, pricing, forecasting, product launch, and marketing programs. He holds a B.S. in Physics from the Virginia Military Institute and an M.B.A. in Marketing from the College of William and Mary.

Ellen S. Quackenbush is responsible for analyzing new market opportunities for Digital's network and communications products. She focuses on mapping information flows within organizations to highlight how Digital's distributed processing can give businesses a competitive advantage. She was a staff member at MIT's Center for Information Systems Research where she investigated the cost of voice network ownership, the emerging partnerships between MIS and line of business organizations, and the impact of PCs on sales force productivity. She holds an M.S. from M.I.T.'s Sloan School of Management and a B.A. in Economics from Smith College.

Jodie N. Ray has been Senior Vice President and Manager of Texas Instruments Industrial Automation Intra-Company Objective. This corporate thrust has been formed to focus TI's industrial automation efforts as applied internally and externally. He was previously senior vice president and manager of the Electro-Optics business entity of TI's Defense Systems and Electronics Group (DSEG). During his 19 years in DSEG, he held various engineering and management assignments. From 1976 to 1981, he was product-customer center manager of the Tactical Weapons and Electro-Optic Seekers departments. From 1981 to 1986, he was manager of the Electro-Optics Division. He has a B.S. in Electrical Engineering Science from M.I.T. and an M.S. in Electrical Engineering from Southern Methodist University.

Carl E. Reichardt is CEO and Director of Wells Fargo & Co. He joined the firm in 1970 and has served as president of Wells Fargo Bank. In the *Forbes* January 1987 "Annual Report on American Industry," Wells Fargo was selected as the "most improved bank." He is a director of Ford Motor Company, Hospital Corporation of America, Pacific Gas & Electric Company, the Irvine Company, Utah International, and Newhall Management Corporation. He is also an active leader in numerous civic organizations, holds a B.A. from the University of Southern California, and is a graduate of Harvard's Advanced Management Program.

Douglas M. Reid is Senior Vice President and senior staff officer for Xerox Corporation. He is responsible for policy and strategic direction for communications, advertising, public affairs, and personnel, as well as, the Xerox quality process. In 1987 he was named executive liaison to Fuji Xerox Company, Xerox's Tokyo-based affiliate. He is a member of the advisory committee to the School of Industrial and Labor Relations at Cornell University and on the board of directors of Xerox Canada, Inc. He received a B.A. in Business Administration from the University of Western Ontario and an M.A. in Industrial and Labor Relations from Cornell University.

Y.K. Shetty is professor of management at the College of Business, Utah State University, Logan, Utah. He holds an M.B.A. and Ph.D. from the Graduate School of Management, University of California, Los Angeles. He is currently engaged in research on the problems of productivity, quality, and innovation at the firm level. His articles have been published in *Academy of Management Journal, California Management Review, Business Horizons, Advanced Management Journal, Management Review, Journal of Management Studies, Management International Review,* and other journals. He co-edited, with V.M. Buehler, *Productivity Improvements: Case Studies of Proven Practices* (AMACOM, June 1981); *Quality and Productivity Improvements: U.S. and Foreign Companies Experiences* (Manufacturing Productivity Center, Illinois Institute of Technology, Chicago, March 1983); *Productivity and Quality Through People: Practices of Well-Managed Companies* (Quorum Books, 1985); *Quality, Productivity and Innovation: Strategies for Gaining Competitive Advantage* (Elsevier Science Publishing Co., 1987); and *Productivity and Quality Through Science and Technology* (Quorum Books, 1988).

Shigeo Shingo is, quite simply, the world's leading expert on improving the manufacturing process. Known as "Dr. Improvement" in Japan, he is the originator of the Single-Minute Exchange of Die (SMED) concept, the Poka-yoke defect-prevention system and one of the developers of the just-in-time (JIT) production system that helped make Toyota the world's most productive automobile manufacturer. His work now helps hundreds of other companies world-wide save billions of dollars in manufacturing costs annually. The most sought-after consultant in Japan, Mr. Shingo has trained more than 10,000 people in 100 companies. He founded and is president of Japan's highly-regarded Institute of Management Improvement and is the author of numerous books, including *Revolution in Manufacturing: The SMED System* and *Zero Quality Control: Source Inspection and the Poka-yoke System.* His most recent book, *The Challenge of Non-Stock Production* concentrates on expanding U.S. manufacturers' understanding of stockless production. Shigeo Shingo's genius is his understanding of exactly why products are manufactured the way they are, and then transforming that understanding into a workable system for low cost, high quality production. In the history of international manufacturing, Shigeo Shingo's name stands alongside such pioneers as Robert

Fulton, Henry Ford, Frederick Taylor, and Douglas McGregor as one of the key figures in the quest for improvement. He was awarded an honorary doctorate by Utah State University in June 1988.

Herbert A. Simon is Richard King Mellon University Professor of Computer Science and Psychology at Carnegie-Mellon University, where he has taught since 1949. During the past 30 years he has been studying decision-making and problem-solving processes using computers to simulate human thinking. He has published over 600 papers and 20 books and monographs. He was elected to the National Academy of Sciences in 1967. He has received awards for his research from the American Psychological Association, the Association for Computing Machinery, the American Political Science Association, the American Economic Association, and the Institute of Electrical and Electronic Engineers. He received the Nobel Memorial Prize in Economics in 1978 and the National Medal of Science in 1986.

Dorsey J. Talley is Vice President of Quality Assurance at the Fort Worth Division of General Dynamics. In this capacity, he is responsible for a work force engaged in maintaining the high quality of all aircraft and radar systems manufactured at the division. Previously, he had a successful career in the USAF retiring with the rank of Colonel. He attended the University of Texas, earned his B.A. in Engineering from Texas A&M, and his M.S. Logistics and Industrial Management from the Air Force Institute of Technology. Recent publications include "Meeting and Beating the DoD Quality Improvement Objectives," *Government Executive Magazine,* (January 1987) and "The Quest for Quality: A Defense Contractor's Story," *Defense Management Journal.* He is a member of National Contract Management Association, National Rifle Association (Life Member), Daedalians, Rotary International, Sigma Iota Ipsilon, and Alph Pi Mu. He has held several offices in the Aerospace Industries Association (AIA).

John H. Taylor received his B.S. in Electrical Engineering from Duke University and did graduate work at the University of Delaware in electrical engineering, computer science, and mathematics. His entire career has been with Du Pont. He joined it in 1962 and held various technical and management positions, including Superintendent of Computer Systems and Services at Du Pont's largest plant, Systems Consultant in the Engineering Department, Specialist Manager and Project Manager in the Engineering Department. He is a member of the Institute of Electrical and Electronic Engineers and has spoken and been interviewed over the last several years regarding scientific and technical computing within Du Pont.

Henry J. Todd has worked at McDonnell Douglas for 30 years in engineering, seven years in operations, three years in program management, and four years as General Manager-MDAC Monrovia Operations. He has managed and directed numerous projects from their inception through production. He recently served as Deputy Program Manager of the Army's successful Mast Mounted Sight Program and was instrumental in the transition of this project from the development to the production stages. He is now Vice President-Product Assurance & Logistics Support (PA&LS) at MDAC-Huntington Beach.

James W. Torvinen is one of the nation's leading experts in the production application of Shigeo Shingo's SMED techniques. He is production superintendent for press shop and assembly operations at Ford Motor Company's Van Dyke plant. He has been a proponent of productivity improvement since his first position at Huss Paper and Pulp Company in 1965. After serving as a communications specialist with the U.S. Army, he joined Ford's stamping operation as a manager. After graduating from Henry Ford Community College, he received his doctorate from Wayne State University.

Larry White is Plant Manager of the Oregon Saw Chain Plant of Omark Industries in Portland. He joined OSC in 1965 and has held numerous management positions before assuming his present one in 1983. He has been directly involved with implementing the disciplines of Just-In-Time Production and Total Quality Control in North America. He holds a B.S. in Industrial Engineering from Oregon State University.

Ronald J. Whittier is Vice President and Director of Marketing of Intel Corporation. He joined Intel in 1970, serving as Components Manufacturing Plant Manager and Director of Technology Development. His duties include managing marketing programs and business development activities. He worked from 1965 to 1970 with the research and development group of Fairchild Semiconductor where he specialized in developing solid state devices. He graduated from the University of California-Berkeley with a B.S. in Chemical Engineering in 1960. After working in the chemical industry, he received a Ph.D. in Chemical Engineering from Stanford University in 1965.

Lynn Williams is the fifth president of the United Steelworkers of America, one of North America's largest unions. He has headed the USWA since 1983, when he was elected temporary acting president following the death of Lloyd McBride. He has been a union man all of his adult life. He has carried organized labor's message into bastions of conservatism, appearing before analysts, economists, business schools, trade associations, and personnel managers. In the process, he has earned a reputation as cerebral, far-minded, idealistic, incorruptible...and tough — a view held by people inside and outside the labor movement.

Roger F. Wolff is Director of Design and Development at Union Carbide Corporation. He has also been Director of Human Resources and Labor Relations Manager. His entire career has been with Union Carbide. He has a B.A. in Psychology from Cornell University and an M.A. in Industrial and Labor Relations from the University of Illinois.

John Young is President and CEO of Hewlett-Packard Company. In 1983 he was appointed by Ronald Reagan to be Chairman of the President's Commission of Industrial Competitiveness, which was chartered to explore means of improving the competitive posture of U.S. industry at home and abroad. In 1986, the Council of Competitiveness, a private-sector group led by Young, was founded to continue the goals of improving U.S. industry's competitive posture. In 1985, he was named Manufacturer of the Year by the California Manufacturers Association; Business Communicator of the Year by the Business/ Professional Advertising Association; and was the recipient of a leadership award by the U.S. Council for International Business.

Topical Index

Chapter 1

Introduction to the book. (page 3)
Productivity and quality. (5)
Increasing market share. (9)
Exploiting information
    technology. (12)
Total quality costs. (13)

Chapter 2

Historical growth of productivity.
    (page 18)
Global economy of the future. (23)
Comparative economic statistics. (26)
Developing nations (LDCs). (28)
A proposal for the future. (30)

Chapter 3

Role of technology in U.S. economic
    growth. (page 33)
Forces that reduce U.S.
    competitiveness. (36)
Importance of creating new
    technology. (40)
Commercializing new
    technology. (42)
Focus on time, cost, and quality. (43)

Chapter 4

A rational information strategy for
    management. (page 46)
Artificial intelligence and its
    future. (51)
Understanding human
    performance. (54)

Chapter 5

The work ethic. (page 55)
Its paradox in economic theory. (56)
Its economic value. (60)
Women's role in the work force. (62)

Chapter 6

Benefits of labor-management
    cooperation. (page 63)
Road blocks to economic justice. (66)
Employee involvement. (74)
Dangers of offshore plants. (76)

Chapter 7

Responding to global competition.
    (page 79)
Factors determining
    competitiveness. (83)
Public-private sector agendas. (86)
Information as a strategic
    resource. (88)

Chapter 8

Building a companywide quality
    program. (page 99)
Renewing U.S. industrial
    leadership. (104)
Three problem areas in managing
    quality. (106)
Return-on-investment (ROI) as
    motivation. (113)

Chapter 9

New economic age replaces age of
    American hegemony. (page 120)

Chapter 9 cont.

New international order. (122)
How Japan's system works. (124)
The fallacy of protectionism. (126)

Chapter 10

The Sperry-Burroughs merger.
(page 129)
How two firms were put together to
form Unisys. (133)
Employee involvement in the new
culture. (135)
The merger: one year later. (138)

Chapter 11

Educational institutions resist
change. (page 144)
Schooling does not equal
education. (145)
Being competitive vs. maintaining
living standard. (148)
Reforming public-policy
making. (156)

Chapter 12

Banks restructure following
deregulation. (page 161)
Acquisitions/mergers can produce
economies of scale. (161)
Sick banks, failing thrifts, huge
Third-World debt losses. (162)
Signs of hope. (164)

Chapter 13

Business women have more
opportunities than constraints.
(page 170)
Dynamic, fast-paced industries favor
women. (171)
Women's innate skills (consensus
building, encouraging participation,
listening) in growing
demand. (173)

Chapter 14

Changing industry's impact on
women. (page 175)
Gains by women in
management. (177)

Can-do attitude. (178)
Need for role model and plan. (179)

Chapter 15

Impact of structure and culture on
career opportunities. (page 182)
Women managers' view of
success. (183)
Profiles of successful women. (185)

Chapter 16

Strategic planning terms. (page 190)
Guiding principles at Ford. (193)
The role of the human resource
staff. (194)
HR's future in strategic planning. (198)

Chapter 17

Xerox's human resource philosophy.
(page 202)
Key HR objectives. (203)
Employee communications. (204)
Affirmative action. (206)

Chapter 18

Pay for performance, non-
performance, and exceptional
performance. (page 209)
Incentive plan tied to goals. (212)
The aging work force. (214)
John Hancock's future. (214)

Chapter 19

Union Carbide's national
comprehensive medical plan.
(page 219)
Switch from short-term to retirement
savings. (220)
New group universal life
program. (221)
New health and dependent day
care. (222)

Chapter 20

Employee attitudes toward benefits
plans. (page 224)
Benefit tradeoff analysis. (226)
Case study of health plan
redesign. (227)

Chapter 21

Issues in rewarding employee inventors. (page 233)
Present reward systems (or lack thereof) in U.S., Japan, Western Europe. (234)
The author's proposal. (236)

Chapter 22

Super achievers vs. workaholics. (page 242)
Envision a mission, be results oriented. (242)
Tap your internal resources. (243)
Enlist team spirit. (244)

Chapter 23

Total employee involvement (TEI). (page 247)
Make work exciting. (249)
Letting employees know the score. (250)
Japanese working habits. (251)

Chapter 24

Workforce ethics at General Dynamics. (page 255)
Setting corporate policies, procedures, and standards. (260)
Rewards, hotlines, and communication. (264)
Appendix: GD's Standards of Business Ethics and Conduct (267)

Chapter 25

How Bonneville promotes employee creativity. (page 279)
Start with top management. (281)
Share ideas. (282)
Provide growth opportunities. (283)

Chapter 26

Networking opens communication lines. (page 287)
Today's business pressures. (288)
Focus on customer and supplier goals. (292)

Networking in the 1990s. (297)

Chapter 27

Open architectures help solve communication. (page 301)
Private networks and hybrid networks flourish. (303)
Extending networks for competitive advantage. (303)

Chapter 28

Defining open systems interconnection (OSI). (page 305)
OSI model. (307)
Vendor conformance testing. (309)
Interoperability. (309)

Chapter 29

Vendors and users benefit from standards. (page 311)
Networking needs multi-vendor environment. (314)
World governments demand interoperation. (315)
Standardization requires conformance testing and licensing. (316)
Demonstrating inter-connectivity. (318)

Chapter 30

Integrated service digital networks (ISDN). (page 321)
ISDN's usage, timing, costs, and pricing. (323)
Timeplex's ISDN program. (324)

Chapter 31

Planning operations systems networks (OSNs) at BellComm. (page 327)
OSN architecture, transition issues, and 4 development phases. (330)

Chapter 32

Integrated Services Digital Networks (ISDN). (page 337)

Chapter 32 cont.

Strategies and development of ISDN. (338)
ISDN pitfalls. (340)
Southern Bell case study. (340)

Chapter 33

Intel as a user of information technology. (page 341)
Administrative productivity: 1975 and 1985. (342)
Order processing: 1975, 1987, and the 1990s. (343)
Why companies and individuals must use information technology effectively. (345)

Chapter 34

Competitive advantage is lead time on a maturity curve. (page 348)
Technology is not the problem — resource deployment is. (348)
Exploiting global electronic mail, artificial intelligence, electronic data interchange, supercomputers, and compound document architecture. (349)

Chapter 35

Computer simulation's value in manufacturing. (page 355)
Modeling and simulation. (355)
How simulation works. (360)
Information out and information in. (363)

Chapter 36

Computing's hidden costs. (page 371)
"Rapture of the deep," a management problem. (372)
Career paths for computer-literate professionals. (378)
Teach more business and less technology. (378)

Chapter 37

Shigeo Shingo's Single-Minute Exchange of Die (SMED) system.

(page 383)
Reducing inventory, setup time, and lot size. (383)
History of production revolutions. (385)
How pre-automation reduces labor costs. (386)
Taylor, Gilbreth, the Hawthorne experiment, and NUMMI. (387)
Source inspection and defect prevention. (391)

Chapter 38

Reducing wasted resources to achieve a pre-selected output result. (page 399)
Using Shingo methods at Granville-Phillips. (400)
Identifying root actions and acting on root causes. (402)

Chapter 39

Employee involvement at Omark Industries. (page 405)
Empowering workers to improve systems. (407)
Stages in self-management. (409)
Productivity results. (411)

Chapter 40

Applying SMED techniques at Ford's Van Dyke plant. (page 413)
SMED's impact on Ford's manufacturing operations. (414)
Changeovers reduced from 6 days to 6 hours. (416)
Appendix: case study. (417)

Chapter 41

How Texas Instruments is successfully implementing computer-integrated manufacturing (CIM). (page 423)
Automation and artificial intelligence. (425)
Lessons learned while integrating TI's factories. (427)

Chapter 42

The quality program at Kodak's Copy
    Products Division. (page 431)
Phases I, II, and III, and their
    success. (433)
Critical Parameter Monitoring's
    screening process performed by
        assembly. (440)
Conforming audits on all
    products. (441)

Chapter 43

How Dr. Juran changed Hewlett-
    Packard's quality program.
        (page 443)
H-P's experience with quality. (445)
TQC in manufacturing, credit
    control, teamwork, and strategic
        planning. (446)

Chapter 44

How McDonnell Douglas manages
    quality and productivity
        improvement. (page 451)
Managing and implementing Natural
    Work Groups (NWGs). (452)
Common objectives, tangible results,
    and maintaining the focus. (454)

Chapter 45

Sustaining quality improvement at
    General Dynamics. (page 457)
GD's program and chronology. (457)
Their results. (462)

Chapter 46

Improving service sector productivity.
    (page 463)
Productivity: the human factor. (467)
Motivating people by integrating
    work and play. (467)
Honoring your own needs. (470)

Chapter 47

ConAgra's approach to quality and
    productivity. (page 473)
Company turnaround: the power of
    the individual. (474)

Family of independent operating
    companies. (476)
Shared visions shape individual
    behavior. (480)

Chapter 48

Managerial guidelines for
    productivity and quality
        improvement. (page 485)
Proven methods being used
    today. (486)
A framework for success. (489)

.

Other Books on
Quality and Productivity

Productivity Press publishes and distributes materials on productivity, quality improvement, and employee involvement for business and industry, academia, and the general market. Many products are direct source materials from Japan that have been translated into English for the first time and are available exclusively from Productivity. Supplemental services include conferences, seminars, in-house training programs, and industrial study missions. Send for free book catalog.

Zero Quality Control
Source Inspection and the Poka-yoke System
by Shigeo Shingo, translated by Andrew P. Dillon

This book demonstrates how source inspection (detecting errors before they become defects) can eliminate the need for statistical quality control. It goes into the nitty-gritty of Poka-yoke and ZQC and shows how to turn out the highest quality products in the shortest period of time.
ISBN 0-915299-07-0 / 305 pages / $65.00

The Idea Book
Improvement Through TEI
(Total Employee Involvement)
Edited by the Japan Human Relations Association

This is a hands-on teaching tool for the most important component of TEI, a vital, total-participation suggestion system. In Japan, suggestion systems are part of ongoing company improvement efforts known as *kaizen*. The Japanese-style system encourages all workers to continually re-examine their jobs and their products to improve the quality of the entire company.
ISBN 0-915299-22-4 / 217 pages / $49.95

Canon Production System
Creative Involvement of the Total Workforce
compiled by the Japan Management Association

A fantastic success story! Canon set a goal to increase productivity by three percent per month — and achieved it! The first book-length case study to show how to combine the most effective Japanese management principles and quality improvement techniques into one overall strategy that improves every area of the company on a continual basis. Shows how the seven new QC tools are applied in a matrix management model.
ISBN 0-915299-06-2 / 232 pages / $36.95

Productivity Press, Dept. BK, P.O. Box 3007, Cambridge, MA 02140 1-800-274-9911

Management for Quality Improvement
The 7 New QC Tools
edited by Shigeru Mizuno

Building on the traditional seven QC tools, these new tools were developed specifically for managers. They help in planning, troubleshooting, and communicating with maximum effectiveness at every stage of a quality improvement program. Only recently made available in the U.S., they are certain to advance quality improvement efforts for anyone involved in project management, quality assurance, MIS, or TQC.
ISBN 0-915299-29-1 / 318 pages / $59.95

Audio Visual Training Aids

The SMED System
by Shigeo Shingo, translated by Andrew P. Dillon

Mr. Shingo visually demonstrates exactly how the Single-Minute Exchange of Die (SMED) system works. Part I explains the theory and conceptual stages. Part II shows practical applications of this major change in the way setups are performed. Slide package contains two binders, each with carousel tray, audio tape and facilitator's guide with work sheets. Video package contains two video tapes and two booklets.

Slides and Audio Cassette (45 min.)	$749.00
Video (45 min.)	$749.00

The Poka-yoke System
by Shigeo Shingo, translated by Andrew P. Dillon

Mr. Shingo visually shows exactly how to implement Zero Quality Control (ZQC) and the Poka-yoke system. He shows how to use source inspection and mistake-proofing devices on the production line. Part I explains the theory and concepts and Part II shows practical applications. Slide package includes two binders, each with carousel tray, audio tape and facilitator's guide with work sheets. Video package contains two video tapes and two booklets.

Slides and Audio Cassette (45 min.)	$749.00
Video (45 min.)	$749.00

Productivity Press, Dept. BK, P.O. Box 3007, Cambridge, MA 02140 1-800-274-9911

BOOKS AVAILABLE FROM PRODUCTIVITY PRESS

Christopher, William F. **Productivity Measurement Handbook**
ISBN 0-915299-05-4 / 1983 / 680 pages / looseleaf / $137.95

Ford, Henry. **Today and Tomorrow** (originally published 1926)
ISBN 0-915299-36-4 / 1988 / 302 pages / hardcover / $24.95

Fukuda, Ryuji. **Managerial Engineering: Techniques for Improving Quality and Productivity in the Workplace**
ISBN 0-915299-09-7 / 1984 / 206 pages / hardcover / $34.95

Hatakeyama, Yoshio. **Manager Revolution! A Guide to Survival in Today's Changing Workplace**
ISBN 0-915299-10-0 / 1984 / 198 pages / hardcover / $24.95

Japan Human Resources Association. **The Idea Book: Improvement Through Total Employee Involvement**
ISBN 0-915299-22-4 / 1988 / 218 pages / $49.95

Japan Management Association and Constance E. Dyer.
Canon Production System: Creative Involvement of the Total Workforce
ISBN 0-915299-06-2 / 1987 / 251 pages / hardcover / $36.95

Japan Management Association. **Kanban and Just-In-Time at Toyota: Management Begins at the Workplace,** Translated by David J. Lu
ISBN 0-915299-08-9 / 1986 / 186 pages / hardcover / $29.95

Karatsu, Hajime. **Tough Words for American Industry**
ISBN 0-915299-25-9 / 1988 / 179 pages / hardcover / $24.95

Karatsu, Hajime. **TQC Wisdom of Japan: Managing for Total Quality Control**
ISBN 0-915299-18-6 / 1988 / 138 pages / hardcover / $29.95

Lu, David J. **Inside Corporate Japan: The Art of Fumble-Free Management**
ISBN 0-915299-16-X / 1987 / 278 pages / hardcover / $24.95

Mizuno, Shigeru (ed.) **Management for Quality Improvement: The 7 New QC Tools**
ISBN 0-915299-29-1 / 1988 / 326 pages / hardcover / $59.95

Nakajima, Seiichi. **Introduction to Total Productive Maintenance**
ISBN 0-915299-23-2 / 1988 / 129 pages / $39.95

Nikkan Kogyo Shimbun. **Poka-Yoke: Improving Product Quality by Preventing Defects**
with a foreword by Shigeo Shingo
ISBN 0-915299-31-3 / 1988 / 288 pages / $49.95

Ohno, Taiichi. **Toyota Production System: Beyond Large-Scale Production**
ISBN 0-915299-14-3 / 1988 / 176 pages / hardcover / $39.95

Ohno, Taiichi. **Workplace Management**
ISBN 0-915299-19-4 / 1988 / 176 pages / hardcover / $34.95

Ohno, Taiichi and Setsuo Mito. **Just-In-Time for Today and Tomorrow: A Total Management System**
ISBN 0-915299-20-8 / 1988 / 176 pages / hardcover / $34.95

Productivity Press, Dept. BK, P.O. Box 3007, Cambridge, MA 02140 1-800-274-9911

Shingo, Shigeo. **Non-Stock Production: The Shingo System for Continuous Improvement**
ISBN 0-915299-30-5 / 1988 / 480 pages / hardcover / $75.00

Shingo, Shigeo. **A Revolution in Manufacturing: The SMED System,** translated by Andrew P. Dillon
ISBN 0-915299-03-8 / 1985 / 383 pages / hardcover / $65.00

Shingo, Shigeo. **Zero Quality Control: Source Inspection and the Poka-Yoke System,** translated by Andrew P. Dillon
ISBN 0-915299-07-0 / 1986 / 328 pages / hardcover / $65.00

Shingo, Shigeo. **The Sayings of Shigeo Shingo: Key Strategies for Plant Improvement,** translated by Andrew P. Dillon
ISBN 0-915299-15-1 / 1987 / 207 pages / hardcover / $36.95

Shinohara, Isao (ed.) **New Production System: JIT Crossing Industry Boundaries**
ISBN 0-915299-21-6 / 1988 / 218 pages / hardcover / $34.95

AUDIO-VISUAL PROGRAMS

Shingo, Shigeo. **The SMED System,** translated by Andrew P. Dillon
ISBN 0-915299-11-9 / 181 slides / 40 minutes / $749.00
ISBN 0-915299-27-5 / 2 videos / 40 minutes / $749.00

Shingo, Shigeo, **The Poka-Yoke System**, translated by Andrew P. Dillon
ISBN 0-915299-13-5 / 224 slides / 45 minutes / $749.00
ISBN 0-915299-28-3 / 2 videos / 45 minutes / $749.00

TO ORDER: Write, phone or fax Productivity Press, Dept. BK, P.O. Box 3007, Cambridge, MA 02140, phone 617/497-5146, fax 617/868-3524. Send check or charge to your credit card (American Express, Visa, MasterCard accepted).

U.S. ORDERS: Add $3 shipping for first book, $1 each additional. CT residents add 7.5% and MA residents 5% sales tax.

FOREIGN ORDERS: Payment must be made in U.S. dollars. For Canadian orders, add $8 shipping for first book, $1 each additional. Orders to other countries are on a proforma basis; please indicate shipping method desired.

NOTE: Prices subject to change without notice.

UTAH STATE UNIVERSITY PARTNERS PROGRAM

Shigeo Shingo Medallion

Shigeo Shingo Prize for Manufacturing Excellence

Announces the 1988-89

Shigeo Shingo Prizes for Manufacturing Excellence

Awarded for Manufacturing Excellence Based on the Work of Shigeo Shingo

For North American Businesses, Students and Faculty

ELIGIBILITY

Businesses: Applicants from North America must apply by January 20, 1989, indicating the quality and productivity improvements achieved through Shingo's manufacturing methods and similar techniques. Letters of intent are required by January 3.

Students: Applicants from accredited schools competing for the 1988-89 school year must apply by letter before November 15, 1988, indicating the nature of research planned.

Faculty: Applicants from accredited schools must apply by letter before November 15, 1988, indicating the scope of papers planned.

CRITERIA

Businesses: Quality and productivity improvements achieved by using Shingo's Scientific Thinking Mechanism (STM) and his methods, such as Single-Minute-Exchange of Die (SMED), Poka-yoke (defect prevention), Just-In-Time (JIT), and Non-Stock Production (NSP), or similar techniques.

Students: Creative research on quality and productivity improvements through the use and extension of Shingo's STM and his manufacturing methods: SMED, NSP, and Poka-yoke.

Faculty: Papers publishable in professional journals based on empirical, conceptual or theoretical applications and extensions of Shingo's manufacturing methods for quality and productivity improvements: SMED, Poka-yoke, JIT, and NSP.

PRIZES

Awards will be made by Shigeo Shingo at Utah State University's fourteenth annual Partners Productivity Seminar in Logan, Utah, on April 27-28, 1989.

Five graduate and five undergraduate student awards of $2,000, $1,500, and $1,000 to first, second, and third place winners, respectively, and $500 to fourth and fifth place winners.

Three faculty awards of $3,000, $2,000 and $1,000, respectively.

Six Shigeo Shingo Medallions to the top three large and small business winners.

SHINGO PRIZE COMMITTEE

Committee members representing prestigious business, professional, academic and governmental organizations worldwide will prescribe guidelines and select winners, assisted by a technical examining board.

Application forms and contest information may be obtained from the Partners Program, College of Business, USU, Logan, UT, 84322, (801) 750-2281. Complimentary copies of Shingo's Non-Stock Production have been furnished by Productivity Press to accredited schools. All English language books by Dr. Shingo can be purchased from the publisher, Productivity Press, P.O. Box 3007, Cambridge, MA 02140: call 1-800-274-9911 or 617-497-5146.

Japan's "Dean of Quality Consultants"

Dr. Shigeo Shingo is, quite simply, the world's leading expert on improving the manufacturing process. Known as "Dr. Improvement" in Japan, he is the originator of the Single-Minute Exchange of Die (SMED) concept and the Poka-yoke defect prevention system and one of the developers of the Just-In-Time production system that helped make Toyota the most productive automobile manufacturer in the world. His work now helps hundreds of other companies worldwide save billions of dollars in manufacturing costs annually.

The most sought-after consultant in Japan, Dr. Shingo has trained more than 10,000 people in 100 companies. He established and is President of Japan's highly-regarded Institute of Management Improvement and is the author of numerous books, including *Revolution in Manufacturing: The SMED System* and *Zero Quality Control: Source Inspection and the Poka-yoke System*. His newest book, *Non-Stock Production*, concentrates on expanding U.S. manufacturers' understanding of stockless production.

Dr. Shingo's genius is his understanding of exactly why products are manufactured the way they are, and then transforming that understanding into a workable system for low-cost, high-quality production. In the history of international manufacturing, Shingo stands alongside such pioneers as Robert Fulton, Henry Ford, Frederick Taylor, and Douglas McGregor as one of the key figures in the quest for improvement.

His world-famous SMED system is known as "The Heart of Just-In-Time Manufacturing" for (1) reducing set-up time from hours to minutes; (2) cutting lead time from months to days; (3) slashing work-in-progress inventory by up to 90%; (4) involving employees in team problem solving; (5) 99% improvement in quality; and (6) 70% reduction in floor space.

> *Shigeo Shingo has been called the father of the second great revolution in manufacturing.*
> — Quality Control Digest

The money-saving, profit-making ideas... set forth by Shingo could do much to help U.S. manufacturers reduce set-up time, improve quality and boost productivity ... all for very little cash.
Tooling & Production Magazine

When Americans think about quality today, they often think of Japan. But when the Japanese think of quality, they are likely to think of Shigeo Shingo,... architect of Toyota's now famous production system.
Boardroom Report

Shingo's visit to our plant was significant in making breakthroughs in productivity we previously thought impossible. The benefits... are more far-reaching than I ever anticipated.
Gifford M. Brown, Plant Mgr.
Ford Motor Company